Los Angeles

by Stephanie Avnet

Macmillan • USA

ABOUT THE AUTHOR

A native of Los Angeles and an avid traveler, antique hound, and pop history enthusiast, **Stephanie Avnet** worked in the music business before becoming a freelance writer. In addition to authoring this guide, Stephanie contributes to *Frommer's California* and *Frommer's California from $60 a Day,* and she is currently at work on *Wonderful Weekends from Los Angeles* (Macmillan Travel).

MACMILLAN TRAVEL

A Simon & Schuster Macmillan Company
1633 Broadway
New York, NY 10019

Find us online at **http://www.mgr.com/travel** or
on America Online at Keyword: **Frommer's.**

ISBN 0-02-861332-5
ISSN 0899-3238

Editor: Cheryl Farr
Contributors: Jim Moore, Mary Susan Herczog, Steve Hochman,
Heidi Siegmund Cuda, Erika Lenkert
Production Editor: Beth Mayland
Digital Cartography: Peter Bogaty and Ortelius Design
Design by Michele Laseau
Maps copyright © by Simon & Schuster, Inc.

SPECIAL SALES

Bulk purchases (10+ copies) of Frommer's and selected Macmillan travel guides are available to corporations, organizations, mail-order catalogs, institutions, and charities at special discounts, and can be customized to suit individual needs. For more information write to: Special Sales, Macmillan General Reference, 1633 Broadway, New York, NY 10019.

Manufactured in the United States of America

Travel Discount Coupon

This coupon entitles you to special discounts
when you book your trip through the

RESERVATION SERVICE

Hotels ◆ Airlines ◆ Car Rentals ◆ Cruises
All Your Travel Needs

Here's what you get: *

◆ A discount of $50 USD on a booking of $1,000** or
more for two or more people!

◆ A discount of $25 USD on a booking of $500** or more
for one person!

◆ Free membership for three years, and 1,000 free miles
on enrollment in the unique Miles-to-Go™ frequent-
traveler program. Earn one mile for every dollar spent
through the program. Earn free hotel stays starting at
5,000 miles. Earn free roundtrip airline tickets starting
at 25,000 miles.

◆ Personal help in planning your own, customized trip.

◆ Fast, confirmed reservations at any property
recommended in this guide, subject to availability.***

◆ Special discounts on bookings in the U.S. and around
the world.

◆ Low-cost visa and passport service.

◆ Reduced-rate cruise packages.

Visit our website at http://www.travnet.com/Frommer or
call us globally at 201-567-8500, ext. 55. In the U.S., call
toll-free at 1-888-940-5000, or fax 201-567-1838. In
Canada, call toll-free at 1-800-883-9959, or fax 416-922-
6053. In Asia, call 60-3-7191044, or fax 60-3-7185415.

---

* To qualify for these travel discounts, at least a portion of your trip must
   include destinations covered in this guide. No more than one coupon discount
   may be used in any 12-month period, for destinations covered in this guide.
   Cannot be combined with any other discount or program.
** These are U.S. dollars spent on commissionable bookings.
*** A $10 USD fee, plus fax and/or phone charges, will be added to the cost of
   bookings at each hotel not linked to the reservation service. Customers
   must approve these fees in advance.

Valid until December 31, 1998. Terms and conditions of the Miles-to-
Go™ program are available on request by calling 201-567-8500, ext 55.

LLA123

Contents

List of Maps

AN INVITATION TO THE READER

In researching this book, we discovered many wonderful places—hotels, restaurants, shops, and more. We're sure you'll find others. Please tell us about them, so we can share the information with your fellow travelers in upcoming editions. If you were disappointed with a recommendation, we'd love to know that, too. Please write to:

Stephanie Avnet
Frommer's Los Angeles, 11th Edition
Macmillan Travel
1633 Broadway
New York, NY 10019

AN ADDITIONAL NOTE

Please be advised that travel information is subject to change at any time—and this is especially true of prices. We therefore suggest that you write or call ahead for confirmation when making your travel plans. The authors, editors, and publisher cannot be held responsible for the experiences of readers while traveling. Your safety is important to us, however, so we encourage you to stay alert and be aware of your surroundings. Keep a close eye on cameras, purses, and wallets, all favorite targets of thieves and pickpockets.

WHAT THE SYMBOLS MEAN

✪ Frommer's Favorites

Hotels, restaurants, attractions, and entertainment you should not miss.

⑤ Super-Special Values

Hotels and restaurants that offer great value for your money.

The following abbreviations are used for credit cards:

AE	American Express	EU	Eurocard
CB	Carte Blanche	JCB	Japan Credit Bank
DC	Diners Club	MC	MasterCard
DISC	Discover	V	Visa
ER	enRoute		

Area Code Change Notice

Please note that, effective June 14, 1997, the phone company plans to split the 818 area code. The eastern portion, including Burbank, Glendale, and Pasadena, will change to the new area code **626.** You will be able to dial 818 until January 17, 1998, after which you will have to use 626.

Postcards from L.A.: Introducing the City of Angels

The entire world knows what Los Angeles looks like. It's a real-life version of one of those souvenir postcard folders, which spill out images accordion-style: tall palm trees sweeping an azure sky; the "Hollywood" sign gleaming white and huge against a shrub-blanketed hillside; freeways flowing like concrete rivers across the landscape; a lone surfer riding the day's last wave silhouetted against the sunset's glow. These seductive images are just a few of many that bring to mind the city that just about everyone loves to hate—and to experience, at least once in a lifetime.

Los Angelenos know that their city will never have the sophisticated style of Paris or the historical riches of London—but we cheerfully lay claim to living in the most fun city in the United States, maybe the world. Home to the planet's first amusement park, L.A. regularly feels like one, as the line between fantasy and reality is so often obscured. From the unattainable, anachronistic glamour of Beverly Hills to the earthy, often-scary street-energy of Venice, each of the city's diverse neighborhoods is like a mini–theme park, offering its own kind of adventure. The colors of the city seem just a little bit brighter—and more surreal—than they do in other cities, the angles just a little sharper. Drive down Sunset Boulevard, and you'll see what I mean: The billboards are just a bit taller, the wacky folks just a touch wackier. Everything seems larger than life. No, you're not in Kansas anymore—you're in Toon Town now.

Part of the fun and spontaneity of L.A. comes from the fact that the city is constantly redefining itself. Things change so quickly here that sometimes everything passes by in a blur. Just like the movies and TV shows that come to life here, the physical landscape, social doctrines, and popular pastimes of the city itself are fluid and unreliable. Will a neighborhood of charming but crumbling bungalows be restored by a zealous community or forsaken by its neighbors and replaced by a glittering paean to some superstar modern architect? Will L.A., driven by racially motivated outbursts and other social inequities, set precedents of tolerance (like the successfully gay-oriented City of West Hollywood), or will its residents continue to retreat to name-calling and NIMBY(Not-In-My-Back-Yard)-ism well into the next century? Will health-conscious Los Angeles succeed in being the world's first entirely nonsmoking city (witness the stringent guidelines on every definable public indoor space), or will the peculiar resurgence of cigar culture undermine decades of effort? Who knows? It could go either way.

Los Angeles gleefully embraces individuality and weirdness and change. Collectively, the city is like a theatrical actor projecting to the very back row: We want everybody else to sit up and take notice—and we're constantly reinventing ourselves so they will. We'd never want our city to be Paris or London or New York for all the Mona Lisas in the world.

1 Frommer's Favorite L.A. Experiences

- **Driving Along the Coast:** This has to be the quintessential Southern California activity—one that never loses its appeal, even for longtime L.A. natives. The ocean has a spirit all its own, in every season of the year: August's cool respite from the glaring heat inland; January's surprise warmth under wide blue skies; March's gray, bleary almost New England–like chill; and the first warm breezes of summer in June. Stop wherever catches your fancy—at a Malibu cantina, a Santa Monica boutique, or a South Bay beach; your day along the shore can be whatever you make it.

- **Watching One of Your Favorite TV Sitcoms Being Taped:** Alternately boring and fascinating, being in the audience is your free admission to wander the soundstage, marvel at the cheesy three-wall sets that look so real on TV, and get an inside look at the bloopers that never make it to broadcast—and are often far more entertaining than the scripted dialogue.

- **Dining at Spago (or The Ivy, or Maple Drive, or the Palm):** Less expensive per capita than admission to Universal or Disneyland, dining at one of L.A.'s *uber*-trendy A-list celebrity watering holes is an experience to be filed under "only in L.A." Hear dialogue straight out of *The Player* while eating some fine meals prepared for some of the world's pickiest eaters.

- **Going to the Getty:** Learn how to spot a fake, ponder van Gogh's *Irises,* then stroll around the gardens high above the Pacific at Malibu's Getty Museum. This outrageously derivative Greek villa will be closing at the end of 1997 for a planned 3-year renovation, so see it while you can.

- **Paying Your Respects at the Cemetery of the Stars:** Visit Humphrey Bogart, Clark Gable, Karen Carpenter, and all their friends at Forest Lawn in Glendale. This palatial and often garish "memorial park" was wryly satirized by expatriate Brit Evelyn Waugh in his classic novel *The Loved One.*

- **Reliving *Rebel Without a Cause:*** For a view of the city—and a film memory—without compare, head to moderne masterpiece Griffith Observatory, virtually unchanged since the 1954 filming of several pivotal scenes from James Dean's quintessential portrayal of youthful angst.

- **Going Gidget:** This is, after all, L.A.—so get thee to a beach! Watch a vollyball tournament in Manhattan Beach, weightlifters doing their thing at Venice Beach, or a bikini contest in Marina del Rey; surfers hang ten at Malibu, and families pitch umbrellas at Zuma.

- **Visiting the Happiest Place on Earth—Disneyland:** Go on a weekday to avoid the crowds, or during the off-season, between January and April. The Park's worldwide appeal is evident in the virtual United Nations of fellow revelers traipsing between Adventureland, Storybookland, and Tomorrowland; you'll hear lots of international voices without even having to endure "It's a Small World."

- **Spending a Day Downtown:** See the city from the observation deck atop City Hall, stop in for a snack at the bustling Grand Central Market, pick up some inexpensive Mexican handcrafts along colorful and historic Olvera Street, then have an authentic dim-sum lunch in Chinatown.

- **Taking a Specialty Tour of the City:** You might think that guided tours are the last resort of the imagination-impaired, but consider the following: a Grave Line Tour (in a hearse) of death and burial sites, from Marilyn Monroe to Divine; an L.A. Conservancy walking tour of downtown's extravagent movie-houses, abandoned with their ornate glory intact; or an "Insomniac's Tour" of builders, bakers, and farmers at work in the wee hours before the sun stirs the city into motion. If you're a committed do-it-yourselfer, opt for one or both of the driving tours in chapter 8.

- **Shopping 'til You Drop:** You'll see "I'd Rather Be Shopping At Nordstrom" license plate frames on Lexuses all over L.A., evidence that spending money is the primary pastime here. Whether it's $3 vintage bowling shirts, $10,000 Beverly Hills baubles, or anything in between, you're sure to find it in L.A.'s cornucopia of consumerism. Even window-shopping doesn't get much better than kooky Melrose Avenue or tony Rodeo Drive.

- **Strolling Wilshire Boulevard's Museum Row:** Natural history meets pop culture meets modern art with the La Brea Tar Pits, the Museum of Miniatures, the Petersen Automobile Museum, the Craft and Folk Art Museum, and the Los Angeles County Museum of Art all shoulder-to-shoulder in the heart of L.A. The only problem is, too much to see in one day! Pick your favorite for an indepth visit, and just browse the bookstore/gift shops at the others.

- **Visiting Venice's Ocean Front Walk:** Rollerblade, or just stroll along, taking in the human carnival swirling around you; nosh on a Jody Maroni's *haute* dog; and pick up some cheap sunglasses, silver jewelry, or ethnic garb, all while enjoying the wide sand beach, blue sea, and assorted busking performers along the boardwalk. You can even rent a bicycle and pedal along the parallel bike path.

- **Seeing a Show at McCabe's:** Spend a memorable evening snacking on cookies and cider while enjoying live acoustic music with a hundred of your closest friends at McCabe's Guitar Shop in Santa Monica. In a city filled with over-amplified rock clubs, McCabe's is a welcome change.

- **Taking a Gourmet Picnic to the Hollywood Bowl:** What better way to spend an L.A. evening than under the stars with a bottle of wine and some naturally amplified entertainment? In addition to being the summer home of the Los Angeles Philharmonic, the Bowl hosts visiting performers ranging from chamber music quartets to jazz greats to folk humorists. The imposing white Frank Lloyd Wright–designed bandshell always elicits appreciative gasps from first-time Bowl-goers.

- **Cruising Mulholland Drive:** Ogle the homes with those million-dollar views, then pull over to catch the view for yourself, particularly at night when the lights of the city twinkle below. Canine lovers should stop by the dog park just west of Laurel Canyon Boulevard; ever since city parks tightened leash laws, many owners have been bringing their pooches to this grassy doggie free-for-all nestled in the hills.

2 Los Angeles Yesterday & Today

TINSELTOWN TODAY Having survived a long, leisurely pioneering infancy, and a slightly uncouth adolescence, Los Angeles has now blossomed into one of the world's major cultural centers. The movies, TV, and music that issues forth from here are seen, heard, and felt throughout the world; the pop products of the city's efforts govern who we are and how we spend our time and how we think more

Dateline
- **1781** Los Angeles is founded.
- **1821** Spain grants independence to Mexico and, thus, to California.
- **1846** The so-called Bear Flag Republic is proclaimed; the

continues

Impressions

If [Los Angeles] is hell, why is it so popular?

—Bryce Nelson, *The New York Times*

U.S. flag is raised in Yerba Buena (San Francisco) and Los Angeles.

- **1850** California becomes the 31st state.
- **1875** The Santa Fe Railroad reaches Los Angeles.
- **1881** The *Los Angeles Times* begins publication.
- **1892** Oil is discovered in downtown Los Angeles, at what is now the intersection of 2nd Street and Glendale Boulevard.
- **1900** The population of California approaches 1.5 million; Los Angeles has more than 102,000 residents.
- **1902** The first movie-house, the Electric Theatre, opens on Main Street.
- **1909** Santa Monica Pier is erected to accommodate cargo and passenger ships.
- **1911** Hollywood's first film studio is established.
- **1912** More than 16 motion-picture companies are operating out of Hollywood; the first U.S. gas station opens at the corner of Grand Avenue and Washington Street.
- **1913** Cecil B. DeMille directs the film industry's first full-length feature, *The Squaw Man,* in a barn near Selma and Vine Streets.
- **1920** Douglas Fairbanks builds the mansion known as "Pickfair" in the foothills of Beverly Hills for his young bride, America's sweetheart, Mary Pickford.
- **1922** The Hollywood Bowl opens.
- **1923** The Hollywood sign is erected to advertise a real estate development.

continues

than we would ever like to admit. The city is America's—and often the world's—tastemaker, its cultural barometer. When it comes to what's hot and what's not, Angelenos can confidently say that they heard—or started—the buzz here first.

In a way, Los Angeles has to be sexier than other cities, because the camera is always on. The evening news carries our dirty laundry, in the form of video-taped indiscretions, out to the rest of the country; lately, it seems like even our crimes are more glamorous than those elsewhere in America: privileged upper-class kids in designer tennis whites gunning down their parents in the rec room of the family's Beverly Hills mansion, or a millionaire sports hero's murder trial catapulting his Armani-clad attorneys to celebrity status and obscuring the issue of whether or not he ambushed his exwife and a stranger, leaving them in a pool of blood in front of a Brentwood condo tourists still take pictures of.

As Los Angeles—and the rest of the planet—hurtles toward the 21st century, the city is going through some drastic changes. Intense growth and increased ethnic diversity have fueled a climate of political and philosophical change; in many ways, there are two L.A.'s, existing in parallel universes, like some weird science fiction plot. There's the beautiful show-biz town, home of starlets and hunks who cruise palm-tree-lined streets in sleek red convertibles on their way to the studio. This L.A. has marble-lobbied hotels, trendy restaurants and nightclubs, and Beverly Hills. The other universe is a multi-ethnic Pacific Rim metropolis, swelling uncomfortably from the influx of new residents, yet growing richer from the cultural diversity they bring. In this other L.A., you'll encounter Vietnamese, Ethiopian, Russian, and Ecuadoran enclaves; formerly rundown parts of town whose architectural treasures are being renewed and pressed into use by a new generation of families. You'll find a city straining to grow technologically into a new century, right next to the town eager to preserve its golden (and sometimes isolationist) roots.

But through it all, there is tourism. Los Angeles, like the shampoo commercial supermodel ("Don't hate me because I'm beautiful"), knows which side its bread is buttered on and will never neglect the careful maintenance of its image. It's not as contrived as it sounds—remember, everyone here was a visitor first.

HISTORY 101 Unlike many of the country's (and the world's) greatest metropolitan destinations, Los Angeles is seen more in the context of the present—even the future—than the past. Young even in relation to the eastern United States, the city is that much more intriguing to the historian, because the past is fresh and easily excavated (both figuratively and literally); the sense of simultaneously having one foot in yesterday and one in tomorrow is part of what makes discovering L.A. intriguing.

The city was founded by the Spanish on the site of a Native American village in 1781, but it wasn't until after the first film studio was established, in 1911, that Los Angeles really took off. Within 5 years, movies like D.W. Griffith's *Birth of a Nation* were being produced by the hundreds. By World War I, the Hollywood studio system was firmly entrenched, with the young trio of Charlie Chaplin, Douglas Fairbanks, and "America's Sweetheart," Mary Pickford, at its fore.

When the box office boomed in the 1920s and 1930s, so did the population of Los Angeles. Easterners—including the dust-bowl refugees depicted in John Steinbeck's *The Grapes of Wrath*—came to the burgeoning urban paradise in droves in order to find their fortunes. The world-famous Hollywood sign, erected in 1923, was built as an advertisement for just one of many fledgling real estate developments that began to crop up on the "outskirts" of the city. Los Angeles, and Hollywood, was all that much more alluring during the Great Depression; the city flourished as Americans ached for an escape from their less-than-inspiring reality, one provided by Hollywood's cinematic fantasies. With each glamorous, idyllic portrayal of California, Los Angeles's popularity—and population—grew.

As the city grew, so did the need for water. Most great American cities grew from small settlements on rivers or lakes, fresh-water sources vital to everyday life and commerce. Not L.A.—it was founded in the middle of an arid basin. The Los Angeles River—on whose banks early El Pueblo de la Reina de Los Angeles was founded—has always been too unpredictable to support the city's growth, and today is merely a series of flood control channels operated by the Department of Water and Power. But the quest for water has provided some of L.A.'s most gripping

- **1927** The first "talkie" is released, *The Jazz Singer,* with Al Jolson.
- **1928** Los Angeles's first airport, Mines Field (on the current site of LAX) opens, with only a single dirt strip as a runway.
- **1929** The Academy of Motion Picture Arts and Sciences bestows its first Oscar.
- **1940** L.A.'s first freeway, the Arroyo Seco Parkway, opens, connecting Hollywood and Pasadena.
- **1945** The world's largest toy manufacturer, Mattel, maker of Barbie, is founded in Hawthorne.
- **1947** The first TV station west of the Mississippi, KTLA, begins broadcasting; the Rams football team comes to Los Angeles from Cleveland, Ohio; the Hollywood Freeway opens, linking L.A. with the San Fernando Valley.
- **1950** L.A.'s population is almost 2 million.
- **1955** Disneyland opens.
- **1956** Capitol Records Tower, the nation's first circular office building, opens for business. The provocative architectural stack is the brainchild of Capitol recording stars Nat King Cole and Johnny Mercer.
- **1961** Hollywood's Walk of Fame is started by the Hollywood Chamber of Commerce.
- **1962** California overtakes New York as the nation's most populous state; Dodger Stadium opens on land purchased by owner Walter O'Malley.
- **1965** Anger over the recent assassination of Martin Luther King, Jr., fuels riots in Watts, leaving 34 dead and over 1,000 injured.

continues

- **1968** Robert F. Kennedy is fatally shot at the Ambassador Hotel after winning California's Democratic Party presidential primary.
- **1980** L.A.'s population is nearly 3 million.
- **1984** Los Angeles hosts the Summer Olympic Games, and raises the national standard of traffic control by implementing flex-time work schedules, metered freeway on-ramps, and sophisticated central computer tracking and diffusing of potential trouble spots.
- **1990** The first of what some consider to be a mass-transit trolley system, MetroRail's Blue Line opens with service between Long Beach and downtown Los Angeles; First Interstate Tower, designed by I.M. Pei, opens for business; it's the tallest building west of Chicago's Sears Tower.
- **1992** In the Los Angeles race riots resulting from the acquittal of the police officers involved in the Rodney King beating, more than 40 are dead, hundreds injured.
- **1994** An earthquake measuring 6.8 on the Richter scale shakes the city; Los Angeles hosts the World Cup soccer finals and closing ceremonies.
- **1995** At the conclusion of the "Crime of the Century" trial, O.J. Simpson is found not guilty of the murders of Nicole Brown Simpson and Ron Goldman.
- **1996** Griffith Park, the country's largest municipal park, celebrates its 100-year anniversary.

real-life drama. As early as 1799, Spanish padres at the new Mission San Fernando dammed the river to provide for their water needs, causing an uprising among settlers downstream. Disputes continued up to the incidents that inspired the movie *Chinatown*, about the early battle for rights to the abundant water William Mulholland and Fred Eaton "stole" from the Owens Valley up north with their new California aqueduct. Resentment from northern California continues up to the present time, as L.A. continues to reap the agricultural, domestic, and electrical benefits of what many claim was never rightfully theirs.

The opening of the Arroyo Seco Parkway in 1940, linking downtown L.A. and Pasadena with the first of what would be a network of freeways, ushered in a new era for the city. From that time on, car culture flourished in Los Angeles; it became perhaps the city's most distinctive feature (for more on this subject, see "From Horseless Carriages to Hot Rods: L.A.'s Love Affair with the Automobile," below). America's automotive industry successfully conspired to undermine Los Angeles's public transportation system by halting the trolley service that once plied downtown, and advocating the construction of auto-friendly roads. The growth of the freeways led to the development of L.A.'s suburban sprawl, turning Los Angeles into a city without a single geographical focus. The suburbs became firmly entrenched in the L.A. landscape during World War II, when shipyards and munitions factories, as well as aerospace giants McDonnell Douglas, Lockheed, Rockwell, and General Dynamics, opened their doors in Southern California.

After the war, the threat of television put the movie industry into a tailspin. But instead of being destroyed by the "tube," Hollywood was strengthened when that industry made its home here as well. Soon afterward, in the '50s and '60s, the avant-garde discovered Los Angeles as well; the city became popular with artists, beats, and hippies, many of whom settled in Venice.

The 1970s gave rise to a number of exotic religions and cults that found eager adherents in Southern California. The spiritual "New Age" born in the "Me" decade found life into the 1980s, in the face of a population growing beyond manageable limits, an increasingly polluted environment, and escalating social ills. At the same time, California became very rich. Real estate values soared, banks and businesses prospered, and the entertainment industry boomed.

In the 1990s Angelenos are on the leading edge of American pop culture. But they've discovered, as the world shakes its collective head and wags its unified finger, that success isn't always all it's cracked up to be. The nation's economic, social, and environmental problems have become the city's own, and have even become amplified in the larger-than-life arena. The spotlight was turned on the city in 1991, when four white police officers were videotaped beating African-American motorist Rodney King. The officers' shocking acquittal in the spring of 1992 sparked 3 days of rioting and looting. Injury was added to insult as Mother Nature seemingly turned on her favorite progeny, sending fires, floods, mudslides, and an earthquake in rapid succession.

After the earthquake on January 17, 1994, half the city proclaimed the disaster as signaling the beginning of the end; they declared that L.A. could never recover. The other half optimistically proclaimed that adversity would unite the fragmented city and it would emerge, phoenix-like, more solid than ever. Both factions were partially correct—but mostly the city has just gone on with the business of being L.A. The earthquake—like all the other ups and downs in the course of the city's history—has become part of the city's collective psyche; but time heals all wounds, and Los Angeles has moved on to the business at hand.

3 Wolfgang Puck & the Birth of California Cuisine

Southern California's own unique cuisine, now known the world over as California Cuisine, can be traced back to 1979, when 25-year-old chef Michael McCarty opened Michael's in Santa Monica. McCarty's combination of French technique with local ingredients is de rigeur today, but was a radical departure from the traditional Parisian cookery that was then the standard on the L.A. dining scene.

Since Michael's opened its doors, California-style cuisine has evolved, integrating techniques and ingredients from the international cultures so prevalent in cosmopolitan Los Angeles, with particular emphasis on Japanese and Mexican cookery. In true L.A. style, preparations are light and health conscious; they're often accompanied by some variation on salsa, from the traditional Mexican-style garnish to nouveau mango chutney.

No one has been more successful in the genre than Wolfgang Puck, a German émigré who made his mark serving wood-fired individual pizzas topped with a galaxy of untraditional ingredients like duck sausage, shiitake mushrooms, leeks, artichokes, and other California-grown ingredients. After the triumph of his still-popular über-restaurant, Spago, Puck duplicated his success with Chinois on Main, a Franco-Chinese eatery taking what McCarty did a step further, and Malibu's Granita, which puts Puck's unique California twist on seafood.

Despite Michael McCarty's undisputed title as the father of California Cuisine, it has been Puck who has brought the nouvelle cuisine not only into its creative own, but beyond the city's limits and into restaurant kitchens across the nation and around the world. He has been its shameless marketer, making appearances everywhere, from the finest European kitchens to the stage of *The Late Show with David Letterman*. With his line of frozen foods and the opening of the first of what is sure to be many

Impressions

If you tilt the whole country sideways, Los Angeles is the place where everything loose will fall.

—Frank Lloyd Wright

People here still believe. The sun comes out every day and smacks them in the face and they march off gamely to face insurmountable odds. Los Angeles may be the most renewable city in the world.

—Tom Shales, *Washington Post*

moderately priced Wolfgang Puck Cafés, L.A.'s superchef has fired up his ovens for the masses, bringing California Cuisine into America's malls—and freezers—across the country.

You'll feel Puck's influence throughout your visit to Los Angeles. In the last 10 years or so, he has managed to be the dining scene's most defining influence; he's been to L.A.'s—one might even say to the world's—kitchens what the Beatles were to pop music. Even more directly, rarely in the kitchen himself, the jet-setting superchef has had an uncanny knack for hiring kitchen help as smart and creative as himself; Spago alumni have gone on to open top restaurants around the city, among them Campanile, Eclipse, and Carrots.

While you're in Los Angeles, be sure to splurge on at least one meal at one of the top restaurants featuring the city's own home-grown—and now world-famous—cuisine. See chapter 6, "Dining," for all the details, and remember to make your reservations well in advance, particularly if you opt for one of the star-studded heavyweights (such as Spago itself). Enjoy!

4 From Horseless Carriages to Hot Rods: L.A.'s Love Affair with the Automobile

The Southern California lifestyle is so closely tied to the automobile that it has given rise to a whole subculture of the car. Since its introduction to the infant city it would grow up with, the automobile has become a pop phenomenon all its own, inextricably intertwined with the personality of Los Angeles—and the identities of its residents. What's more, although the first "horseless carriages" emerged from the Midwest, it has been Hollywood's influence that has defined the entire nation's passion for the car.

During the early 1920s, movie comedians Laurel and Hardy and the Keystone Cops began to blend their brand of physical humor with the popular Ford Model T. And a visionary coach builder named Harley Earl was busy in his shop on South Main Street, building special vehicles for the movies—the Ben Hur racing chariots—and designing flamboyant custom automobiles for the wealthy movie stars of the day. Earl would later be recruited by General Motors, bringing along with him from Hollywood to Detroit an obsession with style over substance that would culminate in the legendary tailfins of the 1950s.

As movie director Cecil B. DeMille once said, both cars and movies captured Americans' love of motion and speed. Car culture as it was depicted in motion pictures continued to set the pace for the country. In *Rebel Without a Cause*, James Dean's troubled teenager and his hot-rodding buddies assert their independence through their jalopies (in several memorable confrontations filmed on the roads around the Griffith Observatory in the Hollywood Hills). As authorities cracked down on dangerous street racing, locally based *Hot Rod Magazine* helped spawn the movement to create legal drag strips, and the sport of professional drag racing was born. The art of auto body customizing also came into being here, pioneered by George Barris, the "King of Kustomizers."

The world watched Southern California's physical landscape change to accommodate the four-wheeled resident. In postwar suburban tracts the garage, which had traditionally been a separate shed, grew attached to the house and became the family's main entrance. The Arroyo Seco Parkway (now the Pasadena Freeway) opened in 1940, its curvaceous lanes modeled after the landscaped parkways of the New York City metropolitan area, each turn placed to open up a series of scenic vistas for the driver. (Later L.A. freeways, reflecting a greater concern with speed, were modeled after the straight, efficient autobahns of Europe.)

Meanwhile, businesses in town built signs in an attempt to catch the eye of the driving customer; as the cars got faster, the signs got larger and brighter. A look at the gargantuan billboards on the Sunset Strip shows where that trend ended up. Another scourge of the modern landscape, the minimall, actually started innocently enough in 1927 with the first "supermarket." The term was coined by Hattem's (at the corner of Western Avenue and 43rd Street), where several grocers lined up side by side, set back from the street to provide plentiful parking and one-stop convenience for their customers.

The 1930s saw the emergence of Streamline Moderne design throughout Los Angeles, and the car's lifeline, the gas station, was no exception to this style. The awnings of 1920s-era stations, which had vanished in most parts of the country, remained in fashion in the Southwest in order to protect motorists from sun and heat; when interpreted by '30s designers, the Moderne canopy became a distinct local variation. Following World War II, L.A. saw the first "Gas-a-teria," ancestor of today's ubiquitous self-serve station.

But perhaps the most enduring feature to arise from the phenomenon of the automobile is the drive-up, drive-in, and drive-through business. In the mid-1920s someone thought to punch through their outer wall in order to serve the motoring customer. By the next decade, Los Angeles boasted the world's largest collection of establishments that you could patronize from the privacy and comfort of your car. There were drive-up bank teller windows (now replaced by ATMs), drive-through florists and dry cleaners, drive-through dairies (Alta Dena still maintains several in the Southland), and drive-up restaurants. These weren't the impersonal fast-food joints of today, but real restaurants (like the popular Dolores Drive-In chain) with cheerful carhops bringing your freshly made order to you on a window tray. (Bob's Big Boy Restaurant in Toluca Lake invites patrons with vintage autos to cruise over and enjoy nostalgic carhop service on Friday and Saturday nights.)

Perhaps the most popular of these drive-in landmarks are the movie theaters. Los Angeles had the second one in the whole country (at the corner of Pico and Westwood boulevards); the city still boasts at least a dozen that screen first-run films, among them the Winnetka in Chatsworth, the Hi-Way 39 in Westminster, and the Foothill in Azusa. At the drive-in theater, you were able to enjoy the picture—along with all those great snack-bar treats—without sacrificing any of the comforts of home. Long established as a teenage make-out haven, one theater gained popularity in a

Impressions

Looks like another perfect day . . . I love L.A.!

—Randy Newman

more spiritual way when Reverend Robert Schuller began to deliver Sunday morning sermons to a comfortably parked audience at the Orange County Drive-In. His
slogan: "Come as you are, in the family car."

The trend to view the car as an extension of the home persists today, with the
marketing of telephones, fax machines, electric shavers, vacuum cleaners, and more,
all car sized and capable of plugging into the dashboard cigarette lighter socket and
functioning inside your car. What more could the auto-loving Angeleno ask for?

For more Southern California automobile lore, visit the Petersen Automotive
Museum; see chapter 7 for details.

Planning a Trip to Los Angeles

2

In the pages that follow, we've compiled everything you need to know to handle the practical details of planning your trip in advance—airlines, weather, a calendar of events, and more.

1 Visitor Information & Money

VISITOR INFORMATION

If you'd like information on the city before you go, contact the **Los Angeles Convention and Visitors Bureau,** 633 W. 5th St., Suite 600, Los Angeles, CA 90071 (☎ **213/624-7300**). If you're on the World Wide Web, check out the L.A. information site at **http://www.ci.la.ca.us/index.html.**

In addition, almost every municipality and economic district in Los Angeles has a dedicated tourist bureau or chamber of commerce that will be more than happy to send you information on their particular area; see "Orientation" in chapter 4 for a complete list.

MONEY

You never have to carry a lot of cash in Los Angeles. Automated teller machines (ATMs) are located at virtually every bank in the city, as well as at supermarkets and major tourist attractions (like theme parks). And all the major credit cards are accepted by the vast majority of L.A.'s hotels, restaurants, attractions, shops, and nightspots.

The ubiquitous **Bank of America** accepts Plus, Star, and Interlink cards; **Wells Fargo Bank** is part of both Cirrus and Star systems. Both banks have dozens of branches all around the city. For the location of the nearest ATM, call **800/424-7787** for the Cirrus network or **800/843-7587** for the Plus system. Most ATMs will make cash advances against MasterCard and Visa. American Express cardholders can write a personal check, guaranteed against the card, for up to $1,000 in cash at American Express offices (see "Fast Facts: Los Angeles" in chapter 4 for locations).

If you're the kind of traveler who prefers the security of traveler's checks, you'll find that they're also widely accepted for goods and services, and can be exchanged for cash at banks and check-issuing offices.

What Things Cost in Los Angeles	U.S. $
Taxi from the airport to downtown	30.00
Super-shuttle from LAX to West Hollywood area	12.00
Bus fare to any destination within the city	1.35
Double room at the Beverly Hills Hotel (very expensive)	300.00
Double room at the Hotel Oceana (expensive)	170.00
Double room at Casa Malibu (moderate)	100.00
Double room at the Hollywood Celebrity Hotel (inexpensive)	60.00
Lunch for one at Cafe Pinot (moderate)	14.00
Chili Double Bacon–Burrito Dog at Pink's	3.60
Dinner for one, without wine, at Morton's (expensive)	40.00
Dinner for one, without wine, at Cha Cha Cha (moderate)	21.00
Dinner for one, without wine, at the Source (inexpensive)	12.00
Cup of coffee at Philippe The Original	.09
Cup of coffee at Peninsula Hotel	3.25
2$^{1}/_{2}$-hour Grave Line Tour of Hollywood	40.00
Admission to Hollywood Wax Museum	9.00
Admission to the J. Paul Getty Museum	Free
Movie ticket	7.50

2 When to Go

Many visitors don't recognize that Los Angeles—with its blue ocean, swaying palm trees, miles of green lawns, and forested foothills—is more desert than anything else. But with the desert climes tempered by sea breezes (which make air-conditioning largely unnecessary even 20 miles inland), and the landscape kept green with water carried by aqueduct from all around the West, L.A. might just be the most perfect desert you've ever visited. No matter how hot it gets, low humidity keeps things dry and comfortable.

Tourism peaks during summer—coastal hotels fill to capacity, restaurant reservations can be hard to come by, and top attractions are packed to the gills with visitors and locals who are off from work or school. Summer can be miserable in the inland valleys, where daytime temperatures—and that famous L.A. smog—can reach stifling levels, but the beach communities almost always remain comfortable.

Moderate temperatures, fewer crowds, and sometimes lower hotel rates make travel to L.A. most pleasurable during the winter. The city is particularly delightful from early autumn to late spring, when the skies are less smoggy. Rain is rare in Los Angeles, but can cause crippling flooding when it does sneak up on the unsuspecting city; precipitation is most likely from February to April, and virtually unheard of between May and November. Los Angeles is a perfect winter destination; even in January, daytime temperature readings regularly reach into the 60s and higher—sometimes even into the 80s.

Pundits claim L.A. has no seasons; it might be more accurate to say we have our own unique seasons instead. Two of them are "June Gloom" and "the Santa Ana's." The first refers to the ocean fog that keeps the beach cities (and often all of L.A.) overcast into early afternoon; it's most common in June (hence the name) but can occur anytime between late April and mid-August. Mid-autumn (October and November) often brings the "Santa Ana's"—strong, hot winds from across the desert that increase brush-fire danger and cause an Indian summer giddiness in animals and people alike.

As you can see below, Los Angeles remains relatively temperate year-round. It's possible to sunbathe throughout the year, but only die-hard enthusiasts and wet-suited surfers venture into the ocean in winter. The water is warmest in summer and fall, but even then the Pacific is too chilly for many.

Los Angeles's Average Temperatures (°F)

	Jan	Feb	Mar	Apr	May	Jun	Jul	Aug	Sept	Oct	Nov	Dec
Avg. High	65	66	67	69	72	75	81	81	81	77	73	69
Avg. Low	46	48	49	52	54	57	60	60	59	55	51	49

LOS ANGELES AREA CALENDAR OF EVENTS

January

- **Tournament of Roses,** Pasadena. A spectacular parade down Colorado Boulevard, with lavish floats, music, and extraordinary equestrian entries, followed by the Rose Bowl Game. Call **818/449-4100** for details, or just stay home and watch it on TV (you'll have a better view). January 1.
- **Oshogatsu,** Los Angeles. Participate in traditional Japanese ceremonies and enjoy foods and crafts at this New Year's celebration at the Japanese American Cultural and Community Center in Little Tokyo. Call **213/628-2725.** First weekend in January.
- **Martin Luther King Parade,** Long Beach. This annual parade down Alameda and 7th Streets ends with a festival in Martin Luther King Park. For more information, contact the Council of Special Events (☎ **310/570-6816**). Third Monday in January.
- **Native American Film Festival,** Los Angeles. Cinematic works by or about Native Americans express their visions, diversity, and ideas. Call the Southwest Museum at **213/221-2164** for schedule and details. Mid-January.
- **Bob Hope Chrysler Classic Golf Tournament,** Palm Springs Desert Resorts. Everyone's favorite celebrity duffer, and the desert's most visible resident, presides over this Pro-Am and PGA event held on four of the areas most challenging courses. For information, call **619/346-8184.** Mid-January.

February

- **Chinese New Year,** Los Angeles. Colorful dragon dancers parade through the streets of downtown's Chinatown. Chinese opera and other events are scheduled. For this year's schedule, contact the Chinese Chamber of Commerce, 977 N. Broadway, Room E, Los Angeles, CA 90012 (☎ **213/617-0396**). Early February.
- **Nissan L.A. Open Golf Tournament,** Pacific Palisades. The PGA Tour makes its only Tinseltown appearance each year at the exclusive Riviera Country Club overlooking the ocean. Expect to see stars in attendance, watching defending champion Craig Stadler going for another L.A. win. For tickets and information, call the Los Angeles Junior Chamber of Commerce (☎ **213/482-1311**). Last week in February.
- **Mardi Gras,** West Hollywood. The festivities—including live jazz and lots of food—take place along Santa Monica Boulevard, from Doheny Drive to La Brea Avenue, and in the alley behind Santa Monica Boulevard. Contact the West

Hollywood Convention & Visitors Bureau (☎ **800/368-6020**) for details. Late February.

- **National Date Festival,** Indio. Celebrating the Coachella Valley's largest and most fanciful crop, this extravaganza includes Arabian nights-themed activities like camel races, Middle Eastern foods and a parade through downtown Indio—plus all the date shakes you can drink. For information, call **619/863-8236.** Second half of February.

March

- **Los Angeles Marathon.** This 26.2-mile run through the streets of Los Angeles attracts thousands of participants, from world champions to the guy next door. The run starts in downtown Los Angeles. Call **310/444-5544** for registration or spectator information. First Sunday in March.
- **California Poppy Blooming Season,** Antelope Valley. Less than an hour's drive north of Los Angeles lies the California Poppy Reserve, part of the state park system. In spring, miles of hillside blaze with brilliant hues of red and orange, dazzling the senses or motorists who flock to witness the display. For information and directions, call **805/942-0662.** Mid-March through mid-May.
- **American Indian Festival and Market,** Los Angeles Natural History Museum. A showcase of Native American arts and culture; the fun includes traditional dances, storytelling, and arts and crafts, as well as a chance to sample Native American foods. Admission to the museum includes festival tickets. For further details, call **213/744-DINO.** Late March.

April

- **Renaissance Pleasure Faire,** San Bernardino. This annual event is one of America's largest Renaissance festivals. Set in the relatively remote Glen Ellen Regional Park, it's a re-created Elizabethan marketplace with costumed performers and living history displays. The fair provides an entire day's activities, shows and festivities, food and crafts. You're encouraged to come in period costume. For ticket information, call **800/523-2473.** Weekends from April through June.
- **Long Beach Grand Prix.** An exciting weekend of Indy-class auto racing and entertainment in and around downtown Long Beach draws world-class drivers from the United States and Europe, plus many celebrity contestants and spectators. Contact the Grand Prix Association, 3000 Pacific Ave., Long Beach, CA 90806 (☎ **800/752-9524** or 310/981-2600), for information. Mid-April.

May

- **Cinco de Mayo,** Los Angeles. A week-long celebration of Mexico's jubilant Independence Day takes place throughout the city. There's a carnival atmosphere with large crowds, live music, dances, and food. The main festivities are held at El Pueblo de Los Angeles State Historic Park, downtown; call **213/628-1274** for information. Other events are held around the city. The week surrounding May 5.
- **Redondo Beach Wine Festival.** This is the largest outdoor wine-tasting event in Southern California. For exact dates and current locations, contact the Redondo Beach Chamber of Commerce, 200 N. Pacific Coast Hwy., Redondo Beach, CA 90277 (☎ **310/376-6912**). Early May.
- **Venice Art Walk,** Venice Beach. An annual weekend event that gives visitors a chance to take docent-guided tours of galleries and studios, plus take a Sunday self-guided art walk through the private home studios of more than 50 emerging and well-known artists. For details, call the Venice Family Clinic, which

coordinates the event (☎ **310/392-8630, ext. 342**), or visit their Internet Web site at **http://www.pureartmkt.com/veniceartwalk**. Mid-May.

- **National Orange Show**, San Bernardino. This 11-day county fair includes various stadium events, celebrity entertainment, livestock shows, and carnival rides. Call **909/888-6788**. Mid-May.
- **Long Beach Lesbian & Gay Pride Parade and Festival**, Shoreline Park, Long Beach. There's more than 100 decorated floats, health-awareness booths, live rock and country music, dancing, and food. Call **310/987-9191**. Mid-May.

June

- **Playboy Jazz Festival**, Los Angeles. Bill Cosby is the traditional master of ceremonies, presiding over top artists at the Hollywood Bowl. Call **310/246-4000**. Mid-June.
- **Cajun & Zydeco Festival**, Long Beach. The spirit of New Orleans comes alive in the Rainbow Lagoon Park during this weekend of celebration. There's Cajun and Creole food, contemporary Cajun and Zydeco music, dancing, dance lessons, and a children's Mardi Gras parade. Call **310/427-3713** for information. First weekend in June.
- **Gay & Lesbian Pride Celebration**, West Hollywood. In its 27th year, this West Hollywood gathering promises to be larger than ever; outdoor stages, disco- and western-dance tents, food, and revelry culminate in Sunday's flamboyant parade down Santa Monica Blvd. Call **213/860-0701**. Last weekend in June.
- **Mariachi USA Festival**, Los Angeles. A 2-day family-oriented celebration of Mexican culture and tradition at the Hollywood Bowl, where festival-goers pack their picnic baskets and enjoy music, folkloric ballet, and related performances by special guests. Call **213/848-7717**. Late June.

July

- **Fourth of July Celebration**, Pasadena. Southern California's most spectacular display of fireworks follows an evening of live entertainment at the Rose Bowl. Call **818/577-3100**. July 4.
- **Fireworks Display at the Marina**, Marina del Rey. Burton Chase Park, at the west end of Mindanao Way on one of the manmade fingers that jut into the marina basin, is a favorite place to ooh and aah at the traditional Fourth of July fireworks. Arrive in the afternoon to get the best parking and viewing sites. July 4.
- **Hollywood Bowl Summer Festival**, Los Angeles. Summer season at the Hollywood Bowl brings the world's best sounds of jazz, pop, and classical to a beautiful open-air setting. The season includes an annual Fourth of July concert. The season runs from July through mid-September; call the box office (☎ **213/850-2000**) for information and this year's schedule.
- **Festival of Arts & Pageant of the Masters**, Laguna Beach. A 60-year tradition in artsy Laguna, the festival features food, live music, and dozens of artists exhibiting and selling their unique works, from pottery to jewelry to wearable art. Each evening, it's the works of the masters that literally come alive: Costumed volunteers re-create famous works of art on stage, in stunningly accurate presentations. General admission is a couple of bucks; pageant tickets range from $15 to $40. Call **714/494-1145** or 800/487-FEST. July and August.

August

- **International Surf Festival**, Hermosa, Manhattan, and Redondo beaches. Four beachside cities collaborate in the oldest international surf festival in California.

Competitions include surfing, boogie boarding, sand-castle building, and other beach-related activities. Call 310/376-6911 for information. Early August.

- **Nisei Week Japanese Festival,** Los Angeles. This week-long celebration of Japanese culture and heritage is held in the Japanese American Cultural and Community Center Plaza in Little Tokyo. Festivities include parades, food, music, arts, and crafts. Call **213/687-7193.** Mid-August.
- **African Marketplace and Cultural Fair.** African arts, crafts, food, and music are featured at this cultural-awareness event. Call **213/734-1164.** Held at Rancho La Cienega Park, 5001 Rodeo Rd.; to get there, take I-10 to the La Brea Avenue exit. Weekends, second week of August through Labor Day.

September

- **Los Angeles County Fair,** Pomona. Horse racing, arts, agricultural displays, celebrity entertainment, and carnival rides are among the attractions at one of the largest county fairs in the world. Held at the Los Angeles County Fair and Exposition Center; call **909/623-3111** for information. Throughout September.
- **Watts Towers Day of the Drum Festival,** Los Angeles. This event celebrates the historic role of drums and drummers throughout the world. A variety of unique performances are staged, from Afro-Cuban folkloricos to East Indian tabla players. Call **213/847-4646.** Late September.

October

- **Catalina Island Jazz Trax Festival.** More than 10 contemporary jazz greats travel to the island to play at the legendary Casino Ballroom. The festival takes place over two consecutive 3-day weekends. Call **800/866-TRAX** or 619/458-9586 for more information. Late September or early October.

November

- **Catalina Island Triathlon.** This is one of the top 100 triathlons in the world. Participants run on unpaved roads, swim in the cleanest bay on the West Coast, and bike on challenging trails. There's also a "kid's tri." Call Pacific Sports at **818/357-9699.** Early November.
- **Doo Dah Parade,** Pasadena. An outrageous spoof of the Rose Parade, featuring such participants as the Briefcase Precision Drill Team and a kazoo-playing marching band. Call **818/795-9311.** Saturday after Thanksgiving.

December

- **Hollywood Christmas Parade.** This spectacular star-studded parade marches down Hollywood Boulevard just after Thanksgiving. For information, call **213/469-2337.**
- **Christmas Boat Parades.** Following long standing tradition, sailors love to decorate their craft with colorful lights for the holidays. Several pleasure-boat harbors along the coast hold nighttime parades showcasing these creations throughout the month of December. Great for kids—it's kind of like Disneyland's Main Street Electrical Parade afloat. At Marina Del Rey (☎ **310/821-0555**); Long Beach's Shoreline Village (☎ **310/435-4093**); and Huntington Harbour (☎ **714/840-7542**).

3　Staying Healthy & Safe in L.A.

INSURANCE

Many travelers are covered by their hometown health insurance policies in the event of an accident or sudden illness while away on vacation. Make sure that your Health Maintenance Organization (HMO) or insurance carrier can provide services for you while you're in California. If there's any doubt, a health insurance policy that specifically covers your trip is advisable.

You can also protect yourself with insurance against lost or damaged baggage and trip-cancellation or interruption costs. These coverages are often combined into a single comprehensive plan, sold through travel agents, credit- and charge-card companies, and automobile and other clubs.

Most travel agents can sell low-cost health, loss, and trip-cancellation insurance to their vacationing clients. Compare these rates and services with those offered by local banks as well as by your personal insurance carrier.

PERSONAL SAFETY

Los Angeles suffers from one of the highest crime rates in the nation, but visitors are rarely victims; only a tiny percentage of the city's tens of millions of annual visitors are targets of crime. Still, there are precautions everyone should take.

Know where you're going in advance. It may feel very unsettling to stray into East and South-Central Los Angeles unknowingly. Don't let your car advertise that you're a visitor. Place maps, travel brochures, this guidebook, and other valuables out of sight—in the glove compartment or trunk. When parking for the night, ask yourself if you've left anything in your car that could be of any value whatsoever—then remove it.

Homelessness is a big problem in Los Angeles. Panhandlers are especially prevalent in Santa Monica, Venice, and downtown. Most homeless people are harmless; however, some are chronic law violators who may infringe on the rights of others. A combination of respect and caution is suggested.

EARTHQUAKES

Some people actually hope to experience this California phenomenon; you might be surprised to learn that their wishes are usually answered, because earthquakes happen dozens of times a day throughout the state. Most are imperceptible to people and only register on finely tuned tracking equipment, so no one ever knows they have occurred. In the rare event of a major earthquake, you should know about a few simple precautions that every California schoolkid is taught:

If you're in a tall building, don't run outside; instead, move away from windows and toward the center of the building. Crouch under a desk or table, or stand in a doorway or against a wall. If you're in bed, get under the bed or stand in the doorway, or crouch under a sturdy piece of furniture. When exiting the building, use stairwells, *not* elevators.

If you're in your car, an earthquake feels as though you have a flat tire (strange, but true!). Simply pull over to the side of the road and stop, but wait until you're away from bridges or overpasses and telephone or power poles and lines. Stay in your car.

If you're out walking, stay outside and away from trees, power lines, and buildings. If you're in an area with tall buildings, stand in a doorway.

4 Tips for Travelers with Special Needs

FOR TRAVELERS WITH DISABILITIES

All of Los Angeles's public museums and tourist attractions are fitted with wheelchair ramps to accommodate physically challenged visitors, and most hotels offer special accommodations and services for wheelchair-bound and other disabled guests. These include large bathrooms, ramps, and telecommunication devices for the deaf. The **California Travel Industry Association** (2500 Wilshire Blvd., Suite 603, Los

Angeles, CA 90057; ☎ **213/384-3178**) provides information and referrals to specially equipped sights and hotels around the city and state. In addition, California issues special license plates to physically disabled drivers and honors plates issued by other states. You'll find specially marked "handicapped" parking spots wherever you go.

The **Los Angeles County Commission on Disabilities** (383 Hall of Administration, 500 W. Temple St., Los Angeles, CA 90012; ☎ **213/974-1053** or TDD 213/974-1707) publishes a free brochure listing services and facilities offered by the city's private- and public-sector agencies. Call to have a copy sent to you.

The **Junior League of Los Angeles** (Farmers Market, 3rd & Fairfax Sts., Gate 12, Los Angeles, CA 90036; ☎ **213/937-5566**) distributes *Round the Town with Ease* free to visitors with disabilities; there is a $2 handling fee for mail orders.

FOR GAY & LESBIAN TRAVELERS

Gay- and lesbian-oriented business and services are concentrated in West Hollywood. There are many gay-oriented publications with information and up-to-date listings, including *The Advocate,* a biweekly national magazine; *Frontiers,* a Southern California–based biweekly; and *Nightlife,* a local weekly with comprehensive listings of entertainment places, complete with maps. These and other periodicals are available at most newsstands citywide.

A Different Light (8853 Santa Monica Blvd., West Hollywood; ☎ **310/854-6601**) is Los Angeles's best gay-oriented bookshop; it's one of the largest of its kind on the West Coast. **Sisterhood Bookstore** (1351 Westwood Blvd., West Los Angeles; ☎ **310/477-7300**) is one of the best sources for lesbian-oriented books, magazines, and newspapers.

West Hollywood is also home to the charming **San Vicente Inn,** a gay-owned and -operated bed-and-breakfast. See chapter 5 for details.

Chapter 10 includes listings of clubs and bars that cater to gays and lesbians.

FOR SENIORS

In California, "senior citizen" usually means anyone 65 or older. Seniors regularly receive discounts at museums and attractions; when available, these discounts are listed in the following chapters under their appropriate headings. Ask for discounts everywhere—at hotels, movie theaters, museums, restaurants, and attractions—and you may be surprised how often you'll be offered reduced rates. When making airline reservations, ask about a senior discount, but find out if there's a cheaper promotional fare before committing yourself.

If you aren't a member of the **American Association of Retired Persons (AARP),** 3200 E. Carson St., Lakewood, CA 90712 (☎ **800/424-3410**), you should consider joining. AARP provides discounts at many lodgings and attractions throughout Southern California (although sometimes you can get a similar discount just by showing your ID).

FOR STUDENTS

A high school or college ID often entitles you to discounts at attractions (particularly at museums), and sometimes to reduced rates at restaurants, shops, and nightspots. Keep your ID with you, and always inquire.

TIPS FOR FAMILIES

When flying with children, plan ahead by requesting children's meals; obtain seat assignments in advance to either specify or avoid bulkhead seats. The advantage of this placement is more legroom where smaller children can play; the disadvantage is having no convenient place to store carry-on bags because there is no row of seats in front of you. It also pays to plan ahead when making lodging arrangements—ask what the cut-off age is for children to stay free in a parent's room. With the rising popularity of suite-style hotels, it can be economic and comfortable to have the kids stay in your suite rather than paying for a second room.

When making car-rental arrangements, request child seats in advance—they are sometimes provided at no charge.

If you need a baby-sitter while you're in L.A., try the **Baby-Sitters Guild** in Glendale (☎ 818/552-2229); or **Sitters Unlimited** (☎ 800/328-1191). The concierge at larger hotels can also usually recommend a reliable sitter. **Babyland** rents strollers, cribs, car seats, and the like from both of their Los Angeles area locations, at 1782 S. La Cienega Blvd. (North of I-10), Los Angeles (☎310/836-2222); and 1901 E. Colorado Blvd. (East of Hill Ave.), Pasadena (☎818/578-7500). Rental rates vary; the charge is 35% of the item's retail price per week.

If you travel often with the family, consider subscribing to *Family Travel Times,* published 10 times a year by **Travel With Your Children** (☎ 212/477-5524). This useful periodical covers destinations, types of vacations, modes of travel, and other useful tips. A year's subscription is $55; or call for a list of available back-issues by topic.

5 Getting There

ARRIVING BY PLANE

All major U.S. carriers serve Los Angeles International Airport (LAX). Domestic airlines flying in and out of LAX include **Alaska Airlines** (☎ 800/426-0333), **America West** (☎ 800/235-9292), **American Airlines** (☎ 800/433-7300), **Delta Air Lines** (☎ 800/221-1212), **Northwest Airlines** (☎ 800/225-2525), **Southwest Airlines** (☎ 800/435-9792), **TWA** (☎ 800/221-2000), **United Airlines** (☎ 800/ 241-6522), and **USAir** (☎ 800/428-4322).

The five biggest domestic airlines—American, Delta, Northwest, TWA, and United—have all considerably raised their domestic fares in the past 2 years, but occasional sales and competition from smaller carriers still makes Los Angeles one of the cheapest cities to reach from almost any other major American city. Across the board, the cheapest seats are currently being offered by no-frills Southwest Airlines, but their service and schedules are much more limited than the big five. The lowest airfares from New York usually fluctuate between $400 and $500, and between $300 and $400 from Chicago; sometimes you can do a little better, especially by calling the airlines directly.

Several smaller carriers are known for the excellent and comprehensive service they provide up and down the California coast. **America West** (☎ 800/235-9292), **American Eagle** (☎ 800/433-7300), **Skywest** (☎ 800/453-9417), **United Express** (☎ 800/241-6522), and **USAir Express** (☎ 800/428-4322) are some of the biggest carriers offering regular service between California cities. The lowest round-trip fare between San Francisco and L.A. is about $198—on occasion, it's even less.

If you're booking less than 30 days prior to travel, and can be a little flexible with your travel dates, you can often get great deals on fares between L.A. and other major U.S. cities by calling a consolidator, such as **Cheap Tickets** (☎ 800/377-1000 or 310/645-5054), **Cheap Seats** (☎ 800/451-7200 or 213/873-2838; http://www.chpseats.com/chpseats), **Travac** (☎ 800/TRAV-800 or 212/563-3303), or **Unitravel** (☎ 800/325-2222 or 314/569-0900).

LAX & THE OTHER LOS ANGELES–AREA AIRPORTS

There are five airports in the Los Angeles area. Most visitors fly into **Los Angeles International Airport** (☎ 310/646-5252). Better known as LAX, this behemoth is situated oceanside, between Marina del Rey and Manhattan Beach. LAX is a convenient place to land, located within minutes of Santa Monica and the beaches, and not more than a half-hour from downtown, Hollywood, or the Westside. Despite its size, the eight-terminal airport has a rather straightforward, easy-to-understand design. Free blue, green, and white **Airline Connections shuttle buses** (☎ 310/646-2911) connect the terminals at LAX and stop in front of each ticket building. Special handicapped-accessible minibuses are also available. **Travelers Aid of Los Angeles** (☎ 310/646-2270) operates booths in each terminal.

One of the area's smaller airports might be more convenient for you, landing you closer to your destination and allowing you to avoid the traffic and bustle of LAX. **Burbank-Glendale-Pasadena Airport** (2627 N. Hollywood Way, Burbank; ☎ 818/840-8840) is the best place to land if you're locating in Hollywood or the valleys. The small airport has especially good links to Las Vegas and other southwestern cities. **Long Beach Municipal Airport** (4100 Donald Douglas Dr., Long Beach; ☎ 310/421-8293), south of LAX, is the best place to land if you are visiting Long Beach or northern Orange County and want to avoid L.A. entirely. **John Wayne Airport** (19051 Airport Way N., Anaheim; ☎ 714/252-5200) is closest to Disneyland, Knott's Berry Farm, and other Orange County attractions. **Ontario International Airport** (Terminal Way, Ontario; ☎ 909/988-2700) is the least popular airport for tourists. Primarily a commuter airport, Ontario is popular with business people heading to San Bernardino, Riverside, and other inland communities. It's very convenient if you're heading to Palm Springs.

TRANSPORTATION FROM (AND TO) LAX

By Car

All the major car-rental firms operate off-site branches that are reached via shuttle from the terminals. See "Getting Around" in chapter 4 for a list of major rental companies.

LEAVING LAX BY CAR To reach Santa Monica and other northern beach communities, exit the airport, take Sepulveda Boulevard north, then follow the signs to Calif. 1 (Pacific Coast Highway or PCH) north.

To reach Redondo, Hermosa, Newport, and the other southern beach communities, take Sepulveda Boulevard south, then follow the signs to Calif. 1 (Pacific Coast Highway) south.

To reach Beverly Hills or Hollywood, exit the airport via Century Boulevard, then take I-405 north to Santa Monica Boulevard east.

To reach downtown or Pasadena, exit the airport, take Sepulveda Boulevard south, then take I-105 east to I-110 north.

A SHORTCUT TO LAX One of the city's busiest interchanges is from the Santa Monica Freeway (I-10) to the San Diego Freeway (I-405) on the way to Los Angeles International Airport. Therefore, when heading to LAX for your flight home, the scenic route may prove to be the fastest. From the Santa Monica Freeway (I-10) westbound, exit south to La Brea Avenue. Go right on Stocker Street, then left on La Cienega Boulevard. Veer right on La Tijera Boulevard and left on Airport Boulevard, then follow the signs. You can use this trick from West Hollywood and Beverly Hills as well—simply take La Cienega south, continuing as above.

By Shuttle

Many city hotels provide free shuttles for their guests; ask about transportation when you make reservations. **Super Shuttle (☎ 310/782-6600)**, a private ride-sharing service, offers regularly scheduled minivans from LAX to any location in the city. The set fare can range from about $10 to $50, depending on your destination. When traveling to the airport for your trip home, reserve your shuttle at least one day in advance.

By Taxi

Taxis line up outside each terminal, and rides are metered. Expect to pay about $30 to Hollywood and downtown, $25 to Beverly Hills, $20 to Santa Monica, and $45 to Pasadena. These prices include a $2.50 service charge for rides originating at LAX.

By Rail

The city's new Metro Green Line connects LAX with Norwalk, an eastern L.A. city where few visitors want to go. At its midsection, though, the Green Line is intersected by the Blue Line, a light-rail service that operates between downtown and Long Beach. By transferring from the Green to the Blue Line, visitors arriving at LAX can now travel from the airport to downtown or Long Beach by train. The service operates from 6am to 9pm and the combined fare is $1.60. Call the **Los Angeles County Metropolitan Transit Authority (MTA)** at **800/252-7433** or 213/626-4455 for information.

By Public Bus

The city's MTA buses also go between LAX and many parts of the city. Phone **MTA Airport Information (☎ 800/252-7433** or 213/626-4455) for the schedules and fares.

ARRIVING BY CAR

Los Angeles is well connected to the rest of the United States by several major highways. Among them are Interstate 5, which enters the state from the north; Interstate 10, which originates in Jacksonville, Florida, and terminates in Los Angeles; and U.S. 101, which follows the western seaboard from Los Angeles north to the Oregon state line. If you're planning to take smaller roads, call the **California Highway Patrol (☎ 213/953-7383)** to check road conditions before heading out.

If you're driving in **from the north,** you have two choices: the quick route, along I-5 through the middle of the state, or the scenic route along the coast.

Heading south along I-5, you'll pass a small town called Grapevine. This marks the start of the mountain pass known as the Grapevine. Once you've reached the southern end of the mountain pass, you'll be in the San Fernando Valley, and you've arrived in Los Angeles County. To reach the beach communities and L.A.'s Westside take I-405 south; to get to Hollywood, take Calif. 170 south to U.S. 101 south (this route is called the Hollywood Freeway the entire way); the I-5 will take you along the eastern edge of downtown and into Orange County.

If you're taking the scenic coastal route in from the north, take U.S. 101 to I-405, I-5, or stay on U.S. 101, following the instructions as listed above to your final destination.

If you're approaching **from the east,** you'll be coming in on I-10. For Orange County, take Calif. 57 south. I-10 continues through downtown and terminates at the beach. If you're heading to the Westside, take the I-405 north. To get to the beaches, take Calif. 1 (PCH) north or south, depending on your destination.

From the south, head north on I-5. At the southern end of Orange County, I-405 splits off to the west; take this road to the Westside and beach communities. Stay on I-5 to reach downtown and Hollywood.

Here are some handy driving times if you're on one of those see-the-U.S.A. car trips: From Phoenix, it's about 350 miles, or 6 hours (okay, 7, if you drive the speed limit), to Los Angeles via I-10. Las Vegas is 265 miles northeast of Los Angeles (about a 4- or 5-hour drive). San Francisco is 390 miles north of Los Angeles (between 6 and 7 hours on I-5), and San Diego is 115 miles (about 2 hours) south.

Before you set out on a big car trip, you might want to join the **American Automobile Association (AAA)** (☎ 800/336-4357), which has hundreds of offices nationwide. Members receive excellent maps (they'll even help you plan an exact itinerary) and emergency road service.

ROAD MAPS   California's freeway signs frequently indicate direction by naming a town rather than a point on the compass. If you've never heard of Canoga Park you might be in trouble, unless you have a map. The best state road guide is the comprehensive *Thomas Bros. California Road Atlas,* a 300-plus-page book of maps with schematics of towns and cities statewide. It costs $21, but is a good investment if you plan to do a lot of exploring. There's also a *Thomas Bros. Guide for Los Angeles County* (about $16). Smaller, accordion-style maps are handy for the state as a whole or for individual cities and regions. These foldout maps usually cost $2 to $3 and are available at gas stations, pharmacies, supermarkets, and tourist-oriented shops everywhere.

ARRIVING BY TRAIN

Amtrak (☎ 800/USA-RAIL) connects Los Angeles with about 500 American cities. Trains bound for Southern California leave daily from New York and pass through Chicago and Denver. The journey takes about $3^1/_2$ days, and seats fill up quickly. At this writing, the lowest round-trip fare was $339 from New York and $269 from Chicago. These heavily restricted tickets are good for 45 days and allow up to three stops along the way.

The *Sunset Limited* is Amtrak's regularly scheduled transcontinental service, originating in Florida and making 52 stops along the way as it passes through Alabama, Mississippi, Louisiana, Texas, New Mexico, and Arizona before arriving in Los Angeles. The train, which runs three times weekly, features reclining seats, a sightseeing car with large windows, and a full-service dining car. Round-trip coach fares begin at $259; sleeping accommodations are available for an extra charge.

Amtrak also runs trains up and down the California coast, connecting Los Angeles with San Francisco and all points in between. A one-way ticket can often be had for as little as $50. The coastal journey, aboard Amtrak's *Coast Starlight,* is a fantastically beautiful trip that runs from Seattle to Oakland; crosses Salinas, the artichoke capital of the world; climbs San Luis Obispo's bucolic hills; drops into Santa Barbara; then runs down the Malibu coast into Los Angeles. You can then continue on to San Diego if you like. It's a popular journey—make reservations well in advance.

Call Amtrak for a brochure outlining routes and prices for the entire system. Ask about special family plans, tours, and other money-saving promotions the rail carrier may be offering.

The L.A. terminus is **Union Station** (800 N. Alameda; ☎ 213/624-0171), on downtown's northern edge. Completed in 1939, the station was the last of America's great train depots—a unique blend of Spanish Revival and Streamline Moderne architecture that still functions as a modern-day transport center (see "Architectural Highlights," in chapter 7, for more details). From the station, you can take one of the many taxis that line up outside the station, or board the Metro Blue Line to Long Beach.

ARRIVING BY BUS

Bus travel is an inexpensive and often flexible option. **Greyhound/Trailways** (☎ **800/231-2222**) can get you here from anywhere, and offers several money-saving multiday passes. Round-trip fares vary depending on your point of origin, but few, if any, ever exceed $200. The main Los Angeles bus station is downtown at 1716 E. 7th Street, east of Alameda (☎ **213/262-1514**). For additional area terminal locations and local fare and schedule information, call the toll-free number listed above.

PACKAGE TOURS

Operators offering escorted tours in Southern California include **Caravan** (401 N. Michigan Ave., Chicago, IL 60611; ☎ 800/227-2826 or 312/321-9800); **Collette Tours** (162 Middle St., Pawtucket, RI 02860; ☎ 800/832-4656 or 401/728-3805); **Gadabout Tours** (700 E. Tahquitz Way, Palm Springs, CA 92262; ☎ 800/952-5068 or 619/325-5556); and **Globus** (5301 South Federal Circle, Littleton, CO 80123; ☎ 800/221-0090 or 303/797-2800).

Independent fly/drive packages (no escorted tour groups, just a bulk rate on your airfare, hotel, and possibly your rental car) are offered by **American Airlines Fly AAway Vacations** (☎ 800/634-5555), **Delta Dream Vacations** (☎ 800/872-7786), **TWA Getaway Vacations** (☎ 800/438-2929), and **United Airlines Vacation Planning Center** (☎ 800/328-6877).

3

For Foreign Visitors

American fads and fashions have spread across other parts of the world to such a degree that the United States may seem like familiar territory before your arrival. But there are still many peculiarities and uniquely American situations any foreign visitor may find confusing or perplexing. This chapter will provide specifics about getting to the United States as economically and effortlessly as possible, plus some helpful information about how things are done in Southern California—from receiving mail to making a local or long-distance telephone call.

1 Preparing for Your Trip

ENTRY REQUIREMENTS

DOCUMENT REGULATIONS Canadian nationals need only proof of Canadian residence to visit the United States. Citizens of the United Kingdom and Japan need only a current passport. Citizens of other countries, including Australia and New Zealand, usually need two documents: a valid passport with an expiration date at least 6 months later than the scheduled end of their visit to the United States and a tourist visa available at no charge from a U.S. embassy or consulate.

To get a tourist or business visa to enter the United States, contact the nearest American embassy or consulate in your country; if there is none, you will have to apply in person in a country where there is a U.S. embassy or consulate. Present your passport, a passport-sized photo of yourself, and an application, available through the embassy or consulate, completed by you. You may be asked to provide information about how you plan to finance your trip or show a letter of invitation from a friend with whom you plan to stay. Those applying for a business visa may be asked to show evidence that they will not receive a salary in the United States. Be sure to check the length of stay on your visa; it is usually 6 months. If you want to stay longer, you may file for an extension with the Immigration and Naturalization Service once you are in the country. If permission to stay is granted, a new visa is not required unless you leave the United States and want to reenter.

MEDICAL REQUIREMENTS No inoculations are needed to enter the United States unless you are coming from, or have stopped over in, areas known to be suffering from epidemics, particularly cholera or yellow fever.

If you have a disease requiring treatment with medications containing narcotics or drugs requiring a syringe, carry a valid signed generic prescription from your physician to allay any suspicions that you are smuggling drugs. The prescription brands you are accustomed to buying in your country may not be available in the United States.

CUSTOMS REQUIREMENTS Every adult visitor may bring in, free of duty: 1 liter of wine or hard liquor; 200 cigarettes or 100 cigars (but no cigars from Cuba) or 3 pounds of smoking tobacco; and $100 worth of gifts. These exemptions are offered to travelers who spend at least 72 hours in the United States and who have not claimed them within the preceding 6 months. It is altogether forbidden to bring foodstuffs (particularly cheese, fruit, cooked meats, and canned goods) and plants (vegetables, seeds, tropical plants, and so on) into the country. Foreign tourists may bring in or take out up to $10,000 in U.S. or foreign currency with no formalities; larger sums must be declared to Customs on entering or leaving.

INSURANCE

Unlike most other countries, the United States does not have a national health system. Because the cost of medical care is extremely high, we strongly advise all travelers to secure health coverage before setting out on their trip. You may want to take out a comprehensive travel policy that covers (for a relatively low premium) sickness or injury costs (medical, surgical, and hospital); loss or theft of your baggage; trip-cancellation costs; guarantee of bail in case you are arrested; costs of accident, repatriation, or death. Such packages (for example, "Europe Assistance" in Europe) are sold by automobile clubs at attractive rates, as well as by insurance companies and travel agencies and at some airports.

MONEY

The U.S. monetary system has a decimal base: One American dollar ($1) = 100 cents (100¢). Dollar bills commonly come in $1 (a "buck"), $5, $10, $20, $50, and $100 denominations (the last two are not welcome when paying for small purchases, and are usually not accepted in taxis or at subway ticket booths). There are six coin denominations: 1¢ (one cent, or "penny"); 5¢ (five cents, or "nickel"); 10¢ (ten cents, or "dime"); 25¢ (twenty-five cents, or "quarter"); 50¢ (fifty cents, or "half dollar"); and the $1 pieces (both the older, large silver dollar and the newer, small Susan B. Anthony coin).

Traveler's checks in U.S. dollars are accepted at most hotels, motels, restaurants, and large stores. Sometimes picture identification is required. American Express, Thomas Cook, and Barclay's Bank traveler's checks are readily accepted in the United States.

Credit cards are the method of payment most widely used: Visa (BarclayCard in Britain), MasterCard (EuroCard in Europe, Access in Britain, Diamond in Japan), American Express, Discover, Diners Club, enRoute, JCB, and Carte Blanche, in descending order of acceptance. You can save yourself trouble by using "plastic" rather than cash or traveler's checks in 95% of all hotels, motels, restaurants, and retail stores. A credit card can also serve as a deposit for renting a car, as proof of identity, or as a "cash card," enabling you to draw money from automated teller machines (ATMs) that accept them.

If you plan to travel for several weeks or more in the United States, you may want to deposit enough money into your credit-card account to cover anticipated expenses and avoid finance charges in your absence. This also reduces the likelihood of your receiving an unwelcome big bill on your return.

You can telegraph (wire) money, or have it telegraphed to you very quickly using the Western Union system (☎ 800/325-6000).

SAFETY

While tourist areas are generally safe, crime is on the increase everywhere, and U.S. urban areas tend to be less safe than those in Europe or Japan. Visitors should always stay alert. This is particularly true of large U.S. cities. It's wise to ask the city's or area's tourist office if you're in doubt about which neighborhoods are safe.

Remember also that hotels are open to the public, and in a large hotel, security may not be able to screen everyone entering. Always lock your room door—don't assume that once inside your hotel you are automatically safe and no longer need be aware of your surroundings.

Also see "Staying Healthy & Safe in L.A." in chapter 2.

DRIVING Safety while driving is particularly important. Question your rental agency about personal safety, or ask for a brochure of traveler safety tips when you pick up your car. Obtain written directions, or a map with the route marked in red, from the agency showing how to get to your destination. And, if possible, arrive and depart during daylight hours.

Recently, more and more crime has involved cars and drivers. If you drive off a highway into a doubtful neighborhood, leave the area as quickly as possible. If you have an accident, even on the highway, stay in your car with the doors locked until you assess the situation or until the police arrive. If you are bumped from behind on the street or are involved in a minor accident with no injuries and the situation appears to be suspicious, motion to the other driver to follow you to a well-lighted area. Never get out of your car in such situations.

If you see someone on the road who indicates a need for help, do not stop. Take note of the location, drive on to a well-lighted area, and telephone the police by dialing 911. Park in well-lighted, well-traveled areas if possible.

Always keep your car doors locked, whether attended or unattended. Never leave any packages or valuables in sight. If someone attempts to rob you or steal your car, do not try to resist the thief/carjacker—report the incident to the police department immediately.

2 Getting to the U.S.

Travelers from overseas can take advantage of APEX (advance purchase excursion) fares offered by all the major U.S. and European carriers. Aside from these, attractive values are offered by Virgin Atlantic from London to Los Angeles.

A number of U.S. airlines offer service from Europe to the United States. If they do not have direct flights from Europe to Los Angeles, they can book you straight through on a connecting flight. You can make reservations by calling the following numbers in London: **American** (☎ 0181/572-5555), **Continental** (☎ 4412/9377-6464), **Delta** (☎ 0800/414-767), and **United** (☎ 0181/990-9900).

And, of course, many international carriers serve LAX. Helpful numbers include **Virgin Atlantic** (☎ 0293/747-747 in London), **British Airways** (☎ 0345/222-111 in London), and **Aer Lingus** (☎ 01/844-4747 in Dublin or 061/415-556 in Shannon). **Qantas** (☎ 008/177-767 in Australia) has flights from Sydney to Los Angeles; you can also take **United** from Australia to Los Angeles. **Air New Zealand** (☎ 0800/737-000 in Auckland or 64-3/379-5200 in Christchurch) also offers service to LAX. Canadian travelers might book flights on **Air Canada** (in Canada ☎ 800/268-7240 or 800/361-8620), which offers direct service from Toronto, Montreal, Calgary, and Vancouver to Los Angeles.

The visitor arriving by air, no matter what the port of entry, should cultivate patience and resignation before setting foot on U.S. soil. Getting through immigration control may take as long as 2 hours on some days, especially summer weekends, so have your guidebook or something else to read handy. Add the time it takes to clear Customs and you will see you should make a very generous allowance for delay in planning connections between international and domestic flights—figure on 2 to 3 hours at least.

In contrast, for the traveler arriving by car or rail from Canada, the border-crossing formalities have been streamlined to the vanishing point. And for the traveler by air from Canada, Bermuda, and some places in the Caribbean, you can sometimes go through Customs and Immigration at the point of departure, which is much quicker.

3 Getting Around the U.S.

BY PLANE   On their trans-Atlantic or trans-Pacific flights, some large U.S. airlines offer special discount tickets for any of their U.S. destinations (**American Airlines' Visit USA** program and **Delta's Discover America** program, for example). The tickets or coupons are not for sale in the United States and must be purchased before you leave your point of departure. This system is the best, easiest, and fastest way to see the United States at low cost. You should obtain information well in advance from your travel agent or the office of the airline concerned, since the conditions attached to these discount tickets can be changed without advance notice. Call the airlines at the numbers listed above for details on these and other intracontinental travel programs.

For more details on arriving in Los Angeles by air from other destinations in the U.S., see "Getting There" in chapter 2.

BY RAIL   International visitors can also buy a **USA Railpass,** good for 15 or 30 days of unlimited travel on Amtrak. The pass is available through many foreign travel agents. Prices in 1996 for a 15-day pass are $229 off peak, $340 peak; a 30-day pass costs $339 off peak, $425 peak (off peak is August 31 to June 15). (With a foreign passport, you can also buy passes at some Amtrak offices in the United States, including locations in San Francisco, Los Angeles, Chicago, New York, Miami, Boston, and Washington, D.C.) Reservations are generally required and should be made for each part of your trip as early as possible. Train travel between cities within the state of California is scenic and economical; prices vary, so call **Amtrak** (☎ **800/USA-RAIL** within the U.S.) or your travel agent for details.

Visitors should also be aware of the limitations of long-distance rail travel in the United States. With a few notable exceptions (for instance, the Northeast Corridor line between Boston and Washington, D.C.), service is rarely up to European standards: Delays are common, routes are limited and often infrequently served, and fares are rarely significantly lower than discount airfares. Thus, cross-country train travel should be approached with caution.

BY BUS   Although bus trips between cities have traditionally been the most economical form of public transit, at this writing, bus passes are priced slightly higher than similar train passes. Short bus trips within the state of California, however, may still prove to be the cheapest way to travel. **Greyhound/Trailways** (☎ **800/**

231-2222), the sole nationwide bus line, offers an **Ameripass** for unlimited travel for 7 days (for $359), 15 days (for $459), and 30 days (for $559). Bus travel in the United States can be both slow and uncomfortable, so this option is not for everyone. In addition, bus stations are often located in undesirable neighborhoods.

FAST FACTS: For the Foreign Traveler

Automobile Organizations   Auto clubs will supply maps, suggested routes, guidebooks, accident and bail-bond insurance, and emergency road service. The major auto club in the United States, with 955 offices nationwide, is the American Automobile Association (AAA). Members of some foreign auto clubs have reciprocal arrangements with the AAA and enjoy its services at no charge. If you belong to an auto club, inquire about AAA reciprocity before you leave. The AAA can provide you with an International Driving Permit validating your foreign license, although drivers with valid licenses from most home countries don't really need this permit. You may be able to join the AAA even if you are not a member of a reciprocal club. To inquire, call 619/233-1000 or 800/222-4357. In addition, some automobile rental agencies now provide these services, so you should inquire about their availability when you rent your car.

Automobile Rentals   To rent a car, you need a major credit or charge card and a valid driver's license, and you usually need to be at least 25 years of age. Some companies do rent to younger drivers but add a daily surcharge. Be sure to return your car with the same amount of gas (petrol) you started out with; rental companies charge excessive prices for gasoline. An exception is if you purchase gas "in advance" from the rental agency, a good option if you think you might not remember or be able to fill up immediately before returning the car. All the major car rental companies are represented in Los Angeles (see chapter 4).

Business Hours   Offices are usually open weekdays from 9am to 5pm. Banks are open weekdays from 9am to 3pm or later on weekdays, and sometimes on Saturday morning. Shops, especially department stores and those in shopping complexes, tend to stay open late—until about 9pm weekdays and until 6pm weekends. Shops are usually open 6 days a week, sometimes Sundays as well.

Climate   See "When to Go" in chapter 2.

Currency   See "Preparing for Your Trip" earlier in this chapter.

Currency Exchange   The "foreign-exchange bureaus" so common in Europe are rare in the United States. They're at major international airports, and there are a few in most major cities, but they're nonexistent in medium-sized cities and small towns. Try to avoid having to change foreign money, or traveler's checks denominated other than in U.S. dollars, at small-town banks, or even at branches in a big city; in fact, leave any currency other than U.S. dollars at home (except the cash you need for the taxi or bus ride home when you return to your own country); otherwise, your own currency may prove more nuisance to you than it's worth.

Drinking Laws   The legal age to purchase and consume alcohol is 21 years; if you are lucky enough to look younger than 30, be prepared to show proof of age in bars, restaurants, and liquor or grocery stores when purchasing alcohol.

Electric Current   The United States uses 110–120 volts, 60 cycles, compared to 220–240 volts, 50 cycles, as in most of Europe. Besides a 100-volt converter, small appliances of non-American manufacture, such as hair dryers or shavers, will require a plug adapter, with two flat, parallel pins. The easiest solution to the power struggle is to purchase dual-voltage appliances that operate on both 110 and 220 volts, and then all that is required is a U.S. adapter plug.

Embassies/Consulates   All embassies are located in Washington, D.C. Listed here are the West Coast consulates of the major English-speaking countries. The **Australian Consulate** is located at 611 N. Larchmont, Los Angeles, CA 90004 (☎ 213/469-4300). The **Canadian Consulate** is at 300 South Grand Ave., Suite 1000, Los Angeles, CA 90071 (☎ 213/346-2700). The **Irish Consulate** is located at 655 Montgomery St., Suite 930, San Francisco, CA 94111 (☎ 415/392-4214). The **New Zealand Consulate** is at 12400 Wilshire Blvd., Los Angeles, CA 90025 (☎ 310/207-1605). Contact the **U.K. Consulate** at 11766 Wilshire Blvd., Suite 400, Los Angeles, CA 90025 (☎ 310/477-3322).

Emergencies   Call 911 for fire, police, and ambulance. If you encounter such traveler's problems as sickness, accident, or lost or stolen baggage, call the **Travelers Aid Society of Los Angeles** (☎ 310/646-2270), an organization that specializes in helping distressed travelers; Travelers Aid also has booths located in each terminal at Los Angeles International Airport (LAX). U.S. hospitals have emergency rooms, with a special entrance where you will be admitted for quick attention.

Gasoline (Petrol)   One U.S. gallon equals 3.75 liters, while 1.2 U.S. gallons equals 1 imperial gallon. A gallon of unleaded gas (short for gasoline), which most rental cars accept, costs about $1.30 if you fill your own tank (it's called "self-serve"); about 10¢ more if the station attendant does it (called "full-service"). Most gas stations in Los Angeles are strictly self-serve stations.

Holidays   On the following national legal holidays, banks, government offices, post offices, and many stores, restaurants, and museums are closed: January 1 (New Year's Day), third Monday in January (Martin Luther King, Jr., Day), third Monday in February (Presidents' Day), last Monday in May (Memorial Day), July 4 (Independence Day), first Monday in September (Labor Day), second Monday in October (Columbus Day), November 11 (Veterans Day/Armistice Day), last Thursday in November (Thanksgiving Day), and December 25 (Christmas Day). The Tuesday following the first Monday in November is Election Day.

Legal Aid   If you are stopped for a minor infraction (for example, of the highway code, such as speeding), never attempt to pay the fine directly to a police officer; you may be arrested on the much more serious charge of attempted bribery. Pay fines by mail, or directly into the hands of the clerk of the court. If accused of a more serious offense, it is best to say and do nothing before consulting a lawyer. Under U.S. law, an arrested person is allowed one telephone call to a party of his or her choice. Call your embassy or consulate.

Mail   You may receive mail c/o General Delivery at the main post office of the city or region where you expect to be. The addressee must pick it up in person, and must produce proof of identity (driver's license, credit card, passport, and so on).

Mailboxes are blue with a white-and-blue eagle logo, and carry the inscription "United States Postal Service." Within the United States, it costs 20¢ to mail a standard-size postcard and 32¢ to send an oversize postcard (larger than 6 by 4¹/₄ inches, or 15.4 by 10.8 centimeters). Letters that weigh up to 1 ounce (that's about five 11-by-8-inch, or 28.2-by-20.5-centimeter, pages) cost 32¢ plus 23¢ for each additional ounce. A postcard to Mexico costs 35¢, a ¹/₂-ounce letter 40¢; a postcard to Canada costs 40¢, a 1-ounce letter 52¢. A postcard to Europe,

Australia, New Zealand, the Far East, South America, and elsewhere costs 50¢, while a $1/2$-ounce letter is 60¢, and a 1-ounce letter is $1.

Medical Emergencies   See "Emergencies," above.

Taxes   In the United States, there is no VAT (value-added tax) or other indirect tax at a national level. There is a $10 Customs tax, payable on entry to the United States, and a $6 departure tax. Sales tax is levied on goods and services by state and local governments, however, and is not included in the price tags you'll see on merchandise. These taxes are not refundable. In Los Angeles, the sales tax is 8.25%. Hotel tax is charged on the room tariff only (which is not subject to sales tax), and is set by the city, ranging from 11% to 16% around Southern California.

Telephone and Fax   Pay phones can be found on street corners, as well as in bars, restaurants, public buildings, and stores and at service stations. Some accept 20¢, most are 25¢. If the telephone accepts 20¢, you may also use a quarter (25¢), but you will not receive change. You're usually allowed 3 minutes for a local call; you'll have to deposit more change for lengthier or long-distance calls.

For long-distance or international calls, it's most economical to charge the call to a telephone charge card or a credit card. If you prefer to use change, be sure to have a lot on hand. The pay phone will instruct you how much to deposit and when to deposit it into the slot on the top of the telephone box.

For long-distance calls in the United States, dial 1 followed by the area code and number you want. For direct overseas calls, first dial 011, followed by the country code (Australia, 61; Republic of Ireland, 353; New Zealand, 64; United Kingdom, 44; and so on), and then by the city code (for example, 171 or 181 for London, 21 for Birmingham, 1 for Dublin) and the number you wish to call.

Before calling from a hotel room, always ask the hotel phone operator if there are any telephone surcharges. There almost always are, and they often are as much as 75¢ or $1, even for a local call. These charges are best avoided by using a public phone, calling collect, or using a telephone charge card.

For reversed-charge or collect calls and for person-to-person calls, dial 0 (zero) followed by the area code and number you want; an operator will then come on the line, and you should specify that you are calling collect, or person-to-person, or both. If your operator-assisted call is international, immediately ask to speak with an overseas operator.

For local directory assistance ("Information"), dial 411; for long-distance information dial 1, then the appropriate area code and 555-1212.

In the past few years, many American companies have installed "voice-mail" systems, so be prepared to deal with a machine instead of a receptionist if calling a business number. Listen carefully to the instructions (you'll probably be asked to dial 1, 2, or 3 or wait for an operator to pick up); if you can't understand, sometimes dialing 0 (zero, not the letter O) will put you in touch with an operator within the company. Be patient; making your way through an automated system can be frustrating even for locals!

Most hotels have fax machines available for their customers, and there is usually a charge to send or receive a facsimile. You will also see signs for public faxes in the windows of small shops.

Telephone Directory   Most hotels and many pay phones provide local directories for your use. The local phone company distributes two kinds of telephone directories. The general directory, called the "white pages," lists personal residences and businesses separately, in alphabetical order. The first few pages are devoted to community-service numbers, including a guide to long-distance and international calling, complete with country codes and area codes.

The second directory, the "yellow pages," lists all local services, businesses, and industries by type, with an index at the back. The listings cover not only such obvious items as automobile repairs by make of car, or drugstores (pharmacies), often by geographical location, but also restaurants by type of cuisine and geographical location, bookstores by special subject and/or language, places of worship by religious denomination, and other information that a visitor might otherwise not readily find. The yellow pages also include city plans or detailed area maps, often showing postal ZIP codes and public transportation.

Time   California is on Pacific time, which is 3 hours earlier than on the U.S. East Coast. For instance, when it is noon in Los Angeles, it is 3pm in New York and Miami; 2pm in Chicago, in the central part of the country; and 1pm in Denver, Colorado, in the midwestern part of the country. California, like most of the rest of the United States, observes daylight saving time during the summer; in late spring, clocks are moved ahead 1 hour and then are turned back again in the fall. This results in lovely long summer evenings, when the sun sets as late as 8:30 or 9pm.

Tipping   Some rules of thumb: bartenders, 10 to 15%; bellhops, at least 50¢ per bag, or $2 to $3 for a lot of luggage; cab drivers, 10% of the fare; cafeterias and fast-food restaurants, no tip; chambermaids, $1 per day; checkroom attendants, $1 per garment; theater ushers, no tip; gas-station attendants, no tip; hairdressers and barbers, waiters and waitresses, 15 to 20% of the check; valet parking attendants, $1.

4

Getting to Know Los Angeles

The freeways crisscrossing the Los Angeles metropolitan area are your lifelines to the sights, but it will take you a little time to master their maze. Even locals sometimes have trouble making their way around this sprawling city. This chapter will familiarize you with the setup of the city and will start you on the road to negotiating it like a native.

1 Orientation

VISITOR INFORMATION CENTERS

The **Los Angeles Convention and Visitors Bureau,** 633 W. 5th St., Suite 600, Los Angeles, CA 90071 (☎ **213/624-7300**), is the city's main source for information. The bureau also staffs a **Visitors Information Center** at 685 S. Figueroa St., downtown between Wilshire Boulevard and 7th Street, which is open Monday through Friday from 8am to 5pm and Saturday from 8:30am to 5pm. Information is also available on the World Wide Web at **http://www.ci.la.ca.us/index.html**.

Many Los Angeles–area communities also have their own information centers:

Beverly Hills Visitors Bureau, 239 S. Beverly Dr., Beverly Hills, CA 90212 (☎ **800/345-2210** or 310/271-8174; fax 310/858-8032), is open Monday through Friday from 9am to 5pm.

Visitor Information Center Hollywood, Janes House, 6541 Hollywood Blvd., Hollywood, CA 90028 (☎ **213/236-2331**), is open Monday through Saturday from 9am to 5pm. **Hollywood Arts Council,** P.O. Box 931056, Dept. 1995, Hollywood, CA 90093 (☎ **213/462-2355**), distributes the magazine *Discover Hollywood* for a $2 postage and handling fee. It contains listings and schedules for the area's many theaters, galleries, music venues, and comedy clubs.

Marina del Rey Chamber of Commerce/Visitor and Convention Bureau (☎ **310/821-0555**) has walk-in hours Monday through Friday from 9am to 5pm at 4371 Glencoe Ave., B-14, Marina del Rey, CA 90292. For information by mail, write 13428 Maxella Ave., Box 441, Marina del Rey, CA 90292. A 24-hour updated bulletin board listing local restaurant, lodging, shopping, boating, and relocation information is available by calling the InfoCenter System at 800/919-0555.

Redondo Beach Chamber of Commerce, 200 N. Pacific Coast Highway, Redondo Beach, CA 90277 (☎ **310/376-6911**), is open Monday through Friday from 8:30am to 5pm.

Santa Monica Convention and Visitors Bureau, 2219 Main St., Santa Monica, CA 90405 (☎ **310/393-7593**), is the source for information about Santa Monica. The Santa Monica Visitors Bureau Palisades Park is located near the Santa Monica Pier, at 1400 Ocean Avenue (between Santa Monica Boulevard and Broadway), and is open daily from 10am to 5pm. You can also visit the city on the Internet at **http://www.ci.santa-monica.ca.us**.

West Hollywood Convention and Visitors Bureau, 8687 Melrose Ave., M-26, West Hollywood, CA 90096 (☎ **800/368-6020** or 310/289-2525; fax 310/289-2529), is open Monday through Friday from 8am to 6pm. Their Web address is **http://www.ci.west-hollywood.ca.us**.

OTHER INFORMATION SOURCES

Local tourist boards are terrific for uncritical information regarding attractions and special events, but they often fail to keep a figurative finger on the pulse of what's really happening, especially with regard to dining, culture, and nightlife. Several city-oriented newspapers and magazines offer up-to-date info on current happenings. *L.A. Weekly,* a free weekly listings magazine, is packed with information on current events around town. It's available from sidewalk newsracks and in many stores and restaurants around the city. The *Los Angeles Times* "Calendar" section of the Sunday paper is an excellent guide to the world of entertainment in and around L.A., and includes listings of what's doing and where to do it. The *Times* also maintains an **Internet "Guide to Tinseltown"** at **http://www.latimes.com/HOME/ENT/TINSEL**.

Los Angeles Magazine and the even trendier upstart *Buzz* are city-based monthlies full of news, information, and previews of L.A.'s art, music, and food scenes. Both are available at newsstands around town. Serious cyber-hounds should visit **At L.A.'s Internet Website** at **http://www.at-la.com**; it's an exceptionally useful guide, with links to over 6,500 sites in 1,000 categories relating to the L.A. area, including many destinations covered in chapter 11, "Side Trips from Los Angeles."

CITY LAYOUT

Los Angeles is not a single compact city, but a sprawling suburbia comprising dozens of disparate communities. Most of the city's communities are located between mountains and ocean, on the flatlands of a huge basin. Even if you've never visited L.A. before, you'll recognize the names of many of these areas: Hollywood, Beverly Hills, Santa Monica, Malibu. Ocean breezes push the city's infamous smog inland, toward dozens of less well-known residential communities, and through mountain passes into the suburban sprawl of the San Fernando and San Gabriel valleys.

Downtown Los Angeles—which isn't where most tourists will situate themselves—is in the center of the basin, about 12 miles east of the Pacific Ocean. Most visitors will spend the bulk of their time either on the coast or on the city's Westside (see "Neighborhoods in Brief," below, for complete details on all of the city's sectors).

MAIN ARTERIES & STREETS

L.A.'s extensive freeway system connects the city's patchwork of communities; they work well together to get you where you need to be, although rush-hour traffic can sometimes be bumper-to-bumper. Here's an overview of the entire system:

The Freeway System

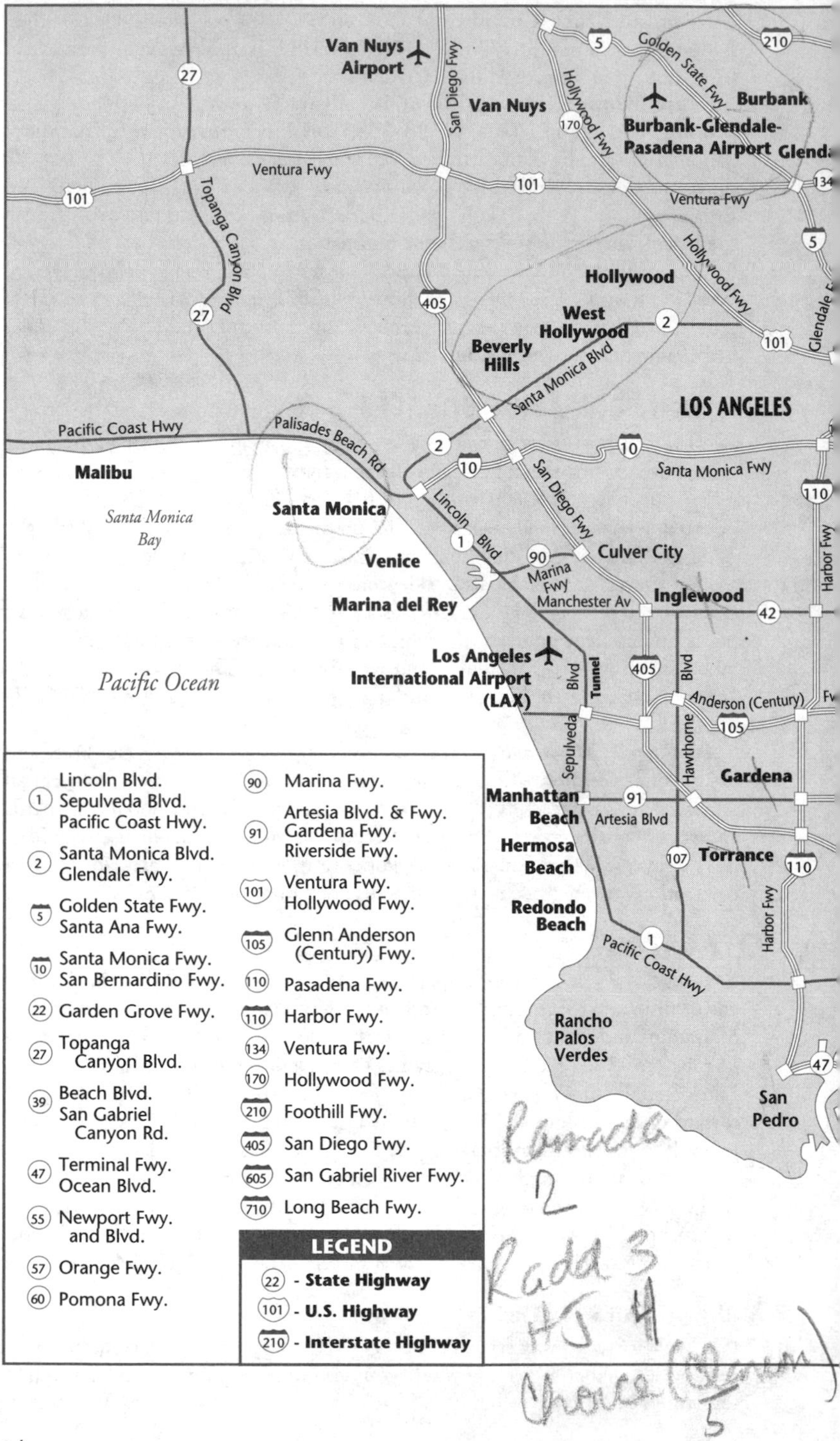

Van Nuys Airport
Van Nuys
San Diego Fwy
Golden State Fwy
Hollywood Fwy
Burbank
Burbank-Glendale-Pasadena Airport
Glenda
Ventura Fwy
Topanga Canyon Blvd
Hollywood
West Hollywood
Beverly Hills
Santa Monica Blvd
Glendale
LOS ANGELES
Pacific Coast Hwy
Palisades Beach Rd
Malibu
Santa Monica Bay
Santa Monica Fwy
Santa Monica
Lincoln Blvd
Venice
Marina Fwy
Culver City
Harbor Fwy
Marina del Rey
Manchester Av
Inglewood
Los Angeles International Airport (LAX)
Sepulveda Blvd
Tunnel
Hawthorne Blvd
Anderson (Century)
Pacific Ocean
Gardena
Manhattan Beach
Artesia Blvd
Hermosa Beach
Torrance
Redondo Beach
Rancho Palos Verdes
San Pedro
1 Lincoln Blvd. Sepulveda Blvd. Pacific Coast Hwy.
2 Santa Monica Blvd. Glendale Fwy.
5 Golden State Fwy. Santa Ana Fwy.
10 Santa Monica Fwy. San Bernardino Fwy.
22 Garden Grove Fwy.
27 Topanga Canyon Blvd.
39 Beach Blvd. San Gabriel Canyon Rd.
47 Terminal Fwy. Ocean Blvd.
55 Newport Fwy. and Blvd.
57 Orange Fwy.
60 Pomona Fwy.
90 Marina Fwy.
91 Artesia Blvd. & Fwy. Gardena Fwy. Riverside Fwy.
101 Ventura Fwy. Hollywood Fwy.
105 Glenn Anderson (Century) Fwy.
110 Pasadena Fwy.
110 Harbor Fwy.
134 Ventura Fwy.
170 Hollywood Fwy.
210 Foothill Fwy.
405 San Diego Fwy.
605 San Gabriel River Fwy.
710 Long Beach Fwy.
LEGEND
22 - State Highway
101 - U.S. Highway
210 - Interstate Highway

1-1085

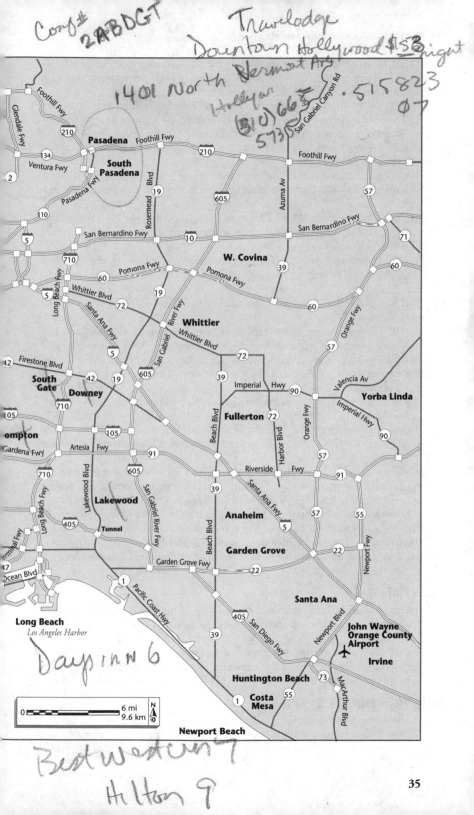

Handwritten annotations on map:

Conf# 2ABDGT

Travelodge
Downtown Hollywood $153 /night

1401 North Vermont Ave
Hollywood
(310) 665-5730

· 515823
07

Dayinn 6

Best western 7
Hilton 9

Map labels:

Glendale Fwy
Foothill Fwy
210
Pasadena
South Pasadena
Ventura Fwy
34
2
Pasadena Fwy
110
Rosemead Blvd
19
Foothill Fwy
210
605
Azuma Av
Foothill Fwy
57
San Gabriel Canyon Rd
San Bernardino Fwy
71
San Bernardino Fwy
5
710
San Bernardino Fwy
10
W. Covina
60
60
39
Pomona Fwy
60
Pomona Fwy
Long Beach Fwy
5
Whittier Blvd
Santa Ana Fwy
72
19
San Gabriel River Fwy
Whittier
Whittier Blvd
5
72
39
Orange Fwy
57
42
Firestone Blvd
South Gate
42
Downey
19
605
39
Imperial Hwy
90
Valencia Av
Yorba Linda
Orange Fwy
Imperial Hwy
90
Beach Blvd
Fullerton
72
Harbor Blvd
105
ompton
710
Gardena Fwy
Artesia Fwy
91
Riverside Fwy
57
91
55
Newport Fwy
710
605
Lakewood Blvd
San Gabriel River Fwy
Lakewood
Tunnel
405
39
Anaheim
5
57
Santa Ana Fwy
Garden Grove
22
Long Beach Fwy
Terminal Fwy
47
Ocean Blvd
1
Pacific Coast Hwy
Garden Grove Fwy
22
Beach Blvd
Santa Ana
405
San Diego Fwy
Newport Blvd
John Wayne
Orange County
Airport
Irvine
Long Beach
Los Angeles Harbor
MacArthur Blvd
73
Huntington Beach
1
Costa Mesa
55
39
Newport Beach

0 — 6 mi
9.6 km
N

35

U.S. 101, called the "Ventura Freeway" in the San Fernando Valley and the "Hollywood Freeway" in the city, runs across L.A. in a roughly northwest–southeast direction, from the San Fernando Valley to the center of downtown.

Calif. 134 continues as the "Ventura Freeway" after U.S. 101 turns into the city and becomes the Hollywood Freeway. This branch of the Ventura Freeway continues directly east, through the valley towns of Burbank and Glendale, to **I-210** (the "Foothill Freeway"), which will take you through Pasadena and out toward the eastern edge of Los Angeles County.

I-5, otherwise known as the "Golden State Freeway" north of I-10, and the "Santa Ana Freeway" south of I-10, bisects downtown on its way from San Francisco to San Diego.

I-10, labeled the "Santa Monica Freeway" west of I-5 and the "San Bernardino Freeway" east of I-5, is the city's major east–west freeway, connecting the San Gabriel Valley with downtown and Santa Monica.

I-405, also known as the "San Diego Freeway," runs north–south through L.A's Westside, connecting the San Fernando Valley with LAX and the southern beach areas.

I-105, Los Angeles's newest freeway—called the "Century Freeway"—extends from LAX east to I-605.

I-110, commonly known as the "Harbor Freeway," starts in Pasadena as **Calif. 110** (the "Pasadena Freeway"); it turns into the interstate in downtown Los Angeles and runs directly south, where it dead-ends in San Pedro. The section that is now the Pasadena Freeway is Los Angeles's historic first freeway, known as the Arroyo Seco when it opened in 1940.

I-710, a.k.a. the "Long Beach Freeway," runs in a north–south direction through East Los Angeles and dead-ends at Long Beach.

I-605, the "San Gabriel River Freeway," runs roughly parallel to the I-710 further east, through the cities of Hawthorne and Lynwood and into the San Gabriel Valley.

Calif. 1—called "Highway 1," the "Pacific Coast Highway," or simply "PCH"—is really a highway (more like a surface thruway) rather than a freeway. It skirts the ocean, linking all of L.A.'s beach communities, from Malibu to the Orange Coast.

The freeways are complemented by a complex web of surface streets. From north to south, the major east–west thoroughfares connecting downtown to the beaches are **Sunset Boulevard, Santa Monica Boulevard, Wilshire Boulevard,** and **Olympic, Pico, and Venice Boulevards.** The section of Sunset Boulevard that runs between Crescent Heights Boulevard and Doheny Drive is the famed **Sunset Strip.**

STREET MAPS

Because Los Angeles is so spread out, a good map of the area is essential. Foldout maps are available at gas stations, hotels, bookshops, and tourist-oriented shops around the city. If you're going to be in Los Angeles for a week or more, or plan on doing some extensive touring, you might want to invest in the all-inclusive *Thomas Guide,* a comprehensive book of city maps that depicts every single road in the city. The ring-bound edition is sold in most area bookstores and costs about $16.

NEIGHBORHOODS IN BRIEF

Los Angeles is a very confusing city, with fluid neighborhood lines and equally elastic labels. We have found that the best way to grasp the city is to break it into five regions—Santa Monica & the Beaches; L.A.'s Westside & Beverly Hills; Hollywood;

Downtown; and the San Fernando Valley—each of which encompasses a more-or-less distinctive patchwork of city neighborhoods and independently incorporated communities.

Throughout the book, the regions are ordered according to their natural geographical progression from west to east (except for the San Fernando Valley, which is roughly north of the city's other major regions, separated from them by the Hollywood Hills). We've structured our coverage this way because you'll be most likely starting out at the beach. Most visitors arrive at Los Angeles International Airport (LAX), which is located on the coast just south of L.A.'s primary beach communities. And unless you're coming to L.A. on business, you're likely to concentrate your visit in the city's western districts, since that's where the majority of attractions, restaurants, and shops are; many visitors never make it as far east as Downtown.

SANTA MONICA & THE BEACHES

These are my favorite L.A. communities. The 60-mile beachfront stretching from Malibu to the Palos Verdes Peninsula has milder weather and less smog than the inland communities, and traffic is nominally lighter—except on summer weekends, of course. The towns along the coast each have their own mood and charm; they're listed below from north to south.

Malibu, at the northern border of Los Angeles County, 25 miles from downtown, was once a privately owned ranch—purchased in 1857 for 10¢ an acre. Today its particularly wide beaches, sparsely populated hills, and relative remoteness from the inner city make it extremely popular with rich recluses. Indeed, the resident lists of Malibu Colony and nearby Broad Beach—oceanfront strips of closely packed mansions—read like a Who's Who in Hollywood. With plenty of green space and dramatic rocky outcroppings, Malibu's rural beauty is unsurpassed in L.A.

Pretty **Santa Monica,** Los Angeles's premier beach community, is known for its long ocean pier, artsy atmosphere, and somewhat wacky residents. It's also noted for its particularly acute homeless problem. The Third Street Promenade, a pedestrian-only outdoor mall lined with great shops and restaurants, is one of the country's most successful revitalization projects.

Venice, a planned community in the spirit of its Italian forebear, was constructed with a series of narrow canals connected by quaint one-lane bridges. The area had become infested with grime and crime over the years, but gentrification is now in full swing. There are scores of great restaurants and boutiques, the existing canals are lined with quaint homes and apartment duplexes, and real estate values are soaring. Some of L.A.'s most innovative and interesting architecture lines funky Main Street. Without question, Venice is best known for its Ocean Front Walk, a sandfront sidewalk that's a nonstop circus of skaters, vendors, and poseurs of all ages, colors, types, and sizes.

Marina del Rey, just south of Venice, is a somewhat quieter, more upscale community best known for its small-craft harbor, one of the largest of its kind in the world.

Manhattan, Hermosa, and **Redondo Beaches,** as well as neighboring **Rancho Palos Verdes,** are relatively sleepy residential neighborhoods with modest homes, mild weather, and easy parking. There are excellent beaches for volleyball players, surfers, and sun-worshippers, but there's not much else about these South Bay suburbs for visitors to get very excited about; when it comes to good restaurants or cultural activities, pickings are quite slim indeed. The drive to downtown L.A. can easily take 45 minutes.

The Neighborhoods in Brief

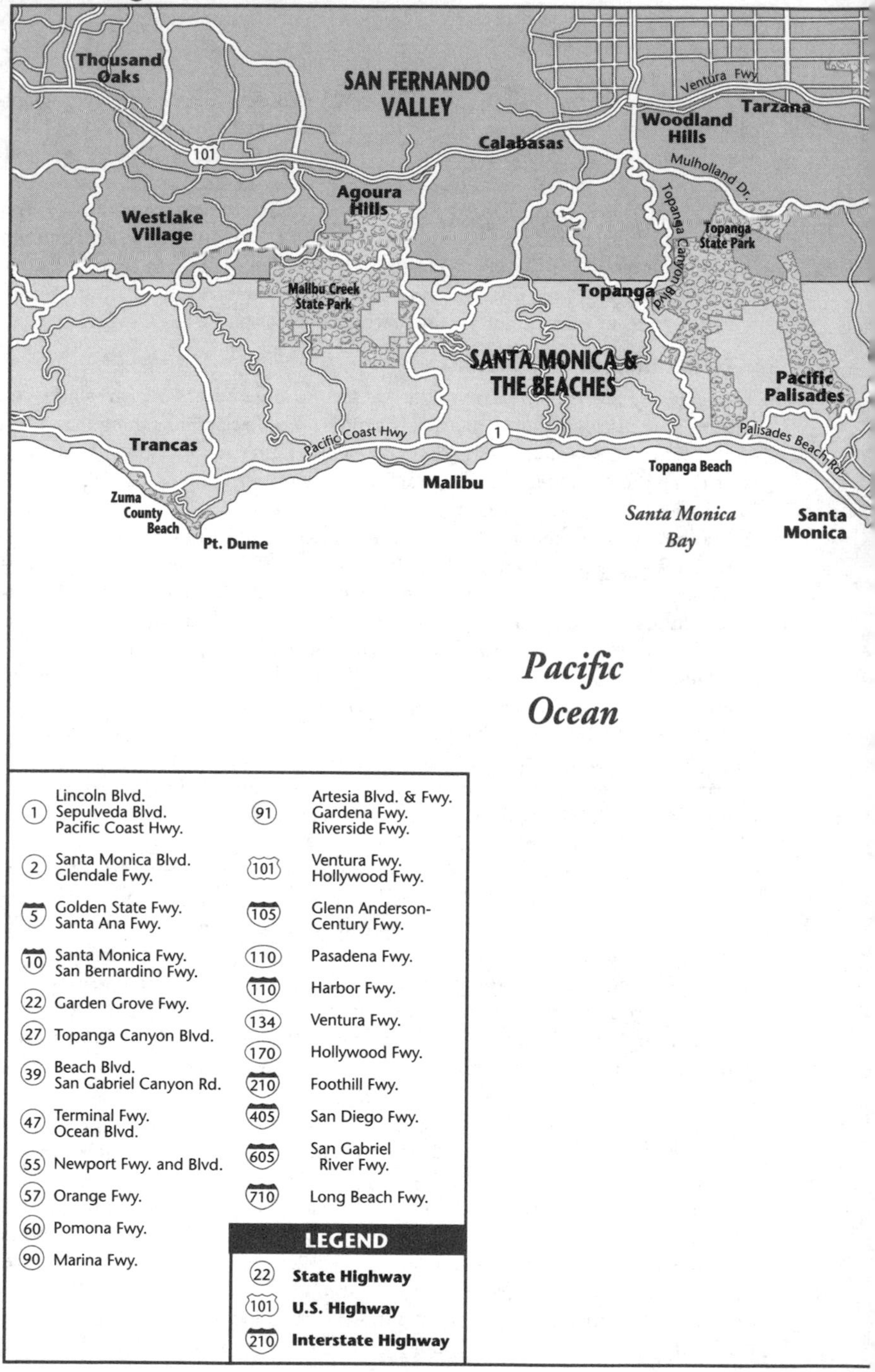
Thousand Oaks
SAN FERNANDO VALLEY
Ventura Fwy
Tarzana
Woodland Hills
Calabasas
101
Mulholland Dr.
Agoura Hills
Topanga Canyon Blvd
Westlake Village
Topanga State Park
Malibu Creek State Park
Topanga
SANTA MONICA & THE BEACHES
Pacific Palisades
Pacific Coast Hwy
1
Palisades Beach Rd
Trancas
Malibu
Topanga Beach
Zuma County Beach
Pt. Dume
Santa Monica Bay
Santa Monica
Pacific Ocean
1 Lincoln Blvd. Sepulveda Blvd. Pacific Coast Hwy.
2 Santa Monica Blvd. Glendale Fwy.
5 Golden State Fwy. Santa Ana Fwy.
10 Santa Monica Fwy. San Bernardino Fwy.
22 Garden Grove Fwy.
27 Topanga Canyon Blvd.
39 Beach Blvd. San Gabriel Canyon Rd.
47 Terminal Fwy. Ocean Blvd.
55 Newport Fwy. and Blvd.
57 Orange Fwy.
60 Pomona Fwy.
90 Marina Fwy.
91 Artesia Blvd. & Fwy. Gardena Fwy. Riverside Fwy.
101 Ventura Fwy. Hollywood Fwy.
105 Glenn Anderson-Century Fwy.
110 Pasadena Fwy.
110 Harbor Fwy.
134 Ventura Fwy.
170 Hollywood Fwy.
210 Foothill Fwy.
405 San Diego Fwy.
605 San Gabriel River Fwy.
710 Long Beach Fwy.
LEGEND
22 State Highway
101 U.S. Highway
210 Interstate Highway

Van Nuys Airport Burbank-Glendale-Pasadena Airport

North Hollywood Burbank Glendale

Van Nuys 170

101 Ventura Fwy

Sherman Oaks Studio City Universal City Golden State Fwy

L.A.'S WESTSIDE & BEVERLY HILLS HOLLYWOOD Griffith Park 5 Glendale Fwy

San Gabriel Valley Pasadena San Marino Foothill Fwy

Hollywood Santa Monica Blvd 101 South Pasadena San Gabriel

Rimby Hills West Hollywood Melrose Ave. 110 San Bernardino Fwy

Westwood Beverly Hills Mid Wilshire Dodger Stadium Historic District 10

entwood Century City Santa Monica Fwy City Center 60 Pomona Fwy

'est Los Angeles Culver City 10 Exposition Park East Los Angeles Whittier Blvd

Lincoln Blvd Marina Fwy DOWNTOWN 710 Santa Ana Fwy

enice Fairfax Ave. Harbor Fwy Long Beach Fwy

Marina del Rey Manchester Av Inglewood

Los Angeles International Airport (LAX) Watts South Gate Firestone Blvd Downey

El Segundo 110 105 Glenn Anderson-Century Fwy

Manhattan Beach Sepulveda Blvd 405 Hawthorne Blvd Western Ave. Compton 105 Lakewood Blvd

Hermosa Beach Artesia Blvd Gardena Gardena Fwy

Redondo Beach Torrance San Diego Fwy Lakewood

Pacific Coast Hwy Long Beach Fwy 710 405 Pacific Coast Hwy

Rancho Palos Verdes Harbor Fwy Terminal Fwy Ocean Blvd Long Beach

San Pedro *Los Angeles Harbor*

0 5 m N
8 km

L.A.'S WESTSIDE & BEVERLY HILLS

The Westside, an imprecise, misshapen "L" sandwiched between Hollywood and the city's coastal communities, includes some of Los Angeles's most prestigious neighborhoods, virtually all with names you're sure to recognize:

Beverly Hills is roughly bounded by Olympic Boulevard on the south, Robertson Boulevard on the east, and the districts of Westwood and Century City on the west; it extends into the hills to the north. Politically distinct from the rest of Los Angeles, this famous enclave is best known for its palm tree–lined streets of palatial homes and high-priced shops. But it's not all glitz and glamor; the healthy mix of filthy rich, wannabes, and tourists that peoples the downtown area creates a unique—and sometimes bizarre—atmosphere.

West Hollywood is a key-shaped community (go ahead, look at your map) whose epicenter is the intersection of Santa Monica and La Cienega Boulevards. It's bounded on the west by Doheny Drive and on the south roughly by Melrose Avenue; the tip of the key extends east for several blocks north and south of Santa Monica Boulevard as far as La Brea Avenue, but it's primarily located to the west of Fairfax Avenue. Nestled between Beverly Hills and Hollywood, this politically independent town can feel either tony or tawdry, depending on which end of the city you're in. In addition to being home to the city's best restaurants, shops, and art galleries, West Hollywood is the center of L.A.'s gay community.

Bel Air and **Holmby Hills,** located in the hills north of Westwood and west of the Beverly Hills city limits, are wealthy residential areas that feature prominently on most maps to the stars' homes.

Brentwood, the world-famous backdrop for the O.J. Simpson melodrama, is really just a tiny, quiet, relatively upscale neighborhood with the typical L.A. mix of homes, restaurants, and strip malls. It's west of I-405 and north of Santa Monica and West Los Angeles.

Westwood, an urban village that the University of California, Los Angeles (UCLA), calls home, is bounded by I-405, Santa Monica Boulevard, Sunset Boulevard, and Beverly Hills. The village, which used to be a hot destination for a night on the town, has lost much of its appeal thanks to overcrowding, general rudeness, and even street violence. There's still a high concentration of movie theaters that draw crowds, but we're all waiting for Westwood to regain the charm it once had.

Century City is a compact, busy, rather bland high-rise area sandwiched between West Los Angeles and Beverly Hills that was once the back lot of 20th Century Fox studios. Its primary draws are the Shubert Theatre and the Century City Marketplace, a very pleasant open-air mall. Century City's three main thoroughfares are Century Park East, Avenue of the Stars, and Century Park West; it's bounded on the north by Santa Monica Boulevard and on the south by Pico Boulevard.

West Los Angeles is a label that generally applies to everything that isn't one of the other Westside neighborhoods. It's basically the area south of Santa Monica Boulevard, north of Venice Boulevard, east of Santa Monica and Venice, and west and south of Century City.

HOLLYWOOD

Yes, they still come. Young hopefuls with stars in their eyes are attracted to this town like moths fluttering in the glare of neon lights. But Hollywood is now much more a state of mind than a glamor center. Many of the neighborhood's former movie studios have moved to less expensive, more spacious venues in Burbank, on the Westside, and in other parts of the city. Hollywood Boulevard has become one of the city's seediest strips. The area is now just a less-than-admirable part of the whole of

Los Angeles, but the legend of the neighborhood as the movie capital of the world endures.

For our purposes, the label "Hollywood" extends beyond the worn central neighborhood of Hollywood itself to surrounding neighborhoods. It generally encompasses everything between Western Avenue to the east and Fairfax Avenue to the west and from the Hollywood Hills (with its dazzling homes and million-dollar views) south.

Seedy **Hollywood,** which centers around Hollywood and Sunset Boulevards, is the historic heart of L.A.'s movie industry. It's home to several important attractions, such as the Walk of Fame and Mann's Chinese Theatre.

Melrose Avenue, a scruffy but fun neighborhood, is the city's funkiest shopping district.

The stretch of Wilshire Boulevard that runs through the southern part of Hollywood is known as the **Mid-Wilshire** district, or Miracle Mile. It's lined with contemporary apartment houses and office buildings. The stretch of the boulevard just east of Fairfax Avenue, now known as Museum Row, is home to almost a dozen museums, including the Los Angeles County Museum of Art, the La Brea Tar Pits, and that shrine to L.A. car culture, the Petersen Automotive Museum.

Griffith Park, up Western Avenue in the northernmost reaches of Hollywood, is one of the country's largest urban parks. It's home to the Los Angeles Zoo and the famous Griffith Observatory.

DOWNTOWN

Roughly bounded by the U.S. 101, I-110, I-10, and I-5 freeways, L.A.'s downtown is home to a tight cluster of high-rise offices, the El Pueblo de Los Angeles Historic District, and the neighborhoods of Koreatown, Chinatown, and Little Tokyo. The construction of skyscrapers—facilitated by earthquake-proof technology—transformed downtown Los Angeles into the business center of the city. Despite the relatively recent construction of numerous cultural centers—including the Music Center and the Museum of Contemporary Art—and a few hip restaurants, downtown isn't the hub that it would be in most cities; the Westside, Hollywood, and the beach communities are all more popular.

For our purposes, the residential neighborhoods of Silverlake and Los Feliz, Exposition Park (home to Los Angeles Memorial Coliseum, the L.A. Sports Arena, and several downtown museums), and East and South-Central L.A., the city's famous barrios, all fall under the Downtown umbrella.

El Pueblo de Los Angeles Historic District, a 44-acre ode to the city's early years, is worth a visit on your way to Los Angeles City Hall and the *Los Angeles Times* buildings. Neither Chinatown nor Little Tokyo is on the scale of its San Francisco equivalents and, quite honestly, neither is especially worth going out of your way for.

Silverlake, a residential neighborhood located just north of downtown, and adjacent **Los Feliz,** just to the west, are arty areas with ethnic cafés, theaters, graffiti, and art galleries—all in equally plentiful proportions.

Exposition Park, just south and west of downtown, is home to the Los Angeles Memorial Coliseum and the L.A. Sports Arena. The park also contains the Natural History Museum of Los Angeles County, the California African-American Museum, and the Museum of Science and Industry. The University of Southern California is next door.

East and South-Central L.A., just east and south of downtown, are home to the city's large, infamous barrios. This is where the 1992 L.A. Riots were centered; it was here, at Florence and Normandie avenues, that a news station's reporter, hovering above in a helicopter, videotaped Reginald Denny being pulled from the cab of his

---

Area Code Change Notice

Please note that, effective June 14, 1997, the phone company plans to split the 818 area code. The eastern portion, including Burbank, Glendale and Pasadena, will change to the new area code **626.** You will be able to dial 818 until January 17, 1998, after which you will have to use 626.

---

truck and beaten by several young men. There are few tourist-oriented sites in these neighborhoods—the Watts Towers being a notable exception—though they are, without question, quite unique.

THE SAN FERNANDO VALLEY

The San Fernando Valley, known locally as "The Valley," was nationally popularized in the 1980s by the notorious mall-loving "Valley Girl" stereotype. Snuggled between the Santa Monica and the San Gabriel mountain ranges, most of the Valley is residential and commercial, and off the beaten track of tourists. But some of its attractions are bound to draw you over the hill:

Universal City, located west of Griffith Park between U.S. 101 and Calif. 134, is home to Universal Studios and the trippy shopping and entertainment complex known as CityWalk. And you may make a trip to **Burbank,** just west of these other suburbs and north of Universal City, to see one of your favorite TV shows being filmed at NBC or Warner Bros. Studios. There are also a few good restaurants and shops along Ventura Boulevard in and around Studio City (see chapter 9, "Shopping").

Glendale is a largely residential community north of downtown, sandwiched between the Valley and Pasadena (see chapter 11, "Side Trips from Los Angeles"). You'll find the city's best sightseeing cemetery, Forest Lawn, there.

2 Getting Around

BY CAR

Need we tell you that Los Angeles is a car city? You're really going to need one to get around. The city's elaborate network of freeways connects this incredible urban sprawl; roads are generally well maintained, but you'll have to learn how to make sense of them and cultivate some patience for dealing with the traffic. The golden rule of driving in Los Angeles is this: Always allow more time to get to your destination than you reasonably think it will take, especially during morning and evening rush hours. (For an explanation of the city layout and details on the freeway system, see "Orientation," above.)

RENTALS

Los Angeles is one of the cheapest places in America to rent a car. Major national car-rental companies usually rent Geo Metros, Ford Escorts, and the like for about $35 per day and $120 per week with unlimited mileage. The best-known firms, with locations at the airport and throughout the city, include **Alamo** (☎ 800/327-9633), **Avis** (☎ 800/331-1212), **Budget** (☎ 800/527-0700), **Dollar** (☎ 800/421-6868), **Enterprise** (☎ 800/325-8007), **Hertz** (☎ 800/654-3131), **National** (☎ 800/328-4567), and **Thrifty** (☎ 800/367-2277). If you're thinking of splurging, however, the place to call is **Budget Rent-a-Car of Beverly Hills,** 9815 Wilshire Blvd., Beverly Hills (☎ 310/274-9173); they rent Mercedes, BMWs, and Porsches for up to $450 per day.

Most rental firms pad their profits by selling Loss/Damage Waiver (LDW), which usually costs an extra $9 or $10 per day. This coverage could come in handy in the unlikely event that you have an accident. Before accepting it, however, check with your insurance carrier and credit- and charge-card companies; many people don't realize that they are already insured by either one or both.

For renters, the minimum age usually falls somewhere between 19 and 25. Some agencies have also set maximum ages. If you're concerned that these limits may affect you, ask about rental requirements at the time of booking to avoid problems later.

Finally, think about splurging on a convertible. Few things in life can match the feeling of flying along the Southern California freeways with the sun smiling on your shoulders and the wind whipping through your hair.

PARKING

Explaining the parking situation in Los Angeles is like explaining the English language—there are more exceptions than there are rules. In some areas, every establishment has a convenient free lot or ample street parking; others are pretty manageable, as long as you have a quick eye and are willing to take a few turns around the block; but there are some frustrating parts of town (particularly around restaurants after 7:30pm), where you'll have to give in and valet park. Valet parking depends more on the congestion of the area than on the elegance of the establishment these days; the size of an establishment's lot often simply won't allow for self-parking.

Restaurants and nightclubs sometimes provide a complimentary valet service, but more often charge between $2.50 and $5. Some areas, like Santa Monica and Beverly Hills, offer self-park lots and garages convenient to the neighborhood action; costs range from $2 to $10. Most of the hotels listed in this book offer off-street parking, for which they charge up to $20 per day.

A Few Parking Tips to Remember:

- **Be prepared for anything.** Always have a pocketful of quarters and a few $1 bills in case you need them. Downtown and Santa Monica are two of the worst areas for free 'n' easy parking.
- **Be creative.** "Case" the immediate area by taking a turn around the block. In many parts of the city you can find an unrestricted street space less than a block away from eager valets.
- **Read posted restrictions carefully.** You'll avoid a ticket if you pay attention to the signs, which warn of street cleaning schedules, rush hour "no parking," and resident "permit only" zones.

DRIVING TIPS

Los Angeles has the most extensive freeway system in the world. In addition to a number, each freeway also has a name, or series of names, as it passes through various communities. See "Orientation," above, and its accompanying map for a listing of major highways and freeways, along with their locally known names.

Many Southern California freeways have designated carpool lanes, also known as High Occupancy Vehicle (HOV) lanes or "white diamond" lanes (after the large diamonds painted on the blacktop along the lane). Some require two passengers, others three. Most on-ramps are metered during even light congestion to regulate the flow of traffic onto the freeway; cars in HOV lanes can pass the signal without stopping. Although there are tales of drivers sitting life-sized mannequins next to them in order to beat the system, don't consider ignoring the stoplights for any reason if you're not part of a carpool—fines begin around $200.

When it comes to radio traffic reporter jargon, the names of L.A.'s freeways (as opposed to their numbers) are usually used. A "SigAlert" is the term used for an unplanned freeway crisis (i.e., a serious accident) that will affect the movement of traffic for 30 minutes or more. (They're named after Lloyd Sigmon, a traffic reporter in the 1950s.) When you hear "A big rig is blocking the number one lane," you can determine the lane by counting out from the center divider.

On surface roads, you may turn right at a red light (unless otherwise indicated) after making a complete stop and yielding to traffic and pedestrians. Pedestrians have the right-of-way at intersections and crosswalks.

BY PUBLIC TRANSPORTATION

We've heard rumors about visitors to Los Angeles who have toured the city entirely by public transportation, but they can't be more than that—rumors. It's hard to believe that anyone can comprehensively tour Auto Land without a car of their own. Still, if you're in the city for only a short time, are on a very tight budget, or don't expect to be moving around a lot, public transport might be for you.

The city's trains and buses are operated by the **Los Angeles County Metropolitan Transit Authority (MTA),** 425 S. Main Street, Los Angeles, CA 90013 (☎ 800/ COMMUTE or 213/626-4455). In addition to offering schedule and trip information, the MTA publishes a handy pamphlet outlining about two dozen self-guided MTA tours, including visits to Universal Studios, Beverly Hills, and Disneyland. A second, more convenient MTA office is located in the ARCO Towers at 515 S. Flower Street.

BY BUS

Spread-out sights, sluggish service, and frequent transfers make extensive touring by bus impractical. For short hops and occasional jaunts, however, buses are both economical and environmentally correct. However, it isn't recommended to ride buses late at night.

The basic bus fare is $1.35 for all local lines, with transfers costing 25¢. Express buses, which travel along the freeways, and buses on intercounty routes charge higher fares; phone for information.

The **Downtown Area Short Hop (DASH)** shuttle system operates buses throughout downtown and the west side of L.A. Service runs every 5 to 20 minutes, depending on the time of day, and costs just 25¢. Phone the MTA for schedules and route information.

BY RAIL

The **MetroRail** system is a sore subject around town. For years they've been digging up the city's streets, sucking away huge amounts of tax money, and installing exhaust vents up through peaceful parkland—and for what? Let's face it, L.A. will never have New York's subway or San Francisco's BART. While it's still in its infancy and used primarily by commuters from outlying suburbs, here's an overview of what's currently in place:

The **Metro Blue Line,** an above-ground rail system, connects downtown Los Angeles with Long Beach. Trains operate daily from 6am to 9pm; the fare is $1.35.

The **Metro Red Line,** L.A.'s first subway, opened in 1993 and currently covers just about 5 miles, making seven stops in the downtown area. The line begins at Union Station, the city's main train depot, and travels west underneath Wilshire Boulevard. The fare is 25¢. The Red Line will be extended to Hollywood and the San Fernando Valley by 1999.

The **Metro Green Line,** opened in 1995, runs for 20 miles along the center of the new I-105, the Glenn Anderson (Century) Freeway, and connects Norwalk in eastern Los Angeles County to LAX. A connection with the Blue Line offers visitors access from LAX to downtown L.A. or Long Beach.

Call the **MTA** (☎ **800/COMMUTE** or 213/626-4455) for information on all Metro lines.

BY TAXI

Distances are long in Los Angeles, and cab fares are high; even a short trip can cost $10 or more. Taxis charge $1.90 at the flagdrop, plus $1.60 per mile. A service charge is added to fares originating at LAX.

Except in the heart of downtown, passing cabs will usually not pull over when hailed. Cab stands are located at airports, at downtown's Union Station, and at major hotels. To assure a ride, order a taxi in advance from **Checker Cab** (☎ **213/654-8400**), **L.A. Taxi** (☎ **213/627-7000**), or **United Independent Taxi** (☎ **213/483-7604**).

FAST FACTS: Los Angeles

American Express   Offices are located at 327 N. Beverly Dr., Beverly Hills; 901 W. 7th St., downtown; and elsewhere around the city. Call either the downtown branch at 213/627-4800 or Travelers Check Services at 800/221-7282 to find the branch nearest you. To report lost or stolen cards, call 800/528-4800. To report lost or stolen traveler's checks, call 800/221-7282.

Area Code   There are currently four area codes in Los Angeles. All numbers east of La Cienega Boulevard, including those in Hollywood and downtown, are within the 213 code. Phone numbers west of La Cienega, including those in the city's beach communities, have the 310 area code. Portions of the county east and south of Los Angeles, including Long Beach, are in the newly established 562 area code. Many inland suburbs, and the San Fernando Valley, are within the 818 calling area. The phone company is planning to split 818 effective June 14, 1997, creating the new area code 626 for the eastern half of the area currently covered by 818, which includes Burbank, Glendale and Pasadena.

Baby-Sitters   If you're staying at one of the larger hotels, the concierge can usually recommend a reliable baby-sitter. If not, contact the Baby-Sitters Guild in Glendale (☎ 818/552-2229); or Sitters Unlimited (☎ 800/328-1191).

Computer Rentals   PCR Personal Computer Rentals, 5777 W. Century Blvd., Suite 110, Los Angeles (☎ 800/322-1001 or 310/417-3007; fax 310/645-8765), rents laptops, printers, and peripherals on a short-term basis on short notice.

Dentists   To find an area dentist, call the national Dental Referral Service (☎ 800/422-8338).

Doctors   Contact the Uni-Health Information and Referral Hotline (☎ 800/922-0000) for a free, confidential physician referral.

Emergencies   For police, fire, highway patrol, or in case of life-threatening medical emergencies, dial **911.**

Hospital   Centrally located (and world-famous), Cedars-Sinai Medical Center, 8700 Beverly Blvd., Los Angeles (☎ 310/855-5000), has a 24-hour emergency room staffed by some of the country's finest MDs.

Library   Gutted by fire in 1986, the Los Angeles Central Library, 630 W. 5th St., downtown (☎ 213/228-7000), reopened in 1993 to become the third largest in America. There are umpteen local branches, and a sophisticated electronic card catalog can find a particular item at any branch (from any terminal, including via modem).

Liquor Laws   Liquor and grocery stores can sell packaged alcoholic beverages between 6am and 2am. Most restaurants, nightclubs, and bars are licensed to serve alcoholic beverages during the same hours. The legal age for purchase and consumption is 21; proof of age is required.

Newspapers/Magazines   The *Los Angeles Times* is a plump, high-quality daily with strong local and national coverage, and meager international offerings. Its Sunday "Calendar" section is an excellent and interesting guide to the world of entertainment in and around L.A. The free weekly events magazine *L.A. Weekly* is packed with news of events and a calendar of happenings around town; it's available from sidewalk newsracks and in many stores and restaurants around the city. *Los Angeles* and *Buzz* are hip monthly magazines with good listings and entertainment news.

Melrose News, at the corner of Melrose and Martel avenues, is one of the city's best outdoor newsstands. World Book & News Co., at 1652 N. Cahuenga Boulevard, near Hollywood and Vine and Mann's Chinese Theater, is equally terrific. Located here for almost 70 years, the shop stocks lots of out-of-town and foreign papers and magazines. No one minds if you browse through the magazines, but you'll be reprimanded for thumbing through the newspapers. It's open 24 hours.

Pharmacies   Horton & Converse has locations around L.A., including 2001 Santa Monica Blvd., Santa Monica (☎ 310/829-3401); 9201 Sunset Blvd., Beverly Hills (☎ 213/272-0488); and 11600 Wilshire Blvd., West Los Angeles (☎ 310/478-0801); hours vary, but the West L.A. location is open until 2am.

Police   In an emergency, dial **911.** For nonemergency police matters, call 213/485-2121; in Beverly Hills, dial 213/550-4951.

Post Office   Call 213/586-1467 to find the one closest to you.

Radio Stations   There are literally dozens of radio stations in L.A. FM classical music stations include KLON (88.1), KUSC (91.5), and KKGO (105.1). The country music station is KZLA (93.9). Rock music stations include KLOS (95.5) and KLSX (97.1); alternative rock can be found on KSCA (101.9) and KROQ (106.7); rock/pop oldies live forever on KCBS (93.1) and KRTH (101.1). The top AM news and information station is KNX (1070).

Taxes   The combined Los Angeles County and California state sales taxes amount to 8.25%; hotel taxes add 12% to 17% to the room tariff.

Taxis   You can order a taxi in advance from Checker Cab (☎ 213/221-2355), L.A. Taxi (☎ 213/627-7000), or United Independent Taxi (☎ 213/483-7604).

Television Stations   All the major networks and several independent stations are represented. They are KCBS, Channel 2; KNBC, Channel 4; KTLA (Warner Bros.), Channel 5; KABC, Channel 7; KCAL (local independent), Channel 9; KTTV (Fox), Channel 11; KCOP (UPN), Channel 13. The local PBS station is KCET, Channel 28.

Time   Call 853-1212 for the correct time (operates in all area codes).

Weather   Call Los Angeles Weather Information (☎ 213/554-1212) for the daily forecast. For beach conditions, call the Zuma Beach Lifeguard recorded information (☎ 310/457-9701).

Accommodations 5

by Jim Moore

A graduate of Wake Forest University, Jim Moore
was an assistant editor at Macmillan Travel before
he abandoned the concrete canyons of New York
City for sunny Southern California.

In sprawling Los Angeles, location is everything. Choosing the right neighborhood as a base can make or break your vacation; if you plan to while away a few days at the beach but base yourself downtown, for example, you're going to lose a lot of valuable relaxation time on the freeway. For business travelers, choosing a location is easy: Pick a hotel near your work—don't commute if you don't have to. For vacationers, though, the decision about where to stay is a more difficult one. Take into consideration where you'll be wanting to spend your time before you commit yourself to a base. But, wherever you stay, count on doing a good deal of driving—no hotel in Los Angeles is convenient to everything.

The relatively smogless coastal areas are understandably popular with visitors—everybody loves to stay at the beach. Trendy Santa Monica and its neighbors are home to lots of hotels; book ahead, because they fill up quickly in the summer, when everyone wants to be by the water. Santa Monica also enjoys convenient freeway access to the popular tourist sights inland. Malibu and the South Bay communities (Manhattan, Hermosa, and Redondo Beaches) are more out of the way, and hence quieter, but you'll have quite a drive to the majority of L.A.'s attractions.

Most visitors stay on the city's Westside, a short drive from the beach and close to most of L.A.'s most colorful sights. The city's most elegant—and expensive—accommodations are in Beverly Hills and Bel Air; a few of the hotels in this neighborhood have become visitor attractions unto themselves. You'll find the city's best hotel values in West Hollywood, an exciting and convenient place to base yourself.

There are fewer hotels in Hollywood than the visitor would expect. The accommodations here, usually moderately priced, are generally well maintained but otherwise unspectacular. Hollywood is very centrally located between downtown and Beverly Hills, and it's within easy reach of Santa Monica. It's a great base if you're planning to do a lot of touring.

In general, downtown hotels are business oriented; they're sometimes popular with groups, but are largely ignored by independent tourists. The top hotels here are very good, but cheaper ones can be downright nasty. If you're on a budget, locate elsewhere.

Families might want to head to the San Fernando Valley to be near Universal Studios, or straight to Anaheim or Buena Park for easy access to Disneyland and Knott's Berry Farm (see chapter 11, "Side Trips from Los Angeles," for places to stay in the Anaheim area).

The hotels listed below are categorized first by area, then by price: under **Very Expensive,** you'll find double rooms for more than $200; under **Expensive,** doubles are $150 to $199; **Moderate** doubles are $100 to $149; and **Inexpensive** doubles are below generally less than $100. Rates given are the rack rates for a standard room for two with private bath (unless otherwise noted); you can often do better. Ask about weekend packages and discounts, corporate rates, family plans, and any other special rates that might be available. The prices given do not include state and city hotel taxes, which run from 14% to a whopping 17%. Be aware that most hotels make additional charges for parking (with in-and-out privileges, except where noted) and levy heavy surcharges for telephone use.

Most L.A. hotels have their own on-site gym facilities; they can vary from a small room with just a few treadmills and Lifecycles to full-service spas. Hotels without facilities often have an arrangement with a nearby club, where you can pay to use their facilities on a per-day basis; charges are usually $8 to $15.

All the top-quality, business-oriented chain hotels (including Four Seasons, Hilton, Hyatt, Sheraton, and Wyndham) offer rooms on exclusive "Club" or "Executive" floors, and most of the city's better hotels offer no-smoking rooms; these special rooms should be requested when making reservations.

Chain-operated toll-free numbers can also help you in your search for accommodations. These "800" numbers will save you time and money when inquiring about rates and availability. **Best Western** (☎ 800/528-1234), **Days Inn** (☎ 800/325-2525), **Holiday Inn** (☎ 800/465-4329), **Motel 6** (☎ 800/437-7486), **Quality Inn** (☎ 800/228-5151), **Ramada Inn** (☎ 800/272-6232), and **Travelodge** ☎ 800/421-3939) all have locations in the Los Angeles area.

RESERVATIONS SERVICES   Several hotel reservations services offer one-stop shopping; they'll tell you what's available at many of L.A.'s hotels and book you into the one of your choice, all at no additional charge. These services are particularly helpful for last-minute reservations, when rooms are often scarce—or discounted. The following companies serve the L.A. area:

Central Reservation Service, 505 Maitland Ave., Suite 100, Altamonte Springs, FL 32701 (☎ **800/548-3311** or 417/339-4116; fax 407/339-4736).

Hotel Reservations Network, 8140 Walnut Hill Lane, Suite 203, Dallas, TX 75231 (☎ **800/96-hotel** or 214/361-7311; fax 214/361-7299).

1 Best Bets

- **Best Luxury Hotel:** The **Hotel Bel-Air** (701 Stone Canyon Rd., Bel Air; ☎ 800/648-4097) wins my vote hands down. Nestled in 11 lush acres of private parkland, this opulent castle-away-from-home is an oasis in the middle of the urban jungle.
- **Best Historic Hotel:** While many might argue that the nearby Biltmore is L.A.'s grand dame, it can hardly match the comparative intimacy of the **Wyndham Checkers Hotel** (535 S. Grand Ave., downtown; ☎ 800/996-3426). Rooms have all the modern amenities that you'd expect from a hotel of this caliber, but the hotel's cultural integrity—including an abundance of original 1927 detail—is intact, so much so that the Wyndham Checkers has been preserved by the city as a cultural landmark. An art deco masterpiece, the **Argyle** (8358 Sunset Blvd., West Hollywood; ☎ 800/225-2637) is also a cultural landmark and makes a fine choice if you're looking for Hollywood digs.
- **Best for Business Travelers:** If you need to stay downtown, The **Hyatt Regency Los Angeles** (711 S. Hope St., downtown; ☎ 800/233-1234) is designed to meet

the needs of today's business traveler. But my favorite L.A. business hotel is still the **Hotel Nikko** (465 S. La Cienega Blvd.; ☎ 800/645-5687); the furnishings are a step above standard-chain fare and room layouts are particularly well thought out, making them functional both as bedrooms and workspaces. There are conference rooms and a full business center for guests' use.

- **Best for a Romantic Getaway:** If a luxurious oceanfront room at **Shutters on the Beach** (1 Pico Blvd., Santa Monica; ☎ 800/334-9000) doesn't put a spring in your relationship, it's hard to imagine that any place will. Walk on the beach, watch the sun set over the Pacific, and order breakfast in bed from One Pico, Santa Monica's finest hotel restaurant.

- **Best Trendy Hotel:** The **Peninsula Beverly Hills** (9882 Little Santa Monica Blvd., Beverly Hills; ☎ 800/462-7899) is the hotel of the moment. Celebrities and Industry insiders from around the globe have abandoned their longstanding allegiances to stalwarts like the Regent Beverly Wilshire in order to pow-wow at this new power spot. The Peninsula's more than a bit contrived, but what else would you expect from today's high-profile trendsetters?

- **Best for Families:** Because it's both close to the beach and the boardwalk and offers the "Splash Club," a great summertime children's program, the **Loews Santa Monica Beach Hotel** (1700 Ocean Ave., Santa Monica; ☎ 800/223-0888) tops our list as L.A.'s best family hotel.

- **Best Moderately Priced Hotel:** The well-maintained, double-decker **Casa Malibu** (22752 Pacific Coast Hwy., Malibu; ☎ 800/831-0858) has a terrific beachfront location and rates left over from more carefree days. I love Casa Malibu; it's L.A.'s best-kept secret—until now, of course.

- **Best Budget Hotel:** Westwood's **Hotel Del Capri** (10587 Wilshire Blvd.; ☎ 800/444-6835) isn't the cheapest hotel in town, but it's well located and a great buy in an expensive neighborhood. It's also very comfortable—more so than its rate card would suggest.

- **Best Alternative Accommodation:** The casual party atmosphere at **Banana Bungalow** (2775 Cahuenga Blvd., West Hollywood; ☎ 800/4-HOSTEL) isn't for everybody, but if you're looking for an unusual place to hang your hat, this is it. Daily activities and free transportation to many of the city's top attractions make this the best place for fun-loving but frugal explorers.

- **Best Service:** The Regent hotel chain built its reputation on the quality of its service, and the **Regent Beverly Wilshire** (9500 Wilshire Blvd., Beverly Hills; ☎ 800/421-4354) is one of its crown jewels. Stewards are at your service on every floor, and you can summon a butler at any time with the bell that sits beside your bed. The service is doting if you want it, discrete if you don't.

- **Best Location: Le Montrose Suite Hotel** (900 Hammond St., West Hollywood; ☎ 800/776-0666), located in West Hollywood, gets marks not only for its convenience to restaurants, clubs, and attractions, but also for its manageable size—which means you won't have to wait forever for your car to be delivered from the valet.

- **Best Health Club:** The state-of-the-art health club at the **Loews Santa Monica Beach Hotel** (1700 Ocean Ave., Santa Monica; ☎ 800/223-0888) is one of L.A.'s best hotel facilities. It's packed with treadmills, StairMasters, Lifecycles, and other cardio and weight machines, as well as a full complement of free weights. And Loews's location just off the beach and the 27-mile running, biking, and skating path that runs along it makes it even more attractive to fitness enthusiasts. In fact, in their February 1996 issue, *Runner's World* magazine stated that this was the best hotel they've seen for runners.

2 Santa Monica & the Beaches

VERY EXPENSIVE

✪ **Loews Santa Monica Beach Hotel.** 1700 Ocean Ave. (south of Colorado Blvd.), Santa Monica, CA 90401. ☎ **800/223-0888** or 310/458-6700. Fax 310/458-6761. 349 rms, 22 suites. A/C TV TEL. $225–$315 double; suites from $450. AE, CB, DC, EU, MC, V. Valet parking $15, self-parking $13.

If it weren't for Shutters, this would be the finest hotel in Santa Monica. Loews isn't exactly beachfront; it's on a hill less than a block away, but the unobstructed ocean views are fabulous. But realize that you're paying for location—the drone of the ice makers is audible in the hallways and the plumbing is noisy at times, blemishes that you wouldn't expect from a hotel of this caliber. But this is still a great hotel. A dramatic, multistory glass and green-steel atrium lobby gives way to ample cookie-cutter rooms that are outfitted with the latest luxury-hotel amenities. This popular hotel doesn't need my recommendation to stir business; the hotel has become something of a darling for Industry functions, and it's booked to capacity in the summer months.

Dining/Entertainment: There are two restaurants and poolside snack service. There's live jazz in the lounge most nights.

Services: Concierge, 24-hour room service, overnight shoeshine, nightly turndown, baby-sitting, valet parking.

Facilities: VCRs on request, outdoor heated pool, Jacuzzi, fitness center with cardio machines, summer children's program, business center, bike and roller-skate rental.

Miramar Sheraton Hotel. 101 Wilshire Blvd. (between Ocean Ave. and 2nd St.), Santa Monica, CA 90401. ☎ **800/325-3535** or 310/576-7777. Fax 310/458-7912. 302 rms, 62 suites. A/C TV TEL. $250–$385 double; suites from $355. AE, DC, EU, DISC, JCB, MC, V. Parking $11.

Miramar is Spanish for "ocean view"—perched on a cliff above Santa Monica Beach, that's just what this 10-story hotel offers. It was originally built in the 1920s; even after an extensive and beautiful 1994 renovation, the elegance of that era remains. The approach is particularly impressive: Wrought-iron gates open to the majestic Moreton Bay fig tree that the hotel was built around. Inside, the spacious rooms have been thoughtfully redecorated; they feel classically stylish and contemporary at the same time. Top floors have great views of the bay clear to Malibu. Casually elegant, the two-story bungalows feature such amenities as three terraces, a sauna, and a two-person Jacuzzi tub. The lush gardens and pretty pool area have led some to refer to the Miramar as the "little Beverly Hills Hotel by the beach."

Dining/Entertainment: The Miramar Grille, a California-style bistro, is open for lunch and dinner; a café serves casual fare all day. Both restaurants offer outdoor seating.

Services: Concierge, 24-hour room service, same-day laundry service, complimentary newspaper, nightly turndown, valet parking.

Facilities: Large outdoor heated pool, health center, sundeck, bicycle rental, car-rental desk, beauty salon, gift shop, women's boutique.

✪ **Shutters on the Beach.** 1 Pico Blvd. (at the beach), Santa Monica, CA 90405. ☎ **800/334-9000** or 310/458-0030. Fax 310/458-4589. 186 rms, 12 suites. TV TEL. $290–$475 double; suites from $675. AE, DC, DISC, EU, MC, V. Parking $16.

Light and luxurious Shutters enjoys one of the city's most prized locations: directly on the beach (this is the only fine hotel to enjoy such a distinction in L.A.), one block from Santa Monica Pier. Rooms fall into two categories: cottagelike beachfront rooms and those housed in a taller tower. Although the beach-cottage rooms are plainly more desirable, when it comes to rates, the hotel doesn't distinguish between them. The views and sounds of the ocean are the most outstanding qualities of the rooms, some of which have fireplaces and Jacuzzis; all have floor-to-ceiling windows that open. Showers come with waterproof radios, toy duckies, and biodegradable bath supplies. Despite this welcome whimsy, there's a relaxed and elegant atmosphere throughout the hotel, which is filled with contemporary art—sort of like staying at the opulent Cape Cod estate of a very well-off friend (except for the quirky parade of humanity along the boardwalk out front). The small swimming pool on an elevated deck and the sunny lobby lounge overlooking the sand are two great places for spotting the celebrities who swear by Shutters as an alternative to smoggy Hollywood.

Dining/Entertainment: One Pico, the hotel's premier restaurant, is very well regarded. The best meals at the more casual Pedals are prepared on the wood-burning grill. The overdesigned Handle Bar offers good happy-hour specials.

Services: Concierge, 24-hour room service, overnight laundry, evening turndown, in-room massage, valet parking.

Facilities: VCRs, outdoor heated pool, exercise room with cardio machines, Jacuzzi, sauna, sundeck, beach equipment rental, bicycle rental.

EXPENSIVE

Hotel Oceana. 849 Ocean Ave., Santa Monica, CA 90403. ☎ **800/777-0758** or 310/393-0486. 63 suites. TV TEL. $170–$325 suite. All rates include breakfast. AE, DC, DISC, MC, V. Parking $10.

If you stayed in the former Oceana Suites Hotel, you won't even recognize the newly renovated and renamed Hotel Oceana. Excellently located in a residential neighborhood right on Ocean Avenue, this all-suite hotel is great for families. Upon entering the hotel, you'll know you've arrived at the beach; light and airy and capped by an enormous skylight, the newly built lobby is covered with Jean Cocteau–inspired floor-to-ceiling murals. With bright Matisse-inspired colors and cushy IKEA-ish furniture, the completely renovated suites appear to have been decorated by the set designer from *Friends.* Some suites have ocean views; VIP suites feature air-conditioning and two-person Jacuzzi tubs. In-room lunch and dinner service is provided by Wolfgang Puck's Cafe, but since all suites come with fully equipped kitchens, cooking for yourself is another option.

Radisson Huntley Hotel. 1111 2nd St. (north of Wilshire Blvd.), Santa Monica, CA 90403. ☎ **800/333-3333** or 310/394-5454. Fax 310/458-9776. 213 rms, 6 suites. A/C TV TEL. $150–$180 double; executive rooms from $180. Ask about the "Supersaver Rates" promotion. AE, CB, DC, DISC, EU, MC, V. Parking $7.50.

This hotel, one of Santa Monica's tallest buildings, offers nondescript, moderate-quality accommodations close to the Third Street Promenade and just two blocks from the beach. All rooms underwent a major renovation in 1995–96. Basic but comfortable, they're available with either ocean or mountain views; and the windows open in all the rooms, perfect for catching ocean breezes. Toppers, the rooftop Mexican restaurant, has a great view, serves very good margaritas, and hosts live entertainment nightly. There's also a classy coffee shop serving American standards.

MODERATE

✪ **Barnaby's Hotel.** 3501 Sepulveda Blvd. (at Rosecrans Ave.), Manhattan Beach, CA 90266. ☎ **800/552-5285** or 310/545-8466. 123 rms. A/C. $144–$169 double. All rates include breakfast. AE, DC, DISC, EU, MC, V. Valet parking $4.

Accommodations in
Santa Monica & the Beaches

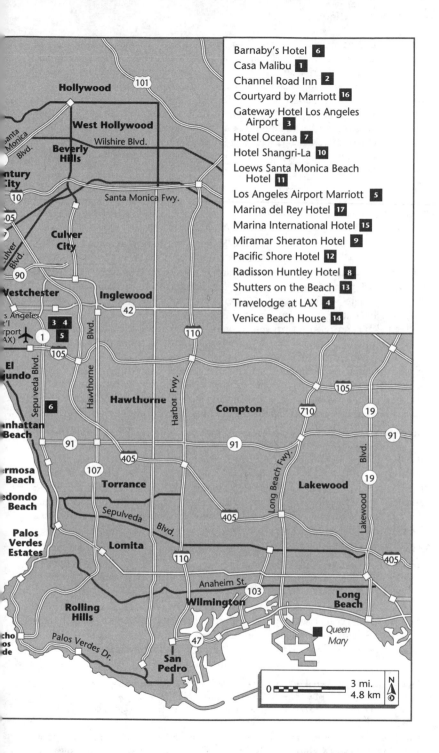

Barnaby's Hotel **6**
Casa Malibu **1**
Channel Road Inn **2**
Courtyard by Marriott **16**
Gateway Hotel Los Angeles
 Airport **3**
Hotel Oceana **7**
Hotel Shangri-La **10**
Loews Santa Monica Beach
 Hotel **11**
Los Angeles Airport Marriott **5**
Marina del Rey Hotel **17**
Marina International Hotel **15**
Miramar Sheraton Hotel **9**
Pacific Shore Hotel **12**
Radisson Huntley Hotel **8**
Shutters on the Beach **13**
Travelodge at LAX **4**
Venice Beach House **14**

Hollywood
101

West Hollywood
Beverly
Hills
Wilshire Blvd.

Santa
Monica
Blvd.

ntury
City
10
Santa Monica Fwy.

05

Culver
City

Culver
Blvd.

90

Vestchester
Inglewood
42

s Angeles
t'l
irport
AX)
3 4
5
1
105

Sepulveda Blvd.

El
undo
6

Hawthorne

Hawthorne

Harbor Fwy.

Compton
105
710
19

nhattan
Beach
91

rmosa
Beach
405

107

edondo
Beach

91

19

91

Torrance
Lakewood

Lakewood Blvd.

Palos
Verdes
Estates
Sepulveda
Blvd.
405

Lomita
110
405

Anaheim St.

cho
os
de

Rolling
Hills

Palos Verdes Dr.

Wilmington
103

Long
Beach

47

San
Pedro

*Queen
Mary*

0   3 mi.
           4.8 km

N

The most unusual hotel on the coast, Barnaby's sounds like a guest house, operates like a bed-and-breakfast, and feels like a quaint old hotel. The hotel's stuccoed pink facade and trademark green awnings give way to European-styled guest rooms; each is decorated with antique headboards, lace curtains, hardcover books, and 19th-century prints. Some rooms feature balconies, chandeliers, and attractive but nonfunctioning fireplaces. The best rooms are in back and overlook the courtyard, where weddings and other functions are held. Romantic Barnaby's is an excellent place for couples and celebrants. Full English breakfasts are served buffet style. The hotel offers complimentary airport service as well as a glass-enclosed heated pool and Jacuzzi and a sundeck.

✪ **Casa Malibu.** 22752 Pacific Coast Hwy. (about a quarter-mile south of Malibu Pier), Malibu, CA 90265. ☎ **800/831-0858** or 310/456-2219. Fax 310/456-5418. 19 rms, 2 suites. TV TEL. $99–$135 double with garden view, $150 double with ocean view, $169 beachfront double. Suites from $169. Room with kitchen $10 extra. AE, EU, MC, V. Free parking.

I'm hesitant to crow too loudly about Casa Malibu—one of my favorite L.A. hotels—for fear that it will be even harder to get a room here. The modest two-story motel wraps around a palm-studded inner courtyard with well-tended flowerbeds and cuppa d'oro vines climbing the facade. Just past the garden is the blue Pacific and a large swath of private Malibu beach for the exclusive use of hotel guests. Rooms are surprisingly contemporary and cheerful, with top-quality mattresses, bathrobes, coffeemaker, and refrigerator; some rooms come with a fireplace and/or air-conditioning. The king-bedded oceanfront rooms have balconies directly over the sand, making them some of the city's most coveted accommodations—they're a great place to watch the pelicans dive for fish in the late afternoon. If you've got a room without a view, you can only see the ocean from the communal balcony; but since the sound of the waves will put you soundly to sleep in any of the rooms, that criticism seems like complaining that the caviar is too cold.

Channel Road Inn. 219 W. Channel Rd., Santa Monica, CA 90402. ☎ **310/459-1920** or 310/454-7577. Fax 310/454-9920. 13 rms, 1 suite. TV TEL. $95–$195 double; $225 suite. AE, MC, V. All rates include full breakfast. Free parking.

When it was built in 1910, this house was located on 2nd Street; later it was moved to its current location on West Channel Road, just one block from the beach. There are only 14 individually decorated rooms in this charming inn. Fitted with pine furnishings and a smattering of antiques, some rooms have four-poster beds covered with hand-sewn Amish quilts, and others enjoy ocean views; two have fireplaces. There's a hot tub on the property and bicycles for guests' use.

Courtyard by Marriott. 13480 Maxella Ave., Marina del Rey, CA 90292. ☎ **800/628-0908** or 310/822-8555. Fax 310/823-2996. 276 rms. A/C TV TEL. $109–$119 double. Children under 10 stay free. AE, DC, DISC, V. Free parking.

This resortlike hotel is conveniently located only a few blocks from the marina and the Villa Marina Center, where you'll find good dining options and shopping. Rooms have been recently renovated and feature two phones and coffeemakers; many have patios or balconies. Take advantage of the spa, pool, sauna, steamroom, and whirlpool; you'll also have free use of a nearby fitness center.

Gateway Hotel—Los Angeles Airport. 6101 W. Century Blvd. (near Sepulveda Blvd.), Los Angeles, CA 90045. ☎ **800/325-3535** or 310/642-1111. Fax 310/410-1267. 807 rms, 91 suites. A/C TV TEL. $135–$175 double; suites from $300. AE, CB, DC, DISC, EU, MC, V. Valet parking $14; self-parking $8.

This 15-story hotel overlooking the runway recently underwent a $16 million renovation. Rooms have a California look with comfortable, light-color furnishings and triple-pane windows that block out even the loudest takeoffs. There's a large, heated outdoor pool, an exercise room with Universal equipment, a Jacuzzi, and three 24-hour restaurants. The hotel also offers 24-hour room service, a rarity in this price range.

Hotel Shangri-La. 1301 Ocean Ave., Santa Monica, CA 90401. ☎ **800/345-STAY** or 310/394-2791. Fax 310/451-3351. 10 rms, 45 suites. A/C TV TEL. $115 studio; suites from $155. AE, EU, DC, DISC, MC, V. Free parking.

Perched right on Ocean Avenue overlooking the Pacific and just two blocks from the Third Street Promenade, the Shangri-La has a great location. The small lobby opens to a large plant-filled courtyard (suprisingly lacking a pool) bordered on the north and west by the hotel. Rooms are accessed motel-style—from outside balconies overlooking the courtyard. The rooms themselves are spacious, and almost all offer ocean views. The overall art deco feel of the hotel carries through into the rooms—the lamps and mirrors, even the faucets and doorknobs evoke the early part of the century. The large Formica-covered furniture, however, evokes the Starship Enterprise more than the Golden Age of Hollywood. Complimentary continental breakfast is served daily, and there's a small ocean-view exercise room.

Los Angeles Airport Marriott. Century Blvd. (at Airport Blvd.), Los Angeles, CA 90045. ☎ **800/228-9290** or 310/641-5700. Fax 310/337-5358. 1,010 rms, 19 suites. A/C TV TEL. $119–$135 double; suites from $375. AE, CB, DC, DISC, EU, MC, V. Weekend rates available. Valet parking $12; self-parking $9.

Built in 1973 and renovated in 1987, this is no cutting-edge hotel, but it's a good airport choice. The hotel is designed for travelers on the fly; there's a laundry room, and ironing boards, irons, and hair dryers available for use. Rooms are decorated in standard chain hotel style; some have balconies. There are two serviceable restaurants, a coffee shop, and a bar. The hotel offers room service, concierge, complimentary airport shuttle, and a car-rental desk. Facilities include a giant outdoor heated pool, swim-up bar, Jacuzzi, garden sundeck, and business center.

Marina del Rey Hotel. 13534 Bali Way (west of Lincoln Blvd.), Marina del Rey, CA 90292. ☎ **800/882-4000**, 800/862-7462 in California or 310/301-1000. Fax 310/301-8167. 154 rms, 6 suites. A/C TV TEL. $140–$205 double; suites from $350. Packages available. AE, CB, DC, EU, MC, V. Free parking.

This hotel, on a pier jutting into the harbor, is bounded on three sides by the world's largest manmade marina. Guest rooms are surprisingly well decorated, with fine contemporary furnishings and a few nautical nods. Most rooms have balconies or patios and harbor views. The entrance and lobby were under renovation when I visited, but should be completed by the time you arrive. The Waterfront Bar & Grill, overlooking the marina, serves California-style cuisine all day. Services and facilities include concierge, room service, complimentary airport limousine, an outdoor heated waterside pool, sundeck, nearby tennis and golf, putting green, and car-rental service.

Marina International. 4200 Admiralty Way (west of Lincoln Blvd.), Marina del Rey, CA 90292. ☎ **800/529-2525** or 310/301-2000. Fax 310/301-6687. 110 rms, 25 bungalows. A/C TV TEL. $125–$300 double; bungalows from $150. AE, CB, DC, EU, MC, V. Free parking.

This hotel's lovely rooms are bright, contemporary, and very, very private. Most rooms are decorated in a casual California style, with soft pastels and textured fabrics; all have balconies or patios. The bungalows are plush and absolutely huge—some are even split-level duplexes—with sitting areas and sofa beds. The Crystal Fountain serves continental fare indoors or out, and the hotel offers concierge, room service, and complimentary airport shuttle. There's an outdoor heated pool, whirlpool, sundeck, nearby golf and tennis, business center, and a tour desk.

Pacific Shore Hotel. 1819 Ocean Ave. (at Pico Blvd.), Santa Monica, CA 90401. ☎ **800/ 622-8711** or 310/451-8711. Fax 310/394-6657. 168 rms. A/C TV TEL. $125–$135 double. AE, EU, MC, V. Free parking.

This rectangular, eight-story glass and concrete monolith, located about a block from the beach, is a good choice for those who want to be in the heart of Santa Monica. There's nothing to get too excited about, but the rooms are decent and well priced. Every room is chain-hotel identical. Great sunsets can be seen from the ocean-facing rooms on the high floors, but you'll have to look over busy Ocean Avenue, a vacant lot, and the roofs of Shutters on the Beach. There are ice and soft-drink machines on every floor, a busy cocktail lounge downstairs, and a heated swimming pool and Jacuzzi out back.

✪ **The Venice Beach House Historic Inn.** 15 30th Ave. (off Pacific Ave.), Venice, CA 90291. ☎ **310/823-1966.** Fax 310/823-1842. 4 rms, 5 suites. TV TEL. $85–$95 double w/shared bath; $130–$165 suite. All rates include continental breakfast. AE, EU, MC, V. Free parking.

This former family home, built in 1911, is now a fine bed-and-breakfast on one of Venice's unique sidewalk streets (a service alley provides access to rear garages). The interiors of this Victorian, with its hardwood floors, bay windows, lattice porch, and large Oriental rugs, will make you forget the hustle and bustle of a beach that's just steps away. Each of the nine guest rooms is different, outfitted with white rattan or antique wood furnishings; some are punctuated with country prints, others with shelves packed with worn hardcover books. One particularly romantic room has an ocean view and a fireplace. Continental breakfast—cereal, breads, juice, and coffee— is served in the comfortable downstairs sitting room; afternoon tea or cool lemonade is served with fresh-baked cookies every day. The inn can prepare picnic baskets for day excursions. *Beware:* The inn can get noisy, and despite its relative homeyness, it's not for everyone. Smoking is not permitted.

INEXPENSIVE

Travelodge at LAX. 5547 W. Century Blvd., Los Angeles, CA 90045. ☎ **800/421-3939** or 310/649-4000. Fax 310/649-0311. 147 rms. A/C TV TEL. $69–$74 double. Extra person $8; children under 18 stay free. Lower rates off season. AE, DISC, DC, MC, V. Free parking.

The lobby is nondescript and the rooms standard at this chain motel, but there's a surprisingly beautiful tropical garden surrounding the pool area. Some units have terraces. No-smoking rooms are available. Services include free airport transportation, baby-sitting, 24-hour room service (a rarity for a hotel in this price range), and a car-rental desk. A Denny's is attached to the hotel.

3 L.A.'s Westside & Beverly Hills

VERY EXPENSIVE

✪ **The Argyle.** 8358 Sunset Blvd., West Hollywood, CA 90069. ☎ **800/225-2637** or 213/ 654-7100. Fax 213/654-9287. 1,963 rms, 48 suites. MINIBAR TV TEL. $225 double; suites from $325. AE, CB, DC, EU, MC, V.

Completed in 1929, this landmark 15-story hotel is one of the most pristine art-deco buildings in the city; it was designed in the Streamline Moderne style, with a gunmetal gray facade, rounded corners, and an intricate stepped pediment that's reminiscent of classical designs. It's also terrifically located, at the base of the Hollywood Hills between Beverly Hills and Hollywood. Formerly the St. James Club (and, before that, Sunset Tower), the hotel has been home to Jean Harlow, Errol Flynn, and John Wayne (who once kept a cow on his balcony so he could have fresh milk every day). More recently, it has made an appearance in *The Player.* Purchased in 1995 by the Lancaster Group (which owns the Jefferson in Washington and the Tremont in Chicago), the Argyle is undergoing interior renovation, and an exterior face-lift, which added dusty rose accents near the roof, was just completed.

Rooms are on the small side, but they're lovely, with deco reproductions and specially commissioned hand-crafted Italian furnishings, such as unique gondola-like beds. Corner rooms have marvelous rounded windows and spectacular city views. Though the hotel appears straight out of the 1920s, modern conveniences haven't been overlooked—all rooms come equipped with VCRs, CD players, fax machines, and space-age phones with display screens that do everything from tell the temperature to control the room's lighting.

Dining/Entertainment: Book a table at Fenix when you reserve your room. Ken Frank, one of the area's most respected restaurateurs, sold his celebrated French restaurant La Toque in order to cook here; it's likely to become one of the neighborhood's most prominent dining rooms.

Services: Concierge, 24-hour room service, laundry service, secretarial services.

Facilities: Heated outdoor pool, small exercise room with free weights and cardio machines, sundeck, car-rental desk.

✪ **Beverly Hills Hotel & Bungalows.** 9641 Sunset Blvd. (at Rodeo Dr.), Beverly Hills, CA 90210. ☎ **800/283-8885** or 310/276-2251. Fax 310/281-2905. 194 rms, 21 bungalows and garden suites. A/C TV TEL. $300–$350 double; bungalows from $300; suites from $595. AE, DC, EU, MC, V. Parking $15.

After a 4¹/₂-year, $100 million restoration, the Pink Palace is back. The famous stucco facade, impeccably landscaped grounds, and grand lobby have been restored to their former over-the-top glory, and then some: Despite declarations that the custom pink color has been painstakingly re-created, most everyone will tell you—myself included—that the hotel should now be known as the "Salmon Palace." Despite this controversy, the reborn hotel is glorious again. This is the kind of place where legends are made—and many were: This was center stage for deal- and star-making in Hollywood's golden days. Howard Hughes long maintained quite a complex here (he even kept a separate room for his personal food-taster). Dean Martin and Frank Sinatra once got into a big fistfight with other guests at the bar. In 1969, John Lennon and Yoko Ono checked into the most secluded bungalow under assumed names, only to station so many armed guards around their cozy hideaway that they might as well have put up a neon sign announcing their arrival. Inside observers claim many of the Beverly Hills Hotel's Old Hollywood faithfuls defected to the nearby Peninsula, and have yet to return following the hotel's 1995 reopening, but plenty of current stars and Industry hot-shots can be found lazing around the pool that Katharine Hepburn once dove into fully clothed.

The hotel was reconfigured to compete in today's luxury market. There are fewer rooms, each more spacious and loaded with modern amenities. Gone is the sorry plumbing and tiny bathrooms of yesteryear; today's larger ones are outfitted with double Grecian marble sinks, TVs, and telephones for sink-side deal making. The best original touches have been retained as well, like a butler at your service with the touch of a button. The bungalows are more luxurious than ever—and who knows who you'll have as a neighbor?

Dining/Entertainment: The iconic Polo Lounge is back, with the original atmosphere and traditional comfort fare, like Dutch apple pancakes or its signature guacamole; their veteran maitre d' is back too, greeting the agents and stars here to close mega-buck movie deals. The adjacent Polo Grill takes up the nouvelle torch, specializing in California cuisine. The famous Fountain Coffee Shop is back. The Tea Lounge is another new addition.

Services: Concierge, 24-hour room service, dry cleaning, laundry service, nightly turndown, airport limo service, massage, valet parking.

Facilities: VCRs, video rentals delivered to room, large outdoor heated pool, fitness room with cardio machines, Jacuzzi, sundeck, car-rental desk, beauty salon, boutiques.

Beverly Hilton. 9876 Wilshire Blvd. (at Santa Monica Blvd.), Beverly Hills, CA 90210. ☎ **800/ 922-5432** or 310/274-7777. Fax 310/285-1313. 581 rms, 46 suites. A/C MINIBAR TV TEL. $230–$260 double; suites from $300. AE, CB, DC, DISC, EU, MC, V. Parking $15.

Easily one of the best in the Hilton chain, this huge convention hotel, owned by Merv Griffin, has been attracting professionals—and a smattering of tourists—since 1955. The eight-story hotel is a self-contained minicity, complete with shopping mall, Olympic-sized swimming pool, and indoor tennis and racquetball courts. Out of the hotel's three buildings, one was renovated in 1993, and the tower (where all the corporate clients are housed) was renovated in 1996; the third is in need of renovation, but it's primarily used for package tours. And beware: The cookie-cutter rooms are not all alike—only some have balconies, and some are decidedly larger than others. During the summer, the ground-level poolside rooms are a good choice thanks to their french doors, which open onto the sundeck.

Dining/Entertainment: It's hard to beat a pu-pu platter and a rum-spiked pineapple punch at the Polynesian-style Trader Vic's. This probably isn't the best place in Beverly Hills for dinner, but it's about the atmosphere, not the food. Griff's is best for Sunday brunch. There is also a lobby bar, and the Red Lion Inn features pool tables in a publike setting.

Services: Concierge, 24-hour room service, laundry and dry cleaning, express checkout, valet parking.

Facilities: Two outdoor heated pools, small exercise room with cardio machines, sundeck, business center, shops.

Four Seasons Los Angeles. 300 S. Doheny Dr. (at Burton Way), Los Angeles, CA 90048. ☎ **800/332-3442,** 800/268-6282 in Canada or 310/273-2222. Fax 310/859-3824. 179 rms, 106 suites. A/C MINIBAR TV TEL. $325–$395 double; suites from $650. AE, DC, EU, MC, V. Valet parking $15; free self-parking.

Four Seasons operates terrific hotels. As the unofficial superintendent of the monied elite, the ultraconservative Canadian chain can always be counted on for impeccable service and the highest standards. This means attention to the slightest details, top-quality food and decor, and a concierge that's famously well connected. This 16-story hotel attracts both old money and new, so you'll see pin-striped financiers and rock stars sharing the elevator. Both groups favor the European art, bathroom TVs, and oversized private balconies. Guest rooms are sumptuous but nevertheless dull; their designs and muted colors won't win any style awards. Plus, bathrooms have only single sinks, and bedrooms are devoid of stereos or VCRs, increasingly common accoutrements in deluxe hotels.

Dining/Entertainment: The Gardens is a terrific California-French restaurant that's often overlooked by locals; service and food are first rate, and Sunday brunch is worth leaving your room for.

Services: Concierge, 24-hour room service, overnight laundry, complimentary shoeshine, nightly turndown, valet parking.

Facilities: Large outdoor heated pool, small outdoor exercise room, Jacuzzi, sundeck, car-rental desk, gift shop, florist.

✪ **Hotel Bel-Air.** 701 Stone Canyon Rd. (north of Sunset Blvd.), Bel Air, CA 90077. ☎ **800/ 648-4097** or 310/472-1211. Fax 310/476-5890. 52 rms, 40 suites. $315–$435 double, suites from $495–$2,500. AE, DC, MC, V. Parking $12.50.

The Hotel Bel-Air is your address if you want to impress. This Mission-style hotel is truly one of the finest—and most beautiful—hotels in Southern California. It regularly wins praise for its attentive service and luxurious rooms. The grounds—11 acres of private park—are strikingly magical, lush with ancient trees, fragrant flowers, and a swan-dotted pond. The welcoming, richly traditional public rooms are filled with fine antiques. Guest villas, decorated in Mediterranean style with compulsive attention to detail, dot the property. Rooms and garden suites are equally stunning; all have two phones, a VCR, and a CD player. Some units have wood-burning fireplaces. The hotel is a natural for honeymooners and other celebrants, but families might be put off by the Bel-Air's relative formality, which is geared more to the jet-setting socialites and professionals who sojourn here.

Dining/Entertainment: It's worth having dinner at The Restaurant. Even if you're not staying, stop in for drinks at the cozy bar.

Services: Concierge, 24-hour room service, evening turndown, valet parking, welcome tea upon arrival.

Facilities: VCRs, large outdoor heated pool, health club with treadmills, StairMasters, Lifecycles, sundeck, nature trails.

✪ **Hotel Nikko.** 465 S. La Cienega Blvd., Los Angeles, CA 90048. ☎ **800/645-5687** or 310/247-0400. Fax 310/247-0315. 300 rms and suites. A/C TV TEL. $295–$395 double; suites from $600. Valet parking $16.50; free self-parking.

Finally—a hotel designed for business travelers whose primary goal isn't mimicking every other business hotel. The Nikko refers to its interior decoration as Pacific Rim (Organic Pacific Rim for the suites, which use all organic textiles), but well-thought-out seems just as appropriate. Thanks to amenities such as in-room fax machines, three two-line phones, and large counter/desk space, rooms function equally well as sleeping quarters and workspaces. And after a long day at work, the huge Japanese soaking tubs that come in all the bathrooms are perfect for unwinding. Registration is done at sit-down desks, and in the guest rooms shoji screens replace curtains, allowing light to filter through or block it out entirely.

Dining/Entertainment: Blending French and American dishes with Asian influences, Pangaea was named "L.A's Best New Restaurant of 1994" by Esquire magazine. On Sunday, Pangaea offers a 14-piece big band brunch. The Nikko also has a cocktail lounge with nightly entertainment.

Services: Concierge, 24-hour room service, evening turndown, same-day dry cleaning and laundry.

Facilities: Heated pool, exercise room, sauna, massage service, business center.

The Peninsula Beverly Hills. 9882 Little Santa Monica Blvd. (at Wilshire Blvd.), Beverly Hills, CA 90212. ☎ **800/462-7899** or 310/551-2888. Fax 310/788-2319. 162 rms, 36 suites. A/C MINIBAR TV TEL. $315–$480 double; suites from $600. AE, CB, DC, DISC, EU, MC, V. Parking $17.

This is an excellent hotel that strives to be more opulent and personalized than its competition, but ends up feeling more than a bit contrived. The squat Renaissance-style hotel, fronted by a flower-hedged circular motorcourt, has a small, postcard-perfect lobby and large, luxurious rooms fitted with antiques, marble floors, and magnificent rugs. The best suites are in the two-story villas; they have their own fireplaces, spa tubs, and terraces.

Dining/Entertainment: Breakfast at the Belvedere is a tradition among agents and clients from nearby CAA. Insiders order the nowhere-on-the-menu banana-stuffed Brioche French Toast, topped with strawberries and powdered sugar. The restaurant also serves lunch and dinner. Light lunches are served seasonally on the 5th floor Roof Garden Terrace—a treat. There's a clublike cocktail lounge, and afternoon tea and cocktails are poured in the Living Room.

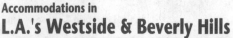

Accommodations in
L.A.'s Westside & Beverly Hills

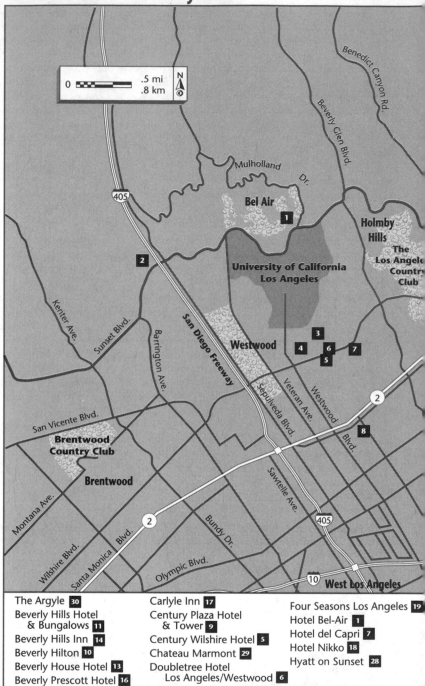

The Argyle **30**
Beverly Hills Hotel
    & Bungalows **11**
Beverly Hills Inn **14**
Beverly Hilton **10**
Beverly House Hotel **13**
Beverly Prescott Hotel **16**

Carlyle Inn **17**
Century Plaza Hotel
    & Tower **9**
Century Wilshire Hotel **5**
Chateau Marmont **29**
Doubletree Hotel
    Los Angeles/Westwood **6**

Four Seasons Los Angeles **19**
Hotel Bel-Air **1**
Hotel del Capri **7**
Hotel Nikko **18**
Hyatt on Sunset **28**

1-1089

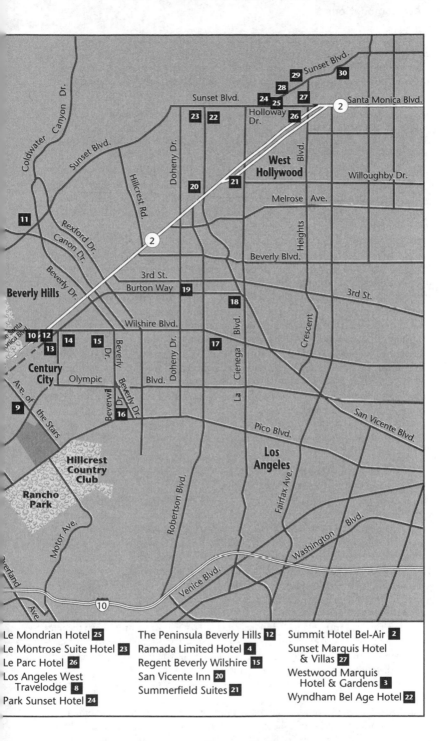

Le Mondrian Hotel 25
Le Montrose Suite Hotel 23
Le Parc Hotel 26
Los Angeles West
  Travelodge 8
Park Sunset Hotel 24

The Peninsula Beverly Hills 12
Ramada Limited Hotel 4
Regent Beverly Wilshire 15
San Vicente Inn 20
Summerfield Suites 21

Summit Hotel Bel-Air 2
Sunset Marquis Hotel
  & Villas 27
Westwood Marquis
  Hotel & Gardens 3
Wyndham Bel Age Hotel 22

Services: 24-hour concierge, 24-hour room service, overnight dry cleaning, courtesy Rolls-Royce service in the area.

Facilities: Outdoor heated rooftop lap pool; tiny exercise room; Jacuzzi; a well-equipped day spa offering body treatments, saunas, and steam rooms; sundeck; business center; sundry shop.

✪ **Regent Beverly Wilshire.** 9500 Wilshire Blvd. (east of Santa Monica Blvd.), Beverly Hills, CA 90210. ☎ **800/421-4354** or 310/275-5200. Fax 310/274-2851. 300 rms, 144 suites. A/C TV TEL. $255–$315 standard double; $335–$405 deluxe double; suites from $425. AE, CB, DC, DISC, EU, MC, V. Parking $15.

If the Beverly Hills Hotel is where new money exhibits itself, then this is the place for seasoned sophisticates. But that doesn't mean that it hasn't seen its share of color: Actor Warren Beatty earned his playboy reputation while living here, and parts of *Pretty Woman* were filmed in one of the palatial suites. You just can't beat the location, close to Rodeo Drive shops and an easy cruise down Wilshire to just about anywhere else. Nobody lingers in the spacious, ornate lobby; tell your friends to meet you in the more private lounge. Rooms are refined, with a mix of period furniture, three phones, three TVs, and special double-glazed windows that ensure absolute quiet. Wilshire Wing rooms are unusually huge, but those on the Beverly side are prettier, and include balconies overlooking the pool. Bathrooms have an extra-deep soaking tub and a glass-enclosed shower that's large enough for two (or more). There's steward service on every floor, and butlers can be called from a bedside bell.

Dining/Entertainment: The elegant dining room here—one of the hottest of the moment—is the only place on the Westside offering fine dining and live dance music. The Lounge, a European-style salon, serves a terrific tea from 3 to 5pm, light menus, and cocktails; at night, it's packed with media moguls and beautiful hangers-on.

Services: Concierge, 24-hour room service, overnight shoeshine, nightly turndown, express checkout, valet parking.

Facilities: Small outdoor heated pool, large health club with cardio and weight machines and free weights, hot tubs, sundeck, massage, business center, shops.

Sunset Marquis Hotel & Villas. 1200 N. Alta Loma Rd. (at Sunset Blvd.), West Hollywood, CA 90069. ☎ **800/858-9758** or 310/657-1333. Fax 310/652-5300. 102 suites, 12 villas. TV TEL. Suites from $235; villas from $450. AE, DC, EU, MC, V.

This is the ultimate music-industry hostelry, regularly hosting the biggest names in rock. Sometimes they even record in the Mediterranean-style hotel's basement studios, retiring afterward to the lobby bar, where their session can be piped in directly. It's a short walk from rowdy Sunset Strip, but the hotel feels a world away, with lush gardens, koi ponds, exotic birds, and tropical foliage. Standard rooms are done in traditional motel style; they're not particularly special, just overpriced. But each comes with a sitting area and a good-size refrigerator. The private villas take hospitality to a totally different level—they even have their own baby grand pianos and butlers. This is where Mick stays.

Dining/Entertainment: The Whiskey is one of L.A.'s most exclusive bars; the likes of Axl Rose and Robert Plant turn it into a celebrity fest Wednesday through Saturday nights. Unless you're staying at the hotel, though, you'll probably never get in. Notes, a seafood and pasta restaurant, is nothing special.

Services: Concierge, room service, dry cleaning, laundry service, in-room massage, valet parking.

Facilities: VCRs, two outdoor heated swimming pools, small exercise room, health spa offering beauty treatments, Jacuzzi, sauna, sundeck, 24-hour business and message center, access to the hotel's 48-track/112-channel automated studio.

Westwood Marquis Hotel and Gardens. 930 Hilgard Ave., Los Angeles, CA 90024-3025. ☎ **800/421-2317** or 310/208-8765. Fax 310/824-0355. 257 suites. A/C MINIBAR TV TEL. Suites from $235; penthouse suites from $325. AE, DC, DISC, JCB, MC, V.

This terrific all-suite hotel near UCLA, which attracts behind-the-scenes Industry types, offers accommodations that are straightforward without being boring. Hidden behind a severe concrete exterior, each stylish room is unique and loaded with amenities. The 15-story hotel underwent a major renovation in 1995; each suite was outfitted with multiline speakerphones and fresh textiles. South-facing suites have the best city and ocean views. *Beware:* The hotel can be noisy during graduation and other large school events.

Dining/Entertainment: The Garden Terrace serves breakfast, lunch, and Sunday champagne brunch; dinner is served in the Dynasty Room. There are cocktails and afternoon tea in the lounge, and cocktails and casual fare at the outdoor café.

Services: Concierge, 24-hour room service, dry cleaning, laundry service, nightly turndown, valet parking.

Facilities: Two outdoor heated pools, Jacuzzi, small fitness center, sundeck, flower shop, gift shop.

Wyndham Bel Age Hotel. 1020 N. San Vicente Blvd. (between Sunset and Santa Monica blvds.), West Hollywood, CA 90069. ☎ **800/434-4443** or 310/854-1111. Fax 310/854-0926. 200 suites. A/C MINIBAR TV TEL. $200–$500 suite. AE, CB, DC, EU, MC, V. Parking $16.

This all-suite hotel is one of West Hollywood's best luxury hotels, and an all-suite darling of the entertainment world—you've seen it pretty regularly on *Beverly Hills, 90210* (the high school days). Original paintings line almost every wall in both the rooms and public spaces, leaving the impression that this is as much a gallery as a hotel. The spacious, amenity-filled suites are fitted with dark pecan and rosewood retro furnishings. The best rooms face south; on a clear day, you can see all the way to the Pacific from their large balconies. Recently acquired by the Wyndham chain, the hotel has just undergone a $6.5 million renovation.

Dining/Entertainment: Make reservations at the Franco-Russian Diaghilev (see chapter 6) long before check-in. The Brasserie is less formal and offers great city views; its bar, which regularly draws top jazz performers, is one of the neighborhood's prettiest.

Services: Concierge, 24-hour room service, laundry service, valet parking.

Facilities: Rooftop outdoor heated pool, small fitness room, Jacuzzi, sundeck, hair salon, gift shop, art gallery, florist.

EXPENSIVE

Beverly Prescott Hotel. 1224 S. Beverwil Dr. (P.O. Box 3065) (north of Pico Blvd.), Beverly Hills, CA 90212. ☎ **800/421-3212** or 310/277-2800. Fax 310/203-9537. 128 rms, 12 suites. A/C TV TEL. $190–$275 double; suites from $250. AE, DC, DISC, EU, MC, V. Parking $15.

This hotel opened its doors in 1993, after a multimillion-dollar renovation that rendered the former Beverly Hillcrest unrecognizable. Managed by the Kimpton Group, owners of about a dozen top-quality "boutique" hotels in San Francisco, the Prescott is knowledgeably run and joyfully decorated; its comfortable, colorful, funky furnishings were carefully chosen by a confidently quirky designer. Thus, it was in perfect character for the hoteliers to commission the late, legendary rock musician and neckwear designer Jerry Garcia to remodel one of the suites. The resulting Garcia Suite is surprisingly sedate, designed with fish themes, subtly psychedelic fabrics, a top-of-the-line sound system, and an eclectic art collection that includes a dozen pieces by Captain Trips himself. Each room has an oversize TV screen, cordless phones, and a private balcony with good city views.

Dining/Entertainment: The former Sylvie is, at least for now, The Chez. Operated by the same folks who run Chez Melange (see chapter 6) and a handful of other local restaurants, it serves up robustly flavored fusion cuisine in a bright, Caribbean-influenced interior. Sylvie is not as good as the restaurant it replaced, but it's still worth staying in for.

Services: Concierge, 24-hour room service, overnight laundry/shoe shine, free morning newspaper, nightly turndown, massage and manicure services, complimentary shuttle service to nearby business centers and shopping.

Facilities: Large outdoor heated pool, fitness room with cardio machines, sundeck, business services.

Century Plaza Hotel and Tower. 2025 Ave. of the Stars (south of Santa Monica Blvd.), Century City, CA 90067. ☎ **800/228-3000** or 310/277-2000. Fax 310/551-3355. 996 rms, 76 suites. A/C TV TEL. $150–$220 double; suites from $250. AE, CB, DC, EU, MC, V. Valet parking $19.50, self-parking $10.

Located on a former Twentieth Century Fox backlot, this Westin-managed property sits on 10 of L.A.'s most centrally located acres. It's so close to film and TV's Century City nerve center that it has become the de facto home-away-from-home for countless rank-and-file Industry execs and creative types. Because it's so huge (the main building has 19 floors; the tower has 30), the hotel is also a natural for conventions and meetings; there's always something going on here. All this makes it the antithesis of warm and cozy, but rooms are large, the freeways are nearby, and your anonymity is assured. Rooms in the Tower building were renovated in 1995 and are considerably nicer—and pricier—than those in the main building. They feature large sitting areas, two sinks, and a separate tub and shower stall—some rooms in the main building have only a shower (no tub). Tower suites are head and shoulders above Hotel ones.

Dining/Entertainment: The hotel has two restaurants and two lounges, but dine in only if you have to.

Services: Concierge, 24-hour room service, same-day laundry service, evening turndown, complimentary car service to and from Beverly Hills, valet parking.

Facilities: Two large outdoor heated pools, a children's pool, free access to an off-premises health club, three Jacuzzis, sundeck, two exercise rooms, business center, conference rooms, car-rental desk, airline desk, ticket agency, tour desk.

○ **Chateau Marmont.** 8221 Sunset Blvd. (between La Cienega and Crescent Heights Blvds.), West Hollywood, CA 90046. ☎ **800/242-8328** or 213/656-1010. Fax 213/655-5311. 63 rms, 53 suites, 4 bungalows. A/C TV TEL. $190 double; suites from $240; bungalows from $550. AE, CB, DC, EU, MC, V. Valet parking $12.50.

The Norman-style Chateau Marmont, perched in a curve of the Sunset Strip, is a landmark from 1920s-era Hollywood; step inside and you expect to find John Barrymore or Errol Flynn holding inebriated court in the baronial living room. Greta Garbo regularly checked in as "Harriet Brown," and Howard Hughes maintained a suite here for a while; Jim Morrison was only one of the many to call this home in later years. This historical monument built its reputation on exclusivity and privacy, a posture that was shattered when John Belushi overdosed in Bungalow No. 2. Chateau Marmont is popular because it's close to the Hollywood action, and a luxurious world away at the same time. The standard rooms have views of the city and the Hollywood Hills; some have kitchenettes. Their faux English and Formica furnishings are not too rustic—just enough that you'll enjoy their kitsch. Suites are large, and most come with cloth-canopied balconies. The poolside Cape Cod bungalows—large, secluded, cozy, with full kitchens—are some of the most coveted in town.

Services: Concierge, 24-hour room service, laundry service, nightly turndown.
Facilities: Large outdoor heated pool, small fitness room, sundeck.

Le Mondrian Hotel. 8440 Sunset Blvd., West Hollywood, CA 90069. ☎ **800/525-8029** or 213/650-8999. Fax 213/650-5215. 224 suites. A/C MINIBAR TV TEL. $185–$425 suite. AE, CB, DC, EU, MC, V. Parking $17.

I wish I could say more about this 12-story all-suite hotel, but when I visited they were about to begin a complete renovation that will change the entire look of the hotel, both outside and in. However, the redesign involves Phillipe Starck, so you can expect something original. The hotel caters primarily to creative-type business travelers (it's often filled with New York advertising execs and a smattering of entertainment people). The new look will probably be much hipper than that found at other business hotels, but that's just my guess—the artist's pencil sketches of what the hotel will look like when completed weren't too enlightening. The hotel sits on the highest part of the Strip; on clear days, you can see all the way to the ocean.

Dining/Entertainment: The café is open all day, and the adjoining lounge presents live jazz nightly.

Services: Concierge, 24-hour room service, nightly turndown, voice mail, currency exchange.

Facilities: Heated outdoor pool, well-equipped fitness center, sauna, steam room, whirlpool, sundeck.

Ⓢ **Le Montrose Suite Hotel.** 900 Hammond St., West Hollywood, CA 90069. ☎ **800/776-0666** or 310/855-1115. Fax 310/657-9192. 125 suites. $160–$475 suite. AE, CB, DC, EU, MC, V. Parking $13.

Nestled on a quiet residential street just two blocks from the bustling Strip, this all-suite hotel features large one-bedroom apartments that feel more like upscale condos than standard hotel rooms. Each has a large bedroom, kitchen, and bathroom, as well as a sizable sunken living room complete with gas fireplace, fax machine, and Nintendo games. You have to go up to the roof for anything resembling a view, but once you're up there, you can swim in the pool or play on the lighted tennis court. For location, quality, and price, this is one of L.A.'s best values. Le Montrose is currently constructing an on-site music and sound studio in order to attract music industry clientele; let's hope that when this place catches on, prices will stay reasonable and reservations won't be hard to come by.

Dining/Entertainment: The Library Restaurant serves continental meals all day. Light bites are served poolside.

Services: Concierge, room service (7am–10:45pm), nightly turndown, voice mail, currency exchange.

Facilities: VCRs, video library, outdoor heated pool, small exercise room, Jacuzzi, sauna, sundeck, one lighted tennis court, complimentary bicycles.

Le Parc Hotel. 733 N. West Knoll Dr., West Hollywood, CA 90069. ☎ **800/5-SUITES** or 310/855-8888. Fax 310/659-7812. 154 suites. A/C TV TEL. $185–$265 suite. AE, DC, EU, MC, V. Parking $12.

Situated on a quiet residential street, Le Parc is a high-quality all-suite hotel with a pleasantly mixed clientele. Designers stay here because it's a few minutes' walk to the Pacific Design Center; patients and medical consultants check in because it's close to Cedars-Sinai Medical Center; and tourists enjoy being near Farmer's Market and Museum Row. The nicely furnished, apartment-like units each have a kitchenette, dining area, living room with fireplace, and balcony. There's a swimming pool, a basketball hoop, and a tennis court (recently resurfaced and lit for night play) on the roof. What this hotel lacks in cachet, it more than makes up for in value. Although your L.A. friends may not have heard of this place, thanks to an overall renovation in 1996, they'll be impressed when you invite them up for drinks. Café Le Parc is open from 6:30am to midnight and features a fully licensed bar.

Summerfield Suites. 1000 Wesmount Dr. (one block west of La Cienega Blvd.), West Hollywood, CA 90069. ☎ **800/833-4353** or 310/657-7400. Fax 310/854-6744. 109 suites. A/C TV TEL. $170–$210 suite. All rates include full breakfast. AE, CB, DC, EU, MC, V. Parking $9.

Situated in a residential West Hollywood neighborhood, this all-suite property (formerly known as Le Dufy Hotel de Luxe) looks and feels much like a high quality apartment building. A relatively unassuming interior and quiet public areas are hallmarks of value—less flash for less cash. Likewise, accommodations are detailed and plush without being excessive in either size or style. Most of the pastel-paletted suites have sunken living rooms, gas fireplaces, contemporary furnishings, and petite balconies overlooking Hollywood or Beverly Hills. All have kitchenettes and pretty good original art.

    Dining/Entertainment: There's a California-style café with an adjacent bar.

    Services: Concierge, room service (7am–11pm), laundry service, dry cleaning, grocery shopping.

    Facilities: Rooftop heated pool, small exercise room with cardio machines, rooftop Jacuzzi, sauna, sundeck.

MODERATE

Beverly Hills Inn. 125 S. Spalding Dr., Beverly Hills, CA 90212 ☎ **800/463-4466** or 310/278-0303. Fax 310/2783-1728. 45 rms, 4 suites. A/C TV TEL. $125–$175 double; suites from $175. All rates include breakfast. AE, DC, EC, EU, MC, V. Free parking.

Once the nondescript Beverly Crest Hotel—so dull that you could pass it a hundred times without ever noticing it—this property underwent an enormous year-long renovation and reopened in 1995; it's now a terrific place to stay. The Beverly Hills Inn is well located, within walking distance of both Rodeo Drive and Century City. Rooms are thoughtfully designed in a slightly Asian style. They tend to be on the small side, but you get what you pay for here; prices go up for the larger rooms. The best accommodations overlook the pool and courtyard; those on the other side can keep an eye on their cars in the parking lot. Every room has a refrigerator. There's a sauna and exercise room, and a small bar aptly named the Garden Hideaway. At press time, a new bar and restaurant were scheduled to open shortly.

☻ **Carlyle Inn.** 1119 S. Robertson Blvd. (south of Wilshire Blvd.), Los Angeles, CA 90035. ☎ **800/322-7595** or 310/275-4445. Fax 310/859-0496. 24 rms, 8 suites. A/C MINIBAR TV TEL. $120–$130 double; $190 suite. All rates include full breakfast. AE, DC, DISC, EU, MC, V. Parking $8.

Hidden on an uneventful stretch of Robertson Boulevard, just south of Beverly Hills, this four-story inn is one of the best-priced finds in Los Angeles. The hotel's exceedingly clever design has transformed an ordinary square lot in a high-density district into a delightfully airy hostelry. Despite its small size and unlikely location, architects have managed to create a multistory interior courtyard, which almost every room faces. Well-planned, contemporary interiors are fitted with recessed lighting, deco wall lamps, pine furnishings, and well-framed classical architectural monoprints. Amenities include coffeemakers and VCRs. The hotel's primary drawback is that it lacks views; curtains must remain drawn at all times to maintain any sense of privacy. Suites are only slightly larger than standard rooms.

Century Wilshire Hotel. 10776 Wilshire Blvd. (between Malcolm and Selby aves.), Los Angeles, CA 90024. ☎ **800/421-7223** (outside CA) or 310/474-4506. Fax 310/474-2535.

42 rms, 58 suites. TV TEL. $105 double; $125 junior suite; $150–$175 one-bedroom suite. All rates include continental breakfast. AE, CB, DC, EU, MC, V. Free parking.

The units here are large, sparsely decorated, and well located, near UCLA and Beverly Hills. Most of the rooms in this three-story hotel have kitchenettes, and some have French doors that open onto balconies; furnishings, however, are worn and outdated. The hotel surrounds a quiet courtyard and has an Olympic-size swimming pool. Breakfast is served each morning either inside or out in the courtyard. For the money, it's hard to do better in Westwood.

Doubletree Hotel Los Angeles/Westwood Holiday Inn Westwood Plaza. 10740 Wilshire Blvd. (at Selby Ave.), Los Angeles, CA 90024. ☎ **800/472-8556** or 310/475-8711. Fax 310/475-5220. 284 rms, 9 suites. A/C MINIBAR TV TEL. $139–$160 double; suites from $230. AE, CB, DC, DISC, EU, MC, V. Parking $12.

This former Holiday Inn changed hands in June 1996. With a good Westwood location, this Doubltree's comfortable guest rooms were updated in late 1994, and another renovation is planned for late 1996–97. Special touches include marble sinks and complimentary morning newspapers delivered to your door. The hotel also provides complimentary shuttle service to the UCLA campus, making it popular with visiting parents. There's an outdoor heated pool, exercise room with cardio machines, sauna, Jacuzzi, sundeck, car-rental desk, concierge, and gift shop. The Bruins' Den is best known for its cocktail lounge; it's popular with the basketball and football players who frequently stay here.

Hyatt on Sunset. 8401 Sunset Blvd. (two blocks east of La Cienega Blvd.), West Hollywood, CA 90069. ☎ **800/233-1234** or 213/656-1234. Fax 213/650-7024. 234 rms, 28 suites. A/C TV TEL. $140–$160 double; $350–$550 suite. Special weekend rates available. AE, CB, DC, DISC, EU, MC, V. Parking $10.

This aging 13-story chain hotel is favored by newly signed rock bands and other Industry types for its Sunset Strip location: close to Tower Records, the Whiskey-A-Go-Go, the Roxy, and House of Blues. Except for its art deco lobby, there's nothing exceptional here, but plans are currently in place for an overall renovation. The rectangular rooms are spacious; some have private balconies, and those on high floors enjoy skyline views. There's a heated rooftop swimming pool, a business center, and room service from 6am to midnight. A restaurant and a sports bar/deli serve sandwiches and pastas.

Summit Hotel Bel-Air. 11461 Sunset Blvd., Los Angeles, CA 90049. ☎ **800/HOTEL-411** or 310/476-6571. Fax 310/471-6310. 108 rms, 53 suites. A/C TV TEL. $139–$179 double; suites from $179. AE, CB, DC, DISC, EU, JCB, MC, V. Parking $5.

This two-story hotel on 8 garden acres has one thing going for it: location, location, location. It's just minutes away from Beverly Hills, Brentwood, Westwood Village, and Century City. The conservatively styled rooms and suites are spacious, airy, and comfortably fitted with furniture that was obviously purchased in bulk; each has a large balcony. Since breaking with the Radisson chain in 1996, the hotel has undergone an overall renovation. Facilities include a heated swimming pool, a single un-lit tennis court, a recently renovated lobby restaurant and bar, and an advanced facial salon, Summit Aromatasée Retreat.

INEXPENSIVE

Beverly House Hotel. 140 S. Lasky Dr., Beverly Hills, CA 90212. ☎ **800/432-5444** or 310/271-2145. Fax 310/276-8431. 50 rms. A/C. $93–$99 double. All rates include continental breakfast. AE, CB, EU, MC, V. Free parking.

I wanted to inlude this small hotel as an affordable option in the heart of Beverly Hills, an easy walk from restaurants, fashionable shops, and department stores.

🏠 Family-Friendly Hotels

The L.A. area's highest concentration of family-friendly accommodations—those that make families with kids their primary concern—are found close to Disneyland (see "Anaheim" in chapter 11). That doesn't mean that families aren't welcome in L.A. hotels—in fact, a few welcome kids with open arms:

Loews Santa Monica Beach Hotel *(see p. 50)* offers comprehensive children's programs throughout the summer. More like a resort than any other L.A. hotel, Loews boasts an unbeatable location; it's right by the beach and the boardwalk. What more could make the kids happy? They also offer baby-sitting services, so you can enjoy a kid-free evening on the town.

Hotel Oceana *(see p. 51)* is a spacious all-suite hotel overlooking the beach at Santa Monica. Kids will love the brightly colored walls and cushy furniture, and all suites come with Nintendo video games.

Century Plaza Hotel and Tower *(see p. 64)* offers spacious, family-sized rooms and lots of facilities, including a children's pool adjacent to the two larger ones. Because it's a veritable city unto itself, older kids love to explore this labyrinthine hotel.

The Sheraton Universal Hotel *(see p. 76)* enjoys a terrifically kid-friendly location, adjacent to Universal Studios and the enormously fun CityWalk mall. Baby-sitting services are available and there's a large game room on the premises.

Le Parc Hotel *(see p. 65)*, **Le Mondrian Hotel** *(see p. 65)*, and **Le Montrose Suite Hotel** *(see p. 65)* are fairly comparable all-suite hotels centrally located in West Hollywood. Multiple rooms means privacy for parents, and kitchenettes can cut down on restaurant and room-service bills.

Unfortunately, the pleasant lobby is all I can comment on—the staff refused to show me a room or the rest of the hotel.

🅢 **Hotel Del Capri.** 10587 Wilshire Blvd. (at Westholme Ave.), Los Angeles, CA 90024. ☎ **800/444-6835** or 310/474-3511. Fax 310/470-9999. 36 rms, 45 suites. A/C TV TEL. $85–$105 double; suites from $110. Rates include continental breakfast. AE, CB, DC, EU, MC, V. Free parking.

The Del Capri is one of the best values in trendy Westwood. This well-located and fairly priced hotel is popular with tourists, business travelers, and parents visiting their UCLA offspring. There are two parts to the property: a four-story building on the boulevard, and a quieter two-story motel that surrounds a kidney-shaped swimming pool. Though the rooms are beginning to show wear and tear, all are of good quality and have electronically adjustable beds—a decidedly novel touch. The more expensive rooms are slightly larger, and have whirlpool baths and an extra phone in the bathroom. Most of the suites have kitchenettes. The hotel provides free shuttle service to nearby shopping and attractions in Westwood, Beverly Hills, and Century City.

Los Angeles West Travelodge. 10740 Santa Monica Blvd. (at Overland Ave.), Los Angeles, CA 90025. ☎ **310/474-4576.** Fax 310/470-3117. 55 rms. A/C TV TEL. $59–$96 double. Rates include continental breakfast. AE, CB, DC, EU, MC, V. Free parking.

This clean and friendly motel offers good value in a high-priced area. The pleasant, modern rooms have been renovated. They come with coffeemakers and refrigerators, though some rooms have only a shower stall (no tub). There's an enclosed, heated swimming pool with a sundeck.

Park Sunset Hotel. 8462 Sunset Blvd., West Hollywood, CA 90069. ☎ **800/821-3660** or 213/654-6470. Fax 213/654-5918. 62 rms, 20 suites. A/C TV TEL. $75–$80 double; $150 suite. AE, CB, DC, DISC, EU, MC, V. Parking $5.

You would think that the Park Sunset's location—right on the Strip—would make this one of the noisiest places to sleep in L.A. But all the guest rooms are in the back of the modest three-story hotel, away from the cars and cacophony. The rooms are well kept and surprisingly well decorated, though the carpets are a bit worn and the bathroom color schemes are a tad dated. Some rooms have balconies and/or kitchens, and corner rooms have panoramic city views. There's a small heated pool in a lush courtyard, and a continental restaurant on the lobby level.

Ⓢ **Ramada Limited Hotel.** 1052 Tiverton Ave. (near Glendon Ave.), Los Angeles, CA 90024. ☎ **800/631-0100** or 310/208-6677. Fax 310/824-3732. 27 rms, 9 suites. A/C TV TEL. $66–$76 double; suites from $75. AE, CB, DC, DISC, EU, MC, V. Free parking.

This place isn't a fancy place by any stretch of the imagination, but the rooms are comfortable and have recently been updated—they're in better condition than those in many hotels that cost more. Some have stoves, refrigerators, and stainless-steel countertops; others have microwave ovens. Bathrooms have marble vanities. Facilities include an exercise room, a lounge, and an activities desk.

San Vicente Inn. 837 N. San Vicente Blvd., West Hollywood, CA 90069. ☎ **310/854-6915.** 20 rms, suites, and cottages. TV TEL. $79–$179 double; suites from $89. All rates include continental breakfast. AE, CB, DC, EU, MC, V. Free parking.

West Hollywood's only gay-owned and -operated bed-and-breakfast is a thoroughly charming place, with rooms that are individually and cozily decorated. Some rooms have kitchens, but you won't really need one; lots of restaurants (and shops and bars) are just steps away. Guests have use of the garden patio, swimming pool, spa-bath, and clothing optional redwood sundeck.

4 Hollywood

To locate these hotels, see "Hollywood Area Accommodations & Dining" map in chapter 6 (pp. 104–105).

MODERATE

Holiday Inn Hollywood. 1755 N. Highland Ave. (between Franklin and Hollywood blvds.), Hollywood, CA 90028. ☎ **800/465-4329** or 213/462-7181. Fax 213/466-9072. 448 rms, 22 suites. A/C TV TEL. $150 double; suites from $170. AE, DC, DISC, EU, MC, V. Parking $6.50.

This 23-story hotel in the heart of Hollywood offers perfectly acceptable rooms that are both pleasant and comfortable—as long as you don't mind being on a busy thoroughfare and sharing the pavement with bikers, wannabe rockers, and the other colorful characters that make up the neighborhood melange. A major guest room renovation was completed in 1995, so the hotel's standard furnishings are now stain-free. Suites, which include small kitchenettes, are particularly good buys. There's a swimming pool, a sundeck, and a revolving rooftop restaurant.

Ⓢ **Hollywood Roosevelt.** 7000 Hollywood Blvd., Hollywood, CA 90028. ☎ **800/252-7466** or 213/466-7000. 311 rms, 19 suites. $109–$129 double, suites from $200. AE, CB, DC, DISC, EU, MC, V. Valet parking $9.50.

This 12-story movie-city landmark is located on a slightly seedy, very touristy part of Hollywood Boulevard, across from Mann's Chinese Theatre and just down the street from the Walk of Fame. The Roosevelt was one of the city's grandest hotels when it opened its doors in 1927, and home to the first Academy Awards ceremony. But, like the starlets who once filled the lobby, its beauty faded; until a relatively recent nip-and-tuck, it seemed well on its way to Forest Lawn. The exquisitely restored two-story lobby features a Hollywood minimuseum. Rooms, however, are typical of chain hotels, far less appealing—in size and decor—than the public areas; but a few are charmed with their original 1920s-style bathrooms. Suites are named after stars who stayed in them during the glory days; some have grand verandas, while others are rumored to be haunted by the ghosts of Marilyn Monroe and Montgomery Clift. High floors have unbeatable skyline views. David Hockney decorated the famous Olympic-size pool. The Cinegrill supper club draws locals with a zany cabaret show and guest chateuses from Eartha Kitt to Cybill Shepherd.

INEXPENSIVE

Ⓢ **Banana Bungalow.** 2775 Cahuenga Blvd. (north of U.S. 101), Hollywood, CA 90068. ☎ **800/4-HOSTEL** or 213/851-1129. Fax 213/851-2022. 200 beds, 25 doubles. TV. $45 double; $12–$18 per person in multibed room. EU, MC, V. Free parking.

With a loose, carefree atmosphere reminiscent of a European backpackers' hostel, this is a great choice if you're under 35. It's probably the most fun place to stay in the city; it's often filled with international guests and there's almost always something going on. Nestled on nearly 7 acres in the Hollywood Hills just a short drive from the Walk of Fame and Universal Studios, Banana Bungalow has double and multishare rooms, kitchen facilities, a restaurant, a lounge, a free movie theater, and an arcade/game room. The hostel offers free airport pickup and regular excursions to the beach, Disneyland, and other L.A.–area destinations. They've started offering tours of the stars' homes as well as tours to Tijuana or the Grand Canyon and Vegas for an additional charge. Last time I was there, the Tijuana tour was billed on the grease board as a "DRINKING and sightseeing tour."

Hollywood Celebrity Hotel. 1775 Orchid Ave. (north of Hollywood Blvd.), Hollywood, CA 90028. ☎ **800/222-7017**, 800/222-7090 in California or 213/850-6464. Fax 213/850-7667. 32 rms, 6 suites. A/C TV TEL. $60–$70 double; suites from $75. All rates include continental breakfast. AE, CB, DC, DISC, EU, MC, V. Free parking.

This small but centrally located hotel is one of the best budget buys in Hollywood. Located just half a block behind Mann's Chinese Theatre, it offers spacious, comfortable, art deco–style units. Breakfast is delivered to your door along with the newspaper every morning. Small pets are allowed, but a $50 deposit is required.

5 Downtown

VERY EXPENSIVE

Regal Biltmore. 506 S. Grand Ave. (between 5th and 6th sts.), Los Angeles, CA 90071. ☎ **800/245-8673** or 213/624-1011. Fax 213/612-1545. 640 rms, 43 suites. A/C TV TEL. $225–$235 double; suites from $350. AE, CB, DC, DISC, EU, MC, V. Parking $20.

Built in 1923, the historic—and opulent—Biltmore is considered the grand dame of L.A. hotels. During the 1930s and 1940s, the Academy Awards were held in the spectacular Crystal Ballroom—the first sketch of the Oscar statuette was scrawled on a linen napkin here—and the hotel was the top choice for presidents and the elite. You've seen the Biltmore in many movies, including *The Fabulous Baker Boys, Beverly Hills Cop,* and Barbra Streisand's *A Star Is Born;* the Crystal Ballroom appeared upside down in *The Poseidon Adventure.*

The 11-story hotel sparkles with Italian marble and traditional French-reproduction furnishings, but the hotel's overall elegance has been compromised by an ugly office tower that was added in the mid-1980s. Still, the sense of refinement and graciousness endures, with a vaulted, hand-painted lobby ceiling, attentively decorated—though small—rooms with marble baths, and some enchanting Old World suites with lofty living rooms and nonworking fireplaces.

Dining/Entertainment: Bernard's features high-quality continental cuisine. Smeraldi's serves homemade pastas and lighter California fare. Afternoon tea and evening cocktails are served in the lobby's stately Rendezvous Court. Libations are also available in the Grand Avenue Sports Bar.

Services: Concierge, 24-hour room service, dry cleaning, laundry service, newspaper delivery, nightly turndown, express checkout, valet parking.

Facilities: Beautiful, original 1923 tile-and-brass–inlaid swimming pool, state-of-the-art health club, Jacuzzi, sauna, well-staffed business center.

✪ **Wyndham Checkers Hotel Los Angeles.** 535 S. Grand Ave., Los Angeles, CA 90071. ☎ 800/996-3426 or 213/624-0000. Fax 213/626-9906. 173 rms, 15 suites. A/C TEL TV. $240 double; suites from $400. AE, DC, DISC, EU, MC, V. Parking $18.

The atmosphere at the Wyndham Checkers, a "boutique" version of the Biltmore across the street, is as removed from "Hollywood" as a top L.A. hotel can get. Built in 1927, the hotel is protected by the City Cultural Heritage Commission as a Historic Cultural Monument. It has the feel of a grand old home, with cozy (and freshly upgraded) public areas such as a wood-paneled library. The top-of-the-line accommodations are outfitted with oversize beds and coffeemakers.

Dining/Entertainment: Checkers Restaurant is one of downtown's finest dining rooms (see chapter 6).

Services: Concierge, 24-hour room service, dry cleaning, laundry service, nightly turndown, express checkout, valet parking.

Facilities: Rooftop spa, heated lap pool, Jacuzzi, sundeck.

EXPENSIVE

Hotel Inter-Continental Los Angeles. 251 S. Olive St., Los Angeles, 90012. ☎ 213/617-3300. Fax 213/617-3399. 418 rms, 15 suites. A/C TV TEL. $190–$210 double; suites from $375. AE, DC, DISC, EU, MC, V. Valet parking $18.

Opened in 1992, this large, ultra-contemporary, 17-story hotel is the first to be constructed downtown in over a decade. Adjacent to the Museum of Contemporary Art and within walking distance of the Music Center, this member of the internationally prestigious Inter-Continental chain is the best-managed property in the neighborhood, run by a doting, eager-to-please staff. Conservatively styled, amenity-packed rooms boast floor-to-ceiling views and oversize baths with separate dressing areas. Public areas are decorated with works of art on loan from the Museum of Contemporary Art.

Dining/Entertainment: The hotel's restaurant offers California cuisine all day.

Services: Concierge, 24-hour room service, dry cleaning, laundry service, newspaper delivery, nightly turndown, express checkout on club floor, valet parking.

Facilities: Large outdoor heated pool, small health club, sundeck, well-staffed business center.

✪ **Hyatt Regency Los Angeles.** 711 S. Hope St. (at 7th St.), Los Angeles, CA 90071. ☎ 800/233-1234 or 213/683-1234. Fax 213/612-3179. 484 rms, 40 suites. A/C TV TEL. $155–$185 double; suites from $250. AE, CB, DC, DISC, EU, MC, V. Parking $15.

This 24-story Hyatt is one of the "anchors" of Broadway Plaza, a 35-store shopping complex in the heart of downtown near the Convention Center, the Music Center, and Dodger Stadium. This Hyatt is functional but sterile, outfitted like any other upscale chain hotel catering to the business traveler. Its most outstanding features are absolutely enormous windows that offer great views of downtown from every room.

Downtown Area Accommodations

Hotel Stillwell **10**
Hyatt Regency Los Angeles **9**
Inter-Continental
   Los Angeles **3**
The Kawada Hotel **2**
New Otani Hotel & Garden **1**
Omni Los Angeles Hotel **8**
Regal Biltmore **6**
Sheraton Grande **4**
Westin Bonaventure **5**
Wilshire Radisson Plaza **11**
Wyndham Checkers Hotel **7**

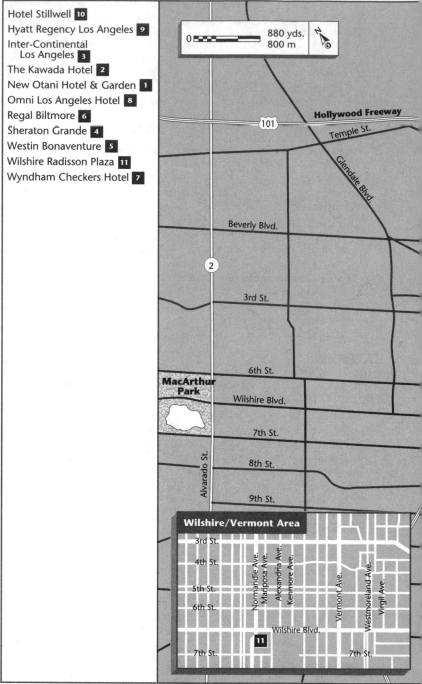

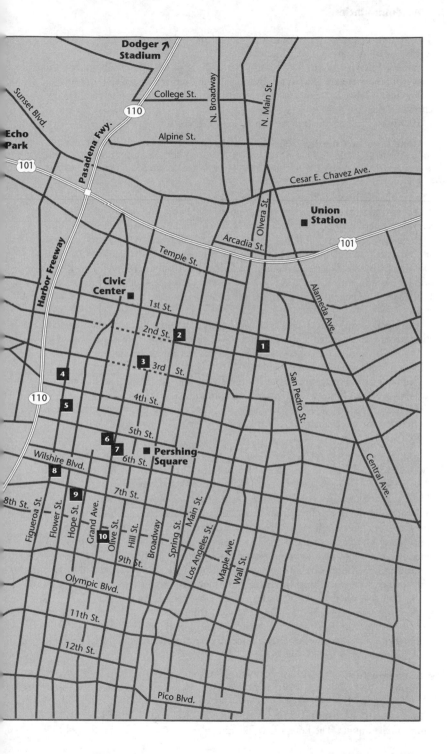

Two floors of Regency Club rooms come with dedicated concierges and complimentary breakfast and afternoon cocktails.

Dining/Entertainment: The Brasserie is nothing to write home about, but the view from the more opulent, distinctive Pavan will keep you lingering for hours.

Services: Concierge, room service (6am to midnight), laundry service, express checkout, valet parking.

Facilities: State-of-the-art fitness club, well-staffed business center.

New Otani Hotel and Garden. 120 S. Los Angeles St. (at 1st St.), Los Angeles, CA 90012. ☎ **800/421-8795,** 800/273-2294 in California or 213/629-1200. Fax 213/622-0980. 434 rms, 20 suites. A/C TV TEL. $160–$250 double; Japanese-style suites from $550. Cultural packages available. AE, CB, DC, EU, MC, V. Parking $11.

Most of the plush rooms in this anonymous 21-story concrete tower are Western style and comparable to other top downtown hotels in quality (and price). The best reason to stay here is to experience the New Otani's unique Japanese-style suites, outfitted with futons on tatami floors, Ofuro baths, and sliding rice-paper shoji screens. Hotel guests have exclusive use of the half-acre rooftop classical tea garden. One- and two-night Japanese Experience cultural packages include suite accommodations, sake and Japanese appetizers served at check-in by a kimono-clad waitress, dinner in any of the hotel's restaurants, shiatsu massages, and a live bonsai tree to take home with you.

Dining/Entertainment: There are two Japanese restaurants, one California-style dining room, and a coffee shop (fresh-baked breads and pastries are a specialty). The beautiful Garden Grill, a Tokyo-style Teriyaki grill featuring rare Japanese Kobe beef (which is beer-fed and massaged daily!). Chefs prepare seafood and prime steaks.

Services: Concierge, room service (6am–11pm), same-day laundry service, nightly turndown, airport limousine service, valet parking.

Facilities: Japanese-style health club (with saunas, baths, and shiatsu massages). Golf and tennis are available at a nearby country club. Car-rental desk, arcade with more than 30 shops.

Sheraton Grande. 333 S. Figueroa St. (between 3rd and 4th sts.), Los Angeles, CA 90012. ☎ **800/325-3535** or 213/617-1133. Fax 213/613-0291. 469 rms, 69 suites. A/C TV TEL. $185 double; suites from $300. AE, CB, DC, DISC, EU, MC, V. Parking $16.50.

The 14-story Sheraton Grande, with its magnificent smoky-mirrored facade, is located right in the heart of the downtown hustle. The airy, skylit lobby and lounge are as spacious and warm as the attractive guest rooms. A 1994 renovation updated already well-chosen room furnishings and refurbished public areas. Floor-to-ceiling windows in every room offer impressive city views.

Dining/Entertainment: The gourmet California-style Scarlatti is helmed by chef Trey Foshee, formerly of Röckenwagner and Abiquiu, so expect a good meal. There's casual dining at the Back Porch, and a pianist performs daily in the lounge.

Services: Concierge, 24-hour room service, laundry service, nightly turndown, express checkout, valet parking.

Facilities: Four movie theaters, downtown's best heated outdoor pool, access to an off-premises health club, sundeck.

Westin Bonaventure. 404 S. Figueroa St. (between 4th and 5th sts.), Los Angeles, CA 90071. ☎ **800/228-3000** or 213/624-1000. Fax 213/612-4800. 1,368 rms, 155 suites. A/C TV TEL. $175–$215 double; suites from $190. AE, CB, DC, EU, MC, V. Parking $18.50.

The 35-story Bonaventure is the hotel that locals most love to hate. It's certainly architecturally unique: The hotel's five gleaming glass silos—like giant mirrored rolls of paper towels—constitute one of downtown's most distinctive landmarks. This is an enormous convention hotel, designed on the scale of a mini-city. The six-story skylit lobby houses splashing fountains, gardens, trees, even a large lake. There's a tangle of concrete ramps and 12 glass-enclosed, high-speed elevators that appear to rise from the reflecting pools. Guest rooms begin on the 10th floor; each has a wall of windows offering good views, but are smaller than similarly priced rooms in the neighborhood. One of the towers is a completely remodeled all-suite facility where rooms come with an additional parlor room and half-bath. There's also an Executive Club level with upgraded facilities and services.

Dining/Entertainment: The rooftop Top of Five features panoramic views along with adequate, but not distinctive, continental cuisine. Ask for an exterior table; they're the only ones with the view. The views from the Bona Vista cocktail lounge are worth the price of a drink. There's nightly entertainment—jazz combos, cocktail-hour dancing—at the Sidewalk Cafe, a California bistro, and the adjacent Lobby Court.

Services: Concierge, 24-hour room service, nightly turndown, express checkout, valet parking.

Facilities: Large outdoor pool, sundeck, business center open Monday through Friday, conference rooms, car-rental desk, five levels of shops and boutiques.

MODERATE

Omni Los Angeles Hotel. 930 Wilshire Blvd. (at Figueroa St.), Los Angeles, CA 90071. ☎ 800/843-6664 or 213/688-7777. 868 rms, 32 suites. A/C TV TEL. $129–$179 double; suites from $425. AE, CB, DC, DISC, EU, MC, V. Valet parking $18.

After taking over this huge hotel from the Hilton chain in 1995, Omni began renovations with the guest rooms; renovation of the impersonal lobby is said to be forthcoming. But it seems from the direction the renovations are going that Omni plans on sticking with the utilitarian feel of the old Hilton, which seems to assume that all business travelers are strictly right-brained. The best rooms overlook the oval swimming pool. The hotel is centrally located, near many downtown attractions. The premium Towers rooms (on the 15th and 16th floors) offer separate check-in facilities, a dedicated concierge, and complimentary continental breakfast and afternoon cocktails. Of the hotel's three restaurants, Cardini, serving northern Italian cuisine, is the only one worth staying in for. The popular City Grill serves breakfast and burgers. Services at the Omni include concierge, room service (6am–11pm), dry cleaning, laundry service, and express checkout; facilities include a large outdoor heated pool, small cardio and weight room, sundeck, car-rental desk, tour desk, and beauty salon.

Wilshire Radisson Plaza. 3515 Wilshire Blvd. (at Normandie Ave.), Los Angeles, CA 90010. ☎ 800/333-3333 or 213/381-7411. Fax 213/385-2653. 373 rms, 26 suites. A/C TV TEL. $129–$139 double; suites from $250. AE, DC, DISC, EU, MC, V. Valet parking $10, self-parking $8.

Close to both Hollywood and downtown, this 12-story hotel is popular with business travelers for its push-button comfort and convenient location. The otherwise nondescript hotel earned a bit of notoriety during the 1981 World Series, when Yankees owner George Steinbrenner broke his hand and busted his lip in a supposed altercation with Dodger fans in the elevator; most people believe he did it to himself, through beating up the elevator in frustration over the third-game loss. The functional, modern rooms are attractively furnished; each has a glass-brick wall. One- and two-bedroom suites have two baths and a living room. There's a heated outdoor pool, a small fitness center, and a business center.

INEXPENSIVE

Hotel Stillwell. 838 S. Grand Ave. (between 8th and 9th sts.), Los Angeles, CA 90017.
☎ **800/553-4774** or 213/627-1151. Fax 213/622-8940. 250 rms. A/C TV TEL. $49 double.
AE, DC, EU, MC, V. Parking $3.

It's far from fancy, but the Stillwell's modestly priced rooms are a good option in an otherwise expensive neighborhood. This relatively clean, basic hotel is conveniently located, close to the Civic Center, the Museum of Contemporary Art, and Union Station. Rooms are simply decorated; some are large enough for families. No-smoking rooms are available. There are two lobby-level restaurants, a business center, and a tour desk.

The Kawada Hotel. 200 S. Hill St. (at 2nd St.), Los Angeles, CA 90012. ☎ **800/752-9232**
or 213/621-4455. Fax 213/687-4455. 115 rms, 1 suite. A/C TV TEL. $79–$119 double; $145
suite. AE, DC, DISC, EU, MC, V. Parking $6.60.

This pretty, well-kept, and efficiently managed hotel is a pleasant oasis in the otherwise gritty heart of downtown. Behind the clean three-story, red-brick exterior are over a hundred pristine rooms, all with handy kitchenettes and simple furnishings. The rooms aren't large, but they're extremely functional, each outfitted with a VCR (movies are available free of charge) and two phones. No-smoking rooms are available. The hotel's lobby-level restaurant features an eclectic international menu all day.

6 The San Fernando Valley

VERY EXPENSIVE

Sheraton Universal. 333 Universal Terrace Pkwy., Universal City, 91608. ☎ **800/325-3535**
or 818/980-1212. Fax 818/985-4980. 417 rms, 25 suites. A/C TEL TV. $225 double; suites from
$300. AE, CB, DC, DISC, EU, MC, V. Valet parking $14, self-parking $10.

This 21-story concrete rectangle, situated on the grounds of Universal Studios, is a good-quality, mixed-use hotel catering to tourists, businesspeople, and Industry folks visiting the studios' production offices. A major 1994 renovation updated every room with contemporary fabrics and floor-to-ceiling windows that actually open; each is equipped with Nintendo games. The hotel is very close to the Hollywood Bowl, and you can practically roll out of bed and into the theme park.

EXPENSIVE

Radisson Valley Center. 15433 Ventura Blvd., Sherman Oaks, CA 91403. ☎ **818/
981-5400.** Fax 818/981-3175. 194 rms, 12 suites. A/C TV TEL. $160 double; suites from $170.
Special discount packages available. AE, CB, DC, EU, MC, V. Parking $5.

This hotel conveniently sits at the crossroads of two major freeways, the San Diego (I-405) and Ventura (U.S. 101). Universal Studios, NBC, Magic Mountain, Griffith Park, Hollywood, and Beverly Hills are all just a short freeway ride away. The spacious rooms have private balconies and are attractively decorated; the baths and furnishings are just beginning to show their age. This Radisson is a comfortable enough place to sleep, and even have a swim or Jacuzzi after a long day of sightseeing. The café is open all day and has an adjacent cocktail lounge.

MODERATE

Beverly Garland Holiday Inn. 4222 Vineland Ave., North Hollywood, CA 91602. ☎ **800/
BEVERLY** or 818/980-8000. Fax 818/766-5230. 258 rms, 12 suites. A/C TV TEL. $139–$149
double; suites from $189. AE, DC, DISC, MC, V. Free parking.

Don't get confused by the name—this hotel is named for its owner, the actress Beverly Garland (of *My Three Sons* fame), not Beverly Hills. Grassy areas and greenery abound at this North Hollywood Holiday Inn, a virtual oasis in the concrete jungle that is most of L.A. The Southern California Mission–style buildings that make up the hotel are a bit dated, but if you grew up with *Brady Bunch* reruns, this only adds to the charm—it looks like something Mike Brady would've designed. Southwestern themed fabrics compliment the natural pine furnishings in the recently renovated guest rooms; unfortunately, the painted cinder-block walls give off something of a college dorm feel. And if you don't smoke, make sure to ask for a nonsmoking room; the smoking rooms smell musty. There are a pool, sauna, and two tennis courts, and all rooms feature balconies. The Paradise Restaurant serves Polynesian-influenced cuisine throughout the day. Complimentary shuttle to Universal is available.

Sportsmen's Lodge. 12825 Ventura Blvd. (west of Coldwater Canyon), Studio City, CA 91604. ☎ **800/821-8511,** 800/821-1625 in California or 818/769-4700. Fax 213/877-3898. 178 rms, 13 suites. A/C TV TEL. $92–$138 double; suites from $180. AE, DC, DISC, EU, MC, V. Free parking.

It's been a long time since this part of Studio City was wilderness enough to justify the lodge's name; this sprawling motel has been enlarged and upgraded since those days, the most recent improvements, sprucing up the worn room furnishings, made within the last 3 years. Walking around the ponds and waterfalls out back, you come upon the surprise luxury of a heated, Olympic-size swimming pool surrounded by a fleet of chaise lounges. It's hard to imagine that busy Ventura Boulevard is just across the parking lot. Rooms are large and comfortable, but not luxurious; many have balconies, and refrigerators are available. The poolside executive studios are the largest and best located of the accommodations here. There's a well-equipped exercise room, a variety of shops and service desks, and both golf and bowling are nearby. Complimentary afternoon tea is served in the lobby at 4pm. Caribou, the latest incarnation of the hotel's stunning glass-enclosed dining room, serves meat and game dishes in a hunting-lodge setting (but hopefully not any of the pretty swans frolicking out back!).

Universal City Hilton and Towers. 555 Universal Terrace Pkwy., Universal City, CA 91608. ☎ **800/HILTONS** or 818/506-2500. Fax 818/509-2031. 446 rms, 26 suites. A/C TV TEL. $125–$165 double; suites from $175. AE, DC, DISC, EU, MC, V. Valet parking $13.

Though it sits right outside of the Universal Studios theme park, there is more of a conservative business traveler feel than the raucous family-with-young-children feel you might expect at this 24-story hotel. The large lobby is built almost entirely of glass, giving it an open feel without feeling hollow or empty. Rooms are tastefully decorated in light earth tones with English-style furniture. Café Sierra serves California cuisine and is open for breakfast, lunch, dinner, and Sunday brunch. Services include concierge, 24-hour room service, dry cleaning and laundry, and express checkout. There's a heated pool, a Jacuzzi, and a privately run health club available for guest use on the premises at no extra charge.

6 | Dining

What a roller-coaster ride Los Angeles gastronomy has been. Barely 15 years ago, Southland gourmands, frustrated by the limited choice in town (between heavy traditional continental fare, rich classic French cuisine, or retro American bar-and-grill) could still be spotted flying up to San Francisco for a "decent" meal. Well, the wealthier ones, that is. Then came Wolfgang Puck and the age of culinary enlightenment—but L.A. got a bad reputation in the heady '80s for ultratrendy restaurants serving bird-size portions of the newly named "California cuisine" with a side order of snooty indifference.

Luckily, as the economy and social atmosphere of the Reagan '80s leveled out into the pragmatic '90s, restaurants quickly changed their tune. No longer faced with full reservation books weeks in advance, restaurant staffs all over the city suddenly remembered that they're in the service industry after all; today, it's a pleasure to dine at even the most cutting-edge, flavor-of-the-month trattoria. Once reticent to provide lowly doggie bags, today's restaurants all cheerfully package any menu item to go, catering to that economic downsize trend of "cocooning." Many went a step further by inventing an adjoining casual alter-ego eatery (Chianti Cucina and Il Pastaio are successful examples). Never one to miss a trend, superstar chef Wolfgang Puck made diversification a veritable art form: In addition to several fine restaurants throughout the Southwest, his name graces a line of frozen foods based on his no-longer-original recipes, as well as a chain of casual Wolfgang Puck Cafes in shopping malls. And while California cuisine has become a staple across the country, here it has already reinvented itself with "fusion," an accurate term describing the introduction of traditional Asian, European, and even (gasp!) American ingredients and techniques.

What about all those old-fashioned, special-dinner-with-the-in-laws retro establishments? Many perennial favorites, notably Chasen's, Scandia, and the Cock 'n' Bull, are gone; but those that remain, such as the eternally hip Musso & Frank, are enjoying a resurgence of popularity among young hipsters and nostalgic baby-boomers, even inspiring relative newcomers like Kate Mantilini and Fenix to offer updated versions of meatloaf, mashed potatoes, pepper steak, and the like. The retro cocktail of choice is, of course, the martini—celebrity chef Joachim Splichal's latest offering, Pinot Hollywood, even has a bar singly devoted to the libation.

The city's restaurants are categorized below first by area, then by price, according to the following guide: **Expensive,** main courses average more than $20; **Moderate,** main courses average between $10 and $20; and **Inexpensive,** main courses average under $10. Keep in mind that many of the restaurants listed as "expensive" are moderately priced at lunch. Reservations are recommended almost everywhere.

1 Best Bets

- **Best Spot for a Romantic Dinner: Camelions** (246 26th St., Santa Monica; ☎ 310/395-0746) unabashedly appeals to lovers: Most of the tables at this intimate restaurant seat only two, and there's not a cold seat in the house. Each of the three 1920s stucco cottages enjoys its own crackling fireplace. On warm nights, you can eat on the ivy-trellised brick patio, where it's not hard to imagine you're in the south of France.
- **Best Spots for a Power Lunch:** Between 12:30 and 2pm, Industry honchos swarm like locusts to a handful of watering holes du jour. Actors, agents, lawyers, and producers flock to perennial favorites **The Ivy** (133 N. Robertson Blvd., West Hollywood; ☎ 310/274-8303) and **Maple Drive** (345 N. Maple Dr., Beverly Hills; ☎ 310/274-9800). The music industry's darling is the L.A. branch of New York's venerable **Palm** (9001 Santa Monica Blvd., West Hollywood; ☎ 310/ 550-8811), a hearty steakhouse where the food is impeccable and the conversations read like dialogue from *The Player.* Lucky for us, the acoustics of this sawdust-strewn room are so bad that even patrons in roomy booths can be clearly overheard across the restaurant.
- **Best Place to Relive Old Hollywood: Musso & Frank Grill** (6667 Hollywood Blvd., Hollywood; ☎ 213/467-7788) is haunted by the ghosts of Faulkner, Fitzgerald, and Hemingway, who drank here during their Hollywood screenwriting days. This comfortable, dark-paneled room, virtually unchanged since 1919, begs you to order up one of L.A.'s best martinis and some hearty chops or legendary chicken pot pie, and listen to the long-timer waitstaff wax nostalgic about the days when Hollywood Boulevard was still fashionable and Orson Welles held court at Musso's.
- **Best Spot for a Celebration:** There are so many restaurants in L.A. that are fantastic for celebrating, it's hard to pick just one. **Citrus** (6703 Melrose Ave., Hollywood; ☎ 213/857-0034) gets my vote, though, because it's open and airy—spacious tables sit under a canopy of cabana umbrellas that soften the lighting and lend an island atmosphere, relaxing the otherwise elegant room. We once sat next to Senator Dianne Feinstein's table and still felt comfortable being casual and festive. The service is friendly, and the terrific food is worth the expense.
- **Best Spot for People Watching:** Nowhere in L.A. is the people watching better than on Venice's Ocean Front Walk, and no restaurant offers a better seat for the action than the **Sidewalk Cafe** (1401 Ocean Front Walk, Venice; ☎ 310/ 399-5547). Unobstructed views of parading skaters, bikers, skateboarders, muscle men, breakdancers, buskers, sword swallowers, and other participants in the daily carnival overshadow the food here, which is a whole lot better than it needs to be.
- **Best Spots for Celebrity Sighting:** Although stars can regularly be spotted at any of the city's best eateries, dinner at **Matsuhisa** (129 N. La Cienega Blvd., Beverly Hills; ☎ 310/659-9639) can almost guarantee a top celebrity sighting most any night of the week. Other Hollywood-heavy restaurants include **Morton's** and **Drai's** (on Mondays), **Eclipse** (Mondays and Tuesdays), and **The Ivy** and **Maple Drive** (Wednesdays to Saturdays).

- **Best Al Fresco Dining:** You'll find that more and more Los Angeles restaurants are eager to create appealing outdoor seating, even if it means placing bistro tables along a busy sidewalk. Taking advantage of the climate? Trying to compensate for the new no-smoking ordinances? Both, really. At the high end of L.A. al fresco is **Four Oaks** (2181 N. Beverly Glen Blvd., Los Angeles; ☎ 310/470-2265), nestled under romantically lit trees in the canyon of Beverly Glen. A more affordable way to enjoy a meal outdoors is by strolling Sunset Boulevard around Sunset Plaza Drive. There are no fewer than a half-dozen exceedingly pleasant sidewalk cafes—and the people watching is extra good!
- **Best Decor:** Campanile (624 S. La Brea Ave., Hollywood; ☎ 213/938-1447), built by Charlie Chaplin in 1928 as his private offices, has been beautifully designed in an understated, postmodern style that takes full advantage of the building's intrinsic charm. The restaurant is both elegantly vintage and crisply contemporary, an imaginative amalgam that makes it one of L.A.'s most beautiful dining rooms.
- **Best View:** Cafe Del Rey (4451 Admiralty Way, Marina del Rey; ☎ 310/823-6395) delivers, with an unparalleled panorama of Marina del Rey's beautiful harbor enhanced by a lively, upbeat atmosphere. Both the restaurant and the views are best at lunch; be sure to reserve a table by the window.
- **Best Wine List:** Wine lovers nationwide felt his pain when restaurateur Piero Selvaggio lost over 20,000 bottles during the 1994 earthquake. Despite the loss, **Valentino** (3115 Pico Blvd., Santa Monica; ☎ 310/829-4313) still boasts L.A.'s best cellar, and has been honored with *Wine Spectator's* highest rating.
- **Best American Cuisine:** Chef Leonard Schwartz cooks the city's greatest meatloaf, chili, and veal chops. Period. He grills a great burger, too. **Maple Drive** (345 N. Maple Dr., Beverly Hills; ☎ 310/274-9800) isn't cheap, but if you'd like to prove to your European friends that American fare isn't all McDonald's and Coca-Cola, this will wordlessly do the trick.
- **Best California Cuisine:** Chef/owner Michael McCarty has had his personal ups and downs in recent years, but his eponymous Santa Monica restaurant, **Michael's** (1147 3rd St., Santa Monica; ☎ 310/451-0843), hasn't suffered because of it. A visit to this ground-breaking eatery makes it clear why McCarty is considered an originator of California cuisine.
- **Best Chinese Cuisine:** While Chinatown is the place to go in search of traditional wonton and chow mein, **Joss** (9255 Sunset Blvd., West Hollywood; ☎ 310/276-1886) is my pick for some provocative twists on Chinese essentials. The sophisticated minimalist decor combined with excellent and personable service make this a great place for a group or a romantic dinner for two—and the food is always superbly presented and heavenly.
- **Best Continental Cuisine: Chaya Brasserie** (8741 Alden Dr., Los Angeles; ☎ 310/859-8833), best known for superb grilled fish and meats, takes continental staples and raises them to a new art form using local flavorings and some Asian techniques. Chef Shigefumi Tachibe is far from traditional, but then again, this is Los Angeles.
- **Best French Cuisine:** Joachim Splichal, one of L.A.'s very best chefs, serves fabulous French fare with a distinctive California twist at **Patina** (5955 Melrose Ave., Los Angeles; ☎ 213/467-1108). The wintertime game dishes are unequaled, and the mashed potatoes and potato truffle chips are second to none.
- **Best Italian Cuisine:** *New York Times* food critic Ruth Reichl called **Valentino** (3115 Pico Blvd., Santa Monica; ☎ 310/829-4313) the best Italian restaurant in

America. This restaurant is very traditional and unusually formal—for L.A.—but the wonderful dining experience is worth dressing up for.

- **Best Mexican Cuisine: El Cholo** (1121 S. Western Ave., Los Angeles; ☎ 213/734-2773) has been an L.A. favorite since 1927; Koreatown has grown up around their traditionally Spanish pink hacienda, but the kitchen still sends out steaming plates of the Mexican specialties Americans love. El Cholo does them better than anyone, though, from their richly dark enchilada sauce to soft handmade tortillas, refreshing margaritas, and the signature green corn tamales that follow the summer harvest.
- **Best Seafood: Water Grill** (544 S. Grand Ave., downtown; ☎ 213/891-0900) is a beautiful contemporary fish house that serves imaginative dishes influenced by America's regional cuisines. An absolutely huge raw bar features the best clams, crabs, shrimp, and oysters available, and the fish is so fresh it practically jumps on the plate.
- **Best Burgers:** They just do one thing at **The Apple Pan** (10801 Pico Blvd., Los Angeles; ☎ 310/475-3585), and they do it well. Choose from the "steakburger" or the saucy "hickory burger"—though regulars know to get hickory sauce on the side instead (for french fry–dipping). You'll feel the '40s live again in the decor and atmosphere of this family-run cottage nestled on the busy Westside . . . I actually suspect the wallpaper dates from opening day in 1947.
- **Best Desserts:** Before French chef Michel Richard ever stirred a sous he was a baker extraordinaire, creating some of the best desserts anywhere. **Citrus** (6703 Melrose Ave., Hollywood; ☎ 213/857-0034) is a great place for dinner, but no one will mind if you show up late just for sweets. Nancy Silverton's creations at **Campanile** come in a close second.
- **Best Afternoon Tea:** Surrounded by botanical gardens, the tearoom at the **Huntington Library** (1151 Oxford Rd., San Marino; ☎ 818/683-8131) is truly an oasis. Located in a fabulously wealthy residential area of Pasadena, the Huntington has the added appeal of pre- and post-tea activities: strolling the theme gardens, viewing the art gallery or library, and visiting the bookstore/gift shop. You can stuff yourself with fresh-baked scones, finger sandwiches, and strawberries with thick Devonshire cream, because the moderately priced tea ($11) is buffet-style; admission to the Huntington is another $7.50. See "Pasadena & Environs" in chapter 11 for details.
- **Best Value:** Feeding teenage boys? A football team? Or just famished after a day of sightseeing? L.A. mayor Richard Riordan's **Original Pantry** (877 S. Figueroa St., downtown; ☎ 213/972-9279) stays open 24 hours a day, serving up large, satisfying plates of traditional American comfort food (meatloaf, cole slaw, ham 'n' eggs, etc.) that won't win any culinary awards, but offers some of the best values in town.
- **Best for Kids:** More theme park than restaurant, **Dive!** (in the Century City Marketplace, 10250 Santa Monica Blvd., Century City; ☎ 310/788-3483) is a festive submarine-theme eatery that's packed with child-pleasing special-effects gadgetry of all kinds. Dive! is a nonstop party for the eyes and ears, but the same can't be said for the palate—the nouveau subs are nothing special.
- **Best Picnic Fare:** Open since 1917, **Grand Central Market** (317 S. Broadway, downtown; ☎ 213/624-2378) is L.A.'s largest and oldest food hall, selling everything from morning-fresh bread to local and exotic produce, fresh fruit juice to smoked meats, Chinese noodles to chili. And the cultural experience of a visit here is a terrific precursor to any picnic.

- **Best Newcomer:** New restaurants open and close at breakneck speed in this town, but **Boxer** (7615 Beverly Blvd., Los Angeles; ☎ 213/932-6178) has been winning fans and accolades since they opened in 1996. It's a small, friendly place whose artistic and inventive take on California cuisine is served with an enthusiastic desire to please—and a price tag that won't break the bank.
- **Best Name: Mo' Better Meatty Meat Burger** (5855 Pico Blvd., Los Angeles; ☎ 213/938-6558). Need we say more?

2 Restaurants by Cuisine

AMERICAN

Du-par's Coffee Shop (San
   Fernando Valley, *I*)
Flora Kitchen (Hollywood, *I*)
Hollywood Hills Coffee Shop
   (Hollywood, *I*)
The Ivy (Westside, *E*)
Kate Mantilini (Westside, *M*)
Maple Drive (Westside, *E*)
The Original Pantry Cafe
   (Downtown, *I*)
Musso & Frank Grill
   (Hollywood, *M*)
Roscoe's House of Chicken 'n'
   Waffles (Hollywood, *I*)
72 Market Street (The Beaches, *E*)
Sidewalk Cafe (The Beaches, *I*)
Swingers (Westside, *I*)

BARBECUE

Benny's Bar-B-Q (The Beaches, *I*)

BREAKFAST

Barney Greengrass (Westside, *M*)
Campanile (Hollywood, *E*)
Cava (Westside, *M*)
Cha Cha Cha (Downtown, *M*)
Chez Melange (The Beaches, *E*)
Du-par's (San Fernando Valley, *I*)
Flora Kitchen (Hollywood, *I*)
Hollywood Hills Coffee Shop
   (Hollywood, *I*)
Jerry's Famous Deli (San
   Fernando Valley, *M*)
Kate Mantilini (Westside, *M*)
Kay 'n Dave's Cantina (The
   Beaches, *I*)
Langer's (Downtown, *I*)
Nate & Al's (Westside, *I*)
The Original Pantry Cafe
   (Downtown, *I*)

Pacific Dining Car (Downtown, *E*)
Philippe the Original
   (Downtown, *I*)
Roscoe's House of Chicken 'n'
   Waffles (Hollywood, *I*)
Sidewalk Cafe (The Beaches, *I*)

CALIFORNIAN

Alice's (The Beaches, *M*)
Boxer (Hollywood, *M*)
Eclipse (Westside, *E*)
Four Oaks (Westside, *E*)
Granita (The Beaches, *E*)
Michael's (The Beaches, *E*)
Morton's (Westside, *E*)
Spago (Westside, *E*)

CALIFORNIA-AUSTRIAN

Checkers Restaurant (Downtown, E)

CALIFORNIA-FRENCH

Cafe Pinot (Downtown, *M*)
Camelions (The Beaches, *M*)
Carrots (The Beaches, *M*)
Citrus (Hollywood, *E*)
Patina (Hollywood, *E*)
Pinot Bistro (San Fernando
   Valley, *E*)

CALIFORNIA-MEDITERRANEAN

Campanile (Hollywood, *E*)

CARIBBEAN

Cha Cha Cha (Downtown, *M*)

CHINESE

Joss (Westside, *M*)
Yang Chow Restaurant (Downtown, *I*)

CONTINENTAL

Checkers Restaurant (Downtown, *E*)
Musso & Frank Grill (Hollywood, *M*)

Key to abbreviations: *E*=Expensive; *I*=Inexpensive; *M*=Moderate; *VE*=Very Expensive

CUBAN
Versailles (Westside, *I*)

DELIS
Barney Greengrass (Westside, *M*)
Jerry's Famous Deli (San Fernando Valley, *M*)
Langer's (Downtown, *I*)
Nate & Al's (Westside, *I*)

FRANCO-CHINESE
Chinois on Main (The Beaches, *E*)

FRANCO-JAPANESE
Chaya Brasserie (Westside, *M*)

FRANCO-RUSSIAN
Diaghilev (Westside, *E*)

FRENCH (CLASSIC)
Drai's (Westside, *E*)

FUSION/PACIFIC RIM
Cafe Del Rey (The Beaches, *M*)
Chez Melange (The Beaches, *E*)

GREEK
Sofi Estiatorion (Hollywood, *I*)

HEALTH FOOD/VEGETARIAN
Inn of the Seventh Ray (The Beaches, *M*)

INDIAN
Bombay Cafe (Westside, *M*)
Clay Pit (Downtown, *M*)

NORTHERN ITALIAN
Ca' Brea (Hollywood, *M*)
Chianti Cucina (Hollywood, *M*)
Il Pastaio (Westside, *M*)
Locanda Veneta (Westside, *M*)
Mezzaluna (Westside, *M*)
Replay Country Store Cafe (Westside, *M*)
Valentino (The Beaches, *E*)

SOUTHERN ITALIAN
Miceli's (San Fernando Valley, *M*)

JAPANESE
Iroha Sushi (San Fernando Valley, *M*)

Matsuhisa (Westside, *E*)
Mishima (Westside, *I*)

MEXICAN
Casa Vega (San Fernando Valley, *M*)
El Cholo (Hollywood, *I*)
Kay 'n' Dave's Cantina (The Beaches, *I*)
La Salsa (Westside, *I*)
La Serenata de Garibaldi (Downtown, *M*)

MIDDLE EASTERN
Skewer (Westside, *I*)

MOROCCAN
Dar Maghreb (Hollywood, *M*)

SANDWICHES/BURGERS/ HOT DOGS
The Apple Pan (Westside, *I*)
Cassell's (Downtown, *I*)
Dive! (Westside, *I*)
Jodi Maroni's Sausage Kingdom (The Beaches, *I*)
Philippe the Original (Downtown, *I*)
Pink's Hot Dogs (Hollywood, *I*)

SEAFOOD
Granita (The Beaches, *E*)
Lawry's The Prime Rib (Westside, *E*)
Water Grill (Downtown, *E*)

SOUTHERN
Aunt Kizzy's Back Porch (The Beaches, *M*)
Georgia (Hollywood, *M*)

SOUTHWESTERN
Authentic Cafe (Hollywood, *M*)

SPANISH
Cava (Westside, *M*)

STEAKS
Lawry's The Prime Rib (Westside, *E*)
Pacific Dining Car (Downtown, *E*)
The Palm (Westside, *E*)

THAI
Talesai (San Fernando Valley, *E*)

3 Santa Monica & the Beaches

EXPENSIVE

Chez Melange. In the Palos Verdes Inn, 1716 Pacific Coast Hwy., Redondo Beach. ☎ **310/ 540-1222.** Reservations required. Main courses $10–$22; lunch $8–$11; breakfast $5–$8. AE, MC, V. Daily 7–11am; Mon–Fri 11:30am–3pm; Mon–Sat 5–11pm, Sun 5–10pm; plus Sat & Sun brunch 7:30am–2:30pm. FUSION/PACIFIC RIM.

Redondo's appropriately named Chez Melange is not only the best restaurant in the South Bay, it's the most eclectic, too. While the combination of sausages and sushi on the same menu should send up red flags in most restaurants, both are well within this kitchen's formidable abilities. Homemade sausages are made with veal, chicken, and lamb, and served with gourmet dipping sauces. Sushi is morning fresh and sliced thick. About a dozen daily specials might include braised rabbit simmered in chicken stock and white wine, or blackened chicken burritos. It's not on the menu, but cognoscenti come for the fresh ahi, which is seared medium rare and blended with sun-dried tomatoes, chopped red onions, horseradish, and a little olive oil, then topped with capers and served on homemade crostini. Call ahead to make sure the fish came in. Required to serve breakfast by the hotel in which they're located, Chez Melange rises to the occasion with kippers and eggs, and scrambled eggs with fried oysters, bacon, and mushrooms. Conceived for serious eaters, the restaurant keeps its clientele with wonderful consistency, a clever newsletter, and lots of special dinners and events.

Chinois on Main. 2709 Main St. (south of Pico Blvd.), Santa Monica. ☎ **310/392-9025.** Reservations required. Main courses $21–$29. AE, DC, MC, V. Wed–Fri 11:30am–2pm; daily 6– 10:30pm. FRANCO-CHINESE.

Widely regarded as Wolfgang Puck's best restaurant, this Franco-Chinese eatery bustles nightly with locals and visitors who are wowed by the eatery's reputation, and rarely disappointed by the food. Groundbreaking in its time, the restaurant still relies on the same quirky East-meets-West mélange of ingredients and technique. The menu is just about equally split between Chinois' signature dishes and new creations by head chef Makoto Tanaka. The most famous of the former are the surprisingly tough baby pork ribs in a cloyingly tangy plum sauce, and farm-raised whole catfish that's perfectly deep fried and dramatically presented—but a bit bland, frankly. Terrific newer dishes include Louisiana shrimp in a mustard-fired plum sauce, and rare roasted loin of venison served in a ginger-spiced Port and sundried cherries sauce. Chef Tanaka will gladly prepare, on request, grilled squab on pan-fried noodles. This off-menu dish comes with a rich garlic-ginger sauce and sautéed shiitake and oyster mushrooms; it's said to be a favorite of regulars Luther Vandross and Shirley MacLaine. The dining room, designed by Puck's wife Barbara Lazaroff, is as colorful as it is loud. The noise level can be deafening, especially if a large party is in the house.

Granita. In the Malibu Colony Plaza, 23725 W. Malibu Rd. (at Webb Way), Malibu. ☎ **310/ 456-0488.** Reservations required. Main courses $21–$26. CB, DC, DISC, MC, V. Wed–Fri 11:30am–2:30pm; daily 6–10:30pm; Sat–Sun 11am–2:30pm. CALIFORNIAN.

In 1995, French-trained Spago alum Lee Hefter took over Wolfgang Puck's toque here, and the menu has never been better. Unfortunately, the restaurant's over-the-top '80s decor, a surreal eruption of oceanic kaleidoscopic art augmented by equally colorful fish swimming in lighted aquariums, is feeling kind of dated. But lovers of seafood don't seem to mind, judging by the ringing phones, crowded bar, and satisfied diners. Hefter's strength is interpreting the everchanging selection of fresh seafood at his disposal; the strongest menu selections are delicate lobster cakes with mango chutney, rare big-eye tuna topped with violet seaweed and quail's egg yolk, or pan-roasted filet of black bass layered with marinated tomatoes. Duck always appears on the menu, whether cooked rare with a delicate smoky essence, served sliced and fanned over roasted golden beets and blood orange segments, or crispy Cantonese-style with ginger and five-spice powder. The least complicated desserts are the best—particularly the warm apple tart or crispy Napoleon.

○ **Michael's.** 1147 3rd St. (west of Wilshire Blvd.), Santa Monica. ☎ **310/451-0843.** Reservations required. Main courses $15–$25. AE, CB, DC, DISC, MC, V. Tues–Fri noon–3pm; Tues–Sat 6pm–10:30pm. CALIFORNIA.

If Wolfgang Puck is the father of contemporary California cuisine, then Michael McCarty is the grandfather. Born in New York and schooled in France, McCarty opened this self-consciously modern American restaurant in 1979, when he was only 25 years old. Those were exciting times: Walls were irreverently hung with works by David Hockney, Cy Twombly, and Jasper Johns; staff uniforms were designed by Ralph Lauren; and the unusually casual dining room had the added novelty of a dining patio and rock garden. Several top L.A. restaurants have since caught up to Michael's—most notably Puck's Spago, Joachim Splichal's Patina, and Michel Richard's Citrus—but this fetching Santa Monica eatery remains one of the city's best. A recent price rollback has made dishes like Michael's simple grilled pork tenderloin with cream sauce and apples, and duck with Grand Marnier and oranges, even more appetizing. Spaghetti tossed in a creamy Chardonnay sauce with large sea scallops, roasted sweet peppers, baby asparagus, and American golden caviar is just one example of the restaurant's delicious, complex pastas. Don't miss Michael's famous goat cheese salad, served warm with walnuts and vinaigrette.

72 Market Street. 72 Market St. (west of Pacific Ave.), Venice. ☎ **310/392-8720.** Reservations recommended. Main courses $12–$26; lunch $7–$14. AE, DC, MC, V. Mon–Fri 11:30am–2:30pm; Mon–Thu 6–10pm, Fri–Sat 6pm–11pm, Sun 5:30pm–9pm. AMERICAN.

Dudley Moore and Tony Bill's "Maple Drive by-the-sea" is a work of art, both architecturally and gastronomically. The single, large, skylit dining room is something of a modern art gallery, with a festival of angles that includes partitions disguised as modern sculpture. Once the trendiest place on the beach, the restaurant has matured; it now has all the hallmarks of permanency. A recent chef change came with a welcome menu revision, but the Franco-American staples that continue to draw loyal crowds haven't budged an inch. A terrific salad niçoise is made with fresh rare-charred tuna, and Dover sole arrives flaky and moist. Meatloaf and chili remain favorites, often reaching the top of local "best" lists. Some regulars opt for the off-menu steak tartare—chopped beef tenderloin with egg, capers, shallots, parsley, mustard, radicchio, snow peas, and tomatoes. A dedicated oyster bar serves up many fresh half-shell selections, along with ceviches, Sevruga caviar, and combinations like calamari with tomatillos.

In 1995, the restaurant began offering exotic box lunches for air travelers. Dishes like Maine lobster salad and veal with wild rice ($18 to $39) are guaranteed to make your flight companions hate you.

○ **Valentino.** 3115 Pico Blvd. (west of Bundy Dr.), Santa Monica. ☎ **310/829-4313.** Reservations required. Pasta $12–$16, meat and fish $18–$25. AE, CB, DC, DISC, MC, V. Fri 11:30am–2:30pm; Mon–Thurs 5:30–10:30pm, Fri–Sat 5:30–11pm. ITALIAN.

All of Los Angeles ached for charming owner Piero Selvaggio when he lost 20,000 bottles of wine in the 1994 earthquake. But elegant Valentino never lost its position as *Wine Spectator* magazine's top wine cellar, and *New York Times* food critic Ruth

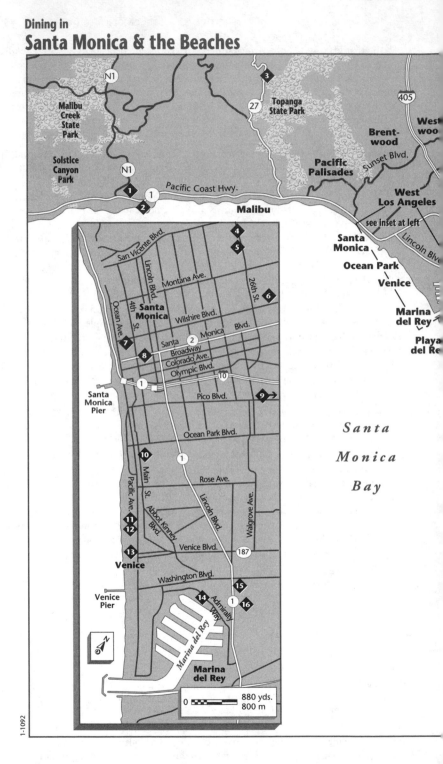

Dining in
Santa Monica & the Beaches

Santa
Monica
Bay

Malibu Creek State Park
Solstice Canyon Park
Topanga State Park
Pacific Coast Hwy.
Malibu
Brentwood
Pacific Palisades
West woo
West Los Angeles
see inset at left
Santa Monica
Ocean Park
Venice
Marina del Rey
Playa del Re

San Vicente Blvd.
Lincoln Blvd.
Montana Ave.
26th St.
Ocean Ave.
4th St.
Santa Monica
Wilshire Blvd.
Santa Monica Blvd.
Broadway
Colorado Ave.
Olympic Blvd.
Santa Monica Pier
Pico Blvd.
Ocean Park Blvd.
Main St.
Pacific Ave.
Rose Ave.
Lincoln Blvd.
Walgrove Ave.
Abbot Kinney Blvd.
Venice Blvd.
Venice
Washington Blvd.
Venice Pier
Admiralty Way
Marina del Rey
Marina del Rey

Sunset Blvd.
Lincoln Blvd

0   880 yds.
     800 m

1-1092

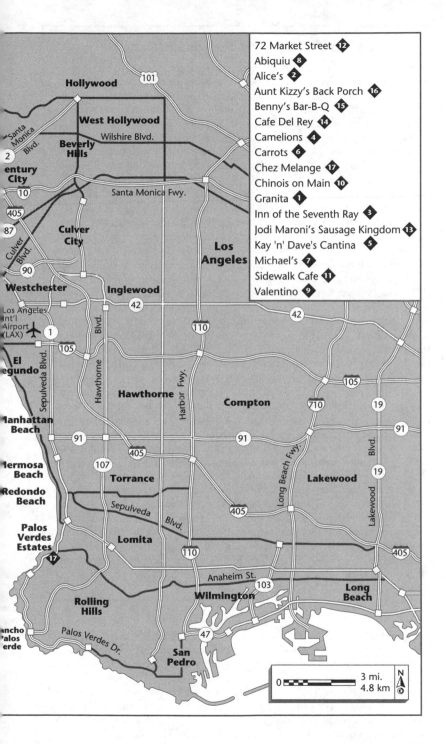

72 Market Street ◆12
Abiquiu ◆8
Alice's ◆2
Aunt Kizzy's Back Porch ◆16
Benny's Bar-B-Q ◆15
Cafe Del Rey ◆14
Camelions ◆4
Carrots ◆6
Chez Melange ◆17
Chinois on Main ◆10
Granita ◆1
Inn of the Seventh Ray ◆3
Jodi Maroni's Sausage Kingdom ◆13
Kay 'n' Dave's Cantina ◆5
Michael's ◆7
Sidewalk Cafe ◆11
Valentino ◆9

L.A.'s Coolest Chefs and Their Hot Restaurants

With the explosion of the Los Angeles restaurant scene, top chefs have joined movie stars as L.A.'s most celebrated residents. Increasingly, the city's chefs have become stars—and scenemakers—in their own right, signing multimillion-dollar, multirestaurant deals, often with celebrity backers. But the top gourmets tend to be held to a different standard than their celluloid-friendly counterparts; the public, happy to forgive and forget a flop of a movie, are much less understanding when it comes to their stomachs. Thus, the chefs who have made it in L.A. tend to be the real thing: culinary Michelangelos who can turn the harshest, most cynical gourmands into their biggest fans.

L.A.'s "Old Guard" are the heavyweight chefs who have been around a dozen years or so—they're the DeNiros, the Stallones, the Schwarzeneggers of the city's kitchens. They're far from formulaic, however; in a scene that will stand for no less, they remain as inventive as ever. In this group is the venerable Piero Selvaggio, whose **Valentino** is one of America's best Italian restaurants. His signature dish, risotto with white truffles, almost smells too good to eat. Sicilian-born Celestino Drago headed other people's kitchens for years before opening his successful pasta palace, **Il Pastaio,** in Beverly Hills. French chef Michel Richard's **Citrus** has proved so consistently popular, it's practically a license to print money. Richard knows a good thing when he sees it, and is currently running around the country opening multiple spin-offs, each called Citronelle. And German-born Wolfgang Puck—the most famous of this group, best known for the gourmet pizzas he began serving at the popular-as-ever **Spago** more than a dozen years ago—has moved into the populist cafe market, as well as into national supermarket freezers.

The "New Guard"—the Brad Pitts, Johnny Depps, Chris O'Donnells of the culinary scene—includes Joachim Splichal (**Patina, Pinot Bistro, Cafe Pinot, Patinette**), who is nosing in on Puck as L.A.'s most successful culinary entrepreneur. John Sedlar of **Abiquiu** is a young American with one of cookery's brightest futures; his innovative cone-shaped tacos will continue to be the talk of the town in 1997. Antonio Tommasi (**Ca' Brea, Locanda Veneta,** and **Ca' Del Sole**), one of the country's best northern Italian chefs, keeps them coming with updated versions of classics like butter squash–stuffed ravioli and shrimp risotto. Mark Peel and Nancy Silverton of **Campanile** are Puck alumni and the city's top husband-and-wife team. Silverton's **La Brea Bakery,** next door, has a devoted following, and delivers to gourmet shops and eateries as far away as Santa Barbara. Nobuyuki Matsuhisa (**Matsuhisa**) is often called L.A.'s most creative chef for his innovative combinations of Japanese flavors with South American spices and salsas. Success has finally gone to his head: Matsuhisa has opened a second restaurant, Nobu, in New York.

Reichl calls this the best Italian restaurant in America. The creations of Selvaggio and his brilliant young chef, Angelo Auriana, make dinners here lengthy multicourse affairs (often involving several bottles of wine). You might begin with a crisp Pinot Grigio paired with caviar-filled cannoli; or crespelle, thin little pancakes with fresh porcini mushrooms and a rich melt of fontina cheese. Handmade pastas tossed with tender baby squid or sweet tiny clams are typical of first courses, though it really depends on what came to market the morning you visit. A rich Barolo is the perfect accompaniment to rosemary-infused roasted rabbit; the fantastically fragrant risotto with white truffles is one of the most magnificent dishes I've ever had. Jackets are all but required in the elegant dining room. What more can I say—go!

MODERATE

Alice's. 23000 Pacific Coast Hwy. (at the Malibu Pier), Malibu. ☎ **310/456-6646.** Reservations recommended. Main courses $9–$18; lunch $7–$15. MC, V. Mon–Fri 11:30am–10pm, Sat–Sun 11am–11pm. CALIFORNIA.

Alice's has a long history as a Malibu fixture, situated on Pacific Coast Highway on the pier above the beach. The dining room is glassed in on three sides and faces the ocean; rear tables sit on a raised platform so that everyone has a million-dollar view. It's a light and airy place, with a casual menu to match. Admittedly, most people are here for the one-of-a-kind atmosphere, but the food is a lot better than it needs to be. Seared yellowtail tuna is served simply, on a bed of spinach, with lemon and tarragon butter. Grilled chicken breast is marinated in garlic and soy and served with tomato-cilantro relish. Pastas and pizzas are also available, and there's a full bar.

Aunt Kizzy's Back Porch. 4325 Glencove Ave. (in the Villa Marina Shopping Center), Marina del Rey. ☎ **310/578-1005.** No reservations accepted. Main courses $8–$13. AE. Mon–Sat 11am–4pm; Sun–Thurs 4–11pm, Fri–Sat 4pm–midnight; Sun 11am–3pm. SOUTHERN.

This is a real Southern restaurant, owned by genuine Southerners from Texas and Oklahoma. Kizzy's chicken Créole, jambalaya, and smothered pork chops are just about as good as it gets in this city. Almost everything comes with vegetables, red beans and rice, and corn muffins. Fresh-squeezed lemonade is served by the mason jar. These are huge meals that, as corny as it sounds, are as filling as they are delicious. Sunday brunches are all-you-can-eat affairs, served buffet style. The biggest problem with Aunt Kizzy's is its location, hidden in a shopping center that has too few parking spaces to accommodate it. Look for the restaurant to the right of Vons supermarket.

Cafe Del Rey. 4451 Admiralty Way (between Lincoln Blvd. and Washington St.), Marina del Rey. ☎ **310/823-6395.** Reservations required. Main courses $13–$29; lunch $9–$15. AE, DC, DISC, MC, V. Mon–Sun 11:30am–2:30pm; Sun 5–10:30pm, Mon–Thurs 5:30–10:30pm, Fri–Sat 5:30–11pm. PACIFIC RIM.

This is a lively, open, high-tech space that makes a meal feel like an event, with a huge menu filled with unusual choices that make ordering fun. And there's a terrific view of the Marina's bobbing sailboats, so you know you're someplace special. The kitchen focuses on creative preparations of fresh, seasonal foods. While most dishes are very good, some are too creative, and too contrived. Cuban black-bean soup, Angus ribeye steaks, and quesadillas stuffed with wild mushrooms and grilled vegetables are all winners; Peking duck with mango chutney, red-chili angel hair pasta with sautéed-shrimps, and penne with wild bacon and fresh tomatoes are not. Get a table by the window, choose wisely, and enjoy yourself.

✪ Camelions. 246 26th St. (south of San Vicente Blvd.), Santa Monica. ☎ **310/395-0746.** Reservations required. Main courses $14–$22; lunch $10–$13. AE, CB, DC, MC, V. Tues–Sun 11:30am–2:30pm; Tues–Sun 6–9:30pm. CALIFORNIA-FRENCH.

Either indoors or out, dining here is one of Los Angeles's most romantic dining experiences. Camelions' three 1920s stucco cottages, each with beamed ceilings and a crackling fireplace, are built around an ivy-trellised brick patio. Contrary to its Provençal setting, the tasty French-inspired cuisine is plenty California trendy. Red lentil crepes arrive garnished with smoked salmon and arrugula salad, and roasted duck breast is sliced thin and fanned out over a plate of walnut-Merlot sauce, accompanied by a risotto and berry timbale. There are traditional French dishes like sautéed rabbit stewed in a clay pot with sweet garlic; in addition, a large selection of sandwiches and salads (like spinach with warm new potatoes, bacon, and mustard vinaigrette) are available at lunch.

Carrots. 2834 Santa Monica Blvd. (between 26th St. and Centinela Ave.), Santa Monica. ☎ 310/453-6505. Reservations recommended on weekends. Main courses $14–$22; lunch $5–$7. MC, V. Wed–Fri 11:30am–2:30pm; Tues–Sun 6–10pm. CALIFORNIA-FRENCH.

Chef/owner Fred Iwasaki, a former sous-chef at Spago and Chinois, was born in the year of the Rabbit—hence Carrots . . . get it? His tiny restaurant, set in an undistinguished minimall, is an understated setting for very good food at very fair prices. Dinners might begin with black mussels in a black bean sauce, shrimp wrapped with julienned potatoes, or a baby green salad with goat cheese. You can't go wrong by ordering grilled salmon, which is sautéed in an onion butter sauce, or New York steak, which is perfectly grilled and thinly sliced. As is the current trend, Carrots offers counter seating for singles; on weekends, even lone diners are happy if they can find a spot here.

Inn of the Seventh Ray. 128 Old Topanga Canyon Rd. (on Calif. 27), Topanga Canyon. ☎ 310/455-1311. Reservations required. Main courses $16–$25. MC, V. Mon–Fri 11:30am–3pm, Sat 10:30am–3pm, Sun 9:30am–3pm; daily 6–10pm. CALIFORNIA HEALTH FOOD.

Topanga Canyon has long been the home of leftover hippies and L.A.'s New-Agers; it's a mountainous, sparsely populated area that is undeniably beautiful, even spiritual. This restaurant, a former church, is in the middle of the aura. No one comes here for the food; people come for a romantic dining experience, far from the bright lights of the city. About half the seating is outdoors, at tables overlooking a creek and endless tangles of untamed vines and shrubs. Inside, the dining room is rustic, with a sloped roof and a glass wall offering mountain views. The Inn was opened about 25 years ago by Ralph and Lucille Yaney, who preach some kind of mumbojumbo about the energy of food, and list menu items in order of their "esoteric vibrational value." Everything is prepared from scratch, and foods are organic and chemical- and preservative-free. The fish are caught in deep water far offshore and served the same day; they even sell unpasteurized wines. Ten main dishes are available daily, and all are served with hors d'oeuvres, soup or salad, and vegetables. The lightest dish, called Five Secret Rays, consists of lightly steamed vegetables served with lemon-tahini and caraway cheese sauces; the densest dish—vibrationally speaking—is a 10-ounce New York steak cut from naturally fed beef.

INEXPENSIVE

Benny's Bar-B-Q. 4077 Lincoln Blvd. (south of Washington Blvd.), Marina del Rey. ☎ 310/821-6939. Sandwiches $4–$6, dinner specials $7–$10. AE, MC, V. Mon–Sat 11am–10pm, Sun 2–10pm. BARBECUE.

It's mostly take-out at this cook shack dive, but there are a few tables, where the city's luckiest diners gorge themselves on Los Angeles's best barbecued pork and beef ribs and hot-link sausages. Like almost everything on the menu, barbecued chicken is bathed in a tangy hot sauce and served with baked beans and a choice of cole slaw, potato salad, fries, or corn on the cob. Beef, ham, and pork sandwiches are also available. To reach Benny's, find Lincoln Boulevard, then follow the heavy aroma.

Jody Maroni's Sausage Kingdom. 2011 Ocean Front Walk (north of Venice Blvd.), Venice. ☎ 310/306-1995. Sandwiches $4–$6. No credit cards. Daily 10am–5:30pm. SANDWICHES/SAUSAGES.

Your cardiologist might not approve, but Jody Maroni's all-natural, preservative-free "haut dogs" are some of the best wieners served anywhere. The grungy walk-up (or

Rollerblade-up) counter looks fairly foreboding—you wouldn't know r met fare behind that aging hot dog–stand facade. At least 14 differenr sandwiches are served here. Bypass the traditional hot Italian and try the garlic, Bombay curried lamb, all-chicken apple, or orange-garlic-cumin. Each is served on a freshly baked onion roll and smothered with onions and peppers. Burgers, hot dogs, BLTs, and rotisserie chicken are also served, but why bother?

Other locations include Santa Monica's Third Street Promenade, the Valley's Universal CityWalk (☎ 818/622-JODY) and inside LAX's Terminal 5, where you can pick up some last-minute vacuum-packed sausages for home.

Ⓢ **Kay 'n' Dave's Cantina.** 262 26th Street (south of San Vicente), Santa Monica. ☎ 310/ 260-1355. Reservations not accepted. Main courses $5–$12. AE, MC, V. Mon–Thurs 7:30am– 9:30pm, Fri 7:30am–10pm, Sat 8am–10pm, Sun 8am–9:30pm. HEALTHY MEXICAN.

A beach community favorite for "really big portions of really good food at really low prices," Kay 'n' Dave's cooks with no lard and has a vegetarian-friendly menu with plenty of meat items, too. Come early for breakfast and be prepared to wait, as local devotees line up for five kinds of fluffy pancakes, zesty omelets, or one of the best breakfast burritos in town. Grilled tuna Veracruz, spinach and chicken enchiladas in tomatillo salsa, seafood fajitas tostada, vegetable-filled corn tamales, and other Mexican specialties really are served in huge portions, making this mostly locals minichain a great choice to energize for (or reenergize after) an action-packed day of beach sightseeing. Bring the family—there's a kids' menu and crayons on every table.

Kay 'n' Dave's also has cantinas in Malibu (18763 Pacific Coast Highway; ☎ 310/ 456-8800) and Pacific Palisades (15246 Sunset Blvd.; ☎ 310/459-8118). The Malibu location opens later in the mornings.

❂ **Sidewalk Cafe.** 1401 Ocean Front Walk (between Horizon Ave. and Market St.), Venice. ☎ 310/399-5547. Reservations not accepted. Main courses $6–$13. MC, V. Sun–Thurs 8am– 11pm, Fri–Sat 8am–midnight. AMERICAN.

Nowhere in L.A. is the people-watching better than along Ocean Front Walk. The constantly bustling Sidewalk Cafe is ensconced in one of Venice's few remaining early 20th-century buildings. The best seats, of course, are out front, around overcrowded open-air tables, all with a perfect view of the crowd, which provides nonstop entertainment. The menu is extensive, and the food is a whole lot better than it has to be at a location like this. Choose from the seriously overstuffed sandwiches or other oversize American favorites: omelets, salads, burgers.

4 L.A.'s Westside & Beverly Hills

EXPENSIVE

Diaghilev. In the Wyndham Bel Age Hotel, 1020 N. San Vicente Blvd. (at Sunset Blvd.), West Hollywood. ☎ 310/854-1111. Reservations recommended. Main courses $23–$27. AE, CB, DC, DISC, MC, V. Tues–Sat 6:30–11pm. FRANCO-RUSSIAN.

In a world where most hoteliers are tearing their hair out trying to persuade guests to spend their dinner dollars in-house, Diaghilev finds itself in the enviable position of having to regularly turn away would-be diners, most of whom aren't even sleeping upstairs. Tucked away in the Wyndham Bel Age Hotel, Diaghilev is a sumptuous turn-of-the-century Franco-Russian theme restaurant where guests lounge on overstuffed loveseats and dine to the soulful strums of a mandolinist. Gilt-framed landscapes hang on silk-covered walls, imported caviar is spooned with ceremony, and seemingly endless varieties of flavored vodkas are sipped from fine crystal. On most nights, host Dimitri hands every lady a long-stemmed rose. Each diner is treated like

ining in L.A.'s Westside & Beverly Hills

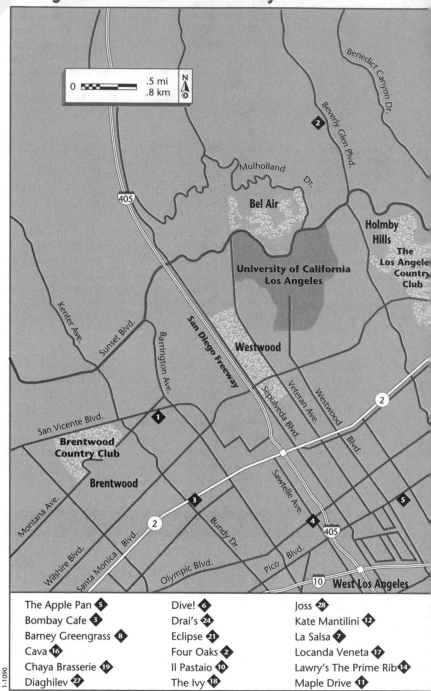

The Apple Pan ⑤
Bombay Cafe ③
Barney Greengrass ⑧
Cava ⑯
Chaya Brasserie ⑲
Diaghilev ㉗

Dive! ⑥
Drai's ㉔
Eclipse ㉑
Four Oaks ②
Il Pastaio ⑩
The Ivy ⑱

Joss ㉘
Kate Mantilini ⑫
La Salsa ⑦
Locanda Veneta ⑰
Lawry's The Prime Rib ⑭
Maple Drive ⑪

1-1090

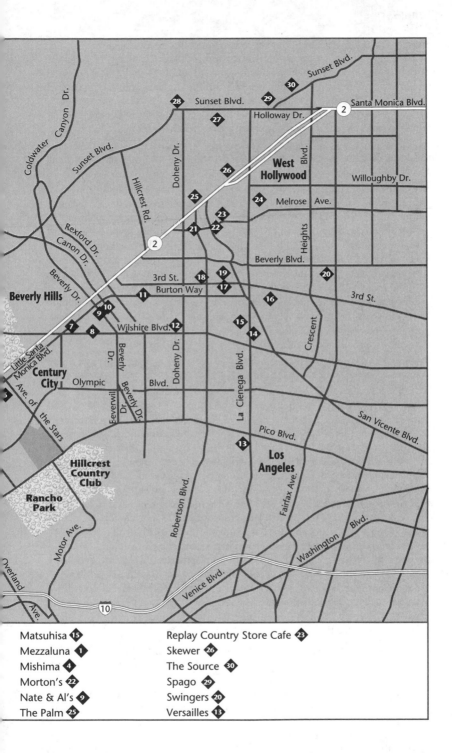

Matsuhisa 15	Replay Country Store Cafe 23
Mezzaluna 1	Skewer 26
Mishima 4	The Source 30
Morton's 22	Spago 29
Nate & Al's 9	Swingers 20
The Palm 25	Versailles 13

a czar by a fawning waitstaff that never lets a glass empty or a cleaned plate lie. For starters, sample the blini topped with Russian vodka and caviar. Better yet, order the zakuski combination plate, which includes smoked salmon, a twirl of egg noodles mixed with veal, and a plump mini–cabbage roll. Main courses include a truffled chicken Kiev and braised veal chop in raspberry vinegar; a moist salmon croquet is wrapped in a wonderful flaky pastry. Diaghilev is delicious, but not cheap; complimentary chocolates served before the check arrives soften the blow.

Drai's. 730 N. La Cienega Blvd. (between Melrose Ave. and Santa Monica Blvd.). ☎ 310/ **358-8585.** Reservations required. Main courses $17–$25. AE, MC, V. Daily 6–10:30pm. CLASSIC FRENCH.

Drai's is the kind of attitude-heavy restaurant that insiders love and outsiders love to hate. Owned by producer-turned-restaurateur Victor Drai, the restaurant is currently going head to head with Morton's for the hip Hollywood Monday night crowd and—at least according to some observers—it's winning. Located on the site of L'Ermitage, a once-famous temple of French haute cuisine, Drai has lightened the menu and turned the front room into a lounge, where diners wait for tables; they're shuttled back after dinner for rushed desserts. The bistro-style offerings include smoked duck salad, baked sweetbreads, beef bourguignonne, and the like. Chef Claude Segal, who's as talented—and confident—as any of the stars in his dining room, doesn't shy away from risk, but he's not always successful. Drai's is a destination restaurant, not just a place for a quick bite; make reservations well in advance, and think about renting a limousine.

Eclipse. 8800 Melrose Ave. (at Robertson Blvd.), West Hollywood. ☎ 310/724-5959. Reservations required. Main courses $18–$30. AE, DC, DISC, MC, V. Daily 5:30–10:30pm. CALIFORNIA.

One of Hollywood's hottest restaurants, Eclipse boasts a flawless pedigree that includes celebrity backers Steven Seagal and Whoopi Goldberg and Spago alumnus maître d' Bernard Erpicum. The restaurant is located in the old Morton's space (Morton's has relocated across the street); on most nights, Eclipse attracts just as many stars and studio heads as its heavyweight neighbor. The restaurant's A-room is both exciting and romantic: It features terra-cotta tones, a high chalet-style ceiling, and large picture windows overlooking a faux forest. On any given night, you can get whiplash while rubbernecking to see the likes of Ovitz, Geffen, or Guber schmoozing with celebs like De Niro, Cruise, or Stone. Unfortunately for most mortals, reservations are required up to one month in advance on weekends, and you're likely to be seated in Siberia. Star power aside, the food is excellent, sometimes even superlative. Chef Serge Falesitch's California Provençal menu emphasizes seafood that's gloriously simple and artfully presented. A bounteous shellfish platter, translucent sashimi, and sesame-studded seared scallops are all great starters. Whole striped bass and John Dory are aromatically infused with basil, tarragon, and fennel and roasted in a brick oven. There's also a superb artichoke risotto, orecchiette with duck ragout, and a thick, perfectly grilled veal chop.

✪ **Four Oaks.** 2181 N. Beverly Glen Blvd., Los Angeles. ☎ 310/470-2265. Reservations required. Main courses $22–$29. AE, MC, V. Tues–Sat 11:30am–9:30pm, Sun 10:30am–2pm; daily 6–10pm. CALIFORNIA.

Just looking at the menu here makes me swoon. The country-cottage ambiance and chef Peter Roelant's superlative blend of fresh ingredients with luxurious Continental flourishes make a meal at the Four Oaks one of my favorite luxuries. Dinner is served beneath trees festooned with twinkling lights. Appetizers like lavender-smoked salmon with crisp potatoes and horseradish crème fraîche complement mouth-watering dishes like roasted chicken with sage, Oregon forest mushrooms, artichoke hearts, and port-balsamic sauce. If you're looking for someplace special, head to this canyon hideaway—you won't be disappointed.

The Ivy. 133 N. Robertson Blvd. (between 3rd St. and Beverly Blvd.), West Hollywood. ☎ **310/274-8303.** Reservations recommended on weekends. Main courses $22–$38; lunch $10–$25. AE, DC, DISC, MC, V. Mon–Sat 11:30am–3pm, Sun 11am–3pm; Mon–Thurs 6–11pm, Fri–Sat 6–11:30pm, Sun 5:30–10:30pm. AMERICAN.

The Ivy attracts one of the most Industry-heavy crowds in the city; it's wildly popular with agents, producers, and plenty of stars. If you like nightclubs with velvet ropes and pick-and-choose doormen, you'll feel at home at this snobby eatery, which treats celebrities and nobodies as differently as Brahmins and Untouchables. Just past the cool reception lies two disarmingly countrified dining rooms filled with rustic antiques, comfortably worn chintz, hanging baskets filled with fragrant flowers—in fact, huge roses bloom everywhere, including out on the charming brick patio (where the highest-profile patrons are seated). The food is excellent. The Ivy's Caesar salad is perfect, as are the plump and crispy crab cakes. Recommended dishes include spinach linguine with a peppery tomato-basil sauce, prime rib dusted with Cajun spices, and succulently tender lime-marinated grilled chicken. They also do a great burger. The wine list is particularly notable, and there's always a terrific variety of desserts (pink boxes are on hand for chocolate-chip cookies to go). If you're willing to pay lots for an admittingly perfect meal, and endure the cold shoulder to ogle L.A.'s celebrities, the Ivy can be very enjoyable.

Lawry's The Prime Rib. 100 N. La Cienega Blvd. (north of Wilshire Blvd.), Beverly Hills. ☎ **310/652-2827.** Reservations required. Main courses $19–$29. AE, CB, DC, DISC, MC, V. Mon–Fri 5–11pm, Sat 4:30–11pm, Sun 4–10pm. PRIME RIB/SEAFOOD.

Most Americans know Lawry's only as a brand of seasoned salt; the seasoning was invented here, conceived to flavor this restaurant's meats. Opened in 1938 by Lawrence Frank, Lawry's remains a serious family enterprise. Going to Lawry's is an Old World event; the only menu offerings are four cuts of prime rib that vary in size from dainty slices to hefty slabs. Every standing rib roast is dry aged for 2 to 3 weeks, sprinkled with Lawry's famous seasoning, then roasted on a bed of rock salt. A carver wheels the cooked beef tableside, then slices it properly, rare to well done. The result is incredibly tender and juicy prime rib, some of the nation's very best. All dinners come with very mushy mashed potatoes, creamy whipped horseradish, and Yorkshire pudding. Each dinner also comes with the Original Spinning Bowl Salad: While mixed greens, hard-boiled eggs, and chopped beets are spinning on a bed of crushed ice, they're drenched with dressing poured straight from the Lawry's bottle.

Lawry's moved across the street from its original location a few years ago, but retained its throwback-to-the-thirties clubroom atmosphere, complete with Persian-carpeted oak floors, high-backed chairs, and original European oils. Couples should opt for a table in either the Vintage or Oval rooms (the latter seats larger parties as well).

✪ **Maple Drive.** 345 N. Maple Dr. (at Alden Dr.), Beverly Hills. ☎ **310/274-9800.** Reservations recommended. Main courses $17–$29; lunch $10–$18. AE, MC, V. Mon–Fri 11:30am–2:30pm; Mon–Thurs 6–10pm, Fri–Sat 6–11pm. AMERICAN.

Owned by Liza Minelli, Dudley Moore, and producer/director Tony Bill (the same celebrity trio that brought 72 Market Street to Venice), Maple Drive is one of the best traditional American restaurants in, well, America. Chef Leonard Schwartz cooks the great meatloaf, terrific chili, and out-of-this-world veal chops (which regulars ask for Milanese style—lightly breaded and served with a squeeze of lemon). The restaurant attracts the biggest celebrities—Barbra, Elton, Arnold, and others who have enjoyed fame for so long they often seem tired of the attention; they enter through a second, more discreet door and sit in relatively secluded booths in back of the multilevel dining room. That's a bonus for us nobodies; on warm nights, the best seats are out on the patio. Maple Drive is a classy place with great food, high prices, and live dinnertime jazz. Even if Clint isn't at the next table, it's worth lingering for the extraordinary desserts.

✪ **Matsuhisa.** 129 N. La Cienega Blvd. (north of Wilshire Blvd.), Beverly Hills. ☎ **310/ 659-9639.** Reservations required. Main courses $14–$22; sushi $20–$30. AE, DC, MC, V. Mon– Fri 11:45am–2:45pm; nightly 5:45 10:15pm. JAPANESE/PERUVIAN.

Japanese chef/owner Nobuyuki Matsuhisa arrived in Los Angeles via Peru and opened what may be the most creative restaurant in the entire city. A true master of fish cookery, Matsuhisa creates fantastic, unusual dishes by combining Japanese flavors with South American spices and salsas. Broiled sea bass with black truffles, sautéed squid with garlic and soy, and Dungeness crab tossed with chiles and cream are good examples of the masterfully prepared delicacies that are available in addition to the thickly sliced nigiri and creative sushi rolls. Matsuhisa is also known for having some of the most hard-to-get tables in town. Both tight and bright, the restaurant's small, crowded main dining room suffers from bad lighting and precious lack of privacy. There's lots of action behind the sushi bar, and a frenetic service staff keeps the restaurant humming at a fiery pace. Stars are commonplace, though many are just walking through on their way to a private room. Matsuhisa is fantastically popular with hard-core foodies, who continually return for the savory surprises that come with every bite. Reserve early, unless you are happy starting your meal at 6 or 10pm.

Morton's. 8764 Melrose Ave. (east of Santa Monica Blvd.), West Hollywood. ☎ **310/ 276-5205.** Reservations required. Main courses $17–$29; lunch $7–$15. AE, MC, V. Mon–Fri noon–11:30pm, Sat 6–11:30pm. CALIFORNIA.

Dining at Hard Rock Cafe–founder Peter Morton's eponymous restaurant has become something of a rite of passage for any Industry insider worthy of the label. Indeed, the restaurant's clientele reads like a who's-who. For years now, on Monday nights, entertainment's high and mighty have considered these the most coveted tables in the city. But this could be changing; after a move across the street and two chef changes, regulars are mumbling that, although the space has improved, the food has been better. The restaurant's seating policy ensures that "nobodies" are placed "in the trees" (by the tall potted plants near the back wall). For those lucky enough not to face the wall, the lofty dining room provides good sightlines, yet remains dark enough to keep it feeling personal. Meals at Morton's are straightforward and good. The menu isn't intimidating, and plates are assembled without a lot of visual froufrou. The emphasis on simplicity, quality, and freshness translates into appetizers like fresh Maryland crab cakes, tuna sashimi, and chopped shrimp and black bean quesadillas. Typical main courses on the seasonal menu include lime-grilled free-range chicken, grilled swordfish, sautéed veal chop, and New York steak. Desserts include hot fudge sundaes and warm fruit tarts.

✪ **The Palm.** 9001 Santa Monica Blvd. (between Doheny Dr. and Robertson Blvd.), West Hollywood. ☎ **310/550-8811.** Reservations required. Main courses $16–$28; lobsters $18 per pound; lunch $8–$15. AE, CB, DC, DISC, MC, V. Mon–Fri noon–3pm, Mon–Sat 5–10pm, Sun 5–9:30pm. STEAK/LOBSTER.

Every great American city has a great steakhouse; in Los Angeles, it's The Palm. The child of the famous New York restaurant of the same name, The Palm is widely regarded by local foodies as one of the best traditional American eateries in the city.

The glitterati seem to agree, as stars and their handlers are regularly in attendance. In both food and ambiance, this West Coast apple hasn't fallen far from the proverbial tree. The restaurant is brightly lit, extremely noisy, and casually decorated, with caricatures on the walls and sawdust on the floor. Live Nova Scotia lobsters are flown in almost daily, then broiled over charcoal and served with big bowls of melted butter. Most are an enormous 3 to 7 pounds and, although they're obscenely expensive, can be shared. Steaks are similarly sized, and some of the choicest cuts of beef available anywhere: New York sirloin, filet mignon, porterhouse, and prime rib are all perfectly grilled to order and served à la carte. Diners also swear by the celebrated Gigi Salad, a mixture of lettuce, shrimp, bacon, green beans, pimento, and avocado. Unfortunately, the wine list is poor and desserts are worse.

Spago. 1114 Horn Ave. (at Sunset Blvd.), West Hollywood. ☎ **310/652-4025.** Reservations required. Main courses $18–$28. DC, DISC, MC, V. Daily 6–11:30pm. CALIFORNIA.

Wolfgang Puck is more than a great chef: He's also a masterful businessman and publicist who has made Spago one of the best-known restaurants in America. Despite all the hoopla—and more than 15 years of service—Spago remains one of L.A.'s top-rated eateries. The bright, clean, colorful dining room is noisy and upbeat. German-born Puck originally won fame serving imaginative "gourmet" pizzas. These individually sized thin-crust pies are baked in a wood-burning oven, topped with goodies like duck sausage, shiitake mushrooms, leeks, and artichokes, and other combinations once considered to be on the culinary edge. Of meat dishes, roast Sonoma lamb with braised shallots and grilled chicken with garlic and parsley are two perennial favorites. The celebrated (and far from secret) off-menu meal is Jewish Pizza, a crispy pie topped with smoked salmon, crème fraîche, dill, red onion, and dollops of caviar. *Note:* The restaurant has plans to move from its quirky, hard-to-find location into Beverly Hills early in 1997, so be sure to call ahead.

MODERATE

Barney Greengrass. 9570 Wilshire Blvd. (in Barney's New York), Beverly Hills. ☎ **310/777-5877.** Reservations suggested. Main courses $12–$23; breakfast $5–$11; lunch $8–$15. AE, DC, MC, V. Mon–Wed and Fri 7:30am–7pm, Thurs 7:30am–8pm, Sat 9am–7pm, Sun 9am–6pm. DELI.

It was a big deal in Beverly Hills when the celebrated New York clothier Barney's opened a satellite store here. But it was a very big deal in Hollywood when New York's celebrated "sturgeon king," Barney Greengrass, opened on the department store's top floor. This upscale deli has quickly become an important power lunch spot for the Industry crowd. Famous for sturgeon and smoked fish—at caviar prices—Barney Greengrass seems more than a bit like a fish out of water here. As soon as you get off the elevator you can tell that the restaurant is joyful, clean, and bright, without the attitude—and none of the atmosphere—of New York's nosheries. In addition to having a separate caviar, champagne, and vodka bar, the restaurant makes its own oven-baked matzos, claims to import their bagels from New York's famed H&H bagelry, and sets their paper-covered tables with designer utensils and stemware. The many smoked specialties include Nova Scotia salmon, sable, chubs, rainbow trout, whitefish, and, of course, sturgeon. The best meals are matzo brei with onions and wild mushrooms, orange-challah french toast, and smoked-salmon soufflé.

Bombay Cafe. 12113 Santa Monica Blvd. (at Bundy Dr.), Brentwood. ☎ **310/820-2070.** Reservations not accepted. Main courses $9–$15. MC, V. Tues–Sun 11:30am–4pm, Tues–Thurs 4–10pm, Fri–Sat 4–11pm. INDIAN.

Indian is the cuisine of the moment in L.A., and nowhere is it done better than at Bombay Cafe. The unlikely McRestaurant interior and storefront location (on the second floor of a nondescript minimall) belie excellent curries and kormas that are typical of South Indian street food. Once seated, immediately order sev puri for the table; these crispy little chips topped with chopped potatoes, onions, cilantro, and chutneys are the perfect accompaniment to what is sure to be an extended menu-reading session. Also recommended are the burrito-like "frankies," juicy little bread rolls stuffed with lamb, chicken, or cauliflower. The best dishes come from the 800° tandoor, and include spicy yogurt-marinated swordfish, lamb, and chicken. The food is served authentically spicy, unless you specify otherwise. The restaurant is phenomenally popular, and gets its share of celebrities: Meg Ryan and Dennis Quaid hired Bombay Cafe to cater an affair at their Montana ranch. Only beer and wine are served.

Cava. In the Beverly Plaza Hotel, 8384 W. 3rd St. (at Orlando Ave.), Los Angeles. ☎ **213/ 658-8898.** Reservations recommended on weekends. Main courses $8–$17; breakfast $3–$9; lunch $4–$14. AE, CB, DC, DISC, MC, V. Daily 6:30am–midnight. SPANISH.

Trendy types in the mood for some fun are attracted to Cava's great mambo atmosphere; their tapas bar is made festive with flamboyant colors and loud, lively flamenco that's live on weekends. The dining room is less raucous, with velvet drapes and tassels adorning the walls and comfortable booths. The cuisine is Spanish livened up with Caribbean touches (Cava is the invention of the team responsible for Cha Cha Cha in Silverlake), an influence reflected in dishes like black bean tamales with tomatillo salsa and golden caviar; thick, dark tortilla soup; jerk chicken with sweet jams; and pan-seared shrimp in spicy peppercorn sauce. Spanish paella is stewed up three ways—with seafood, chicken and sausage, or all-vegetable—and is featured in Monday's all-you-can-eat "Paella Festival." If you have room for dessert, try the ruby-colored pears poached in port, the rice pudding, or the flan.

✪ **Chaya Brasserie.** 8741 Alden Dr. (west of Robertson Blvd.). ☎ **310/859-8833.** Reservations recommended on weekends. Main courses $11–$24; lunch $9–$16. AE, CB, DC, MC, V. Mon–Fri 11am–2:30pm; Mon–Thurs 6–10:30pm, Fri–Sat 6–11pm, Sun 6–10pm. FRANCO-JAPANESE.

Now open for a dozen years, Chaya has become well ensconced as one of Los Angeles's finest restaurants. Popular with film agents during lunch and a particularly beautiful assembly of stars at night, the restaurant is loved for its exceptionally good food and refreshingly unpretentious atmosphere. Despite a high noise level, the stage-lit dining room feels sensuous and swoony. On warm afternoons and evenings, the best tables are on the outside terrace, overlooking the busy street. A continental bistro with Asian overtones, Chaya is best known for superb grilled fish and meats, like seared soy-marinated Hawaiian tuna and Long Island duckling. Chef Shigefumi Tachibe's lobster ravioli with pesto-cream sauce is both stylish and delicious, as is a deceptively simple off-menu dish of spaghetti dressed in dry red chilies, garlic, and olive oil. Hot and cold starters include seaweed salad with ginger-soy rice vinaigrette and sautéed foie gras over hearts of daikon. Chaya is a hot late-night rendezvous for their short but choice supper menu, serving 'til midnight Tuesday through Saturday.

⑤ **Il Pastaio.** 400 N. Canon Dr. (at Brighton Way), Beverly Hills. ☎ **310/205-5444.** Reservations not accepted. Main courses $12–$23; lunch $7–$12. AE, MC, V. Mon–Sat 11am–11pm. ITALIAN.

Sicilian-born Celestino Drago is a terrific chef who has been helming the kitchens of high-profile L.A. restaurants for years. Branching out on his own, Chef Drago hit the jackpot with this hugely successful, value-priced eatery. The restaurant is a simple pasta place with white walls, a long bar, and a pasta-making area; it's as narrow as a bowling alley and almost as loud. Only starters, pastas, and desserts are served, but the selections are vast and great for grazing. Swordfish carpaccio with shaved fennel and blood oranges, and seafood and spaghetti in a flaky filo envelope are Drago's signature dishes. Chef Drago offered a sautéed foie gras appetizer with a buttery balsamic vinegar glaze when he worked at Chianti, and he continues to serve it here—to those who know enough to ask for it. Pastas include lobster-stuffed ravioli in a silky lobster reduction, and garganelli: wheat pasta curls in amatriciana sauce (puréed tomato, pancetta, pecorino, and onion). Two risotti are offered nightly, and both usually hit the proverbial bull's-eye. Unfortunately, Il Pastaio is too small. There's almost always a wait, and an uncomfortable one at that. But by meal's end, it always seems worth it.

A second Il Pastaio, on South Lake Street in Pasadena (☎ 818/795-4006), is identical in spirit but thankfully larger inside.

✪ **Joss.** 9255 Sunset Blvd. (west of Doheny Dr.), West Hollywood. ☎ **310/276-1886.** Reservations suggested. Main courses $8–$18; dim sum $3.75 per order. AE, DC, DISC, MC, V. Mon–Fri noon–3pm; daily 6–11pm. HAUTE CHINESE.

Located on the fringe between Beverly Hills and the Sunset Strip, Joss has a minimalist yet welcoming decor of beige linen chairs, white tablecloths, and tiny halogen lights suspended over each table. The entryway's ever-present sherry decanter hints at the surprisingly well-chosen and affordable wine list, compiled by owner Cecile Tang Shu Shuen, whose inventive menu takes Chinese essentials beyond your expectations—not by creating fussy "fusion" dishes, but by subtly manipulating ingredients and preparations according to her superb artist's palate. Fried rice is spiked with the tang of dried black beans and ginger; velvety curry sauce is creamed with coconut milk and tossed with chicken; and tender beef is marinated with spicy red chiles but mellowed with tangerine liqueur. You could make a meal of the dozen dim sum varieties, which include delicately steamed dumplings (spinach and chicken, shrimp with bamboo shoot, or vegetable and black mushroom) served in stacked bamboo steaming trays, crisp-bottom potstickers filled with Peking duck or lamb and leeks, and crispy wonton or spring rolls. Desserts, never overly sweet, complement Joss's sublime meals perfectly. The restaurant's location draws many celebrities and Industry honchos—but gawking is definitely uncool.

Kate Mantilini. 9101 Wilshire Blvd. (corner of Doheny Dr.), Beverly Hills. ☎ **310/278-3699.** Reservations suggested. Main courses $7–$16. AE, MC, V. Mon–Thurs 7:30am-1am, Fri 7:30am–3am, Sat noon–3am, Sun 10am–midnight. AMERICAN.

It's rare to find a restaurant that feels comfortably familiar yet trendy and cutting edge . . . and is one of L.A.'s few late-night eateries. Kate Mantilini fits the bill perfectly. One of the first to bring meatloaf back into fashion, Kate's offers a huge menu of upscale truckstop favorites like "white" chili (made with chicken, white beans, and Jack cheese), grilled steaks and fish, a few token pastas, and just about anything you could crave. At 2am, nothing quite beats a steaming bowl of lentil vegetable soup and some garlic-cheese toast—unless, of course, your taste runs to fresh oysters and a dry martini. No matter—Kate's has it all. The huge mural of the Hagler-Hearns boxing match that dominates the stark, open interior provides the only clue to the namesake's identity—Mantilini was an early female boxing promotor, circa 1947.

✪ **Locanda Veneta.** 8638 W. 3rd St. (between San Vicente and Robertson blvds.). ☎ **310/274-1893.** Reservations required. Main courses $10–$22. AE, DC, DISC, MC, V. Mon–Fri 11:30am–2:30pm; Mon–Thurs 5:30–10:30pm, Fri–Sat 5:30–11pm. ITALIAN/VENETIAN.

Locanda Veneta's citywide renown belies its tiny size and unpretentious setting. Its location, across from the unsightly monolith that is Cedars-Sinai Hospital, is a far cry from Venice's Grand Canal. And the single, loud, tightly packed dining room can sometimes feel like Piazza San Marco at the height of tourist season. But the sensible prices reflect the restaurant's efficient decor, and while the dining room is decidedly unfancy, the kitchen is dead serious. The restaurant has become a kind of temple for knowledgeable foodies, who flock here to sample the latest creations of chef Massimo Ormani, a gifted artist and culinary technician who's building a national reputation. Soups are excellent, seafood dishes extraordinary, and pastas are as good as they can get. Signature dishes include pasta and bean soup, veal chops, lobster ravioli, shrimp risotto, and perfectly grilled vegetables. Insiders order linguine with rock shrimp, baby asparagus, and tomatoes—an uncharacteristically light off-menu meal.

Mezzaluna. 11750 San Vicente Blvd., Brentwood. ☎ 310/447-8667. Reservations required. Main courses $10–$22; lunch $7–$13. AE, DC, DISC, MC, V. Mon–Sat 11:30am–10pm, Sun 5–10pm. ITALIAN.

Thanks to windfall P.R., this once-trendy little neighborhood restaurant is now bursting at the seams with tourists. Everyone, it seems, wants to taste a bit of history, no matter how macabre. Mezzaluna, you'll recall, is where Ronald Goldman waited tables, and where Nicole Brown Simpson, a regular customer, ate her last meal—rigatoni melanzane. Theatrically lighted, colorfully tiled, and stylishly furnished, Mezzaluna has the same upper middle–class atmosphere as its sister restaurants in New York and Aspen. Gastronomically speaking, the restaurant is best known for its crispy pizzas, topped in traditional California style with smoked meats, porcini mushrooms, pestos, and the like. Pastas are equally creative and good, but not great. The carpaccios are more likable, paired with sautéed olives and tomatoes or hearts of palm and avocado. Locals grumble that Mezzaluna was better before the O.J. scandal; luckily, the throngs of snapshot-snappers are already subsiding.

Replay Country Store Cafe. 8607 Melrose Ave. (between San Vicente and La Cienega blvds.), West Hollywood. ☎ 310/657-6404. Reservations suggested on weekends. Main courses $6–$13. AE, DISC, MC, V. Daily 10am–10pm. ITALIAN/CONTINENTAL.

The two things to remember at Replay are: one, don't buy the clothes, and two, always order the soup. Most of the cafe's tables are on the wraparound wood porch of the overpriced boutique it's attached to. This faux-country-general-store on trendy Melrose near the Pacific Design Center won't fool anyone into plunking down $150 for denim overalls, but their restaurant is one of West Hollywood's hidden treasures. Everything on their casual, vaguely Italian menu is outstanding, from gourmet pizzas and pasta with delicately puréed tomato/basil sauce to the Warm Chicken Salad's surprise combination of blue cheese, walnuts, and mandarin orange wedges. Each day a different soup, always a simple purée allowing the fresh ingredients to shine through, is ladled into wide bowls at your table from heavy copper saucepans. Be sure to save room for dessert; the pastries are exquisite.

INEXPENSIVE

✪ **The Apple Pan.** 10801 Pico Blvd. (east of Westwood Blvd.). ☎ **310/475-3585.** Main courses $6–$7. No credit cards. Tues–Thurs and Sun 11am–midnight; Fri–Sat 11am–1am. SANDWICHES/BURGERS.

There are no tables, just a U-shaped counter, at this classic American burger shack and L.A. landmark. Open since 1947, The Apple Pan is a diner that looks—and acts—the part. It's famous for juicy burgers, bullet-quick service, and its authentic frills-free atmosphere. The hickory burger is best, though the tuna sandwich also has its huge share of fans. Ham, egg salad, and swiss cheese sandwiches round out the menu. Definitely order fries and, if you're in the mood, the home-baked apple pie, too.

Dive! In the Century City Marketplace, 10250 Santa Monica Blvd. ☎ **310/788-3483.** Reservations accepted only for parties of 10 or more. Main courses $6–$15. AE, DC, MC, V. Sun–Thurs 11:30am–10pm, Fri–Sat 11:30am–11pm. SANDWICHES/AMERICAN.

"Prepare to dive!" the public address system cries without warning. Red lights flash, the room darkens, water bubbles through "portholes," video monitors go black . . . and a waitress casually delivers another coke to an adjacent table. Owned by Steven Spielberg and Jeffrey Katzenberg, two thirds of the new mega-company Dreamworks SKG, Dive! is the first of what the investors hope to be a series of submarine-themed restaurants. The restaurant-cum-theme-park's insulated underwater ambiance is the ultimate in dining entertainment. Except for the fries and the thin-cut onion rings, however, the same cannot be said of the food, which is decent at best and bad at worst. The menu is mainly submarine sandwiches (get it?), along with salads and some wood-roasted dishes like salmon served with assorted dipping sauces, such as homemade ketchup and cheddar cheese sauce. Stick with the subs. The restaurant is perpetually packed; waiting patrons get a beeper that conveniently won't work outside, so they have to wait at the expensive bar, where there's a voyeuristic periscope exposing the goings-on down on Santa Monica Boulevard. At the requisite gift shop, you can purchase a souvenir menu sprinkled with puns and quotations. It costs $5, but it lights up.

La Salsa. 9631 Little Santa Monica Blvd. (between Camden and Bedford drives), Beverly Hills. ☎ **310/276-2373.** Main courses $5–$7. MC, V. Mon–Fri 10:30am–9:30pm, Sat 10:30am–9pm, Sun 10:30am–7pm. MEXICAN.

L.A.'s best Mexican fast food is served at this bright and spotless taquaria chain, well known throughout the city for its excellent, healthful, lard-free burritos and tacos. The Gourmet Burrito is a hefty mix of grilled chicken or steak, cheese, and guacamole; the Grande adds rice and beans. True to its name, La Salsa excels in the preparation of fresh sauces, offering four types varying in spiciness, texture, and flavor. The restaurants serve soda and beer, and (sometimes) horchata, a traditional Mexican drink made with rice flour and cinnamon. Order at the counter.

Other locations include Third Street Promenade, Santa Monica (☎ **310/587-0755**); 22800 Pacific Coast Hwy., Malibu (☎ **310/456-6299**); downtown at 727 Flower St. (☎ **213/892-8227**); 44 N. Fair Oaks Ave., Pasadena (☎ **818/793-0723**); and 245 Pine Ave., Long Beach (☎ **310/491-1104**).

Mishima. 11301 Olympic Blvd. (at Sawtelle Blvd.). ☎ **310/473-5297.** Reservations not accepted. Main courses $4–$9. MC, V. Tues–Sun 11:30am–9pm. JAPANESE.

Hidden on the second floor of an unobtrusive strip mall, this small Japanese eatery has nevertheless become extraordinarily popular with neighborhood residents and workers. A dead ringer for any number of noodle shops in Tokyo, Mishima sports a contemporary Asian decor, complete with matte black tables and chairs, Japanese prints on white walls, and plastic reproductions of every menu item. A loyal clientele fills the small, bright dining room with noodle slurps and clicking chopsticks. Udon (thick wheat noodles) or soba (narrow buckwheat linguine) are the main choices here; both are served either hot or cold in a variety of soups and sauces that true aficionados might find too bland and too thin. Sushi, chicken dishes, and a variety of tempuras are also available. It all seems so authentically Japanese—except, thankfully, the prices.

Nate & Al's. 414 N. Beverly Dr. (at Brighton Way), Beverly Hills. ☎ **310/274-0101.** Main courses $8–$13. AE, DISC, MC, V. Daily 7:30am–9pm. DELI.

Despite its location, in the center of Beverly Hills's "Golden Triangle," Nate & Al's has remained unchanged since they opened in 1945, from the naugahyde booths to the motherly waitresses, who treat you the same whether you're a house-account celebrity regular or just stopping in for an overstuffed pastrami on rye. Their too-salty chicken soup keeps Nate & Al's from being the best L.A. deli (actually, I'd be hard pressed to choose any one deli as the city's best), but staples like chopped liver, dense potato pancakes, blintzes, borscht, and well-dilled pickles more than make up for it. If you want to know where Jimmy Stewart, Debbie Reynolds, and other rich-and-famous types go for comfort food, look no further.

⑤ **Skewer.** 8939 Santa Monica Blvd. (between Robertson and San Vicente blvds.), West Hollywood. ☎ **310/271-0555.** Main courses $7–$9; salads and pitas $4–$7. AE, MC, V. Daily 11am–midnight. MIDDLE EASTERN.

From the zesty marinated carrot sticks you get the moment you're seated to sweet, sticky squares of baklava for dessert, this Mediterranean grill is sure to please. Skewer's sidewalk tables, right on Santa Monica Boulevard—the commericial strip at the heart of colorful West Hollywood—are a great place to sit and watch the world go by. If you opt for an inside table, you'll find a New York–like narrow space with changing artwork adorning the bare brick walls. The naturally healthy cuisine features baskets of warm pita bread for scooping up traditional salads like baba ghanoush (grilled eggplant with tahini and lemon) and tabbouleh (cracked wheat, parsley, and tomatoes). Try marinated chicken and lamb off the grill, or dolmades (rice and meat-stuffed grape leaves) seared with a tangy tomato glaze.

Swingers. 8020 Beverly Blvd. (west of Fairfax). ☎ **213/653-5858.** Reservations not accepted. Most items under $8. AE, MC, V. Sun–Thu 6am–2am; Fri–Sat 9am–4am. DINER/AMERICAN.

Resurrected from a motel coffee shop so dismal I can't even remember it, Swingers was transformed by a couple of L.A. hipster nightclub owners into a '90s version of comfy Americana. The interior seems like a slice of the '50s until you notice the plaid upholstery and Warhol-esque graphics, which contrast nicely with the retro red-white-and-blue "Swingers" logo adorning *everything*. Guests from the attached Beverly Laurel Motor Hotel chow down alongside body-pierced Industry hounds from nearby Maverick Records (Madonna's company) while a soundtrack that runs the gamut from punk rock to "Schoolhouse Rock" plays in the background. It's not all attitude here, though—you'll enjoy the menu of high-quality diner favorites spiked with trendy crowd-pleasers: steel-cut Irish oatmeal, challah French toast, grilled Jamaican jerk chicken, and a nice selection of tofu-enhanced vegetarian dishes are just a few of the eclectic offerings. Sometimes I just "swing" by (ha ha) for a malt or milkshake to go—theirs are among the best in town.

Versailles. 1415 S. La Cienega Blvd. (south of Pico Blvd.). ☎ **310/289-0392.** Reservations not accepted. Main courses $5–$11. AE, MC, V. Daily 11am–10pm. CUBAN.

Outfitted with Formica tabletops and looking something like an ethnic International House of Pancakes, Versailles feels very much like any number of Miami restaurants that cater to the exiled Cuban community. Because meals are good, bountiful, and cheap, there's often a wait to get in here. The menu reads like a veritable survey of Havana-style cookery and includes specialties like Moors and Christians (flavorful black beans with white rice), ropa vieja (a stringy beef stew), eastin lechón (suckling pig with sliced onions), and fried whole fish (usually sea bass). Shredded roast pork is particularly recommendable, especially when tossed with the restaurant's trademark garlic-citrus sauce. But what everyone comes for is the chicken—succulent, slow roasted for an eternity, smothered in onions and the garlic-citrus sauce or barbecue sauce. Most everything is served with black beans and rice. Wine and beer are available.

Additional Versailles restaurants are located in Culver City at 10319 Venice Blvd. (☎ **310/558-3168**); and in Encino at 17410 Ventura Blvd. (☎ **818/906-0756**).

5 Hollywood

EXPENSIVE

✪ **Campanile.** 624 S. La Brea Ave. (north of Wilshire Blvd.). ☎ **213/938-1447.** Reservations required. Main courses $18–$28. AE, MC, V. Mon–Fri 7:30am–2:30am, Sat–Sun 8am–1:30pm; Mon–Thurs 6–10pm, Fri–Sat 5:30–11pm. CALIFORNIA-MEDITERRANEAN.

Built as Charlie Chaplin's private offices in 1928, this lovely building has a multi-level layout, with flower-bedecked interior balconies, a bubbling fountain, and a skylight through which diners can see the campanile (bell tower). Crisply contemporary, the dining rooms are successful amalgams of vintage and modern, making this one of the most attractive spaces in Los Angeles. The kitchen, headed by Spago alumnus chef/owner Mark Peel, gets a giant leg up from baker (and wife) Nancy Silverton, who runs the now-legendary La Brea Bakery next door. Meals here might begin with fried zucchini flowers drizzled with melted mozzarella, or lamb carpaccio surrounded by artichoke leaves—a dish that arrives looking like one of Van Gogh's sunflowers. Chef Peel is particularly known for his grills and roasts; try grilled prime rib smeared with black olive tapenade or papardelle with braised rabbit, roasted tomato, and collard greens. And don't skip dessert here; the restaurant's many enthusiastic sweets fans have turned Nancy Silverton's dessert book into a best-seller.

✪ **Citrus.** 6703 Melrose Ave. (west of Highland Ave.). ☎ **213/857-0034.** Reservations recommended. Main courses $25–$30; lunch $10–$16. AE, MC, V. Mon–Fri noon–2:30pm; Mon–Thurs 6–10pm, Fri–Sat 6–10:30pm. CALIFORNIA-FRENCH.

Second in culinary celebrity only to Wolfgang Puck, innovative French chef Michel Richard originally made his mark as a pastry wunderkind, wowing the most refined sweet tooths on two continents. Richard's seamless transition to main courses is showcased nightly at this popular glass-wrapped bistro, which has matured into a cherished L.A. institution. When he's not gallivanting around the world opening spin-off Citronelles or cooking at international benefits, the portly, bearded Richard personally works wonders in the kitchen, which overlooks the dining room's umbrella-topped tables. Beautifully presented contemporary bistro fare includes starters like shiitake mushroom and garlic napoleon, escargot in a potato basket, and sautéed scallops with Maui onion rings. Roasted duck with couscous and lemon sauce, Chilean sea bass with crayfish and pearl pasta, and roasted venison loin with potato risotto are typical main courses. Citrus has one of the best-selected wine lists (offering several good buys) in town. Whatever you do, save room for dessert; it's still Richard's best course, and showcases his inventiveness with concoctions like ginger-citrus rice pudding garnished with one perfectly translucent candied star-fruit slice.

✪ **Patina.** 5955 Melrose Ave. (west of Cahuenga Blvd.). ☎ **213/467-1108.** Reservations required. Main courses $18–$26. AE, DC, DISC, MC, V. Tues–Fri 11:30am–2pm; Sun–Thurs 6–9:30pm, Fri–Sat 6–10:30pm. CALIFORNIA-FRENCH.

Joachim Splichal, arguably L.A.'s very best chef, is also a genius at choosing and training top chefs to cook in his kitchens while he jets around the world. Patina routinely wins the highest praise from demanding gourmands, who are happy to empty their bank accounts for unbeatable meals that almost never miss their intended mark. The dining room is straightforwardly attractive, low key, well lit, and professional, without the slightest hint of stuffiness. The menu is equally disarming: "Mallard Duck with Portobello Mushrooms" gives little hint of the brilliant colors and flavors that

Hollywood Area Accommodations & Dining

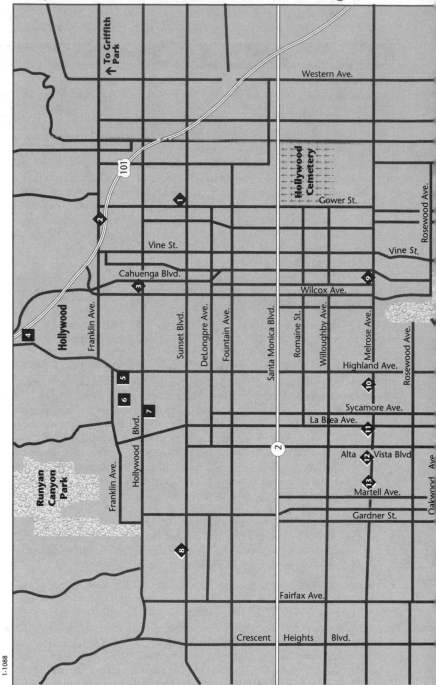

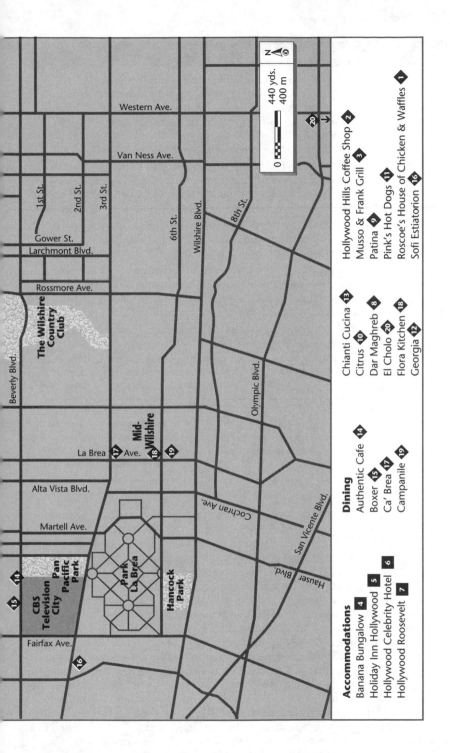

Western Ave.

Van Ness Ave.

1st St.
2nd St.
3rd St.

Gower St.
Larchmont Blvd.

Rossmore Ave.

6th St.

Wilshire Blvd.

8th St.

The Wilshire Country Club

Beverly Blvd.

Olympic Blvd.

Mid-Wilshire

La Brea 17 Ave. 18 19

Alta Vista Blvd.

Cochran Ave.

Martell Ave.

San Vicente Blvd.

Hauser Blvd.

Pan Pacific Park

Park La Brea

Hancock Park

15 14

CBS Television City

16

Fairfax Ave.

N

440 yds.
400 m
0

20 →

Accommodations
Banana Bungalow 4
Holiday Inn Hollywood 5
Hollywood Celebrity Hotel 6
Hollywood Roosevelt 7

Dining
Authentic Cafe 14
Boxer 15
Ca' Brea 17
Campanile 19

Chianti Cucina 13
Citrus 10
Dar Maghreb 8
El Cholo 20
Flora Kitchen 18
Georgia 12

Hollywood Hills Coffee Shop 2
Musso & Frank Grill 3
Patina 9
Pink's Hot Dogs 11
Roscoe's House of Chicken & Waffles 1
Sofi Estiatorion 16

🅰 Family-Friendly Restaurants

Prices notwithstanding, **Musso & Frank Grill** *(see p. 108),* Hollywood's oldest restaurant, is a simple family place that offers something for everyone. Located directly on the Walk of Fame, the restaurant is in the heart of touristland. Kids are pleased by the extensive menu, which has something for everyone. For adults, the restaurant offers unmistakable quality. And who else will serve you peas and cubed carrots—with absolutely no irony—just like Mom used to?

On the other end of the scale is **Pink's Hot Dogs** *(see p. 109),* an institution in its own right that has been serving politically incorrect franks for what seems like forever. Everyone loves Pink's chili dogs, but you may never get the orange stains out of your kid's clothes.

Dive! *(see p. 101)* was created by Steven Spielberg and Jeffrey Katzenberg with kids specifically in mind. It's a fun, theme parkish place, with surroundings designed to take your mind off the food.

Miceli's *(see p. 117)* in Universal City is a cavernous Italian restaurant that the whole family is sure to love. The gimmick? The waitstaff sings showtunes or opera favorites in between serving dinner (and sometimes instead of). Kids will love the boisterous atmosphere, which might even drown them out.

Jerry's Famous Deli *(see p. 117)* in Studio City is frequented mostly by industry types who populate this Valley community; their kids often sport baseball caps or production T-shirts from Mom or Dad's latest project. With the most extensive deli menu in town and a casual, coffee-shop atmosphere, families flock to Jerry's for lunch, early dinner, and (crowded) weekend breakfast.

appear on the plate. The seasonal menu features partridge, pheasant, venison, and other game in winter, and spotlights exotic local vegetables in warmer months. Seafood is always available; if Maine lobster cannelloni or asparagus-wrapped John Dory is on the menu, order it. Patina is justifiably famous for its mashed potatoes and potato truffle chips; be sure to include one (or both) with your meal.

MODERATE

✪ **Boxer.** 7615 Beverly Blvd., Los Angeles. ☎ **213/932-6178.** Reservations required. Main courses $10–$18. AE, MC, V. Tues–Fri 11:30am–2:30pm; Tues–Sun 6–11pm; Sat–Sun brunch 10:30am–2:30pm. CALIFORNIA.

L.A. foodies are watching Boxer carefully—and quickly coming to a consensus that young, enthusiastic chef Neal Fraser has definitely stumbled onto something at this intimate eatery, on the same block as the ever-expanding Authentic Cafe. The dark wood and weathered wrought-iron decor is simple, classy, and welcoming for the suited yuppies, Chanel-garbed socialites, and chunky-shoed twentysomethings who blend inside as well as the varied ingredients on the menu. At first glance, the menu appears fussy, an illusion created by the listing of every component in a dish; the perception is heightened by the almost architectural arrangement of food on the plate. Fraser does invent some fanciful combos, like pancetta-wrapped Numidean hen with caramelized shallot sauce, grilled pork chop served with a tower of apple slices and sage polenta discs, and goat cheese and fennel–crusted swordfish with gazpacho vinaigrette. Side dishes are carefully chosen—you get the overall feeling that your satisfaction is of primary importance to the chef. Spago used to be this way in the early days. Desserts are equally inventive and tasty, ranging from tangerine flan with a pomegranate glaze to bread pudding baked in a small pumpkin.

Eschew the valet for the always-plentiful street parking, and bring your own wine; there's a nominal $3 corkage fee.

Ca' Brea. 346 S. La Brea Ave. (north of Wilshire Blvd.). ☎ **213/938-2863.** Reservations recommended. Main courses $9–$21; lunch $7–$20. AE, CB, DC, MC, V. Mon–Sat 11:30am–2:30pm; Mon–Thurs 5:30–10:30pm, Fri–Sat 5:30pm–midnight. NORTHERN ITALIAN.

When Ca' Brea opened in 1991, its talented chef/owner Antonio Tommasi was catapulted into a public spotlight that's shared by only a handful of L.A. chefs—Wolfgang Puck, Michel Richard, Joachim Splichal. Since then, Tommasi has opened two other celebrated restaurants, Locanda Veneta in Hollywood and Ca' Del Sole in the Valley, but, for many, Ca' Brea remains tops. The restaurant's refreshingly bright two-story dining room is a happy place, hung with colorful, oversize contemporary paintings and backed by an open prep-kitchen where you can watch as your seafood cakes are sautéed and your Napa cabbage braised. Booths are the most coveted seats; but with only 20 tables in all, be thankful you're sitting anywhere. Detractors might complain that Ca' Brea isn't what it used to be since Tommasi began splitting his time between three restaurants; but Tommasi stops in daily and keeps a very close watch over his hand-picked staff. Consistently excellent dishes include the roasted pork sausage, butter squash–stuffed ravioli, and a different risotto each day—always rich, creamy and delightfully indulgent.

Chianti Cucina. 7383 Melrose Ave. (between Fairfax and La Brea aves.). ☎ **213/653-8333.** Reservations recommended. Main courses $12–$20. AE, CB, DC, MC, V. Chianti Cucina: Mon–Thurs, and Sun 11:30am–11:30pm, Fri–Sat 11:30am–midnight. Ristorante Chianti: Sun–Thurs 5:30–10:30pm, Fri–Sat 5:30–11pm. NORTHERN ITALIAN.

Innocent passersby, and locals in search of a secret hideaway, go to the dimly lit, crimson-colored Ristorante Chianti, where waiters whip out flashlights so customers can read the menu. Cognoscenti, on the other hand, bypass that 60-year-old standby and head straight for Chianti Cucina, the bright, bustling eat-in "kitchen" of the more formal restaurant next door. Chianti Cucina features excellent meals at fair prices. The menu, which changes frequently, is always interesting and often exceptional. Hot and cold appetizers range from fresh handmade mozzarella and prosciutto to lamb carpaccio with asparagus and marinated grilled eggplant filled with goat cheese, arugula, and sun-dried tomatoes. As for main dishes, the homemade pasta is both superior and deliciously inventive. Try the black tortellini filled with fresh salmon, or the giant ravioli filled with spinach and ricotta.

Dar Maghreb. 7651 Sunset Blvd. (between Fairfax and La Brea aves.). ☎ **213/876-7651.** Reservations recommended. Fixed-price dinner $29. AE, CB, DC, MC, V. Tues–Fri 6–11pm, Sat 6:30–11pm, Sun 5:30–10:30pm. MOROCCAN.

If you're a lone diner in search of a quick bite, this isn't the place for you. Dinner at Dar Maghreb is an entertaining dining experience that increases exponentially the larger your party is and the longer you linger. Enter an exotic Middle Eastern world of genie waitresses who wash your hands with lemon water and belly dancers who shimmy around an exquisite fountain in the center of a Koranic patio. You'll feel like a guest in an ornately tiled palace as you dine at traditional tables, seated on either low sofas or goatskin cushions. Nothing is available à la carte; the fixed-price meal is a multicourse feast, starting with bread and traditional Moroccan salads, followed by *b'stilla,* an appetizer of shredded chicken, eggs, almonds, and spices wrapped in a flaky pastry shell and topped with powdered sugar and cinnamon. All is eaten with your hands; it's a sensual experience that grows on you as the night progresses. The main courses, your choice of lamb, quail, chicken, and more, are each sublimely seasoned and delectable. Perhaps it's the exotic atmosphere that makes everyone eat more than they expected, but you'll be thankful that desert is a simple fruit and nut basket, accompanied by warm spice tea poured dramatically into traditional glasses.

Georgia. 7250 Melrose Ave. (at Alta Vista Ave.). ☎ **213/933-8420.** Reservations recommended. Main courses $14–$20. AE, MC, V. Mon–Sat 6:30–11pm, Sun 5:30–10pm. SOUTHERN.

Soul food and power ties come together at this calorie-unconscious ode to southern cooking in the heart of Melrose's funky shopping district. Owned by a group of investors that includes Denzel Washington and Eddie Murphy, the restaurant is popular with Hollywood's African-American crowd and others who can afford L.A.'s highest-priced pork chops, fried chicken, and grits. It's great for people-watching. The antebellum-style dining room is built to resemble a fine southern house, complete with mahogany floors, Spanish moss, and wrought-iron gates; a bourbon bar continues the theme. Smoked baby back ribs are particularly good and, like many other dishes, are smothered in onion gravy or remoulade, and sided with corn pudding, grits, string beans, or an excellent creamy garlic coleslaw. Other recommendations include turtle soup, grilled gulf shrimp, and a Creole-style catfish that is more delicately fried than it would traditionally be.

✪ **Musso & Frank Grill.** 6667 Hollywood Blvd. (at Cahuenga Blvd.). ☎ **213/467-7788.** Reservations recommended. Main courses $13–$22. AE, CB, DC, MC, V. Tues–Sat 11am–11pm. AMERICAN/CONTINENTAL.

A survey of Hollywood eateries that leaves out Musso & Frank is like a study of Las Vegas showrooms that fails to mention Wayne Newton. It's not that this is the best restaurant in town, nor is it the most famous; but as L.A's oldest eatery (since 1919), Musso & Frank is the paragon of Old Hollywood grill rooms, an almost kitschy glimpse into a meat-and-potatoes world that's remained the same for generations. This is where Faulkner and Hemingway drank during their screenwriting days, where Orson Welles used to hold court. The restaurant is still known for their bone-dry martinis and perfectly seasoned Bloody Marys. The setting is what you'd expect: oak-beamed ceilings, red-leather booths and banquettes, mahogany room dividers (complete with coathooks), chandeliers with tiny shades. The extensive menu is a veritable survey of American/Continental cookery. Hearty dinners include veal scaloppine marsala, roast spring lamb with mint jelly, and broiled lobster. Grilled meats are the restaurant's specialties, as is the Thursday-only chicken pot pie. Regulars also flock in for Musso's trademark "flannel cakes," crepe-thin pancakes flipped to order.

INEXPENSIVE

✪ **Authentic Cafe.** 7605 Beverly Blvd. (at Curson Ave.). ☎ **213/939-4626.** Reservations not accepted. Main courses $8–$13; lunch $8–$13. AE, MC, V. Mon–Thurs 11:30am–10pm, Fri 11:30am–11pm, Sat 10am–11pm, Sun 10am–10pm. SOUTHWESTERN.

True to its name, this excellent restaurant serves authentic southwestern food in a casual atmosphere; it's a winning combination that has made it an L.A. favorite. The trendy dining room is known for hip people-watching, large portions, and good food; thankfully, they recently expanded the dining room, easing what used to be an unbearable wait for tables. You'll sometimes find an Asian flair to Chef Roger Hayot's southwestern-style meals. Look for brie, papaya, and chili quesadillas; other worthwhile dishes are the chicken casserole with a cornbread crust; fresh corn and red peppers in chile-cream sauce; and meatloaf with caramelized onions.

✪ **El Cholo.** 1121 S. Western Ave. (south of Olympic). ☎ **213/734-2773.** Reservations recommended. Main courses $7–$13. AE, DC, MC, V. Mon–Thurs 11am–10pm, Fri–Sat 11am–11pm; Sun 11am–9pm. MEXICAN.

There's authentic Mexican, and then there's traditional Mexican—El Cholo is comfort food of the latter variety, the south-of-the-border cuisine traditionally craved by Angelenos. They've been serving it up in their pink adobe hacienda since 1927, even though the once-outlying Mid-Wilshire neighborhood around them has turned into Koreatown. El Cholo's expertly blended margaritas, invitingly messy nachos, and classic combination dinners don't break new culinary ground, but their kitchen has perfected these standards over 70 years, and El Cholo is the best of the bunch—I wish they bottled their rich, dark red enchilada sauce! Other specialties include seasonally available green corn tamales, and creative sizzling vegetarian fajitas that go way beyond just eliminating the meat. The atmosphere is festive, as people from all parts of town dine happily in the many rambling rooms which comprise the restaurant. There's valet parking as well as a free self-park lot directly across the street.

Flora Kitchen. 460 S. La Brea Ave. (at 6th St.). ☎ 213/931-9900. Reservations not accepted. Main courses $5–$10. AE, MC, V. Sun–Thurs 8am–10pm, Fri–Sat 8am–11pm. AMERICAN.

Picture an upscale, funky Carrow's or Denny's, and you've imagined Flora Kitchen. Known for its tuna and chicken salads served on exalted La Brea Bakery breads, the restaurant is equally comfortable dishing out more eclectic fare like cayenne-spiced potato soup, poached salmon with dill sauce, and seared ahi with roast vegetables. Flora is popular with art-gallery strollers by day, and with music lovers, who take the restaurant's dinners, boxed, to the Hollywood Bowl, on warm summer nights. Unfortunately, service at Denny's is better.

Hollywood Hills Coffee Shop. 6145 Franklin Ave. (between Gower and Vine sts.). ☎ 213/467-7678. Reservations not accepted. Most items under $8. AE, DISC, MC, V. Tues–Sat 7am–10pm; Sun–Mon 7am–4pm. AMERICAN/INTERNATIONAL.

Having served for years as the run-of-the-mill coffee shop for the attached freeway-side Best Western, this place took on a life of its own when chef Susan Fine commandeered the kitchen and spruced up the menu with quirky Mexican and Asian touches. Hotel guests still spill in from the lobby; however, now they rub noses with the actors, screenwriters, and other artistic types who converge from nearby canyons to await that sitcom casting call or feature film deal. (This community was immortalized in the 1996 film *Swingers*; scenes were actually taped in the restaurant.) Prices have gone up (to pay for the industrial-strength cappuccino-maker visible behind the counter?), and the dinner menu now features surprisingly sophisticated entrees instead of blue-plate specials. But breakfast and lunch are still bargains, and the comfy Americana atmosphere is a nice break from the bright lights of nearby Hollywood Boulevard.

Pink's Hot Dogs. 709 N. La Brea Ave. (at Melrose Ave.) ☎ 213/931-4223. Hot dogs $2.10. Sun–Thurs 9:30am–2am, Fri–Sat 9:30am–3am. HOT DOGS.

Pink's isn't your usual guidebook recommendation, but then again, this crusty corner stand is not your usual doggery. The heartburn-inducing chili dogs are so decadent that otherwise upstanding, health-conscious Angelenos crave them; Bruce Willis reportedly proposed to Demi Moore at the 58-year-old shack, which grew around the late Paul Pink's 10¢ wiener cart. Pray the bulldozers stay away from this little nugget of a place.

Roscoe's House of Chicken 'n' Waffles. 1514 N. Gower St. (at Sunset Blvd). ☎ 213/466-7453. Main courses $4–$11. No credit cards. Sun–Thurs 9am–midnight, Fri–Sat 9am–4am. AMERICAN.

It sounds like a bad joke: Only chicken and waffle dishes are served here, a rubric that also encompasses eggs and chicken livers. Its close proximity to CBS Television

City has turned this simple restaurant into a kind of de facto commissary for the network. A chicken-and-cheese omelet isn't everyone's ideal way to begin the day, but it's de rigeur at Roscoe's. At lunch, few calorie-unconscious diners can resist the chicken smothered in gravy and onions—a house specialty that's served with waffles or grits and biscuits. Large chicken-salad bowls and chicken sandwiches also provide plenty of cluck for the buck. Homemade cornbread, sweet-potato pie, homemade potato salad, and corn on the cob are available as side orders, and wine and beer are sold.

Roscoe's can also be found at 4907 W. Washington Blvd., at La Brea Ave. (☎ 213/936-3730), and 5006 West Pico Blvd. (☎ 213/934-4405)

✪ Sofi Estiatorion. 8030³/₄ W. Third Street (between Fairfax and Crescent Heights). ☎ 213/651-0346. Reservations suggested. Main courses $7–$14. AE, DC, MC, V. Mon–Sat noon–2:30pm; Sun–Thurs 5:30–10:30pm, Fri–Sat 5:30–11pm. GREEK.

Look for the Aegean-blue awning over the narrow passageway leading from the street to this hidden Athenian treasure. Be sure to ask for a table on the romantic patio amidst twinkling lights, and immediately order a plate of their thick, satisfying tzatziki (yogurt-cucumber-garlic spread) and a basket of warm pitas for dipping. Other specialties (recipes courtesy of Sofi's Old-World grandmother) include herbed rack of lamb with rice, fried calamari salad, saganaki (kasseri cheese flamed with ouzo), and other hearty taverna favorites. Located near Farmer's Market in a popular part of town, Sofi's odd, off-street setting has made it an insiders' secret (until now!).

6 Downtown

EXPENSIVE

Checkers Restaurant. In the Wyndham Checkers Hotel, 535 S. Grand Ave. (between 5th and 6th sts.). ☎ 213/624-0000. Reservations recommended. Main courses $18–$28; lunch $15–$19; weekend brunch $9–$18. AE, DC, MC, V. Mon–Fri 11:30am–2:30pm; Sat–Sun 10:30am–2:30pm; daily 5:30–9:30pm. AUSTRIAN-CALIFORNIA.

Nine-to-fivers looking to grab a quick, inexpensive bite are the bread and butter of most eateries in this neighborhood. Not so at Checkers; this peaceful restaurant represents the pinnacle of elegance. The warm, velvet-lined formal dining room is so plush and conservatively ornate that it feels like you're dining inside a Fabergé egg. Lunchtime is dominated by suits from the nearby office high-rises, but dinner is always special; you might begin with smoked duck breast carpaccio or rum-soaked salmon terrine layered with cream cheese and capers. Main courses include lentil and caraway–crusted pork tenderloin and tiger prawns with soba noodles. À la carte brunches mean everything from granola with sun-dried fruit to duck hash with rosemary and poached eggs.

Pacific Dining Car. 1310 W. 6th St. (at Witmer St.). ☎ 213/483-6000. Reservations recommended. Main courses $20–$42; lunch $14–$29; breakfast $11–$20. AE, MC, V. Daily 24 hours (breakfast 11pm–11am). STEAKS.

It's 4am and you're in the mood for a well-marbled, patiently aged New York steak. Well, even in these health-conscious times, there are still enough nocturnal carnivores in Los Angeles to justify not one, but two, all-night Pacific Dining Car steakhouses. The flagship location, just a few short blocks from the epicenter of downtown, is dark and clubby, a vestige of an age when diners guiltlessly indulged in fist-sized medallions of beef. The mesquite-charred steaks are terrific indeed, a cut above the restaurant's other hearty offerings, like lamb and chicken. There's a good wine selection. A separate breakfast menu features egg dishes, salads, and ministeaks.

A second restaurant is located in Santa Monica, at 2700 Wilshire Blvd., one block east of 26th Street (☎ 310/453-4000).

✪ **Water Grill.** 544 S. Grand Ave. (between 5th and 6th sts.). ☎ **213/891-0900.** Reservations recommended. Main courses $14–$22; lunch $9–$15. AE, DC, DISC, MC, V. Mon–Tues 11:30am–9pm, Wed–Fri 11:30am–10pm, Sat 5–10pm, Sun 4:30–9pm. SEAFOOD.

Popular with the suit-and-tie crowd at lunch, the restaurant attracts concertgoers en route to the Music Center by night. The dining room is a stylish and sophisticated fusion of wood, leather, and brass, but it gets a lighthearted lift from cavorting papier-mâché fish that play against an aquamarine ceiling painted with bubbles. Water Grill, considered by many to be L.A.'s best seafood house, is best known for its shellfish. Among the appetizers are a dozen different oysters; Discovery Bay Flats and Goosepoints (both from Washington State), two of my favorites, are particularly sweet and clean. Main courses are imaginative dishes influenced by the cuisines of Hawaii, the Pacific Northwest, New Orleans, and New England. Black linguine is topped with calamari, rock shrimp, and bay scallops in a spicy sauce; Dungeness crab is stuffed into a Maine lobster; grilled mahimahi is served with zucchini noodles; and seared sea scallops are paired with house-smoked salmon.

MODERATE

Cafe Pinot. 700 W. 5th St. (between Grand and Flower sts.). ☎ **213/239-6500.** Reservations recommended. Main courses $13–$22. AE, MC, V. Mon–Sat 11:15am–2:30pm, Mon 5–9pm, Tues–Sat 5–9:30pm. CALIFORNIA-FRENCH.

Chef Joachim Splichal is quickly becoming the most dominant force on the L.A. restaurant scene. Modeled after his top-ranked restaurant, Patina, Cafe Pinot is designed to be less formal in atmosphere and lighter on the palate—and the pocketbook—than his flagship eatery. Opened in 1995 in the gardens of the L.A. Public Library, Cafe Pinot's tables are mostly on the patio, shaded by umbrellas and the well-landscaped library courtyard. The restaurant's location makes it a natural for downtown business folk; at night, there's free shuttle transportation to the Music Center. Splichal has installed a giant rotisserie in the kitchen, and the best meals come from it. The moist, tender mustard-crusted roast chicken is your best bet unless it's Friday night, when you can order the roast suckling pig with its unique crackling skin. Other recommendable dishes include duck leg confit, grilled calf's liver, and seared peppered tuna.

Cha Cha Cha. 656 N. Virgil Ave. (at Melrose Ave.), Silverlake. ☎ **213/664-7723.** Reservations recommended. Main courses $8–$15. AE, DC, DISC, MC, V. Sun–Thurs 8am–10:30pm; Fri–Sat 8am–11:30pm. CARIBBEAN.

Cha Cha Cha serves the West Coast's best Caribbean food in a fun and funky space on the seedy fringe of downtown. The restaurant is a festival of flavors and colors that are both upbeat and offbeat. It's impossible to feel down when you're part of this eclectic hodgepodge of pulsating Caribbean music, wild decor, and kaleidoscopic clutter; still, the intimate dining rooms cater to lively romantics, not obnoxious frat boys. Claustrophobes should choose seats in the airy covered courtyard. The very spicy black-pepper jumbo shrimp gets top marks, as does the paella, a generous mixture of chicken, sausage, and seafood blended with saffroned rice. Other Jamaican/Haitian/Cuban/Puerto Rican–inspired recommendations include jerk pork and mambo gumbo, a zesty soup of okra, shredded chicken, and spices. Hardcore Caribbeanites might visit for breakfast, when the fare ranges from plantain, yucca, onion, and herb omelets to scrambled eggs with fresh tomatillos served on hot grilled tortillas.

Downtown Area Dining

Cafe Pinot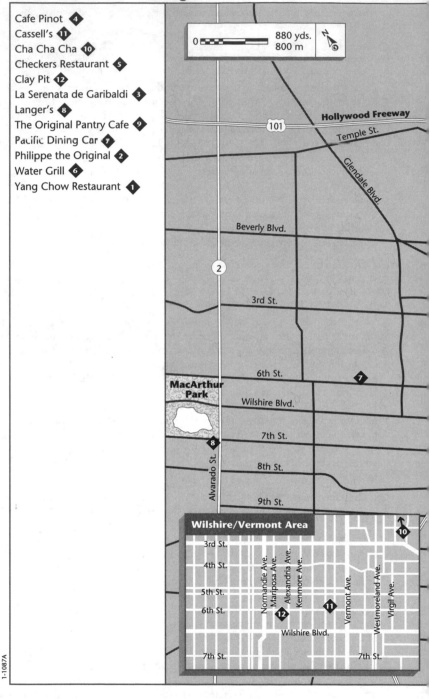

Cassell's 11

Cha Cha Cha 10

Checkers Restaurant 5

Clay Pit 12

La Serenata de Garibaldi 3

Langer's 8

The Original Pantry Cafe 9

Pacific Dining Car 7

Philippe the Original 2

Water Grill 6

Yang Chow Restaurant 1

1-1087A

Clay Pit. In Chapman Market, 3465 W. 6th St. (between Normandie and Vermont aves.). ☎ **213/382-6300.** Reservations recommended on weekends. Main courses $12–$17; lunch $7–$11; weekday lunch buffet $7.75; Sunday brunch buffet $9.95. AE, CB, DC, DISC, MC, V. Mon–Sat 11:30am–2:30pm; daily 5:30–10pm; Sun 11:30am–2:30pm. INDIAN.

When you're in the mood for very good, inexpensive Indian cooking, you can do no better than this cozy and reliable mid-Wilshire tandoori room. Physically, Clay Pit is just an unremarkable neighborhood place, with standard furnishings and decor. But, in nice weather, you can dine by the splashing fountain on an outdoor patio overlooking the action in the landmark Chapman Market arcade. Doting waiters serve flavorful traditional curries, some with California twists. If you're in the mood for authentic, order creamy *saag paneer* (spinach and homemade cheese), chunky *aloo motor kabi* (potato and peas in a coriander-based tomato sauce), or juicy *lamb tikka* (marinated in a yogurt sauce and cooked in the clay oven). If you're not, order rosemary-scented lamb, succulent pork chops, or moist ahi. Excellent naan breads and unbeatable all-you-can-eat buffets keep this value-packed place popular.

✪ **La Serenata de Garibaldi.** 1842 E. 1st St. (between Boyle and State sts.), Boyle Heights. ☎ **213/265-2887.** Reservations recommended. Main courses $9–$18; lunch $6–$11. AE, MC, V. Tues–Sun 11am–10pm. MEXICAN.

Once a humble neighborhood hangout indistinguishable from the many tiny and thriving Latino businesses on this Boyle Heights street, La Serenata grew to prominence as word of their superior cuisine spread to business lunchers in nearby downtown. Soon, affluent patrons were coming from far and wide, including O.J.'s legal "dream team," who lunched here often during the trial. Seafood is the focus of the hardworking kitchen; trademark dishes include shrimp in cilantro sauce and Mexican sea bass fillets in a tangy chipotle sauce, plus a rich, simmered-all-day mole sauce served on giant shrimp or chicken. This brand of authentic Mexican cuisine, done so expertly, has made La Serenata a consistent draw despite its dodgy surroundings. You'll enjoy the earthy ethnic neighborhood, across the street from Mariachi Plaza (where colorfully attired ensembles wait, instruments in hand, for an evening's work). The menu prices are decidedly more Westside than East L.A. these days, but the food is worth the drive.

To get there from the Hollywood Freeway (U.S. 101), take the First Street exit east to the restaurant. It's also within ¼ mile of I-10 and I-5, which, with U.S. 101, form a triangle around the neighborhood it's in. The restaurant has a secure rear parking lot.

A smaller-scale sister restaurant called La Serenata Gourmet recently opened near the Westside Pavilion, 10924 W. Pico Blvd. (near Overland Ave.), Los Angeles (☎ **310/441-9667**).

INEXPENSIVE

Cassell's. 3266 W. 6th St. (west of Vermont Ave.). ☎ **213/480-8668.** Hamburgers $4–$7. No credit cards. Mon–Sat 10:30am–4pm. BURGERS.

Cassell's yellow Formica tables and linoleum floors are the definitions of "dive"; but a loyal pinstriped-suit set from nearby Wilshire Boulevard high-rise offices lines up each day for simple, large burgers that come ready to dress as you like from the condiment buffet. Regulars rave about the restaurant's homemade mayonnaise, used to create superior potato and egg salads. Also praiseworthy are the deliciously crispy onion rings, which, like the rest of the artery-clogging menu, are made fresh in-house. The restaurant is only open for lunch.

Langer's. 704 S. Alvarado St. (at 7th St.). ☎ **213/483-8050.** Main courses $6–$14. MC, V. Mon–Sat 8am–4pm. DELI.

A leader in L.A.'s long-running deli war, Langer's makes some of the best stuffed kishka and matzoh-ball soup this side of the Hudson. For many, however, it's the fresh chopped liver and lean and spicy hot pastrami sandwiches that make Langer's L.A.'s best deli. Langer's has been serving the business community and displaced New Yorkers for almost 50 years. After the riots, when things got dicey around this neighborhood, the restaurant began a curbside delivery service: Phone in your order with an ETA, and they'll be waiting for you at the curb—with change.

Ⓢ **The Original Pantry Cafe.** 877 S. Figueroa St. (at 9th St.). ☎ **213/972-9279.** Main courses $6–$11. No credit cards. Daily 24 hours. AMERICAN.

An L.A. institution if there ever was one, this place has been serving huge portions of comfort food around the clock for more than 60 years; they don't even have a key to the front door. Owned by L.A. Mayor Richard Riordan, the Pantry is especially popular with politicos, who come here for weekday lunches, and conference-goers en route to the nearby L.A. Convention Center. The well-worn restaurant is also a welcoming beacon to late-night clubbers (downtown becomes a virtual ghost town). A bowl of celery stalks, carrot sticks, and whole radishes greets you at your Formica table, and creamy coleslaw and sourdough bread come free with every meal. Famous for quantity rather than quality, the Pantry serves huge T-bone steaks, densely packed meatloaf, macaroni and cheese, and other American favorites. A typical breakfast (served all day) might consist of a huge stack of hotcakes, a big slab of sweet cured ham, home fries, and coffee.

Philippe the Original. 1001 N. Alameda St. (at Ord St.). ☎ **213/628-3781.** Reservations not accepted. Main courses $3–$7. No credit cards. Daily 6am–10pm. SANDWICHES/AMERICAN.

Good old-fashioned value is what this legendary landmark cafeteria is all about. Popular with both South-Central project dwellers and Beverly Hills elite, Philippe's decidedly unspectacular dining room is a microcosm of the entire city; it's one of the few places, it seems, where everyone can get along. Philippe's claims to have invented the French-dipped sandwich at this location in 1908; these remain the most popular menu items. Patrons push trays along the counter and watch while their choice of beef, pork, ham, turkey, or lamb is sliced and layered onto crusty French bread that's been dipped in meat juices. Other menu items include homemade beef stew, chili, and pickled pigs' feet. A hearty breakfast, served daily until 10:30am, is worth attending if only for Philippe's uncommonly good cinnamon-dipped French toast. Beer and wine are available.

Yang Chow Restaurant. 819 N. Broadway (at Alpine St.), Chinatown. ☎ **213/625-0811.** Reservations recommended on weekends. Main courses $8–$12. AE, MC, V. Daily 11:30am–2:30pm; Sun–Thurs 5–9:30pm, Fri–Sat 5–10:30pm. MANDARIN/SZECHUAN.

Open for more then 30 years, family-operated Yang Chow is one of downtown's more popular Chinese restaurants. It's not the dining room's bland and functional decor that accrues accolades, however; what makes Yang Chow so popular is an interesting menu of seafood specialties complementing well-done Chinese standards. After covering the Mandarin and Szechuan basics—sweet and sour pork, shrimp with broccoli, moo shu chicken—the kitchen leaps into high gear, concocting dishes like spicy Dungeness crab; a tangy and hot sautéed squid; and sautéed shellfish with a pungent hoisin-based dipping sauce. A house specialty is plump steamed pork dumplings presented on a bed of fresh spinach. Portions here are generous, but overall quality can be uneven; you may end up with dry rice or overcooked duck.

7 The San Fernando Valley

EXPENSIVE

Pinot Bistro. 12969 Ventura Blvd. (west of Coldwater Canyon Ave.), Studio City. ☎ 818/990-0500. Reservations required. Main courses $16–$22; lunch $7–$13. AE, DC, DISC, MC, V. Mon–Fri 11:30am–2:30pm; Mon–Thurs 6–10pm, Fri 6–10:30pm, Sat 5:30–10:30pm, Sun 5:30–9:30pm. CALIFORNIA-FRENCH.

When the Valley crowd doesn't want to make the drive to Patina, they pack into Pinot Bistro, one of restaurateur Joachim Splichal's other hugely successful restaurants. The Valley's only great bistro is designed with dark woods, etched glass, and cream-colored walls that scream "trendy French" almost as loudly as the rich, straightforward cooking. The menu is a symphony of California and continental elements that includes a beautiful warm potato tart with smoked whitefish, and baby lobster tails with creamy polenta; both are studies in culinary perfection. The most popular dish here is Chef Octavio Becerra's Frenchified Tuscan bean soup, infused with oven-dried tomatoes and roasted garlic and served over crusty ciabatta bread. Generously portioned main dishes continue the gourmet theme: baby lobster risotto; braised oxtail with parsley gnocchi; and puff pastry stuffed with bay scallops, Manila clams, and roast duck. The service is good—attentive and unobtrusive. Many regulars prefer Pinot Bistro at lunch, when a less expensive menu is served to a more easygoing crowd.

Talesai. 11744 Ventura Blvd. (between Colfax Ave. and Laurel Canyon Blvd.), Studio City. ☎ 818/753-1001. Reservations recommended. Main courses $9–$18. AE, DC, MC, V. Mon–Fri 11:30am–2:30pm; daily 5:30–10:30pm. THAI.

Thai food fans will either love or hate this "haute Thai" sibling to a Sunset Strip institution. Talesai's minimalist decor punctuated by crisp white tablecloths complements a sophisticated and innovative Thai cuisine that elevates the usual take-out favorites. Prices reflect this aesthetic, but if you're sick of gummy pad thai and tough satay, Talesai will be a welcome change. Meat dishes accented with curry, coconut milk, and mint can be prepared as spicy or mild as you wish; two Talesai specialties are "Hidden Treasures," in which chili- and coconut-soaked shrimp and crabmeat are baked in tiny clay pots; and "Heavenly BBQ Chicken," marinated in spices and coconut milk then grilled to "heavenly" perfection.

You can find Talesai's Sunset Strip outpost at 9043 Sunset Boulevard (at Doheny Drive), West Hollywood (☎ 310/275-9724).

MODERATE

Casa Vega. 13371 Ventura Blvd. (at Fulton Ave.), Sherman Oaks. ☎ 818/788-4868. Reservations recommended. Main courses $5–$11. AE, MC, V. Daily 5pm–1am. MEXICAN.

I believe that everyone loves a friendly dive; Casa Vega is one of my local favorites. A faux-weathered adobe exterior with no windows conceals red Naugahyde booths lurking amongst fake potted plants and 1960s amateur oil paintings of dark-eyed Mexican children and red-cape–waving bullfighters. At Christmas the decor achieves critical mass, with tinsel garlands dripping everywhere. Locals love it for good, cheap margaritas (order on the rocks), bottomless baskets of hot, salty chips, and traditional combination dinners (order by number) that all come with Casa Vega's patented tostada-style dinner salad. Street parking is plentiful here, so use the valet only as a last resort.

Iroha Sushi. 12953 Ventura Blvd. (west of Coldwater Canyon Ave.), Studio City. ☎ **818/ 990-9559.** Reservations recommended. Main courses $7–$12; sushi $3–$7. AE, DC, MC, V. Mon–Sat 5:30–10:15pm. JAPANESE.

You can't help feeling special at this tiny Japanese cottage hidden behind an ethnic art gallery; there are only about a dozen tables and a short sushi bar. Enter from a zen garden–like gravel courtyard to the demure welcome of kimono-clad waitresses and bowing waiters. Service is discreetly efficient, and everything on the simple menu is excellent, from the airy tempura to tangy teriyaki, and especially the sushi. Dinner ends with an artistically carved orange to sweetly cleanse the palate . . . then it's back to the reality of busy Ventura Boulevard.

Jerry's Famous Deli. 12655 Ventura Blvd. (at Coldwater Canyon Ave.), Studio City. ☎ **818/ 980-4245.** Reservations not accepted. Main courses $9–$14; breakfast $2–$11; sandwiches and salads $4–$12. AE, MC, V. Daily 24 hours. DELI.

Just east of Coldwater Canyon Avenue there's a simple yet sizable deli where all the Valley's hipsters go to relieve their late-night munchies. This place probably has one of the largest menus in America—a tome that spans cultures and continents, from Central America to China to New York. From salads to sandwiches to steak and seafood platters, everything, including breakfast, is served all day. Jerry's is consistently good at lox and eggs, pastrami sandwiches, potato pancakes, and all the deli staples. It's an integral part of L.A.'s cultural landscape, and favorite of the show-business types who populate the adjacent foothill neighborhoods. It also has a full bar.

Miceli's. 3655 Cahuenga Blvd. (east of Lankershim Blvd.), Universal City. ☎ **818/508-1221.** Reservations not accepted. Main courses $7–$12; pizza $9–$15. AE, DC, MC, V. Mon–Thurs 5pm–midnight; Fri 5pm–1am; Sat 4pm–1am; Sun 4–11pm. ITALIAN.

Mostaccioli marinara, lasagna, thin-crust pizza, and eggplant parmigiana are indicative of the Sicilian-style fare at this cavernous, stained-glass-windowed Italian restaurant, whose waitstaff sings show tunes or opera favorites in between serving dinner (and sometimes instead of). Make sure you have enough Chianti to get into the spirit of it all. This is a great place for kids, but way too rollicking for romance.

INEXPENSIVE

Du-par's Coffee Shop. 12036 Ventura Blvd. (1 block east of Laurel Canyon Blvd.), Studio City. ☎ **818/766-4437.** All items under $10. AE, MC, V. Sun–Thurs 6am–1am; Fri–Sat 6am–4am. AMERICAN/DINER.

It's been called a "culinary wax museum," the last of a dying breed . . . the kind of coffee shop Donna Reed took the family to for blue-plate specials. This isn't a trendy new theme place, it's the real deal—that motherly waitress who calls everyone under 60 "hon" has probably been slinging hash here for 20 or 30 years. Popular among old-timers who made it part of their daily routine decades ago, show-business denizens who eschew the industry watering holes, a new generation who appreciates a tasty, cheap meal . . . well, everyone, really. It's common knowledge that Du-par's makes the best buttermilk pancakes in town, though some prefer the eggy, perfect French toast (extra crispy around the edges, please). Mouthwatering pies (blueberry cream cheese, coconut cream, etc.) line the front display case, and can be had for a song.

Also in Los Angeles at Farmer's Market, 6333 W. Third St., ☎ **213/933-8446** (but they don't stay open as late).

7 What to See & Do in Los Angeles

These are exciting times in Los Angeles. The city is currently enjoying the same fame, fortune, and power that London had in the 18th century, Paris possessed in the 19th century, and New York enjoyed at the turn of this century. Museums are opening, culture is flourishing, and the entire world is fascinated by what's going on in L.A.

New museums, such as the Petersen Automotive Museum and the Museum of Tolerance, have popped up over the last few years, and many of the older ones are expanding and improving: The Los Angeles County Museum of Art, the Petersen, George C. Page Museum of Tar Pit Discoveries, the Museum of Miniatures, and the Craft & Folk Art Museum were united along their common stretch of Wilshire Boulevard under the auspices of the newly named Museum Row; the Hammer has just merged with UCLA; and the Getty is putting the finishing touches on a new $750 million complex in the Brentwood hills.

But it's not just the museums that are experiencing a renaissance. The city and its planners know what side their bread is buttered on: The Walk of Fame, the Hollywood sign, Santa Monica Pier, and other traditional tourist draws are being spruced up; new ones, like Universal CityWalk, have been added to L.A.'s repertoire; and L.A.'s theme parks are continually adding new attractions.

Bisected by the Santa Monica Mountains and fronted by long stretches of beach, Los Angeles is also one of the best cities in the world for nature and sports lovers. Where else can you hike in the mountains, in-line skate along the beach, take a swim in the ocean, enjoy a gourmet meal, then take in a basketball or ice hockey or baseball game—all in the same day?

There's plenty to do in L.A.; the problem is, you have to drive everywhere to do it. To get the most out of the city, advance planning is necessary, as is a good map. Plan your days geographically to get the most from them; the itineraries below contain some good suggestions for maximizing a whole day in the beach cities, for example, or spending a day in the heart of Hollywood.

To find out what's going on while you're in town, pick up a copy of the free tabloid *L.A. Weekly,* the monthly magazine *Los Angeles,* or the Sunday *Los Angeles Times* "Calendar" section; each has detailed listings covering what's going on around town, often accompanied by entertaining and helpful commentary on which activities might be worth your while.

In case you want to see the world.

At American Express, we're here to make your journey a smooth one. So we have over 1,700 travel service locations in over 120 countries ready to help. What else would you expect from the world's largest travel agency?

do more

AMERICAN
EXPRESS

Travel

http://www.americanexpress.com/travel

In case you want to be welcomed there.

We're here to see that you're always welcomed at establishments everywhere. That's why millions of people carry the American Express® Card — for peace of mind, confidence, and security, around the world or just around the corner.

do more

AMERICAN EXPRESS

Cards

In case you're running low.

We're here to help with more than 118,000 Express Cash locations around the world. In order to enroll, just call American Express before you start your vacation.

do more

SUGGESTED ITINERARIES

If You Have 1 Day

Spend the morning on Hollywood Boulevard; see the stars on the Walk of Fame, compare your hands and feet with the famous prints outside Mann's Chinese Theatre, and pick up some memorabilia at one of the souvenir shops. Then cruise Sunset Boulevard to the sea. This 45-minute drive will take you through an entertaining cross-section of all that is L.A: from seedy Hollywood to flamboyant West Hollywood, past glittering Beverly Hills and the practical Westside, into the big-city beach town of Santa Monica, the secluded enclave of Pacific Palisades, and finally to the sea. It's a fun drive, often curvy and always scenic; surf music fans can spot all the locations Jan & Dean sing about in "Dead Man's Curve." Lunch on the way at Sunset Plaza, sidewalk-café central of West Hollywood.

Spend the afternoon breathing the fresh sea air all the way from Malibu to Venice Beach's carnival-like Ocean Front Walk. Need some cheap sunglasses? This is the place to stock up! In the evening, after dinner (restaurant choices abound), you might check out the club and music scene in Hollywood and West Hollywood (just pick up an *L.A. Weekly* to see what's going on). Or, with a little planning ahead, you could easily take in a play or concert at downtown's music center or one of the many smaller theaters in Hollywood.

If You Have 2 Days

Spend your first day entirely in Hollywood and the Westside, saving the beach cities for Day 2. On Day 1, check out the Walk of Fame, Mann's Chinese, and one of the show-biz museums along Hollywood Boulevard—a schmaltzy one like the Hollywood Wax Museum, or a serious one like the Hollywood Entertainment Museum. If that's not your style, tour one of the TV or movie studios in Hollywood or just over the hill in the Valley. Do a little shopping along boisterous, trendy Melrose Avenue, or in Beverly Hills's "Golden Triangle." Both areas have great lunch options where you can rest your feet, recharge your body, and restore your spirit. If you have some more energy, take in one of the attractions of Museum Row; perhaps a single exhibit at the Los Angeles County Museum of Art, or just the main floor of the Petersen Automotive Museum. In the evening, if you don't have theater tickets, have a special dinner at one of L.A.'s premier restaurants—perhaps Citrus, Locanda Veneta, or Patina (be sure to reserve a table at least a few days in advance). Afterward, drive up to the Griffith Observatory for a starry city view.

On Day 2, head to the beach; you might want to visit one of Santa Monica's art gallery complexes or outdoor shopping meccas. Have lunch overlooking the ocean, then work it off by renting bikes or skates and joining the human carnival along Venice Beach. Cap off the day with sunset cocktails before heading back to your hotel.

If You Have 3 Days

Three days in L.A. is enough to devote one to the Happiest Place on Earth. After you've spent your first 2 days in Hollywood and at the beach (see above), it's time to go to Disneyland. Arrive early to beat the crowds; you can party all day in Mickey's Anaheim wonderland and still be back in L.A. by dinnertime.

If Disneyland's not for you, you may want to stimulate your senses by putting on your hiking boots, grabbing some deli sandwiches to go, and exploring L.A.'s parks: rural Will Rogers and Temescal overlooking the ocean, or central Griffith Park, which straddles the city and Valley. Or you may prefer to stimulate the economy—there's more great shopping here than can be appreciated in just one day. Be creative: Head to L.A.'s West Third Street or La Brea Avenue, even to Studio City in the San Fernando Valley. All three have a warm neighborly feel, and goods won't be priced out of reach.

If You Have 4 or 5 Days

With 4 or 5 days in the Southland, you definitely should spend one at Disneyland or Universal Studios; both perhaps, if you love amusement parks, or just can't say "no" to the kids! Or use the extra time to explore downtown L.A., an area usually ignored by tourists, but one rich in visual treats and historical adventures. Plan to arrive hungry, and choose between authentic Mexican on Olvera Street, Chinese treats in Chinatown, a variety of fresh ethnic offerings in the Grand Central Market, or an old-fashioned roast beef dip sandwich at Philippe the Original, the downtown institution.

If you're a museum buff, revisit Museum Row, since you have a little extra time to appreciate it. The whole family will enjoy the La Brea Tar Pits and adjoining George C. Page Museum, as well as the Museum of Miniatures across the street. Think early Christmas shopping . . . they all have great museum shops.

1 The Top Attractions

SANTA MONICA & THE BEACHES

✪ **J. Paul Getty Museum.** 17985 Pacific Coast Hwy. (Calif. 1), Malibu. ☎ **310/458-2003.** Free admission. Tues–Sun 10am–5pm (last entrance at 4:30pm).

When it opened in 1974, the Getty Museum was mocked as a filthy-rich upstart with a spotty art collection. It didn't help that the museum was pompously designed after a Roman villa buried at Pompeii. With about $60 million a year to spend, the Getty has repeatedly made headlines by paying record prices for some of the art world's trophies. But far from snatching up everything in sight, the museum is buying intelligently and selectively—perhaps realizing its detractors' worst fears—methodically transforming what was once a rich man's pastime into a connoisseur's delight.

The most notable piece in the rich antiquities collection is *The Victorious Athlete,* a 4th-century B.C. Greek sculpture known as the Getty Bronze; it's believed to have been crafted by Lysippus, court sculptor to Alexander the Great. But the most compelling antiquity is the *Kouros,* a Greek sculpture of a nude youth. It's now largely believed to be fake, but, after years of scientific testing and scholarly debate, the legitimacy of the statue has yet to be resolved. In a classic example of turning lemons into lemonade, rather than shirking from the controversial spotlight, the museum has turned the debate into the focal point of their exhibit, displaying all the evidence both for and against the statue's authenticity.

By the end of 1997, construction of the new Getty Center in Brentwood will be completed, and the Malibu villa will close for 3 years' renovation. Some pieces will be displayed at the new center, which will have extensive research facilities in addition to public galleries. The Malibu Getty is a quintessential L.A. experience, however; try to visit while you still can.

Important: Parking is free, but you must phone for a parking reservation 7 to 10 days in advance. If you can't get a reservation, your best bet is to park in the lot of any restaurant on P.C.H. and phone a cab (see "Getting Around" in chapter 4). Walk-in visitors are not permitted.

Venice Ocean Front Walk. On the beach, between Venice Blvd. and Rose Ave.

This has long been one of L.A.'s most colorful areas. Founded at the turn of the century, the town of Venice was a theme development inspired by its Italian namesake. Authentic Venetian gondolas plied miles of inland waterways lined with rococo palaces. In the 1950s, Venice became the celebrated stomping grounds of Jack Kerouac, Allen Ginsberg, William S. Burroughs, and other beats. In the '60s, this was the epicenter of L.A.'s hippie scene.

Today, Venice is still one of the world's most engaging bohemias. It's not an exaggeration to say that no visit to L.A. would be complete without a stroll along the famous beach path, an almost surreal assemblage of every L.A. stereotype—and then some. Among stalls and stands selling cheap sunglasses, Mexican blankets, and "herbal ecstasy" pills swirls a carnival of humanity that includes bikini-clad in-line skaters, tattooed bikers, muscle-bound pretty boys, panhandling vets, urban gangbangers, beautiful wannabes, and plenty of tourists and gawkers. On any given day, you're bound to come across all kinds of performers: white-faced mimes, breakdancers, buskers, chainsaw jugglers, talking parrots, an occasional apocalyptic evangelist. Last time I was there, a man stood behind a table and railed against the evils of circumcision. "It's too late for us, guys, but we can save the next generation." But a chubby guy singing "Kokomo"—out of tune but with all his heart—cheered me up.

L.A.'s WESTSIDE & BEVERLY HILLS

Rancho La Brea Tar Pits/George C. Page Museum. 5801 Wilshire Blvd., Los Angeles. ☎ 213/857-6311. Admission $6 adults, $3.50 seniors (62 and older) and students with I.D., $2 children 5–12, kids 4 and under free; free to all the second Tuesday of every month. Museum, Tues–Sun 10am–5pm; paleontology laboratory, Wed–Sun 10am–5pm; tar pits, Sat–Sun 10am–5pm. From the Santa Monica Fwy. (I-10), exit onto La Brea Ave. north, continue for 3 miles, and turn left onto Wilshire Blvd. The museum and tar pits are about 10 blocks ahead, between Fairfax and La Brea aves.

An odorous, murky swamp of congealed oil continuously oozes to the earth's surface in the middle of Los Angeles. No, it's not a low-budget horror movie set: It's the La Brea Tar Pits, an awesome, primal pool right on Museum Mile, where hot tar has been bubbling from the earth for over 40,000 years. The glistening pools, which look like murky water, have enticed thirsty animals throughout history. Thousands of mammals, birds, amphibians, and insects—many of which are now extinct—mistakenly crawled into the sticky sludge and stayed forever. In 1906 scientists began a systematic removal and classification of entombed specimens, including ground sloths, giant vultures, mastodons, camels, bears, lizards, even prehistoric relatives of today's beloved super-rats. The best finds are on display in the adjacent George C. Page Museum of La Brea Discoveries, where an excellent 15-minute film documenting the recoveries is also shown. Archaeology work is ongoing; you can watch as scientists clean, identify, and catalog new finds in the paleontology laboratory.

The tar pits themselves are open only on weekends; guided tours are given Saturdays and Sundays at 1pm. Swimming is prohibited.

HOLLYWOOD

Hollywood Sign. At the top of Beachwood Dr., Hollywood.

These 50-foot-high white sheet-metal letters have come to symbolize both the movie industry and the city itself. Erected in 1923 as an advertisement for a fledgling real estate development, the full text originally read "HOLLYWOODLAND." Actress Peg Entwistle leapt to her death from the "H" in 1932; an earthquake-monitoring seismograph is now buried near its base. The recent installation of motion detectors around the sign just made this graffiti tagger's coup a target even more worth boasting

Los Angeles Attractions at a Glance

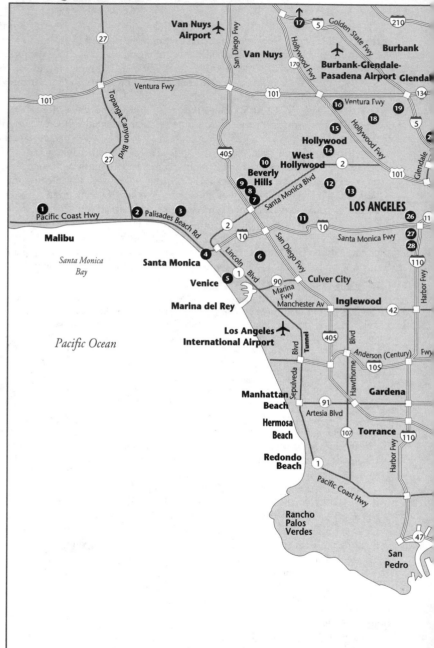

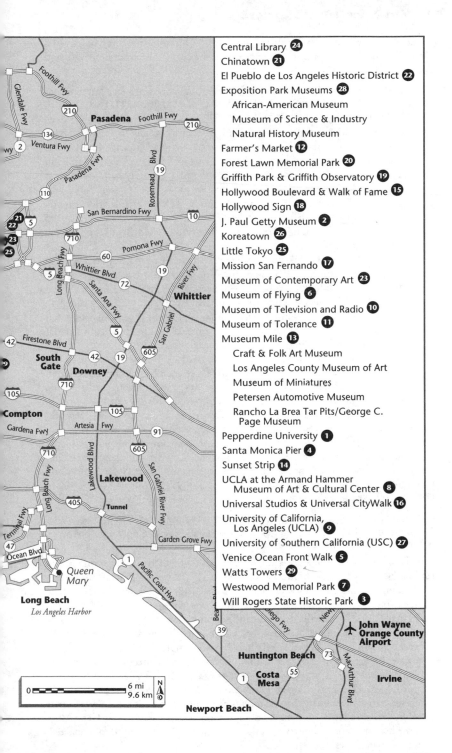

Central Library **24**
Chinatown **21**
El Pueblo de Los Angeles Historic District **22**
Exposition Park Museums **28**
   African-American Museum
   Museum of Science & Industry
   Natural History Museum
Farmer's Market **12**
Forest Lawn Memorial Park **20**
Griffith Park & Griffith Observatory **19**
Hollywood Boulevard & Walk of Fame **15**
Hollywood Sign **18**
J. Paul Getty Museum **2**
Koreatown **26**
Little Tokyo **25**
Mission San Fernando **17**
Museum of Contemporary Art **23**
Museum of Flying **6**
Museum of Television and Radio **10**
Museum of Tolerance **11**
Museum Mile **13**
   Craft & Folk Art Museum
   Los Angeles County Museum of Art
   Museum of Miniatures
   Petersen Automotive Museum
   Rancho La Brea Tar Pits/George C. Page Museum
Pepperdine University **1**
Santa Monica Pier **4**
Sunset Strip **14**
UCLA at the Armand Hammer Museum of Art & Cultural Center **8**
Universal Studios & Universal CityWalk **16**
University of California, Los Angeles (UCLA) **9**
University of Southern California (USC) **27**
Venice Ocean Front Walk **5**
Watts Towers **29**
Westwood Memorial Park **7**
Will Rogers State Historic Park **3**

about. A thorny hiking trail leads toward it from Durand Drive near Beachwood Drive, but the best view is from down below, at the corner of Sunset Boulevard and Bronson Avenue.

Hollywood Walk of Fame. Hollywood Blvd., between Gower St. and La Brea Ave.; and Vine St., between Yucca St. and Sunset Blvd. For information, ☎ 213/469-8311. From U.S. 101, exit onto Highland Blvd. and turn left onto Hollywood Blvd.

Over 2,500 celebrities are honored along the world's most famous sidewalk. Each bronze medallion, set into the center of a granite star, pays homage to a famous television, film, radio, theater, or recording personality. Although about a third of them are just about as obscure as Andromeda—their fame simply hasn't withstood the test of time—millions of visitors are thrilled by the sight of famous names like James Dean (at 1719 Vine St.), John Lennon (at 1750 Vine St.), Marlon Brando (at 1765 Vine St.), Rudolph Valentino (at 6164 Hollywood Blvd.), Greta Garbo (6901 Hollywood Blvd.), Louis Armstrong (7000 Hollywood Blvd.), and Barbra Streisand (6925 Hollywood Blvd).

The sight of leather-clad bikers, long-haired metalheads, druggies, hookers, and hordes of disoriented tourists, all treading on memorials to Hollywood's greats, makes for quite a bizarre tribute indeed. But the Hollywood Chamber of Commerce has been doing a terrific job sprucing up the pedestrian experience with filmstrip crosswalks, rows of swaying palms, accent lighting, and landscaped medians. And at least one weekend a month, a privately organized group of fans calling themselves Star Polishers busy themselves scrubbing tarnished medallions.

Recent subway digging under Hollywood Boulevard has caused the street to sink several inches. When actor John Forsythe's star cracked, authorities removed many others to prevent further damage. In the next few years, up to 250 stars, including those of Marilyn Monroe (6744 Hollywood Blvd.) and Elvis Presley (6777 Hollywood Blvd.), will be temporarily removed as the subway project expands.

The legendary sidewalk is continually adding new names. Celebrities (or their fan clubs) pay about $4,000 for the honor of a star. But not anyone can buy one; the honoree has to be deemed worthy. The public is invited to attend dedication ceremonies; the celebrity honoree is usually in attendance. Contact the **Hollywood Chamber of Commerce,** 6255 Sunset Blvd., Suite 911, Hollywood, CA 90028 (☎ 213/469-8311) for information on who's being honored this week.

Mann's Chinese Theatre. 6925 Hollywood Blvd. ☎ 213/461-3331. Movie tickets $7.50. Call for show times. From U.S. 101, exit onto Highland Blvd. and turn right onto Hollywood Blvd. The theater is three blocks ahead on your right.

This is one of the world's great movie palaces, and one of Hollywood's finest landmarks. The Chinese Theatre was opened in 1927 by entertainment impresario Sid Grauman, a brilliant promoter who's credited with originating the idea of the paparazzi-packed movie "premiere." Outrageously conceived, with both authentic and simulated Chinese embellishments, gaudy Grauman's theater was designed to impress. Original Chinese heaven doves top the facade, and two of the theater's exterior columns once propped up a Ming Dynasty temple.

Visitors flock to the theater by the millions, not for its architectural flamboyance, but for its world-famous entry court, where stars like Elizabeth Taylor, Paul Newman, Ginger Rogers, Humphrey Bogart, Frank Sinatra, Marilyn Monroe, and about 160 others set their signatures and hand- and footprints in concrete. It's not always hands and feet, though: Betty Grable made an impression with her shapely leg, Gene Autry with the hoofprints of his horse Champion, and Jimmy Durante and Bob Hope used their trademark noses.

Farmer's Market. 6333 W. 3rd St. (near Fairfax Ave.). ☎ **213/933-9211.** Mon–Sat 9am–6:30pm, Sun 10am–5pm.

The original Market was little more than a field clustered with stands set up by farmers during the Depression so they could sell directly to city dwellers. It slowly grew into permanent buildings recognizable by the trademark shingled 10-story clocktower, and has evolved into a sprawling food marketplace with a carnival atmosphere, a kind of "turf" version of San Francisco's surfy Fisherman's Wharf. About 100 restaurants, shops, and grocers cater to a mix of workers from the adjacent CBS Television City complex, locals, and tourists, who are brought here by the busload. Retailers sell greeting cards, kitchen implements, candles, and souvenirs; but everyone comes here for the food stands, which offer oysters, Cajun gumbo, fresh-squeezed orange juice, roast beef sandwiches, fresh-pressed peanut butter, and all kinds of international fast foods. You can still buy produce here—no longer a farm-fresh bargain, but a better selection than the grocery stores.

Don't miss Kokomo, an outdoor gourmet coffee shop that has become a power breakfast spot for show-biz types. Red turkey hash and sweet potato fries are the dishes that keep them coming back.

Griffith Observatory. 2800 E. Observatory Rd. (in Griffith Park, at the end of Vermont Ave.). ☎ 213/664-1191; Internet Web site http://www.griffithobs.com; ☎ 213/663-8171 for the Sky Report, a recorded message on current planet positions and celestial events. Planetarium show tickets $4 adults, $2 kids 5–12, $3 seniors 65+. Sept–May Tues–Fri 2–10pm, Sat–Sun 12:30–10pm; June–Aug daily 12:30–10pm. From U.S. 101, take Vermont Ave. north into Griffith Park.

Made world famous in the film *Rebel Without a Cause*, Griffith Observatory's bronze domes have been Hollywood Hills landmarks since 1935. Most visitors never actually go inside; they come to this spot on the south slope of Mt. Hollywood for unparalleled views of Los Angeles, which sometimes reach all the way to the ocean. On warm nights, with the city lights twinkling below, this is one of the most romantic places in L.A.

The main dome houses a planetarium, where narrated projection shows reveal the stars and planets that are hidden from the naked eye by the city's lights and smog. Mock excursions into space search for extraterrestrial life, or examine the causes of earthquakes, moonquakes, and starquakes. The show has been a grammar-school staple in L.A. for eons; the seats aren't too comfortable for adults, but the Observatory is currently fund-raising to refurbish the auditorium and install updated, high-tech projection equipment. Presentations last about an hour, and showtimes vary; call for information.

The adjacent Hall of Science holds exhibits on galaxies, meteorites, and other cosmic objects, including a telescope trained on the sun; a Foucault Pendulum; and 6-foot-diameter earth and moon globes. On clear nights you can gaze at the heavens through the powerful 12-inch telescope.

DOWNTOWN

El Pueblo de Los Angeles Historic District. Enter on Alameda Ave., across the street from Union Station. ☎ 213/628-1274.

This Los Angeles Historic District was built in the 1930s, on the site where the city was founded, as an alternative to the wholesale razing of a particularly unsightly slum. The result is a contrived nostalgic fantasy of the city's beginnings, a kitschy theme park portraying Latino culture in a Disneyesque fashion. Nevertheless, El Pueblo has proven wildly successful, as L.A.'s Latinos have adopted it as an important cultural monument.

Hollywood Area Attractions

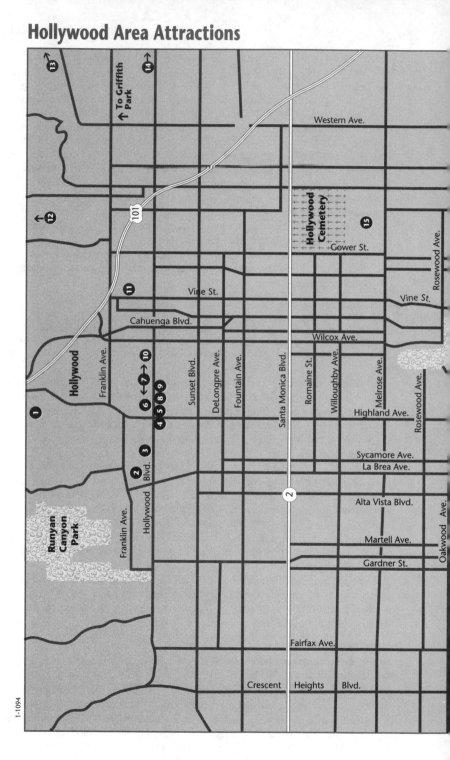

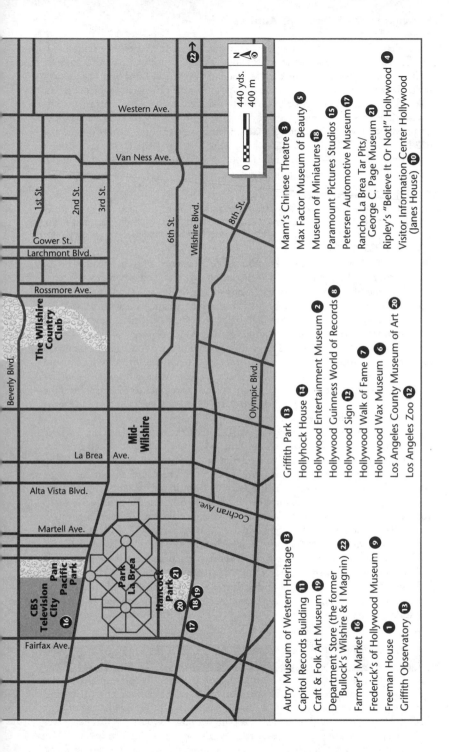

Western Ave.

Van Ness Ave.

1st St.
2nd St.
3rd St.

Gower St.
Larchmont Blvd.

Rossmore Ave.

Beverly Blvd.

The Wilshire Country Club

6th St.

Wilshire Blvd.

8th St.

La Brea   Ave.

Mid-Wilshire

Olympic Blvd.

Cochran Ave.

Alta Vista Blvd.

Martell Ave.

Pan Pacific Park

Park La Brea

Hancock Park ㉑

CBS Television City ⑯

Fairfax Ave.

N

0   440 yds.
    400 m

Mann's Chinese Theatre ③
Max Factor Museum of Beauty ⑤
Museum of Miniatures ⑱
Paramount Pictures Studios ⑮
Petersen Automotive Museum ⑰
Rancho La Brea Tar Pits/
  George C. Page Museum ㉑
Ripley's "Believe It Or Not!" Hollywood ④
Visitor Information Center Hollywood
  (Janes House) ⑩

Griffith Park ⑬
Hollyhock House ⑭
Hollywood Entertainment Museum ②
Hollywood Guinness World of Records ⑧
Hollywood Sign ⑫
Hollywood Walk of Fame ⑦
Hollywood Wax Museum ⑥
Los Angeles County Museum of Art ⑳
Los Angeles Zoo ⑫

Autry Museum of Western Heritage ⑬
Capitol Records Building ⑪
Craft & Folk Art Museum ⑲
Department Store (the former
  Bullock's Wilshire & I Magnin) ㉒
Farmer's Market ⑯
Frederick's of Hollywood Museum ⑨
Freeman House ①
Griffith Observatory ⑬

127

El Pueblo is not entirely without authenticity. Some of L.A.'s oldest extant buildings are located here, and the area really does exude the ambiance of Old Mexico. At its core is a Mexican-style marketplace on old Olvera Street, the district's primary pedestrian thoroughfare. The carnival of sights and sounds is heightened by mariachis, colorful piñatas, and more than occasional folkloric dancing. Olvera Street and adjacent Main Street, are home to about two dozen 19th-century buildings; one houses an authentic Mexican restaurant, **La Golondrina.** Stop in at the **Visitor's Center** at 622 N. Main St. (☎ **213/628-1274;** Monday to Saturday 10am to 3pm). And don't miss **Avila Adobe** at E-10 Olvera St. (Monday to Saturday 10am to 5pm); built in 1818, it's the oldest building in the city.

THE SAN FERNANDO VALLEY

Universal Studios. Hollywood Fwy. (Lankershim Blvd. exit), Universal City. ☎ **818/ 508-9600;** Internet Web site http://www.mca.com/unicity/thehill.html. Admission $34 adults, $28 seniors (65 and older) and children 3–11, kids under 3 free. Parking $5. Summer daily 7am– 11pm; rest of the year daily 9am–7pm.

Believing that filmmaking itself was a bona fide attraction, Universal Studios began offering tours to the public in 1964. The concept worked. Today, Universal is more than just one of the largest movie studios in the world—it's one of the biggest amusement parks, attracting more than five million visitors a year. After walking through the trippy Universal CityWalk mall (see chapter 9), visitors descend into a valley of rides via a set of lengthy outdoor escalators.

The main attraction continues to be the Studio Tour, a 1-hour guided tram ride around the company's 420 acres. En route, you pass stars' dressing rooms and production offices before visiting famous back-lot sets that include an eerily familiar Old West town, a clean New York City street, and the famous town square from the *Back to the Future* films. Along the way, the tram encounters several staged "disasters," which I won't divulge here, lest I ruin the surprise for you.

Other attractions are more typical of high-tech theme park fare, but all have a film-oriented slant. On Back to the Future–The Ride, you're seated in mock time-traveling DeLorean and thrust into a fantastic multimedia rollercoasting extravaganza—it's far and away Universal's best ride. The Backdraft ride surrounds you with brilliant balls of very real fire spewing from imitation ruptured fuel lines. Kids love it. Like the movie that inspired it, the E.T. Adventure appeals to the heart; you ride simulated bicycles on an extraordinary special-effects adventure through principal parts of the film. A Waterworld live-action stunt show is thrilling to watch (and probably more successful than the film that inspired it). The latest special effects showcase, Jurassic Park–The Ride, is short in duration but tall on dinosaur illusions and computer magic lifted from the Universal blockbuster.

Universal Studios is really a fun place. But, just like any theme park, lines can be long; the wait for a 5-minute ride can sometimes last more than an hour. In summer, the stifling Valley heat can dog you all day. To avoid the crowds, skip weekends, school vacations, and Japanese holidays.

2 TV Tapings

Being part of the audience for the taping of a television show might be the quintessential L.A. experience. This is a great way to see Hollywood at work, to find out how your favorite sitcom or talk show is made, and to catch a glimpse of your favorite TV personalities. But you might end up with tickets to a show that may never make an appearance in your *TV Guide* rather than for one of your favorites, like *Mad About You* or *Friends.* Tickets to top shows are in greater demand than others, and getting your hands on them usually takes advance planning—and possibly some time waiting in line.

Request tickets as far in advance as possible. Several episodes may be shot on a single day, so you may be required to remain in the theater for up to 4 hours (in addition to the recommended 1-hour early check-in). If you phone at the last moment, you may luck into tickets for your top choice. More likely, however, you'll be given a list of shows that are currently filming, and you won't recognize many of the titles; studios are always taping pilots, few of which end up on the air. But you never know who may be starring in them—look at all the famous faces that have launched new sitcoms in the past couple of years. Tickets are always free, usually limited to two per person, and are distributed on a first-come, first-served basis. Many shows do not admit children under the age of 10; in some cases, no one under the age of 18 is admitted.

Audiences Unlimited (☎ **818/506-0043;** ticket information hotline 818/ 506-0067) distributes tickets for the top sitcoms, including *Murphy Brown, Seinfeld,* and *Frasier.* **Television Tickets** (☎ **213/467-4697**) distributes tickets for the most popular talk and game shows. Their services are free, and you can reserve by phone. Or you can get tickets directly from the networks:

ABC, 4151 Prospect Ave., Hollywood, CA 90027 (☎ **310/557-7777**). Taped messages on the hotline let you know what's currently going on. Order tickets for a taping either by writing 3 weeks in advance or by showing up the day of the taping.

CBS, 7800 Beverly Blvd, Los Angeles, CA 90036 (☎ **213/852-2345;** ticket information hotline 213/852-2458). Call to see what's being filmed while you're in town. Tickets for tapings are distributed on a first-come, first-served basis; you can write in advance to reserve them or pick them up directly at the studios up to an hour before taping.

NBC, 3000 West Alameda Ave, Burbank, CA 91523 (☎ **818/840-4444** or 818/ 840-3537). Call to see what's on while you're in L.A. Tickets for NBC tapings, including *The Tonight Show with Jay Leno,* can be obtained in two ways: Pick them up on the day of the show you want to see at the NBC ticket counter—they're distributed on a first-come, first-served basis at the ticket counter off California Avenue; or, at least 3 weeks before your visit, send a self-addressed, stamped envelope with your ticket request to the address above.

Shows that appear on FOX, WBN, and UPN as well as many "Big Three" network shows are taped at a variety of studio complexes throughout the city. It's best to call one of the ticket services listed above if you don't have the individual production office numbers or each show. (There are far too many production offices, and production schedules change too frequently, to include a list of them here; you can always try calling information for the number of the company that appears at the end of your favorite show, or calling the network at the numbers listed above for the production office phone number.)

3 More City Sights & Attractions

ARCHITECTURAL HIGHLIGHTS

Los Angeles is a veritable Disneyland of architecture. The city is home to an amalgam of distinctive styles, from art deco to Spanish revival to coffee-shop kitsch to suburban ranch to postmodern—and much more.

The movie industry, more than anything else, has defined Los Angeles. The process of moviemaking isn't—and never has been—confined to studio offices and back

Confessions of a Former Game Show Contestant

People are still impressed when they hear that I was a game show contestant, even though it's been more than 9 years since I won $28,224 on The *$25,000 Pyramid*. There's definitely a pop-culture cachet to a game show appearance: shaking hands with Alex Trebek or Wink Martindale . . . maybe matching wits with up-and-coming or has-been sitcom stars... pulling out bits of grade-school logic or otherwise worthless pop trivia from the vast recesses of your brain . . . your friends and family watching your winnings tally up on the LED readout from home.

Perhaps you've been thinking of taking a chance on fame and fortune next time you're in L.A. Both are more attainable than you might think—actress Markie Post's career began with her audition for a game show; and as far as fortune goes, someone has to win the $100,000 *Jeopardy!* championship!

If you're serious about trying to get on a show, be sure you have some flexibility in your schedule; although most production companies go out of their way to give priority to out-of-town contestants, you should be prepared to return to Los Angeles one or more times for a final audition and/or taping. My own journey from first interview to a victory hug from host Dick Clark took 4 months. Here are some tips that might help you prepare:

The Bubblier the Better: Be friendly, cheerful, and bright at your audition as well as during taping. Be good-natured when you lose or make mistakes and, above all, be exuberant if you win the "big money." When you're onstage, nothing feels quite real; I really did have to remind myself to look thrilled when I suddenly had 25 grand more than I had 60 seconds earlier.

Dress for Success, Part One: Contestant coordinators look for players who won't put off viewers. It's awfully hard for a granny in the heartland to relate to a trendy big-city type. So dress as conservatively as possible for your auditions.

Dress for Success, Part Two: Have you ever noticed that women contestants are always clad in solid blue, red, or green dresses? Producers will dissuade you

---

lots; it's staged in the city's public spaces, it spills out into the streets. The city is an extension of the movie set, and Angelenos have always seen it—and used it—that way. Thus, all of Los Angeles has an air of Hollywood surreality about it that plays itself out in the architecture; the whole city seems a bit larger than life. Cutting-edge, over-the-top styles that would be out of place in other cities, from Tail o' the Pup to the mansions lining the streets of Beverly Hills, are perfectly at home in L.A. The world's top architects, from Frank Lloyd Wright to Frank Gehry, have flocked to L.A., reveling in the artistic freedom they have here. Between 1945 and 1966, *Arts & Architecture* magazine focused the design world's attention on L.A. with its series of "Case Study Houses," modern prototypes for post-war living, many of which were designed by prominent émigrés like Pierre Koenig, Richard Neutra, and Eero Saarinen. Los Angeles has taken some hard criticism as not being a "serious" architectural center, but in terms of innovation and personal style, the city couldn't get higher marks.

Although much of it is gone, you'll still find some prime examples of the kitschy roadside art that defined L.A. in earlier days. The famous Brown Derby is gone, but you can still find an oversized hot dog (the aforementioned **Tail o' the Pup;** see below), and a neon-lit **'50s gas station/spaceship** (at the corner of Little Santa Monica Boulevard and Cresent Drive in Beverly Hills), in addition to some new

from wearing white, black, neutrals, stripes, large prints, or metallics, most of which require lighting and camera adjustments they'd rather not make just for you. Men have an easier time of it; most of you guys already own a suitable jacket or suit.

Most Unglamorous Advice: Remember income taxes. Should you be lucky enough to win big, bear in mind that the retail value of all your prizes will be reported to the IRS as earnings, as well as any cash winnings.

Some Game Shows Currently in Production: In addition to those listed below, shows sometimes advertise for contestants on the front page of the *Los Angeles Times* classified section.

The Price Is Right (Network)   Contestants are chosen from the studio audience to test their shopping expertise. Write for tickets to The Price Is Right, CBS Television City, 7800 Beverly Blvd., Los Angeles, CA 90036.

Supermarket Sweep (Cable)   Do this one with a partner—teams of two use their knowledge of trivia and their supermarket navigation skills to win. Call 213/960-2444.

Shop Till You Drop (Cable)   Pairs compete in games of skill in a replica shopping-mall setting, in which they "shop" to acquire prizes. Call 213/463-7677.

Jeopardy! (Syndicated)   Trivia quiz not for the fainthearted (contestant, that is. It doesn't hurt nearly so much to watch!). Call 310/280-5367.

Wheel of Fortune (Syndicated)   Less about your skill with the "hangman"-style puzzles than your luck spinning the carnival wheel. Call 213/520-5555.

Debt (Cable)   Erase part—or all—of your personal debt by matching wits with veteran game show host Wink Martindale on this wacky hit game show from the Lifetime network. Call 213/468-3300.

structures carrying on the tradition, like the **Chiat/Day/Mojo offices** in Venice (see below).

SANTA MONICA & THE BEACHES

When you're flying in or out of LAX, be sure to stop for a moment to admire the **Control Tower and Theme Building.** The spacey Jetsons-style Theme Building, which has always loomed over LAX, has been joined by a brand-new silhouette. The main control tower, designed by local architect Kate Diamond to evoke a stylized palm tree, is tailored to present Southern California in its best light. You can go inside to enjoy the view from the Theme Building's observation lounge.

Chiat/Day/Mojo Headquarters. 340 Main St., Venice.

What would otherwise be an unspectacular contemporary office building is made fantastic by a three-story pair of binoculars that frames the entrance to this advertising agency. The sculpture is modeled after a design created by Claes Oldenburg and Coosje van Bruggen.

Wayfarers Chapel. 5755 Palos Verdes Drive S., Rancho Palos Verdes. ☎ 310/377-1650.

Constructed on a broad cliff with a steep face, the Wayfarers Chapel enjoys a fantastic spot overlooking the lashing waves of the Pacific. Designed by Frank Lloyd Wright, Jr., son of the more celebrated architect, the church is constructed of glass, redwood, and native stone. Known locally as the "glass church," Wayfarers is a memorial to Emanuel Swedenborg, an 18th-century Swedish philosopher who claimed to have visions of spirits and heavenly hosts. Rare plants, some of which are native to Israel, surround the building. Open daily 9am to 5pm. Phone in advance to arrange a free escorted tour.

L.A.'s WESTSIDE & BEVERLY HILLS

In addition to the design center, don't miss the **Argyle** and **Beverly Hills Hotels** (see chapter 5), and be sure to wind your way through the streets of Beverly Hills off Sunset Boulevard (see "Hollywood at Home" driving tour in chapter 8).

Church of the Good Shepherd. 505 N. Bedford Dr., Beverly Hills.

Built in 1924, this is Beverly Hills's oldest house of worship. However, it's more famous thanks to the share of public tragedy it has seen: In 1950, Elizabeth Taylor and her first husband, Nicky Hilton, were married here; and the funerals of Alfred Hitchcock, Gary Cooper, and Jimmy Durante were all held here.

Pacific Design Center. 8687 Melrose Ave., West Hollywood. ☎ **310/657-0800.**

Designed by Argentinean architect Cesar Pelli, the bold architecture and overwhelming scale of the Pacific Design Center aroused plenty of controversy when it was erected in 1975. Sheathed in cobalt-blue glass that's designed with a gentle curve, the seven-story building houses over 750,000 square feet of wholesale interior design showrooms, and is known to locals as "the blue whale." When the property for the design center was acquired in the 1970s, almost all of the small businesses that lined this stretch of Melrose Avenue were demolished. Only tenacious Hugo's Plating, which still stands in front of the center, successfully resisted the wrecking ball. In 1988 a second box, dressed in equally dramatic kelly green, was added to the design center and surrounded by a protected outdoor plaza.

Rudolph M. Schindler House. 835 No. Kings Rd. (north of Melrose Ave.), West Hollywood. ☎ **310/651-1510.** Admission $5 adults, free to children 18 and under.

A protégé of Frank Lloyd Wright and contemporary of Richard Neutra, Austrian architect Rudolph Schindler designed this innovative modern house for himself in 1921–22. Now restored and home to the Los Angeles arm of Austria's Museum of Applied Arts (MAK), the house—noted for its complicated interlocking spaces, the interpenetration of indoors and out; simple, unadorned materials; and technological innovations—is open Wednesday through Sunday from 11am to 6pm; docent-guided tours are conducted at no additional charge on weekends only.

The MAK Center offers guides to L.A. area buildings by Schindler and other Austrian architects, and presents visiting related exhibitions and creative arts programming. Call for schedule.

☼ Tail o' the Pup. San Vicente Blvd. (between Beverly Blvd. and Melrose Ave.), West Hollywood. ☎ **310/652-4517.**

At first glance, you might not think twice about this hot dog–shaped bit of kitsch just across from the Beverly Center. But locals adored this closet-sized wiener dispensary so much that when it was threatened by the developer's bulldozer, they spoke out en masse to save it. One of the last remaining examples of '50s representational architecture, the "little dog that could" also serves up a great Baseball Special.

HOLLYWOOD

In addition to those listed below, don't miss the **Griffith Observatory** and **Mann's Chinese Theatre** (see "The Top Attractions," above), and the **Hollywood Roosevelt Hotel** (see chapter 5).

Capitol Records Building. 1750 Vine St. ☎ **213/462-6252.**

Opened in 1956, this 12-story tower, just north of the legendary intersection of Hollywood and Vine, is one of the city's most recognizable buildings. Often, but incorrectly, rumored to have been made to resemble a stack of 45's under a turntable stylus (it kinda does, really), this circular tower is nevertheless unmistakable. Nat "King" Cole, songwriter Johnny Mercer, and other 1950s Capitol artists populate a giant exterior mural.

Department Store. 3050 Wilshire Blvd. (at Vermont Ave.).

Formerly Bullock's, then I. Magnin, this classy art-deco gem features a stylish interior with mottled marble wall panels, cubist wall reliefs, and luxurious wood veneers. The main entrance faces the parking lot in the rear; the street-side facade was meant to be admired while flying past.

Freeman House. 1962 Glencoe Way (off of Hillcrest, near Highland and Franklin aves.). ☎ **213/851-0671.** Admission $10 adults, $5 students with I.D.

Frank Lloyd Wright's Freeman House, built in 1924, was designed as an experimental prototype of mass-produced affordable housing. The home's richly patterned "textile-block" exterior was Wright's invention, and is the most famous aspect of the home's design. Situated on a dramatic site overlooking Hollywood, Freeman House is built with the world's first glass-to-glass corner windows. Dancer Martha Graham, bandleader Xavier Cugat, art collector Galka Sheye, photographer Edward Weston, and architects Philip Johnson and Richard Neutra all lived or spent significant time at this house, which became known as an avant-garde salon. The house is open to the public for tours every Saturday at 2pm and 4pm; call ahead to see if scheduled restorations have affected operations.

Hollyhock House. In Barnsdall Park, 4800 Hollywood Blvd. ☎ **213/485-4581.** Admission $2 adults, $1 seniors; kids 12 and under free.

Built between 1917 and 1920, this was the first Frank Lloyd Wright residence to be constructed in Los Angeles. Designed as the centerpiece of an art-filled park, the house was commissioned by oil heiress Aline Barnsdall, yet another in a long line of rich eccentrics who hosted artistic salons in L.A. It's interesting to note that the hilltop park would actually be much larger and extend completely to Hollywood Boulevard and Vermont Avenue if the prudish city of L.A. had not refused Barnsdall's additional gift of land, citing her scandalously born-out-of-wedlock daughter as their cause. Eventually sold to private developers, that apron now holds some of the ugliest strip-mall shopping in the area! Barnsdall Art Park is still quite sizable, however, housing a Municipal Art Gallery and several art workshops in addition to the Wright home, which operates as a small gallery and house museum; the house is currently undergoing extensive repairs for structural damage from the 1994 earthquake. Guided tours of Hollyhock House—which is named for the tall, slender flower whose shape is a recurring motif throughout the home—are offered Tuesday through Sunday at noon, 1pm, 2pm, and 3pm; tours last 45 minutes.

DOWNTOWN

Bradbury Building. 304 S. Broadway (at 3rd St.). ☎ **213/626-1893.**

Built in 1893, this National Historic Landmark is Los Angeles's oldest commercial building, and one of the city's most revered architectural achievements. Capped by a magical five-story skylight, Bradbury's courtyard combines glazed brick, Mexican tile, rich Belgian marble, handsome oak paneling, and lacelike wrought-iron railings. The glass-topped atrium is often used as a movie and TV set; you've seen it in Chinatown and Blade Runner. Open daily 9am to 5pm.

Central Library. 630 W. 5th St. (between Flower St. and Grand Ave.). ☎ **213/228-7000.**

This is one of L.A.'s early architectural achievements. The city rallied to save the library when an arson fire nearly destroyed it in 1986; the triumphant result has returned much of its original splendor. Working in the early 1920s, architect Bertram G. Goodhue employed the Egyptian motifs and materials popularized by the recent discovery of King Tut's tomb, and combined them with a more modern use of concrete block to great effect.

Parking in this area can involve a heroic effort. Try visiting on the weekend and using the Flower Street parking entrance; the library will validate your ticket and you can escape for only $2.

City Hall. 200 N. Spring St.

Built in 1928, the 27-story triangular Los Angeles City Hall remained the tallest building in the city for over 30 years. The structure's distinctive ziggurat roof was featured in the film *War of the Worlds,* but is probably best known as the headquarters of the *Daily Planet* in the *Superman* TV series. When it was built, City Hall was the sole exception to an ordinance outlawing buildings taller than 150 feet. On a clear day, the top-floor observation deck (open Monday to Friday from 10am to 4pm) offers views to Mount Wilson, 15 miles away.

El Alisal. 200 E. Avenue 43, Highland Park. ☎ **213/222-0546.** Free admission.

El Alisal is a small, rugged, two-story "castle," built from 1889 to 1910 from large rocks and telephone poles purchased from the Santa Fe Railroad. The architect and creator was Charles F. Lummis, a Harvard graduate, archaeologist, and writer, who walked from Ohio to California and coined the slogan "See America First." A fan of Native American culture, Lummis is credited with popularizing the concept "Southwest," referring to New Mexico and Arizona. He often lived the lifestyle of the Indians, and founded the nearby Southwest Museum, a repository of Indian artifacts (see "More Museums & Galleries," below). In his castle, Lummis held fabulous parties for the theatrical, political, and artistic elite; his guest list often included Will Rogers and Teddy Roosevelt. The most outstanding feature of his house is the fireplace, which was carved by Mount Rushmore creator Gutzon Borglum. The home's lawn has been turned into an experimental garden of water-conserving plants. Open Friday to Sunday from noon to 4pm.

Union Station. Alameda St. (at Cesar E. Chavez Ave.).

Union Station, completed in 1939, is one of the finest examples of California mission–style architecture, built with the opulence and attention to detail which characterize 1930s W.P.A. projects. The cathedral-size, richly paneled ticket lobby and waiting area of this fantastic cream-colored structure stand sadly empty most of the time, but the MTA does use Union Station for Blue Line commuter trains. When strolling through these grand historic halls, it's easy to imagine the glamorous movie stars who once boarded *The City of Los Angeles* and *The Super Chief* to journey back East during the glory days of rail travel; I like to picture the many joyous reunions between returning soldiers and loved ones following the victorious end to World War II in the station's heyday.

Watts Towers & Art Center. 1765 E. 107th St., Los Angeles. ☎ **213/847-4646.** Gallery open Tues–Sat 10am–4pm and Sun noon–4pm; call for tower tour schedule and directions.

Watts became notorious as the site of violent riots in the summer of 1965, in which 34 people were killed and over 1,000 injured. Today, a visit to Watts is a lesson in inner-city life; it's a high-density land of gray strip malls, well-guarded check-cashing shops, and fast-food restaurants; but it's also a neighborhood of hard-working families struggling to survive in the midst of gangland. Although there's not much for the casual tourist here, the Watts Towers are a truly unique attraction, and the adjoining art gallery illustrates the fierce determination of area residents to maintain cultural integrity against all odds.

The Towers are colorful, 99-foot-tall cement and steel sculptures ornamented with mosaics of bottles, sea shells, cups, plates, generic pottery, and ceramic tiles. They were completed in 1954 by folk artist Simon Rodia, an immigrant Italian tile-setter who worked on them for 33 years in his spare time. True fans of decorative ceramics will enjoy the fact that Rodia's day job was at the legendary Malibu Potteries (are those fragments of valuable Malibu tile encrusting the Towers?). Next to these designated Cultural Landmarks is the Art Center, which has a fascinating collection of ethnic musical intruments as well as several visiting art exhibits throughout the year.

THE SAN FERNANDO VALLEY

Walt Disney Corporate Offices. 500 S. Buena Vista St. (at Alameda Ave.), Burbank. ☎ 818/560-1000.

At first glance, this is just another neoclassical building. But wait a minute: Those aren't Ionic columns holding up the building's pediment—they're the Seven Dwarfs (giant-size, of course).

COLLEGES & UNIVERSITIES
SANTA MONICA & THE BEACHES

Pepperdine University. 24255 W. Pacific Coast Hwy. (Calif. 1), Malibu. ☎ 310/456-4000.

If you drive up the Pacific Coast Highway, you can't miss the Malibu campus of Pepperdine University. The school's enormous rolling green lawn is the size of several football fields—and as inviting as seats at the 50-yard line. Pepperdine is affiliated with the Church of Christ, and has campuses in both Los Angeles and Heidelberg, Germany. The school, which takes a friendly ribbing as "Beach U," boasts a terrific performing arts program with year-round offerings ranging from community theater to visiting opera divas, pop groups like The Kingston Trio, and summertime "Concerts by the Sea" held picnic-style on the lawn mentioned above; call for schedules.

L.A.'s WESTSIDE & BEVERLY HILLS

University of California, Los Angeles (UCLA). Bounded by LeConte St., Sunset Blvd., Gayley Ave., and Hilgard Ave., Westwood. ☎ 310/206-8147.

UCLA enjoys a parklike setting in swanky Westwood and makes for a nice stroll. Most of UCLA's buildings are unspectacular, but you might want to seek out the romanesque Royce Hall and the Morgan Center Hall of Fame, where trophies and memorabilia of the Bruins athletic departments are on display. The prettiest section is North Campus, where you can walk through the Franklin Murphy Sculpture Garden, home to works by Gaston Lachaise and Henry Moore. Although the school only became a full-fledged institution in 1927, UCLA inherited Berkeley's rich academic tradition and is, qualitatively, that top school's peer. Like USC, UCLA is well known for its film school, and end-of-the-year student screenings are some of the hottest tickets in town.

Free 90-minute tours are offered Monday to Friday; reservations are required.

DOWNTOWN

University of Southern California (USC). Bounded by Figueroa, Jefferson, Exposition, and Vermont aves. ☎ 213/740-2300.

Founded by the Methodist Episcopal Church in 1879, the University of Southern California (USC) is the West Coast's oldest private university, and is one of the

West's best schools. The campus was the cultural center of an otherwise rural area when the school was founded more than 100 years ago. Today this downtown site, adjacent to Exposition Park, is more than a bit dodgy, and not high on most tourists' sightseeing lists. If you do go, seek out Widney Hall, a two-story clapboard from 1880 that's the oldest building on campus.

Free 1-hour campus tours are offered Monday through Friday from 10am to 2pm; they depart on the hour from the Admissions Center. USC's football Trojans play in the adjacent Los Angeles Coliseum, centerpiece of the 1984 Summer Olympics.

ETHNIC NEIGHBORHOODS

Los Angeles has the highest concentration of Mexicans outside Mexico, Koreans outside Korea, even Samoans outside Samoa. Tiny Russian, Ethiopian, Armenian, and even British enclaves coexist throughout L.A. But to call it a "melting pot" wouldn't be quite accurate; to paraphrase Alex Haley, it's really more of a tossed salad, comprised of distinct, nearly intact cultures.

The following neighborhoods all fall under the loose "Downtown" label, as we've defined it in "Orientation" in chapter 4.

Boyle Heights. East of downtown; bounded by U.S. 101, I-10, Calif. 60, and Indiana St.

In the first decades of the 20th century, Boyle Heights was inhabited by Jewish immigrants, who have since migrated west to the Fairfax district and beyond. They left behind the oldest orthodox synagogue in Los Angeles, and Brooklyn Avenue, which has since been renamed Cesar E. Chavez Avenue. Boyle Heights is now the heart of the Latino barrio.

Westsiders come "slumming" for Mexican cuisine at **La Serenata dei Girabaldi** (see chapter 6), but many miss my favorite Boyle Heights sight: Near the corner of Boyle Avenue and First Street is **Mariachi Plaza,** a colorful streetcorner where 3-, 4-, and 5-man mariachi bands stand ready to entertain each afternoon and evening. Resplendent in matching ruffled shirts and tailored bolero jackets with a rainbow of embroidery, the mariachis loiter beneath three-story murals of their forebears with guitars at the ready; it's actually commonplace to see someone drive up in a minivan, offer a price for a night's entertainment, and carry off an ensemble to play a private party or other gathering.

Chinatown. Downtown; bounded by North Broadway, North Hill St., Bernard St., and Sunset Blvd.

Hordes of Chinese settled in this once rural area during the second half of the 19th century. Today most Angelenos of Chinese descent are well integrated into the city's suburbs; few can be found living in this rough pocket of downtown. Though it hardly compares in quality or size to the Chinese quarters of London, San Francisco, or New York, Chinatown's bustling little mom-and-pop shops and profusion of ethnic restaurants provide an interesting downtown diversion.

Reconstructed in 1938 a few blocks from its original site just south of Dodger Stadium, Chinatown centers on a mall, **Mandarin Plaza,** at 970 N. Broadway. Go on a Sunday morning for a dim sum brunch at **Ocean Seafood,** 747 N. Broadway (☎ **213/687-3088**), then browse through the curious collection of shops jammed with Chinese slippers, cheap jewelry, and china. You'll also find some upscale stores specializing in inlaid furniture, Asian art, fine silks, and other quality imports.

Chinatown is especially worth going out of your way for during Chinese New Year, a monthlong celebration that usually begins in late January. The neighborhood explodes into a colorful fantasy of sights and sounds with the Golden Dragon Parade, a beauty pageant, and 5K/10K run. There are plenty of firecrackers and all the Lin Go New Year's cakes you can eat.

Koreatown. West of downtown; bordered by Olympic Blvd., Western Ave., I-10, and U.S. 110.

Unlike Chinatown or Little Tokyo, Koreatown isn't a contrived cultural theme park; it's the living, breathing hub of a relatively new Korean-American population, Los Angeles's largest Asian community. Koreans are well known in L.A. as hardworking shopkeepers who have penetrated every corner of the city with nail salons, souvenir shops, groceries, and many other businesses. Many of the shops in Koreatown are run by and for Koreans, often displaying signs only written in their native language. A cruise along Olympic Boulevard between Vermont and Western Avenues discloses strip malls full of food, video, laundry, pet supply, and other workaday shops oriented to Korean tastes.

Leimert Park. Southwest of downtown; bounded by Crenshaw Blvd., Vernon Ave., Leimert Blvd., and 43rd Place.

Fast becoming the center of African American artistic life and historical focus, the neighborhood around tiny Leimert Park features art galleries, restaurants, and shops filled with local crafts and African imports. Throughout the year folks flock to jazz clubs that evoke the heyday of L.A.'s Central Avenue jazz scene, when greats like Ella Fitzgerald mesmerized audiences at swingin' nightclubs. In December, Kwanzaa celebrations enliven Leimert Park even further.

Little Tokyo. Downtown; bounded by 1st, Alameda, 3rd, and Los Angeles sts.

Like nearby Chinatown, this redeveloped ethnic neighborhood southeast of the Civic Center isn't home to the majority of Angelenos of Japanese ancestry; suburban Gardena has that distinction. But Little Tokyo still functions as the community's cultural focal point, and is home to several small-scale paved malls filled with bakeries, bookshops, restaurants, and boutiques, as well as the occasional Buddhist temple. The **Japanese American National Museum** (see "More Museums & Galleries," below) is here, as is the **Japanese American Cultural and Community Center,** 244 S. San Pedro St. (☎ **213/628-2725**), where traditional Kabuki dramas and modern music concerts are regularly performed.

Little Tokyo is shabbier than most any district in the Japanese capital, and has difficulty holding a visitor's attention for much longer than the time it takes to eat lunch. Exceptions to this rule come twice yearly, during the Cherry Blossom Festival in spring, and Nisei Week in late summer. Both heritage festivals celebrate Japanese culture with parades, traditional Ondo street dancing, a carnival, and an arts fair.

MISSIONS

In the late 18th century, Franciscan missionaries established 21 missions up the California coast, from San Diego to Sonoma. Each uniquely beautiful mission was built one day's trek from the next, along a path known as El Camino Real (the Royal Road), remnants of which still exist today. Their construction marked the end of the Indian era and the beginning of the European age. The two L.A. area missions are located in the valleys that took their names. In addition to the one listed below, see Mission San Gabriel in "Pasadena & Environs" in chapter 11.

Mission San Fernando. 15151 San Fernando Mission Blvd., Mission Hills. ☎ **818/361-0186.** Admission $4 adults, $3 seniors and children under 13. Daily 9am–5pm. From I-5, exit at San Fernando Mission Blvd. east and drive 5 blocks to the mission.

Established in 1797, Mission San Fernando once controlled more than 1^1/2 million acres, employed 1,500 Native Americans, and boasted over 22,000 heard of cattle and extensive orchards. The fragile adobe mission complex was destroyed several times, but was always faithfully rebuilt with low buildings surrounding grassy courtyards. The aging church was replaced in the 1940s, and again in the 1970s after a particularly destructive earthquake. The Convento, a 250-foot-long colonnaded structure dating from 1810, is the compound's oldest remaining part. Some of the mission's rooms, including the old library and the private salon of the first bishop of California, have been restored to their late 18th-century appearance. A half-dozen padres and many hundreds of Shoshone Indians are buried in the adjacent cemetery.

MORE MUSEUMS & GALLERIES

Also see "The Top Attractions," above.

SANTA MONICA & THE BEACHES

Museum of Flying. At Santa Monica Airport, 2772 Donald Douglas Loop North, Santa Monica. ☎ **310/392-8822.** Admission $7 adults, $5 seniors, $3 children. Wed–Sun 10am–5pm.

Once headquarters to the McDonald Douglas corporation, the Santa Monica Airport is the birthplace of the DC-3 and other pioneers of commercial aviation. This museum celebrates this bit of local history, with 24 authentic aircraft displays and some interactive exhibits. In addition to antique Spitfires and Sopwith Camels, there's a new kid-oriented learning area, where "hands-on" exhibits detail airplane parts, pilot procedures, and the properties of air and aircraft design. The shop is full of scale models of World War II birds; the coffee-table book *The Best of the Past,* available at the museum shop, beautifully illustrates 50 years of aviation history.

L.A.'S WESTSIDE & BEVERLY HILLS

The Museum of Television and Radio. 465 N. Beverly Drive (at Santa Monica Blvd.), Beverly Hills. ☎ **310/786-1000;** Internet Website http://www.mtr.org/camsm.html. Admission $6 adults, $4 students and seniors, $3 children under 13. Wed–Sun noon–5pm (Thursdays untill 9pm). Closed Thanksgiving, Christmas, and New Year's Days, July 4.

Wanna see the Beatles on *The Ed Sullivan Show* (1964) or Edward R. Murrow's examination of Joseph McCarthy (1954), watch Arnold Palmer win the 1958 Masters Tournament, relive childhood's *Winky Dink and You,* or listen to radio excerpts like FDR's first *Fireside Chat* (1933) and Orson Welles's famous *War of the Worlds* UFO hoax (1938)? All these, plus a gazillion episodes of *The Twilight Zone, I Love Lucy,* and other beloved series are available for viewing within the stark white walls of architect Richard Meier's neutral, contemporary museum building.

Once you gawk at the celebrity and industry-honcho names adorning every hall, room, and miscellaneous area, it becomes quickly apparent that "library" would be a more fitting name for this collection, since the main attractions are requested via sophisticated computer catalogs and viewed in private consoles. Although no one sets out to spend their vacation watching TV, it can be tempting once you start browsing the archives. The West Coast branch of the 20-year-old New York facility succeeds in treating our favorite pastime as a legitimate art form, with the respect history will prove it deserves.

Museum of Tolerance. 9786 W. Pico Blvd. (at Roxbury Dr.). ☎ **310/553-8403.** Admission $8 adults, $6 seniors, $5 students, $3 children 3–12, children under 3 free. Advance purchase recommended. Mon–Thurs 10am–5pm, Fri 10am–3pm (until 1pm Nov–Mar), Sun 11am–5pm. Closed many Jewish and secular holidays; call for schedule.

The Museum of Tolerance is designed to expose prejudices and teach racial and cultural tolerance; it's located in the Simon Wiesenthal Center, an institute founded by the legendary Nazi-hunter. While the Holocaust figures prominently here, this is not just a Jewish museum; it's an academy that broadly campaigns for a live-and-let-live world. Tolerance is an abstract idea that's hard to display, so most of this $50-million museum's exhibits are high tech and conceptual in nature. Fast-paced interactive displays are designed to touch the heart as well as the mind, and engage both serious investigators and the MTV crowd. One of two major museums in America which deal with the Holocaust, the Museum of Tolerance is considered by some to be inferior to its Washington, D.C., counterpart, and visitors can be frustrated by the policy insisting that you follow a proscribed 2¹/₂-hour route through the exhibits.

UCLA at the Armand Hammer Museum of Art and Cultural Center. 10899 Wilshire Blvd. (corner of Westwood Blvd.). ☎ **310/443-7000.** Admission $4.50 adults, $3 students and seniors 55 and over, $1 kids 17 and under; free to everyone Thurs 6–9pm. Tues–Wed and Fri–Sat 11am–7pm; Thurs 11am–9pm; Sun 11am–5pm.

Created in 1990 by the former chairman and CEO of Occidental Petroleum, the Armand Hammer Museum had a hard time winning the respect of critics and the public alike. Barbs are usually aimed at both the museum's relatively flat collection and its patron's tremendous ego. Ensconced in a two-story Carrara marble building attached to the oil company's offices, the Hammer is better known for its high-profile and often provocative visiting exhibits, such as the opulent pre-Revolution treasures of Russian ruler Catherine the Great, or an exhibition entitled "Sexual Politics" assembed around avant-garde artist Judy Chicago's controversial 1970s feminist creation *The Dinner Party.* In conjunction with UCLA's Wight Gallery, a feisty gallery with a reputation for championing contemporary political and experimental art, the Hammer continues to present often daring and usually popular special exhibits; it's most definitely worth calling ahead to find out what will be there during your visit to L.A.

The permanent collection (Armand Hammer's personal collection, which had been promised to the L.A. County Museum but was withdrawn in 1990 amidst great controversy and criticism) consists mostly of traditional Western European and Anglo-American art; it contains noteworthy paintings by Toulouse-Lautrec, Degas, and van Gogh. Several canvases warrant special notice: John Singer Sargent's dramatic *Dr. Pozzi at Home* (1881) feels as though the doctor were an actor about to go on stage; it's a sophisticated masterpiece of Salon painting. Rembrandt's *Juno* (1662), painted as a loving tribute to the artist's mistress, is one of the museum's most important pieces, and one of the finest Dutch paintings in any American collection.

HOLLYWOOD

The first four museums listed below are clustered around Hancock Park, adjacent to the La Brea Tar Pits (see "The Top Attractions," above) on Wilshire Boulevard's Museum Row.

Craft & Folk Art Museum. 5800 Wilshire Blvd. (at Curson Ave.). ☎ **213/937-5544.** Admission $4 adults, $2.50 seniors students, children under 12 free. Open Tues–Sat 11am–5pm.

In 1965, a small restaurant and gallery called the Egg and the Eye began serving up eclectic arts and crafts exhibitions along with modest meals. The restaurant no longer exists, but the gallery has grown into one of the city's largest, opening in a prominent Miracle Mile building in 1995. "Craft and folk art" is quite a large rubric that encompasses everything from clothing, tools, religious artifacts, and other everyday objects to wood carvings, papier-mâché, weaving, and metalwork. The museum displays folk objects from around the world, but its strongest collection is masks from India, United States, Mexico, Japan, and China. Special exhibitions planned for 1997 include a retrospective of California woodworker Sam Maloof (whose custom-made chairs grace many a celebrity home) and a collection examining parallels between Italy's rich textile heritage and traditional bread shapes and textures. The museum is well known for its annual International Festival of Masks, a colorful and ethnic celebration held each October in Hancock Park, across the street.

☼ **Los Angeles County Museum of Art.** 5905 Wilshire Blvd. ☎ **213/857-6111,** or 213/ 857-6000 for recorded information; Internet Web site http://www.lacma.org. Admission $6 adults, $4 students and seniors (62 and over); $1 children 6–17, children under 6 free; regular exhibitions free the second Wed of every month. Tues–Thurs 10am–5pm, Fri 10am–9pm, Sat– Sun 11am–6pm. From the Hollywood Fwy. (U.S. 101), take the Santa Monica Blvd. exit west to Fairfax Ave., then turn left onto Wilshire Blvd.; follow it to the museum.

This is one of the finest art museums in the United States. The huge complex was designed by three very different architects over a span of 30 years; the architectural fusion can be migraine inducing, but this city landmark is well worth delving into. If you fear getting lost forever, head straight for the Japanese Pavilion, designed specifically to accommodate Japanese works and holding the museum's highest concentration of great art. Its exterior walls are made of Kalwall, a translucent material that, like shoji screens, permits the entry of soft natural light. Inside is an internationally known collection of Japanese Edo paintings that's rivaled only by the holdings of the emperor of Japan.

The Anderson Building, the museum's contemporary wing, is home to 20th-century painting and sculpture. Here you'll find works by Matisse, Magritte, and a good number of Dada artists.

The Ahmanson Building houses the rest of the museum's permanent collections. Here you'll find everything from 2,000-year-old pre-Colombian Mexican ceramics to John Singer Sargent's portrait of Mrs. Edward L. Davis and her son, Livingston Davis (1890), one of the museum's most important holdings. There's a unique glass collection, spanning Roman times to the 19th century, as well as a renowned collection of mosaics and monumental silver. The museum also has one of the nation's largest holdings of costumes and textiles, and an important Indian and Southeast Asian art collection.

The Hammer Building is primarily used for major special loan exhibitions. Free guided tours covering the museum's highlights depart on a regular basis from this building. The museum shop is located here, too, and sells merchandise related to current exhibits. You can usually find Japanese teapots, ikebana vases, and sushi accoutrements, as well as interesting jewelry.

The Bing Theater is locally beloved for screening films ranging from silent greats to Golden Age musicals to contemporary favorites; each month's offerings are united by a theme like "Katherine Hepburn Tribute," "Masterpieces of Cinematography," or "The Changing Role of the Heroine"; call for current schedule.

Museum of Miniatures. 5900 Wilshire Blvd. ☎ **213/937-MINI.** Admission $7.50 adults, $6.50 seniors, $5 students, $3 children. Tues–Sat 10am–5pm, Sun 11am–5pm.

With almost 200 exhibits, the Museum of Miniatures is the world's largest repository of diminutive mansions, pint-size automobiles, and intricately decorated minirooms. Completely unbeknownst to most, miniatures-making is a thriving and popular art; almost everything here has been created within the last 15 years. And we're not talking mere dollhouses here (though they have those too): The Museum of Miniatures has perfect $1/12$-scale minis of an antebellum mansion, a Benedictine abbey, and an entire Victorian village. They even have an intricately detailed mini re-creation of Judge Lance Ito's now-famous courtroom, complete with prosecutors and the defense "dream team." Miniature 18K-gold train cars full of rubies, sapphires, and emeralds are pulled by an engine encrusted with almost 200 diamonds. The wonderful museum gift shop has lilliputian tea sets, very small clocks, and tiny Louis XV "chair" brooches; bring your life-size wallet.

✪ Petersen Automotive Museum. 6060 Wilshire Blvd. (at Fairfax Ave.). ☎ **213/930-2277;** Internet Web site http://www.lam.mus.ca.us/petersen. Admission $7 adults, $5 seniors and students, $3 children 5–12, children under 5 free. Tues–Sun 10am–6pm.

When the Petersen opened in 1994, many locals were surprised that it had taken this long for the City of Freeways to salute its most important shaper. Indeed, this museum says more about the city than probably any other one in L.A. Named for Robert Petersen, the publisher responsible for *Hot Rod* and *Motor Trend* magazines, the four-story museum displays over 200 cars and motorcycles, from the historic to the futuristic. Cars on the first floor are depicted chronologically, in period settings. Other floors are devoted to frequently changing shows of race cars, early motorcycles, and famous movie vehicles. Recent exhibits have included the Flintstones' fiberglass and cotton movie car; a customized dune buggy, with seats made from surfboards, created for the Elvis Presley movie *Easy Come, Easy Go;* and a three-wheeled scooter that folds into a Samsonite briefcase, created in competition by a Mazda engineer.

✪ The Autry Museum of Western Heritage. 4700 Western Heritage Way, in Griffith Park. ☎ **213/667-2000;** Internet Web site http://www.questorsys.com/autry-museum. Admission $7 adults, $5 seniors (60 and over) and students 13–18, $3 children 2–12, children under 2 free. Tues–Sun 10am–5pm.

If you're under the age of 45, you might not be familiar with Gene Autry, a Texas-born actor who starred in 82 westerns and became known as the "Singing Cowboy." Opened in 1988, Autry's museum is one of L.A.'s best. The enormous collection of art and artifacts of the European conquest of the West is remarkably comprehensive and intelligently displayed. Evocative exhibits illustrate the everyday lives of early pioneers, not only with antique firearms, tools, saddles, and the like, but with many hands-on exhibits that successfully stir the imagination and the heart. There's footage from Buffalo Bill's *Wild West Show,* movie clips from the silent days, contemporary films, the works of Wild West artists, and plenty of memorabilia from Autry's own film and television projects. The "Hall of Merchandising" displays Roy Rogers bedspreads, Hopalong Cassidy radios, and other items from the collective consciousness—and material collections—of baby boomers.

The Frederick's of Hollywood Museum. 6608 Hollywood Blvd. ☎ **213/466-8506.** Free admission. Mon–Sat 10am–6pm, Sun noon–5pm.

God bless Frederick Mellinger, inventor of the push-up bra, originally known as the "Rising Star." Frederick's of Hollywood opened this world-famous purple-and-pink art deco panty shop in 1947, and dutifully installed a small exhibition saluting all the stars of stage, screen, and television who glamorized lingerie. The collection includes Madonna's pointy-breasted corset, a pair of Tony Curtis's skivvies, and a Cher-autographed underwire bra (size 32B). Some exhibits were lost during the 1992 L.A. riots, when looters ransacked the exhibit. Mercifully, the bra worn by Milton Berle on his '50s TV show was saved. Stop in for a smile, check out Frederick's extensive collection of crotchless panties, and pick up a catalog.

Hollywood Entertainment Museum. 7021 Hollywood Blvd. (at Sycamore Ave.). ☎ **213/469-9151.** Admission $7.50; discounts for students, seniors, and children. Tues–Sun 10am–6pm.

Scheduled to open in October 1996, this facility in the heart of Hollywood's tourist district is devoting itself to the entertainment arts, and plans to display rotating selections from their sizable collection of original sets and props from film, TV, and radio. Initial exhibits will include the complete *Cheers* bar and the Starship Enterprise bridge from the original *Star Trek* series. Fans of the former Max Factor Museum of Beauty will be happy to learn the collection from Hollywood's premiere motion-picture cosmetic designer will be shown at the Entertainment Museum—antique make up pots, glamor photos, and superstar toupees intact.

DOWNTOWN

The first three museums listed below are located in Exposition Park, just southwest of downtown.

California African-American Museum. 600 State Dr., Exposition Park. ☎ 213/744-7432. Free admission; donation requested. Tues–Sun 10am–5pm. Closed Thanksgiving, Christmas, New Year's Day. Parking $3.

This small museum is both a celebration of successful African Americans and a living showplace of contemporary culture. The best exhibits are temporary, and touch on themes as varied as the human experience. Recent shows have included a sculpture exhibit examining interpretations of home; a survey of African puppetry; and a look at black music in Los Angeles in the 1960s. Multimedia biographical retrospectives are also commonplace: An exhibit honoring jazz genius Duke Ellington included his instruments and hand written music. In the gift shop you'll find sub-Saharan wooden masks and woven baskets, as well as hand-embroidered Ethiopian pillows. There are also posters, children's books, and calendars. The museum offers a full calendar of lectures, concerts, and special events; call for the latest.

California Museum of Science and Industry. 700 State Dr., Exposition Park. ☎ 213/744-7400; IMAX theater ☎ 213/744-2014. Free admission to the museum; IMAX theater $6 adults, $4.75 ages 18–21, $4 seniors and children. Multishow discounts available. Daily 10am–5pm.

Celebrating Los Angeles's longstanding romance with the aerospace industry, this museum is best known for its collection of airplanes and other flying objects, including a Boeing DC-3 and a DC-8, as well as several rockets and satellites. Other industrial science exhibits include a working winery and a behind-the-scenes look at a functioning McDonald's restaurant. Exhibits on robotics and fiber optics thrill kids, as does the hatchery, where almost 200 chicks are born daily. Temporary exhibits are well planned and thoughtfully executed. One recent pro–evolution theory exhibit compared the development of chicks, frogs, and humans.

The museum's IMAX theater shows up to three different films daily, from about 10am to 9pm. Most of the films are truly awesome exposés of events on earth and in space; the early shows are often packed with school groups. The two gift shops are brimming with science and aviation toys, model kits, Slinkys, gemstones, and freeze-dried astronaut snacks.

Natural History Museum of Los Angeles County. 900 Exposition Blvd., Exposition Park. ☎ 213/744-3466; Internet Web site http://www.lam.mus.ca.us/facmnh. Admission $6 adults; $3.50 children 12–17, seniors, and students with ID; $2 children 5–12; children under 5 free; free to all the first Tues of every month. Tues–Sun 10am–5pm; closed Thanksgiving, Christmas, and New Year's Day. Free docent-led tours are offered daily at 1pm.

The "Fighting Dinosaurs"—they're not a high-school football team but the trademark symbol of this massive museum: *Tyrannosaurus rex* and *Triceratops* skeletons poised in a stance so realistic that every kid feels inspired to imitate their Jurassic Park bellows. Opened in 1913 in a beautiful columned and domed Spanish Renaissance building, the museum is a 35-hall warehouse of Earth's history, chronicling the planet and its inhabitants from 600 million years ago to the present day. There's a mind-numbing number of exhibits of prehistoric fossils, bird and marine life, rocks and minerals, and North American mammals. The best permanent displays include the world's rarest shark, a walk-through vault of priceless gems, and an Insect Zoo. Dioramas depict animals in their natural habitats, and other exhibits explore human cultures, including one on North Americans from 1660 to 1914.

The Dinosaur Shop sells ant farms and exploding volcano and model kits. The Ethnic Arts Shop has one-of-a-kind folk art and jewelry from around the world. The bookstore has an extensive selection of scientific titles and hobbyists' field guides.

Japanese American National Museum. 369 E. First St. (at Central Ave.). ☎ **213/ 625-0414.** Admission $4 adults, $3 seniors and children ages 6–17, $2 students. Tues–Thurs and Sat–Sun 10am–5pm, Fri 11am–8pm.

Located in a beautifully restored historic building in Little Tokyo, the Japanese American National Museum is a private nonprofit institute created to document and celebrate the history of Japanese in America. The museum's fantastic permanent exhibition chronicles Japanese life in America, while temporary exhibits highlight distinctive aspects of Japanese-American culture.

Museum of Contemporary Art (MOCA). 250 S. Grand Ave. and 152 N. Central Ave. ☎ **213/621-2766.** $6 adults, $4 seniors and students, children under 12 free. Tues–Wed and Fri–Sun 11am–5pm, Thurs 11am–8pm.

This is Los Angeles's only institution exclusively devoted to art from 1940 to the present. Displaying works in a variety of media, the museum is particularly strong in works by Cy Twombly, Jasper Johns, and Mark Rothko, and shows are often superb. For many experts, MOCA's collections are too spotty to be considered world-class, and the conservative museum board blushes when offered controversial shows (they passed on a Whitney exhibit that included photographs by Robert Maplethorpe); but the museum fills what had been a void in L.A.

MOCA is one museum with two buildings that are close to one another, but not within walking distance, and one admission is good for both. The Grand Avenue main building is a contemporary red sandstone structure by renowned Japanese architect Arata Isozaki. The museum restaurant, **Patinette** (☎ **213/626-1178**), located here, is the casual dining creation of celebrity chef Joachim Splichal (see Patina in chapter 6, "Dining"). The museum's second space, on Central Avenue in Little Tokyo, was the "Temporary" Contemporary while the Grand structure was being built, and now houses a superior permanent collection in a fittingly neutral warehouse-type space. An added feature here is a detailed timeline corresponding to the progression of works. Unless there's a visiting exhibit of great interest at the main museum, I recommend you start at the Temporary—it's also easier to park down there.

The Southwest Museum. 234 Museum Dr., in the Highland Park District. ☎ **213/ 221-2164,** or 213/221-2163 for recorded information. Admission $5 adults, $3 seniors (over 55) and students, $2 children 7–18, children 6 and under free. Tues–Sun 11am–5pm. From the Pasadena Fwy. (Calif. 110), exit onto Ave. 43; turn right onto Figueroa and follow the signs zigzagging up the hill to the museum at Museum Dr.

Located on top of a steep hill northeast of downtown, this is the city's oldest museum, considered by some a "best-kept secret" that suffers from lack of recognition and space for its superlative collection. Founded in 1907 by amateur historian and Native American expert Charles F. Lummis (who also designed downtown's landmark "castle," El Alisal; see "Architectural Highlights," above), this privately funded anthropological museum contains the finest examples of Native American art and artifacts found anywhere, including rare paintings, weapons, and a Cheyenne summer tepee. The largest exhibition chronicles 10,000 years of history of the people of the American Southwest. The California Hall focuses on the lifestyles of the first Californians; a separate two-level hall is dedicated to the culture of cold-climate tribes. The museum has a particularly active events calendar that includes a Native

Downtown Area Attractions

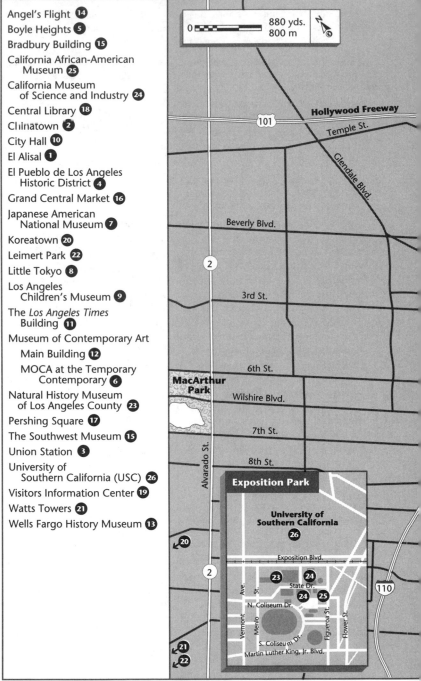

Angel's Flight 14

Boyle Heights 5

Bradbury Building 15

California African-American Museum 25

California Museum of Science and Industry 24

Central Library 18

Chinatown 2

City Hall 10

El Alisal 1

El Pueblo de Los Angeles Historic District 4

Grand Central Market 16

Japanese American National Museum 7

Koreatown 20

Leimert Park 22

Little Tokyo 8

Los Angeles Children's Museum 9

The *Los Angeles Times* Building 11

Museum of Contemporary Art

Main Building 12

MOCA at the Temporary Contemporary 6

Natural History Museum of Los Angeles County 23

Pershing Square 17

The Southwest Museum 15

Union Station 3

University of Southern California (USC) 26

Visitors Information Center 19

Watts Towers 21

Wells Fargo History Museum 13

1-0848

Dodger Stadium

1

College St.

110

Hill St.

N. Broadway

N. Main St.

Sunset Blvd.

Alpine St.

2

Echo Park

101

Pasadena Fwy.

Cesar E. Chavez Ave.

Olvera St.

3 Union Station

4

Arcadia St.

101

5

Temple St.

Harbor Freeway

Civic Center

9

1st St.

10

13 **12**

2nd St.

11

7 **6**

110

3rd St.

8 San Pedro St.

14

4th St.

16 **15**

5th St.

18

17

Pershing Square

Wilshire Blvd.

6th St.

19

7th St.

Central Ave.

8th St.

Figueroa St.

Flower St.

Hope St.

Grand Ave.

Olive St.

Hill St.

Broadway

Spring St.

Main St.

Los Angeles St.

Maple Ave.

Wall St.

9th St.

Olympic Blvd.

11th St.

12th St.

Pico Blvd.

Ready . . . Set . . . Fun! Los Angeles for Kids

Much of larger-than-life L.A. is as appealing to kids as it is to adults. Many of the city's best attractions, like the **Venice Ocean Front Walk,** Hollywood's **Farmer's Market,** and downtown's **Olvera Street** (part of the El Pueblo de Los Angeles Historic District) have a kid-friendly, carnival-like atmosphere. The novelty of sights such as the **Walk of Fame** and **Mann's Chinese Theatre** appeals to kids from 6 to 60 and beyond; curious kids of all ages also love the **Rancho La Brea Tar Pits** and **Griffith Observatory.** (For all of these kid-friendly places, see "The Top Attractions," above.) Older kids, in particular, also love to go on studio tours (see "Studio, Sightseeing & Other Organized Tours," below) and to TV tapings (see above), both of which take them behind the scenes of their favorite shows.

The **Los Angeles Children's Museum,** 310 N. Main St., downtown (☎ 213/ 687-8800), is a thoroughly enchanting place where kids learn by doing. Everyday experiences are demystified with interesting interactive exhibits displayed in a playlike atmosphere. In the Art Studio, kids are encouraged to make finger puppets from a variety of media, and shiny rockets out of Mylar. Turn the corner, and you're in an unrealistically clean and safe City Street, where kids can sit on a policeman's motorcycle or pretend to drive a bus or a firetruck. Kids of all ages can see their shadows freeze in the Shadow Box, board a mock METRO subway train complete with a real ticket machine and video maps, and play with giant foam-filled, Velcro-edged building blocks in Sticky City. And, because this is Hollywood, the museum wouldn't be complete without its own recording and TV studios, where kids can have a taste of fame. Many of the exhibits let kids dress up in costumes and play with stuff that's off-limits to them in real life. The museum hosts many special activities, from cultural celebrations to T-shirt decorating and musical instrument–making workshops. There's a 99-seat theater, where live performances are scheduled every weekend.

The **Los Angeles Zoo,** in Griffith Park, 5333 Zoo Dr. (☎ 213/666-4090) is an easy place to tote the kids around. Animal habitats are divided by continent. The best features are the zoo's walk-in aviary and Adventure Island, an excellent children's zoo that re-creates mountain, meadow, desert, and shoreline habitats.

In addition to these kid-specific attractions, young tourists will also love the wacky **Universal CityWalk** (see chapter 9, "Shopping"), the carousel at **Santa Monica Pier** (see "Piers," below), and the **Travel Town Transportation Museum** in Griffith Park (see "Parks," below). And if all this doesn't keep the kids happy, there's always **Universal Studios** (see "The Top Attractions," above), **Disneyland** (see chapter 11), and the beaches (see below).

American Film Festival, regular lectures, and special children's programs. Phone for the latest. In the shop you'll find authentic Native American drums, kachina dolls, pottery, and sterling-silver jewelry by Native American artist Vernon Begaye.

Wells Fargo History Museum. 333 S. Grand Ave. ☎ **213/253-7166.** Free admission. Mon–Fri 9am–5pm. Closed bank holidays.

Wells Fargo—the Federal Express of its day—was founded just after the Gold Rush as a fast freight and passenger line of horse-pulled stagecoaches; the firm of Henry Wells and William Fargo then branched out into banking. The company's history is inextricably intertwined with the opening of the West; that's proven to be this bank's most fetching marketing gimmick. This compact museum is not as large as the one at the company's main office in San Francisco, but it's worth stopping in for a quick peek at the authentic 19th-century Concord stagecoach and the Challenge nugget—a 2-pound gold lump of 76% purity found in 1975. Visitors can also sit inside a half-built coach and listen to taped excerpts from the diary of a young Englishman who made the arduous journey across America in a similar carriage.

OUTDOOR ART

L.A. boasts an astonishing collection of public art, from nationally acclaimed pieces requiring an endowment for their installation to an ever-increasing panorama of murals, some little more than inspired graffiti. Local freeway corridors are being blessed with new works every day; see how many you can spot in your travels. Here are a couple of areas of the city that are rich with free public works of art.

L.A.'s WESTSIDE AND BEVERLY HILLS

Beverly Gardens Park. Santa Monica Blvd. (between Rexford Dr. and Wilshire Blvd.), Beverly Hills.

This shady, grass-carpeted park skirts busy Santa Monica Boulevard for roughly 2 miles, and is a favorite of Beverly Hills fitness buffs and lunchtime escapees from the nearby work-a-day world. The city frequently displays provocative outdoor art here. There's not been a formal study (that I know of), but I'll bet traffic accidents increase as motorists slow down to examine the latest offerings, which are usually in the sculptural medium—a recent feature was a series of bronze nudes in repose, several times life-size with unbelievably plump, rotund physiques. The park extends from Doheny Drive to Whittier Drive, but the art displays are primarily between Rexford Drive and Wilshire Boulevard.

Downtown

Downtown Los Angeles is a treasure trove of outdoor art, part of a concerted effort during the last decade to rattle the "skyscrapers or skid row" blinders that most residents and visitors cling to. Check out **Pershing Square** (bounded by Fifth, Sixth, Olive, and Hill streets), which was transformed from an overgrown, crime- and drug-ridden eyesore into a modern art park.

L.A.'s own **"Spanish Steps,"** across 5th Street from the Central Library, reflect an artistic intent, with their sensuous shape winding alongside a flowing stream. Meanwhile, the **Central Library's** front courtyard (on Flower Street), was filled with commissioned art for the 1993 grand reopening. Each bench, fountain, and wall bears an inscription, representing the passions of a varied collection of artists. The centerpiece is Judd Fine's "Spine," a cascading series of pools leading up to the library's entrance. From the bottom upward, the components of each level (stair risers, carved inscriptions, pool sculptures, and water spouts) work together to represent evolution in terms of language and intellect. Luckily, you don't need a degree in art appreciation to truly enjoy this work.

For more information on downtown's public art, contact the **Los Angeles Conservancy** (☎ 213/623-2489) or the **Museum of Contemporary Art** (☎ 213/621-2766).

PARKS

In adition to the two excellent examples of urban parkland discussed below, check out **Pan Pacific Park,** a hilly little retreat near Farmer's Market and CBS Studios, named for the art-deco auditorium that, unfortunately, no longer stands at its edge.

SANTA MONICA & THE BEACHES

Will Rogers State Historic Park. 1501 Will Rogers State Park Rd., Pacific Palisades. ☎ 310/454-8212. Park entrance $5 per vehicle. From Santa Monica, take Pacific Coast Hwy. (Calif. 1) north; turn right onto Sunset Blvd., and continue to the park entrance.

Will Rogers (1879–1935) was born in Oklahoma and became a cowboy in the Texas Panhandle before drifting into a Wild West show as a folksy philosophizing roper. The "cracker-barrel philosopher" performed lariat tricks while carrying on a humorous deadpan monologue on current events. The showman moved to Los Angeles in 1919, where he become a movie actor as well as the author of numerous books detailing his down-home "cowboy philosophy."

Located between Santa Monica and Malibu, Will Rogers State Historic Park was once Will Rogers's private ranch and grounds. Willed to the state of California in 1944, the 168-acre estate is now both a park and historic site, supervised by the Department of Parks and Recreation. Visitors may explore the grounds, the former stables, and the 31-room house filled with the original furnishings, including a porch swing in the living room and many Native American rugs and baskets. Charles Lindbergh and his wife, Anne Morrow Lindbergh, hid out here in the 1930s during part of the craze that followed the kidnap and murder of their first son.

The park is open daily 8am to 7pm during the summer, until 5pm the rest of the year. The house opens at 10am, and guided tours can be arranged for groups of 10 or more. There are picnic tables, but no food is sold, so bring your own.

HOLLYWOOD

Griffith Park. Entrances from Los Feliz Blvd., Vermont Ave., Fern Dell (Western Ave.), and Riverside Dr. ☎ **213/665-5188.**

Mining tycoon Griffith J. Griffith donated these 4,000 acres of parkland to the city in 1896. Today, Griffith Park is the largest city park in America. There's a lot to do here, including hiking, horseback riding, golfing, swimming, biking, and picnicking (see "Golf, Hiking & Other Fun in the Surf & Sun," below). For a general overview of the park, drive the mountainous loop road that winds from the top of Western Avenue, past Griffith Observatory, and down to Vermont Avenue. For a more extensive foray, turn north at the loop road's midsection, onto Mt. Hollywood Drive. To reach the golf courses or **Los Angeles Zoo** (see "Ready . . . Set . . . Fun! Los Angeles for Kids," above), take Los Feliz Boulevard to Riverside Drive, which runs along the park's western edge.

Near the Zoo, in a particularly dusty corner of the park, you'll find the **Travel Town Transportation Museum,** 5200 Zoo Drive (☎ **213/662-5874**), a little-known outdoor museum with a small collection of vintage locomotives and old airplanes. Kids love it. The museum is open Monday to Friday from 10am to 4pm, Saturday to Sunday from 10am to 5pm; admission is free.

PIERS

Even though Mother Nature constantly fights back, humankind cannot resist trying to extend its hold from the shoreline into the ocean's domain. Piers have been a tradition in Southern California since its 19th-century seaside resort days; many have long since disappeared (like the beloved Palisades Park, an entire amusement park perched on piles extending offshore), and many others have been shortened by battering storms and are a shadow (or perhaps, stump) of their former selves.

Slightly raffish and somewhat shabby, **Santa Monica Pier,** Ocean Ave. at the end of Colorado Blvd. (☎ **310/458-8900**), is everything an old wharf is supposed to be. Built in 1909 as a passenger and cargo ship pier, the wooden wharf is now home to seafood restaurants and amusement arcades, as well as a gaily colored turn-of-the-century indoor wooden carousel (which Paul Newman operated in *The Sting*). Fishing enthusiasts head to the end to angle, and nostalgia buffs to view the photographic display of the pier's history. This is the last of the great pleasure piers, offering rides, romance, and perfect panoramic views of the bay and mountains. The Pier is about 1 mile up Ocean Front Walk from Venice; it's a great round-trip stroll. The carousel is open every day except Monday.

For more Southland piers locations, see "Beaches," below, as well as "The Orange Coast" in chapter 11.

TOURIST TRAPS

You've heard of all of the following attractions, of course—but you should know exactly what you're in for before you part with your dollars. Not surprisingly, they're all located in the heart of Hollywood on Hollywood Boulevard.

Hollywood Guinness World of Records. 6746 Hollywood Blvd., Hollywood. ☎ 213/463-6433. Admission $7.95 adults, $4.95 children ages 6–12, $6.50 seniors. Sun–Thurs 10am–midnight, Fri–Sat 10am–2am.

Scale models, photographs, and push-button displays of the world's fattest man, biggest plant, smallest woman, fastest animal, and other superlatives don't make for a superlative experience.

The Hollywood Wax Museum. 6767 Hollywood Blvd., Hollywood. ☎ 213/462-8860. Admission $9 adults, $7.50 seniors, $7 children 6–12, free for kids under 6. Sun–Thurs 10am–midnight, Fri–Sat 10am–2am.

Cast in the Madame Tussaud mold, the Hollywood Wax Museum features dozens of lifelike figures of famous movie stars and events. The "museum" isn't great, but it can be good for a cheeky laugh or two. A "Chamber of Horrors" exhibit includes the coffin used in *The Raven,* as well as a diorama from the Vincent Price classic, The *House of Wax.* The "Movie Awards Theatre" exhibit is a short film highlighting Academy Award presentations from the last four decades.

Ripley's "Believe It Or Not!" Hollywood. 6780 Hollywood Blvd. ☎ 213/466-6335. Admission $8.95 adults, $7.95 seniors, $5.95 children ages 5–11.

Believe it or not, this amazing and silly "museum" is still open. A bizarre collection of wax figures, photos, and models depicts unnatural oddities from Robert Leroy Ripley's infamous arsenal. My favorites include the skeleton of a two-headed baby, a statue of Marilyn Monroe sculpted with shredded money, and a portrait of John Wayne made from laundry lint.

VIEWS

It's not always easy to get a good city view. Even if you find a good vantage, the smog may keep you from having any kind of panorama. But, as they say, on a clear day you can see forever. One of the best views of the city can be had from **Griffith Observatory** (see "The Top Attractions," above). The view of Santa Monica bay from the end of **Santa Monica Pier** is also great.

Angel's Flight. Hill St., between 3rd and 4th sts., downtown. ☎ 213/977-1794.

A once-popular downtown landmark constructed in 1901, Angel's Flight was a tiny, open-car cable railway, or funicular, that transported passengers up the steep eastern slope of Bunker Hill, from Hill Street (in the business sector) to Olive Street (then a neighborhood of Victorian homes). Residents agreed to see it torn down in 1969, with the promise that the pieces would be stored and someday reassembled. They got their wish in 1996, as the world's shortest railroad reopened and began offering rides for 25¢. Bunker Hill always offers a great overview of downtown; it's even better from the windows of Angel's Flight as it makes the climb.

Mulholland Drive. Between Coldwater Canyon Dr. and U.S. 101.

Mulholland Drive coasts along the peaks of the Hollywood Hills, straddling Hollywood and the San Fernando Valley. The curvy road provides some amazing views of the city, and offers many opportunities to pull over and simply enjoy. Watch out for drag racers.

4 Stargazing in L.A.: Top Spots About Town for Sighting Celebrities

WHERE TO LOOK FOR YOUR FAVORITE STARS

Celebrities pop up everywhere in L.A. If you spend enough time here, you'll surely bump into a few of them. If you're only in the city for a short time, however, it's best to go on the offensive.

Restaurants are your surest bet. **Matsuhisa, The Ivy,** and **Maple Drive** can almost guarantee sightings any night of the week (see chapter 6, "Dining"). If you're not up to committing yourself to dining at one of these pricey hot spots, try having a cocktail at some of the hotels frequented by out-of-town celebrities, like the **Sunset Marquis, Shutters on the Beach,** or the **Beverly Wilshire** (see chapter 5, "Accommodations"). The trendiest clubs and bars—the **Whiskey-A-Go-Go,** the **Viper Room, The Gate,** and **Roxbury**—are second-best for star-sighting, but cover charges can be astronomical and the velvet ropes oppressive (see chapter 10, "Los Angeles After Dark"). And it's not always Mick and Rod and Madonna; a recent night on the town turned up only Yanni, Ralph Macchio, and Dr. Ruth.

Often, the best places to see members of the A-list aren't as obvious as a back-alley stage door or the front room of Spago. Shops along Sunset Boulevard, like **Tower Records** and the **Virgin Megastore,** are often star-heavy. **Book Soup,** that browser's paradise across the street from Tower, is usually good for a star or two. You'll often find them casually browsing the international newsstand (if they're not there to sign their latest tell-all autobiography). You might even pop into **Sunset Strip Tattoo,** where Cher, Charlie Sheen, Lenny Kravitz, and members of Guns 'n' Roses all got inked. (See chapter 9, "Shopping.")

And don't forget that celebrities keep their larders stocked just like the rest of us . . . you haven't lived until you've stumbled upon Ralph Bellamy or Rosanna Arquette sifting for unbruised tomatoes in the supermarket. Good bets are **Gelson's,** at Sunset Boulevard and Swarthmore Avenue in Pacific Palisades; **Hughes Market,** at Ventura Boulevard and Coldwater Canyon Avenue in Studio City; and **Mayfair Market,** at Franklin and Bronson avenues in Hollywood Hills.

There's no science to any of this. Just keep your eyes peeled—everyone does in L.A.—and you'll more than likely be rewarded. And don't feel bad if you only see Bob Denver. What greater sighting than Gilligan himself?

STARGAZING, PART II: THE LESS-THAN-LIVELY SET
by Mary Susan Herczog

Mary Herczog is a second-generation L.A. native and freelance writer
who thinks that cemeteries and the peccadilloes of famous dead
people are perfectly acceptable hobbies.

Almost everybody who visits L.A. hopes to see a celebrity—they are, after all, our most common export item. Celebrities usually don't cooperate, failing to gather in readily viewable herds. They occasionally trod predictable paths, frequenting certain watering holes, but on the whole, celeb-spotting is a chancy proposition. To increase their odds, many a celeb watcher takes advantage of either Tours Of or Maps To the Stars' Homes—tracking them right to the nest, so to speak.

Heck with that. How can you be sure Mr. or Mrs. Big Star won't have picked that very moment to be out at the grocery store? (Like celebrities do their own grocery shopping—but let's humor them.) There's a much much better alternative. An absolutely guaranteed method of being within 6 feet of your favorite star.

Cemeteries.

Okay, so there's a catch. Favorite Star must be dead. Don't be picky. But let me tell you, cemeteries are the place for star (or at least, headstone) gazing: The star is always available, and you're going to get a lot more up-close and personal than you probably would to anyone who's actually alive.

Nobody lives forever, and sometimes it seems like celebrities, particularly in L.A., have a way of dropping like flies. And they gotta go somewhere. (Yes, some are cremated. Party poops.) L.A.'s a big place, with a lot of cemeteries—and there are a lotta stars in them thar hills. What follows is a guide to the most fruitful.

Note: Some cemeteries, most notably the sullen Forest Lawn, actively discourage star gazing—or at least won't help you find a famous person unless you can prove you're related to them. There isn't enough room to publish details of all grave locations, so the cemeteries will be listed in order (more or less) of friendliness. Some provide maps to the notables; others, if they have the time, will show you around.

For further guides (useful if you don't want to bother a busy cemetery), check out *Permanent Californians* by Judi Culbertson and Tom Randall (Chelsea Green, 1989), and *This Is Hollywood* by Ken Schessler, both of which provide explicit directions to many of the following resting places. The *Hollywood Death Book*, by James Robert Parish (Pioneer, 1992), gives the birth and death dates of all (and we do mean all) Hollywood types, along with the burial places of many.

Hollywood Memorial Park. 6000 Santa Monica Blvd., Hollywood. ☎ **213/469-1181.** Maps to the stars' graves are available at the cemetery.

Weathered Victorian and deco memorials add to the decaying charm of this graveyard, which shares a wall with Paramount Studios. Fittingly, there's a terrific view of the Hollywood sign over the graves, as many of the founders of the community rest here. You'll see their names on the nearby street signs: the Gowers, the Wilcoxes, the Coles. Harvey Wilcox's wife Daeida was traveling on a train when her traveling companion mentioned her estate "Hollywood." Daeida was so enchanted by the name that she gave it to her new property (around Cahuenga and Hollywood Boulevards).

As an older cemetery, Hollywood Memorial quickly became the resting place of choice for many a silent star. Its most notable tenant is Rudolph Valentino; he rests in an interior crypt, originally borrowed from June Mathis, who discovered him. It was supposed to be temporary, until plans for a massive tomb, fitting Rudy's fame, could be built. When Mathis died abruptly shortly thereafter, Rudy was nearly evicted, but his brother quietly purchased the crypt for good. In the same building rests silent star Barbara LaMarr, who made 22 movies and married five husbands before dying at 30 of either anorexia or a barbiturate overdose, or perhaps both (not to mention exhaustion). And there's silent director William Desmond Taylor (under his real name, William Deane Tanner), whose 1922 murder was an enormous Hollywood mystery and scandal, ruining the careers of silent stars Mary Miles Minter and Mabel Normand, who were considered guilty by association. (Sidney Kirkpatrick's excellent *A Cast of Killers* delves into this decades-old mystery in great detail, even solving the crime at last.)

Outside are Tyrone Power, Jr., complete with quote from Hamlet identical to the one on Douglas Fairbanks, Sr.'s, tomb (notice how modest and humble the latter is); Cecil B. DeMille (facing Paramount, his old studio); Alfalfa from the *Little Rascals* (who died after being shot over a disagreement concerning a missing hunting dog. Check out the dog on his grave—contrary to what you might think, that's not Petey); Hearst mistress Marion Davies; Charlie Chaplin's mother Hannah; Bebe Daniels; Valentino's *Sheik* costar Agnes Ayres; John Huston; and a headstone for Jayne Mansfield—she's really buried in Pennsylvania with family. (The odd-looking, tatty grave next to Mansfield's belongs to professional Valentino mourner, the "Woman in Black." Sometimes her ancient daughter is there, cleaning it up.) In other mausoleums are the Talmadge Sisters; Chaplin's son Charlie, Jr.; "Bugsy" Siegel; and Darla from the *Little Rascals.*

There's also Virginia Rappe, the woman who brought down Fatty Arbuckle's movie career. Arbuckle, in the original "Crime of the Century" (or one of them, anyway), was charged with Rappe's rape and murder. Forget what you may have heard: Arbuckle was completely innocent (indeed, he was acquitted of the crime). Not only did he never touch her (much less rape her), Rappe actually died of a botched abortion.

Finally, there's Florence Lawrence. She was originally billed, like all the other actors in Hollywood, as "The Biograph Girl." She fought for her name on the credits and eventually won, becoming the first movie star known by name. But her career faded and she eventually committed suicide—and was buried in an unmarked grave. The woman who fought for recognition in life had the ultimate anonymity in death. (So much for poetic endings, however; recently, Lawrence was given a headstone. Go say hi.)

Holy Cross Cemetery. 5835 W. Slauson Ave., Culver City. ☎ **310/670-7697.** Maps to the stars' graves are available at the cemetery.

This Catholic cemetery is the perfect example of how religion makes for strange bed—er, grave—fellows: In one area, within feet of each other, lie Bing Crosby, Bela Lugosi (buried in his Dracula cape), and Sharon Tate (her unborn son Richard is also on her marker—she was more than 8 months pregnant when the Manson family murdered her); not far away are Rita Hayworth and Jimmy Durante. Also interred here are Tin Man Jack Haley and Scarecrow Ray Bolger; Mary Astor; John Ford; Bonita Granville; Spike Jones; gossip queen Louella Parsons; Mack Sennett; Elizabeth Taylor's first husband, Conrad "Nicky" Hilton; and Rosalind Russell.

And then there's Gloria Morgan Vanderbilt and her twin, Thelma Furness. Gloria was involved in an incredibly prominent custody battle for her daughter, then called "Little Gloria." She lost. Despite the media circus surrounding this event (chronicled in *Little Gloria, Happy At Last* and Gloria, Jr.'s own autobiographies), Little Gloria is now best known for her jeans-hawking. Thelma was another society beauty, who lost her most prominent beau, the Prince of Wales, to one Wallis Simpson, thus changing the course of history.

Evelyn Nesbitt is also buried here. As a teenage chorus girl and the model for the Gibson Girl, she embarked on an affair with Madison Square Garden architect Stanford White. The romance came back to haunt her after her marriage to wealthy—and insanely jealous—Harry K. Thaw. He shot White in a murder that was the subject of the first "Trial of the Century" (unless I've lost count), during which the beautiful Evelyn became quite notorious. (Several books and movies, including the fictional *Ragtime,* deal with this event.)

Hillside Memorial Park. 6001 Centinela Ave., Baldwin Hills. ☎ **310/641-0707.** The front office can provide a guide.

This Jewish cemetery is home to an L.A. landmark: the behemoth tomb of Al Jolson, another humble star. His rotunda (complete with bronze reproduction of Jolson in his Mammy pose) and cascading fountain are visible from the San Diego Freeway (I-405). Also on hand are Georgie Jessel, husband and wife Jack Benny and Mary Livingstone, Eddie Cantor, Vic Morrow, and Fugitive David Janssen. There's also comic Dick Shawn, who may win the award for Best Celebrity Death: In 1988, during his one-man show, he fell to the stage in what the audience assumed was a piece of performance art; it was some time before anyone actually recognized his fatal heart attack.

Westwood Memorial Park. 1218 Glendon Ave., Westwood. ☎ **310/474-1579.** The staff can direct you around.

You just know developers get stomachaches looking at Westwood Memorial. Smack-dab in the middle of some of L.A.'s priciest real estate, surrounded by high-rise office buildings, it couldn't be more incongruous—and, to developers' minds, it couldn't be a bigger waste of land. But it's not going anywhere. Especially when you consider its most famous resident: Marilyn Monroe.

In addition to Marilyn, they've got Truman Capote; John Cassavetes; Armand Hammer; Donna Reed; John Waters's Egg Lady, Edith Massey; Natalie Wood; Playboy playmate Dorothy Stratten (who was murdered by her husband—remember *Star 80*?); Darryl Zanuck; and Will and Ariel Durant, the husband and wife historian/writer team (most notably, the 11-volume *Story of Civilization*), who died within days of each other after a nearly 70-year romance. Peter Lawford was here, but he got evicted after nonpayment of rent, and his ashes were scattered.

Forest Lawn Glendale. 1712 South Glendale Ave., Glendale. ☎ **213/254-3131.** Pretends it has no celebrities.

The most prominent of L.A. cemeteries, Forest Lawn is also the most humorless, which is pretty silly when you realize they've done their darndest to turn their graveyard into an amusement park. What else would you call their regular "dramatic" (read: cheesy) unveilings (complete with music and narration) of such works of "art" as a reproduction of daVinci's *Last Supper* in stained glass, as well as *The Crucifixion* and *Resurrection,* two of the world's largest (and ugliest) paintings? The place is full of Bad Art; it's all part of the continuing vision of founder Hubert Eaton, bane of cemetery buffs everywhere. Eaton thought cemeteries—excuse me, *memorial parks*—should be happy places, uninterrupted by nasty thoughts of, ick, death. So he banished all those gloomy upright tombstones and monuments in favor of flat, pleasant, character-free slabs that are flush to the ground. Voila! A rolling, parklike vista, easy on the eyes and easy to mow.

(If you can, do buy a copy of otherwise exemplary reporter Adele Rogers St. Johns's unintentionally hilarious hagiography of Eaton, *First Step Up Towards Heaven* (available in the gift shop). Otherwise, you can just read *The Loved One* by Evelyn Waugh. It's supposed to be a satire of Eaton and Forest Lawn, but Waugh got away with virtually telling it straight; compare the two books and you'll see what we mean.)

You'd think a place that encourages people to visit just for fun would understand what the real attraction is, but no; Forest Lawn will not tell you where any of their illustrious guests are, so don't even bother asking. This is where the above-mentioned guidebooks come in handy. Forest Lawn Glendale in particular is also immense—and, frankly, dull in comparison to the previously mentioned cemeteries (unless you can get into the kitsch value of the Forest Lawn approach to art). It's really too big just to wander and hope you stumble on someone, but you can always try asking a possibly more accommodating groundsperson for directions.

Contrary to what you've heard, Walt Disney was not frozen and placed under Cinderella's castle at Disneyland. He was cremated and resides in a little garden to the left of the Freedom Mausoleum. Turn around and just behind you are Errol Flynn (in the Garden of Everlasting Peace) and Spencer Tracy (to the right of the George Washington statue). In the Freedom Mausoleum are Alan Ladd, Clara Bow, Nat "King" Cole, Chico Marx, Gummo Marx, Larry Fine (of the Three Stooges), and Gracie Allen—finally joined by George Burns. In a columbarium near the Mystery of Life is Humphrey Bogart. Keep moving to your left, and you should find Mary Pickford (there is a statue of three women and four children in her honor). *Wizard of Oz* author L. Frank Baum is in Section G, while *An American Tragedy* scribe Theodore Dreiser is on the crest of the Whispering Pines hill.

Unfortunately, some of the best celebs are in the Great Mausoleum, which you often can't get into unless you're visiting a relative. If you can get in, you'll see W.C. Fields, Lon Chaney, Clara "Auntie Em" Blandick, Clark Gable and Carole Lombard, Jean Harlow, Irving Thalberg and Norma Shearer, and Theda Bara.

Forest Lawn Hollywood Hills. 6300 Forest Lawn Dr. ☎ **800/204-3131.**

No, it's not actually in the Hollywood Hills—it's more like Burbank adjacent. This Forest Lawn is slightly less anal than the Glendale branch, but the same basic attitude prevails.

On the right lawn, beside the wall near the statue of George Washington, is Buster Keaton. Marty Feldman is in front of the next garden, over on the left. From Buster's grave, go up several flights of stairs to the last wall on the right—there's Stan Laurel.

The Courts of Remembrance are rich ground (so to speak): There you can find Lucille Ball; Charles Laughton; Freddie Prinze; George Raft; Forrest Tucker; and the not-quite-gaudy-enough tomb of Liberace, with his mother and brother George. Outside, in a vault on the Ascension Road side, is Andy Gibb. Bette Davis's sarcophagus is in front of the wall, to the left of the entrance to the Courts. Also on the grounds are Ozzie Nelson; Ricky Nelson; Sammy Davis, Jr.; Ernie Kovacs; Jack Soo; Jack Webb; and John Travolta's mother, Helen.

5 Studio, Sightseeing & Other Organized Tours

STUDIO TOURS
HOLLYWOOD

Paramount Pictures. 5555 Melrose Ave. ☎ **213/956-1777.** Tours $15 per person. Mon–Fri 9am–2pm.

Paramount's double-gated main entrance on Melrose Avenue may look familiar, but it's really an early-1980s reproduction of the original arched Bronson Street gate through which Gloria Swanson was driven in the cinema classic Sunset Boulevard. Paramount, originally known as the Famous Players Film Company, was founded in 1912 by motion picture pioneer Adolph Zukor; the producer merged with the Jesse J. Lasky Feature Play Company and director Cecil B. DeMille to create *The Squaw Man,* the industry's first full-length feature.

Paramount's 2-hour walking tour around their Hollywood headquarters is both a historical ode to filmmaking and a real-life look at a working studio. Tours depart hourly; the itinerary varies, depending on what productions are in progress. Visits might include a walk through the sound stages of TV shows like *Entertainment Tonight, Frasier,* and *Wings.* Cameras, recording equipment, and children under 10 are not allowed.

THE SAN FERNANDO VALLEY

NBC Studios. 3000 W. Alameda Ave., Burbank. ☎ **818/840-3537.** Tours $6 adults, $5.50 seniors, $3.75 children ages 6–12. Weekdays 9am–3pm.

According to a security guard, John Wayne and Redd Foxx once got into a fight here after Wayne refused to ride in the same limousine as Foxx, who called the movie star a "redneck." Well, your NBC tour will probably be a bit more docile than that. The guided 1-hour tour includes a behind-the-scenes look at the *Tonight Show* set, wardrobe, makeup, and set-building departments, and several sound studios. The tour includes some cool video demonstrations of high-tech special effects.

✪ **Warner Brothers Studios.** Olive Ave. (at Hollywood Way), Burbank. ☎ **818/972-TOUR.** Admission $29 per person. Mon–Fri 9am–4pm, Sat (summer only) 10am–2pm.

Warner Brothers offers the most comprehensive—and the least theme park–like— of the studio tours. The tour takes visitors on a 2-hour informational drive-and-walk jaunt around the studio's faux streets. After a brief introductory film, you'll pile into glorified golf carts and cruise past parking spaces marked "Clint Eastwood," "Michael Douglas," and "Sharon Stone," then walk through active film and television sets. Whether it's an orchestra scoring a film or a TV show being taped or edited, you'll get a glimpse of how it's done. Stops may include the wardrobe department or the mills where sets are made. Whenever possible, guests visit working sets to watch actors filming actual productions. Reservations are required; children under 10 are not admitted.

SIGHTSEEING TOURS

Oskar J's Tours (☎ 818/501-2217) operates regularly scheduled panoramic motorcoach tours of the city. Buses (or plush minivans) pick up passengers from major hotels for morning or afternoon tours of Sunset Strip, the movie studios, Farmer's Market, Hollywood, homes of the stars, and other attractions. Tours vary in length (from 2 to 5 hours) and cost ($25 to $50), so call for details and to make reservations.

Next Stage Tour Company offers a unique **Insomniacs' Tour of L.A.** (☎ 213/ 939-2688), a 3am tour of the predawn city that usually includes trips to the Los Angeles Times; flower, produce, and fish markets; and to the top of a skyscraper to watch the sun rise over the city. The fact-filled tour lasts about $6^1/_2$ hours and includes breakfast. Tours cost $47 per person; phone for schedule, reservations, and to hear about Next Stage's other unusual special-interest city tours.

Grave Line Tours (☎ 213/469-4149) is a terrific journey through Hollywood's darker side. You're picked up in a renovated hearse and taken to the murder sites and final residences of the stars. You'll see the Hollywood Boulevard hotel where female impersonator-actor Divine died, the liquor store where John Belushi threw a temper tantrum shortly before his drug overdose, the telephone pole that Montgomery Clift crashed his car into, and the modest graves and palatial crypts where famous folks "live" out their days. Tours cost $40 per person and last about $2^1/_2$ hours. They depart daily at 9:30am from the intersection of Orchid Street and Hollywood Boulevard, by Mann's Chinese Theatre. Reservations are required.

The **L.A. Conservancy** (☎ 213/623-2489) hosts guided walking tours of downtown Los Angeles. The Conservancy conducts a dozen fascinating, information-packed tours of historic downtown L.A., seed of today's sprawling metropolis.

The most popular is "Broadway Theaters," a loving look at movie palaces; other intriguing ones include "Marble Masterpieces," "Art Deco," "Mecca for Merchants," "Terra-Cotta," and tours of the landmark Biltmore Hotel and City Hall. They're usually held on Saturday mornings, and cost $5. Call Monday through Friday between 9am and 5pm for exact schedule and information.

A BIRD'S-EYE VIEW OF THE CITY

Heli USA Helicopter Adventures (☎ 800/443-5487) cruises the Paramount, Universal, Burbank, and Disney studios; hovers over the mega-estates of the stars in Beverly Hills and Bel Air; then winds up over Hollywood's Mann's Chinese Theatre, the Sunset Strip, and the Hollywood sign. The cost of this helicopter "flightseeing" tour, including lunch or dinner, ranges from $99 to $149, depending on the itinerary.

　　Mile High Adventures (☎ 310/450-4447) actually takes passengers on a starlight flight over Los Angeles in a private cabin equipped with a featherbed, a down-filled duvet, king-size pillows, music, a bottle of champagne, strawberries, and chocolate truffles. The flight takes 1 hour and departs from the Santa Monica airport; the price is $229 per couple. Only in L.A.!

GUIDED RUNS

Off 'N Running Tours (☎ 800/523-TOUR or 310/246-1418) combines sporting with sightseeing, taking out-of-town joggers on guided jaunts through the streets of Los Angeles. One-on-one tours are customized to take in the most beautiful areas around your hotel, and can accompany any skill level for 4 to 12 miles. It's a smart way to get the most out of your first morning's jog. Tours cost about $35 (for 6 miles).

BEHIND THE SCENES OF A BIG CITY DAILY

The *Los Angeles Times,* Times Mirror Square, 202 W. 1st St., downtown (☎ 800/ 528-4637 or 213/237-5757), offers editorial tours of the nation's largest metropolitan newspaper. You'll see the newsroom, photo composition facilities, and the test kitchen, where recipes for the food section are developed. Tours of the paper's enormous Olympic Production Plant at 2000 E. 8th St. are also available. Both tours are free; they're offered Monday to Friday at 11:15am and 3pm.

6 Beaches

Los Angeles County's 72-mile coastline sports over 30 miles of beaches, most of which are operated by the **Department of Beaches & Harbors,** 13837 Fiji Way, Marina del Rey (☎ 310/305-9503). County-run beaches usually charge for parking ($4 to $8). Alcohol, bonfires, and pets are prohibited, so you'll have to leave Fido at home. For recorded **surf conditions** (and coastal weather forecast), call **310/ 457-9701.** The following are the county's best beaches, listed from north to south:

EL PESCADOR, LA PIEDRA & EL MATADOR BEACHES　These relatively rugged and isolated beaches front a 2-mile stretch of the Pacific Coast Highway (Calif. 1) between Broad Beach and Decker Canyon Roads, about a 10-minute drive from the Malibu Pier. Picturesque coves with unusual rock formations, they're perfect for sunbathing and picnicking; but swim with caution, as there are no lifeguards or other facilities. These beaches can be difficult to find, as they're marked only by small signs on the highway. Visitors are limited by a small number of parking spots atop the bluffs. Descend to the beach via stairs that cling to the cliffs.

ZUMA BEACH COUNTY PARK   Jampacked on warm weekends, L.A. County's largest beach park is located off the Pacific Coast Highway (Calif. 1), 1 mile past Kanan Dume Road. While it can't claim to be the most lovely beach in the Southland, Zuma has the most comprehensive facilities: plenty of restrooms, lifeguards, playgrounds, volleyball courts, and snack bars. The southern stretch, toward Point Dume, is Westward Beach, separated from the noisy highway by sandstone cliffs. A trail leads over the point's headlands to Pirate's Cove, once a popular nude beach.

PARADISE COVE   This private beach in the 28000 block of the Pacific Coast Highway charges $15 to park and $5 per person if you walk in. Changing rooms and showers are included in the price. The beach is often full by noon on weekends.

✪ MALIBU LAGOON STATE BEACH   Not just a pretty white-sand beach, but an estuary and wetlands area as well, Malibu Lagoon is the historic home of Chumash Indians. The entrance is on Pacific Coast Highway south of Cross Creek Road; there's a small admission charge. Marine life and shorebirds teem where the creek empties into the sea, and waves are always mild. The historic Adamson House is here, a showplace of Malibu tile now operating as a museum.

SURFRIDER BEACH   Without a doubt, these are L.A.'s best waves. One of the city's most popular surfing spots, this beach is located between the Malibu Pier and the lagoon. In surf lingo, few "locals only" wave wars are ever fought here—surfing is not as territorial here as it can be in other areas, where out-of-towners can be made to feel unwelcome. Surrounded by all of Malibu's hustle and bustle, Surfrider isn't recommended for those seeking peace and quiet.

TOPANGA STATE BEACH   Noise from the highway prevents solitude at this short, narrow strip of sand located where Topanga Canyon Blvd. emerges from the mountains. Why go? Ask the surfers who wait in line to catch Topanga's excellent breaks. There's restrooms and lifeguard services, but little else.

WILL ROGERS STATE BEACH   Three miles along Pacific Coast Highway between Sunset Boulevard and the Santa Monica border are named for the American humorist whose ranch (now a state historic park) is nestled above the palisades, which provide the striking backdrop for this popular beach. A pay parking lot extends the entire length of Will Rogers, and facilities include restrooms, lifeguards, and a snack hut in season. While sufing is only so-so, the waves are friendly for swimmers of all ages.

SANTA MONICA STATE BEACH   The beaches on either side of the Santa Monica Pier are popular for their white sands and easy accessibility. There are big parking lots, eateries, and lots of well-maintained bathrooms. A paved beach path runs along here, allowing you to walk, bike, or skate to Venice and points south. Colorado Boulevard leads to the pier; turn north on Pacific Coast Highway below the coastline's striking bluffs, or south along Ocean Avenue; you'll find parking lots in both directions.

VENICE BEACH   Moving south from the city of Santa Monica, the paved pedestrian Promenade becomes Ocean Front Walk, and gets progressively weirder until it reaches an apex at Washington Boulevard and the Venice fishing pier. Although people swim and sunbathe here, Venice Beach's character is defined by the sea of humanity which gathers here, plus the bevy of boardwalk vendors and old-fashioned "walk-streets," lined with beach cottages, a block away. Park on the sidestreets or in plentiful pay lots west of Pacific Avenue.

N1

27 Topanga
State Park

405

Malibu
Creek
State
Park

Brent-
wood

West-
wood

Pacific
Palisades

10

Sunset Blvd.

Solstice
Canyon
Park

N1

West
Los Angeles

7

Pacific Coast Hwy.

9

13

8

1

Lincoln Blvd.

Malibu

Santa
Monica

11

12

14

15

16

Venice

17

Marina
del Rey

Playa
del Rey

see inset map at right

Beaches

El Pescador, La Piedra,
& El Matador Beaches **3**
Hermosa Beach **19**
Leo Carrillo Beach **2**
Long Beach **25**
Manhattan Beach **18**
Marina del Rey Beach **17**
North County Line Beach **1**
Paradise Cove **6**
Point Dume Beach **5**
Redondo Beach **20**
Santa Monica Beach **11**
Seal Beach **26**
Surfrider Beach **8**
Torrance Beach **21**
Venice Beach **15**
Zuma Beach **4**

Sights & Attractions

Chiat/Day/Mojo Headquarters **14**
J. Paul Getty Museum **9**
Museum of Flying **13**
The Narrowest House **23**
Pepperdine University **7**
Queen Mary **24**
Venice Ocean Front Walk **16**
Wayfarers Chapel **22**
Will Rodgers State Historic Park **10**
Santa Monica Pier **12**

Santa

Monica

Bay

1-1095

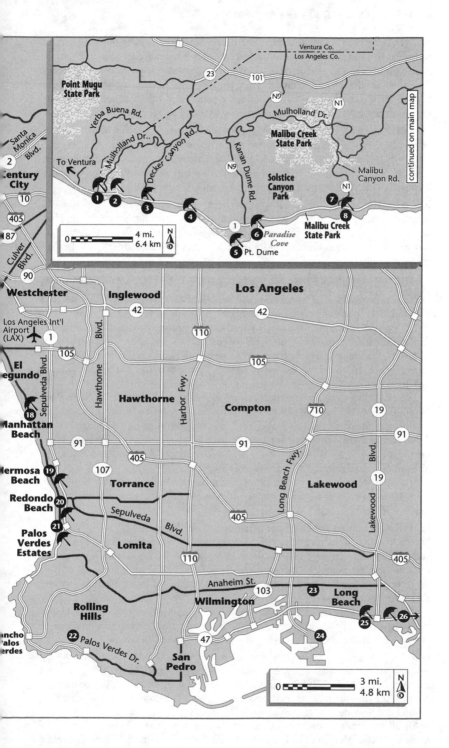

Point Mugu State Park

Yerba Buena Rd.

Mulholland Dr.

Ventura Co.
Los Angeles Co.

23

101

N9

N1

Mulholland Dr.

Malibu Creek State Park

Decker Canyon Rd.

Karan Dume Rd.

N9

Solstice Canyon Park

Malibu Canyon Rd.

To Ventura

Santa Monica Blvd.

2

Century City

10

405

87

Culver Blvd.

90

Mulholland Dr.

1

2

3

4

1

6 *Paradise Cove*

5 Pt. Dume

N1

7

8

Malibu Creek State Park

continued on main map

0   4 mi.
      6.4 km

N

Westchester

Inglewood

Los Angeles

Los Angeles Int'l Airport (LAX) **1**

42

42

110

105

105

Blvd.

Hawthorne

Harbor Fwy.

710

19

El Segundo

Sepulveda Blvd.

Hawthorne

Compton

18

Manhattan Beach

91

91

91

Hermosa Beach **19**

107

405

Torrance

Lakewood

19

Lakewood Blvd.

Redondo Beach **20**

21

Sepulveda Blvd.

405

Long Beach Fwy.

Palos Verdes Estates

Lomita

110

405

Anaheim St.

Rolling Hills

22 Palos Verdes Dr.

Rancho Palos Verdes

Wilmington

103

23

Long Beach

47

San Pedro

24

25

26

0   3 mi.
      4.8 km

N

159

MANHATTAN STATE BEACH   The Beach Boys used to hang out (and surf, of course) at this wide, friendly beach backed by beautiful ocean-view homes. Plenty of parking on 36 blocks of sidestreets (between Rosecrans Avenue and the Hermosa Beach border) draw weekend crowds from the L.A. area. Manhattan has some of the best surfing around, along with restrooms, lifeguards, and volleyball courts; Manhattan Beach Boulevard leads west to the fishing pier and adjacent seafood restaurants.

HERMOSA CITY BEACH   A very, very wide white-sand beach with tons to recommend it, Hermosa extends to either side of the pier and includes "The Strand," a pedestrian lane that runs its entire length. Main access is at the foot of Pier Avenue, which itself is lined with interesting shops. There's plenty of street parking, restrooms, lifeguards, volleyball courts, fishing pier, playgrounds, and good surfing.

REDONDO STATE BEACH   Popular with surfers, bicyclists, and joggers, Redondo's white sand and ice plant-carpeted dunes is just south of tiny King Harbor, along "The Esplanade" (S. Esplanade Drive). Get there via Pacific Coast Highway or Torrance Boulevard. Facilities include restrooms, lifeguards, and volleyball courts.

7 Golf, Hiking & Other Fun in the Surf & Sun

BICYCLING   Los Angeles is great for biking. If you're into distance pedaling, you can do no better than the flat 22-mile paved **Ocean Front Walk** that runs along the sand from Pacific Palisades in the north to Torrance in the south. The path attracts all levels of riders, so it gets pretty busy on weekends. For information on this and other city bike routes, phone the **Metropolitan Transportation Authority** (☎ 213/ 244-6539).

The best place to mountain bike is along the trails of **Malibu Creek State Park** (☎ 800/533-7275 or 818/880-0350), in the Santa Monica Mountains between Malibu and the San Fernando Valley. Fifteen miles of trails rise to a maximum of 3,000 feet and are appropriate for intermediate to advanced bikers. Pick up a trail map at the park entrance, 4 miles south of U.S. 101 off Las Virgenes Road, just north of Mulholland Highway. Park admission is $5 per car.

Sea Mist Rental, 1619 Ocean Front Walk, Santa Monica (☎ 310/395-7076), rents 10-speed cruisers for $5 per hour and $14 per day; 15-speed mountain bikes rent for $6 per hour and $20 per day.

FISHING   **Marina del Rey Sport Fishing,** 13759 Fiji Way (☎ 310/822-3625), known locally as "Captain Frenchy's," has four deep-sea boats departing daily on half- and full-day ocean fishing trips. Of course, it depends on what's running when you're out, but bass, barracuda, halibut, and yellowtail tuna are the most common catches on these party boats. Excursions cost from $20 to $25, and include bait and tackle. Phone for reservations.

No permit is required to cast from shore or drop a line from a pier. Local anglers will hate me for giving away their secret spot, but the best saltwater fishing spot in all of L.A. is at the foot of Torrance Boulevard in Redondo Beach.

GOLF   The greater Los Angeles area has more than 100 golf courses, which vary in quality from abysmal to superb. **American Golf Corp.,** 1633 26th St., Santa Monica (☎ 800/468-7952 or 310/829-4653; fax 310/829-4990), guarantees reserved tee times at more than 16 top area courses. The company can also arrange lessons and provide information on local tournaments.

Of all the city's courses, you can't get more central than **Rancho Park Golf Course,** 10460 W. Pico Blvd. (☎ 310/838-7373), located smack-dab in the middle of L.A.'s Westside. The par-71 course has lots of tall trees, but not enough to dot out the towering Century City buildings next door. Greens fees are $17 Monday through Friday, and $22 on weekends. Reservations are only granted to golfers registered with the city but anyone can show up, sign in, and take their chances, which are generally pretty good on weekdays after 11am or so. Rancho also has a 9-hole par-3 that costs $6 on weekends, $5 weekdays (☎ 310/838-7561).

Industry Hills Golf Club, 1 Industry Hills Pkwy., City of Industry (☎ 818/810-4455), has two 18-hole courses designed by William Bell. Together they encompass 8 lakes, 160 bunkers, and long fairways. The Eisenhower Course, which consistently ranks among *Golf Digest's* top 25 public courses, has extra-large undulating greens and the challenge of thick kikuyu rough. An adjacent driving range is lit for night use. Greens fees are $45 on Monday through Thursday and $60 on Friday through Sunday, including cart; call in advance for tee times.

HANG GLIDING   Up and down the California coast, it's not uncommon to see people poised on the crests of hills, hanging from enormous colorful kites. You can, too. **Windsports International,** 16145 Victory Blvd., Van Nuys (☎ 818/988-0111), offers flight instruction and rentals for both novices and experts. A 1-day lesson in a solo hang glider on a bunny hill costs $99. If it's more of a thrill you're looking for, choose the $125, 3,000-foot high tandem flight, where you are physically connected to an instructor. Lessons take off from varying spots in the San Fernando Valley, depending on the winds. Phone for reservations.

HIKING   The **Santa Monica Mountains,** a small range that runs only 50 miles from Griffith Park to Point Mugu, on the coast north of Malibu, makes Los Angeles a great place for hiking. The mountains peak at 3,111 feet and are part of the Santa Monica Mountains National Recreation Area, a contiguous conglomeration of 350 public parks and 65,000 acres. Many animals make their homes in this area, including deer, coyote, rabbit, skunk, rattlesnake, fox, hawk, and quail. The hills are also home to almost 1,000 drought-resistant plant species, including live oak and coastal sage.

Hiking is best after spring rains, when the hills are green, flowers are in bloom, and the air is clear. Summers can be very hot; hikers should always carry fresh water. Beware of poison oak, a hearty shrub that's common on the West Coast. Usually found among oak trees, poison oak has leaves in groups of three, with waxed surfaces and prominent veins. If you come into contact with this itch-producing plant, bathe yourself in calamine lotion, or the ocean.

For trail maps and more information, contact the **National Parks Service** (☎ 818/597-1036), or stop by their visitor center at 30401 Agoura Rd., Suite 100, in Agoura Hills. They're open Monday to Friday from 8am to 5pm, and Saturday and Sunday from 9am to 5pm. Some areas are administered by the **California Dept. of Parks** (☎ 818/880-0350); their offices are located in Calabasas at 1925 Las Virgenes Rd.

Santa Ynez Canyon, in Pacific Palisades, is a long and difficult climb that rises steadily for about 3 miles. At the top, hikers are rewarded with fantastic views over the Pacific. Also at the top is Trippet Ranch, a public facility providing water, restrooms, and picnic tables. From Santa Monica, take Pacific Coast Highway (Calif. 1) north. Turn right onto Sunset Boulevard, then left onto Palisades Drive. Continue for 2¹/₂ miles, turn left onto Verenda de la Montura, and park at the cul-de-sac at the end of the street, where you'll find the trailhead.

Temescal Canyon, in Pacific Palisades, is far easier than the Santa Ynez trail and, predictably, far more popular. A favorite of locals, this is one of the quickest routes into the wilderness. Hikes here are anywhere from 1 to 5 miles. From Santa Monica, take Pacific Coast Highway (Calif. 1) north; turn right onto Temescal Canyon Road, and follow it to the end. Sign in with the gatekeeper, who can also answer your questions.

Will Rogers State Historic Park, Pacific Palisades, is also a terrific place for hiking. An intermediate-level hike from the park's entrance ends at Inspiration Point, a plateau from which you can see a good portion of L.A.'s Westside. See "Parks," above, for complete information.

HORSEBACK RIDING

The **Los Angeles Equestrian Center,** 480 Riverside Dr., Burbank (☎ 818/ 840-9066), rents horses by the hour for western or English riding through Griffith Park's hills. There's a 200-pound weight limit, and children under 12 are not permitted to ride. Horse rental costs $13 per hour, and there's a 2-hour rental maximum. The stables are open Monday through Friday 8am to 7pm and Saturday and Sunday 8am to 4pm.

Sunrise Downs Equestrian Center, 11900 Big Tujunga Canyon Rd., Tujunga (☎ 818/353-9410), offers 2-, 3-, and 4-hour guided day or evening horseback tours through the San Gabriel Mountains and the scenic San Fernando Valley. They charge $25 per hour, per person; there's a two-person minimum.

JET SKIING   Nature Tours, 1759 9th St., Suite 201, Santa Monica (☎ 310/ 452-7508), offers Personal Watercraft (PWC) rentals and lessons, teaching all levels of riders how to get the most out of jet skis and the more popular, sit-down style WaveRunners. Riders of all levels learn in the harbor's calm water then venture into open Santa Monica Bay. Rates range from $62 to $80 an hour for different size crafts—the larger ones even have a small ice-chest built in under the seat!

SEA KAYAKING   Sea kayaking is all the rage in Southern California; if you've ever tried it, you'll know why. Unlike river kayaks, in which your legs are actually inside the boat's hull, paddlers sit on top of sea kayaks and can maneuver them more easily than canoes.

Southwind Kayak Center, 2801 W. Pacific Coast Hwy. (☎ 800/768-8494 or 714/261-0200), rents sea kayaks for use in the bay or open ocean at rates of $8 to $10 per hour; instructional classes are available on weekends only. They also conduct bird-watching kayak expeditions into Upper Newport Bay Ecological Reserve at rates of $40 to $65.

Island Packers, 1867 Spinnaker Dr., Ventura (☎ 805/642-1393), arranges small group tours to Channel Islands National Park. Half- and whole-day excursions allow you to enjoy the rugged coastline, sea lions, and teeming tidepools of Anacapa, Santa Barbara, or Santa Rosa Islands. Bring a picnic lunch and enjoy the wild beauty of this National Park. Fares range from $21 to $65 for adults, $14 to $45 for kids 12 and under. Camping is available on three islands; permits are required and fares are slightly higher. Two-day adventures to secluded and unspoiled San Miguel Island can also be arranged, with meals and berth accommodations included, for $215 to $235.

SKATING   The 22-mile-long Ocean Front Walk that runs from Pacific Palisades to Torrance is one of the premiere skating spots in the country. In-line skating is especially popular, but conventionals are often seen here, too. Skating is allowed just about everywhere bicycling is, but beware that cyclists have the right of way. **Spokes 'n' Stuff,** 4175 Admiralty Way, Marina del Rey (☎ 310/306-3332), is just one of many places to rent wheels near the Venice portion of Ocean Front Walk. Skates cost $5 per hour; knee pads and wrist guards come with every rental.

SURFING Surfing was invented by the Polynesians; Captain Cook made note of it in Oahu in 1778. George Freeth (1883–1918) is widely credited with introducing the sport to California; he first surfed Redondo Beach in 1907. But the sport didn't catch on until the '50s, when California Institute of Technology graduate Bob Simmons invented a more maneuverable lightweight fiberglass board. The Beach Boys and other surf-music groups popularized Southern California in the minds of beach-babes and -dudes everywhere, and the rest, as they say, is history.

Boards are available for rent at shops near all top surfing beaches in the L.A. area, including **Zuma Jay Surfboards,** 22775 Pacific Coast Hwy, Malibu (☎ 310/ 456-8044); you'll find the shop about a quarter mile south of Malibu Pier. Rentals are $20 per day, plus $8–$10 for wetsuits in winter.

TENNIS While soft-surface courts are more popular on the East Coast, hard surfaces are most common in California. If your hotel doesn't have a court and can't suggest any courts nearby, try the well-maintained, well-lit **Griffith Park Tennis Courts,** on Commonwealth Road, just east of Vermont Avenue (☎ 213/485-5555). Or call the **City of Los Angeles Department of Recreation and Parks** (☎ 213/ 485-5555) to make a reservation at a municipal court near you.

WINDSURFING Invented and patented by Hoyle Schweitzer of Torrance in 1968, windsurfing, or sailboarding, is a fun sport that's much more difficult than it looks. The **Long Beach Windsurfing Center,** 3850 E. Ocean Ave., Long Beach (☎ 310/433-1014), offers lesson and rentals in Alamitos Bay. Twenty-five dollars will get you the use of a board for 4 hours; an $89 learner's package includes instruction from 8am to noon, use of board and wetsuit, and a certificate for a free half-day rental once you've gotten the hang of it.

8 Spectator Sports

BASEBALL Los Angeles has two major-league baseball teams. The **Los Angeles Dodgers** (☎ 213/224-1500) play at Dodger Stadium, 1000 Elysian Park, near Sunset Boulevard. If you're lucky, you just may get to see Hideo Nomo, the Dodgers' Japanese sensation, pitch before a hometown crowd (Hideo is actually the second Japanese player to play in the Big Leagues, but the first of any merit). If you go to a game, don't be surprised by the apparent apathy of the crowd; traffic is so bad getting to and from Dodger Stadium that the fans usually arrive late, around the second or third inning, and leave early—the stands empty out during the seventh inning. Dodgers' fans are an odd bunch.

The Disney-owned **California Angels** (☎ 714/634-2000) call Anaheim Stadium, at 2000 S. State College Boulevard (near Katella Avenue) in Anaheim, home. More often than not, games are populated by displaced fans there to see the visiting team rather than diehard Angels' supporters. If you go to cheer on your hometown Yankees, White Sox, or Twins, you'll probably be right at home in the crowd.

Since 1995's baseball strike, tickets to ball games have been very easy to get, though the best seats still go to season ticket holders.

BASKETBALL Los Angeles has two National Basketball Association franchises: the **L.A. Lakers** (☎ 310/419-3100), who play at the Great Western Forum, 3900 W. Manchester Boulevard (at Prairie Avenue) in Inglewood; and the **L.A. Clippers** (☎ 213/745-0400), who hold court in the L.A. Sports Arena, 3939 S. Figueroa

St., near downtown. Good seats to Lakers games are all but impossible to acquire, though tickets in the nosebleed section are often available. They're practically giving away tickets to Clippers games—except for when they're playing the Lakers, of course.

FOOTBALL   Football fans are out of luck in L.A. now. The two former Los Angeles–area NFL teams both left town in 1995: the Raiders went back to Oakland, and the Rams ran for St. Louis.

HORSE RACING   The scenic **Hollywood Park Racetrack,** 1050 S. Prairie Ave., in Inglewood (☎ 310/419-1500), with its lakes and flowers, features thoroughbred racing from early April through July as well as in November and December. The $1-million Hollywood Gold Cup is also run here. Well-placed monitors project views of the back stretch as well as stop-action replays of photo finishes. The track restaurant, Citation (named after the Triple Crown–winning thoroughbred), features an eclectic menu that includes chicken, beef, pork, and ostrich dishes, but no horse meat, of course. Races are usually held Wednesday through Sunday. Post times are 1pm in summer (at 7pm on Friday), and 12:30pm in the fall. General admission is $6, $25 to the clubhouse.

One of the most beautiful tracks in the country, **Santa Anita Racetrack,** 285 W. Huntington Dr., Arcadia (☎ 818/574-7223), offers thoroughbred racing from October through mid-November and December through late April. The track was featured in the Marx Brothers' film *A Day at the Races,* and in the 1954 version of *A Star Is Born.* On weekdays during the racing season, the public is invited to watch morning workouts from 7:30 to 9:30am. Post time is 12:30 or 1pm. Admission is $4.

ICE HOCKEY   The NHL's **L.A. Kings** (☎ 310/673-6003) play at the Great Western Forum, 3900 W. Manchester Boulevard (at Prairie Avenue), in Inglewood. The Disney-owned **Mighty Ducks** play at Arrowhead Pond, Anaheim (☎ 714/704-2500).

Cruising L.A.: Exploring the City by Car

1 Hollywood at Home: A Driving Tour

Ever since the days before talkies, visitors to Los Angeles have wanted to see just how the rich and famous live. Today it's big business—maps of dubious accuracy are sold on Sunset Strip street corners, and at least a dozen tour operators shuttle vanloads of looky-loos daily through Beverly Hills.

Sure, it's nice and easy to lay out your cash, climb on the bus, and sit back for the ride and the regular spiel. But it's much more fun to do it yourself. By setting your own pace, you can skip the cookie-cutter mansions—yes, there is such a thing—of yawn-inspiring celebs and take your time poking around the sites associated with the legendary (or just plain famous) folks that really give you a thrill.

Go where the tour vans can't—deep into the surrounding hillsides to spy on the rustic star retreats dating from Hollywood's Golden Age. Swaying palms silhouetted against a clear, sunny Los Angeles sky seem an unlikely backdrop for tragedy, but don't be fooled: Some of the homes you'll see are more than the humble abodes of their famous residents; they're the notorious stage sets for some of the movie world's greatest scandals. Behind their innocent facades and unassuming walls, a few even hide the truths to Hollywood mysteries that may never be solved.

Have fun!

Start: 8400 block of Santa Monica Boulevard in West Hollywood.

Finish: Sunset Boulevard at Beverly Glen in Bel-Air.

Time: Allow 3 to 4 hours, not including time spent dining.

Best and Worst Times: Anytime during daylight hours is good for the drive itself, but try to avoid the 12:30 to 1:30pm show-biz lunch rush at the eateries listed.

Related Tip: Notice the streetlamps all along the way—some of the city's loveliest and most elaborate fixtures line the route.

☕ **STARTING OUT** Your mother was right, you know—the best way to start the day is with a power breakfast at one of these local hangouts:

You're as likely to see Hollywood names dining with their high-powered agents at **Hugo's,** 8401 Santa Monica Blvd., at King's Rd.

(☎ 213/654-3993), as you are grungy struggling artists strolling in from the surrounding apartment buildings. Everyone is lured by the casual restaurant's legendary tasty breakfast fare, served throughout the day. Hugo's also offers a selection of pastas and other dishes, many imbued with a refreshingly unique Indian flavor.

Or, try another old Hollywood standby, **Barney's Beanery,** just west of Hugo's at 8447 Santa Monica Boulevard (☎ 213/654-2287). A reliable roadhouse since the days when old Route 66 passed this spot, Barney's draws crowds eager to enjoy a game of pool, a round of beers, and plates generously piled with chili burgers, seasoned fries, and other delicious diner fare (including all-day breakfast favorites). In keeping with the newly nutrition-conscious rock 'n' roll crowd, Barney's Beanery also serves great turkey and veggie burgers.

After fortifying yourself with a hearty meal, begin your adventure by heading west to:

1. **8563 Holloway Drive** and
2. **8573 Holloway Drive.** These apartment buildings share a garden courtyard as well as an infamous past. In 1976, washed-up actor Sal Mineo (best known for his role opposite James Dean in *Rebel Without a Cause*) was mysteriously stabbed to death in the carport beneath the fuschia-colored bougainvillea vines. Earlier, before these buildings were run down, Marilyn Monroe shared number 8573 with fellow starlet Shelly Winters. It would be only one of the dozens of places Marilyn lived in L.A. during her lifetime; you'll pass several more later on this tour.

Continue along Holloway to Sunset Boulevard and turn left, then left again on Larrabee. Follow Larrabee to Cynthia Street, and turn right; proceed to Doheny Drive. On the southeast corner of Doheny and Cynthia is:

3. **882 North Doheny Drive,** an austere white apartment building where Marilyn Monroe was living when she began her ill-fated courtship with her second husband, baseball great Joe DiMaggio.

Turn right onto Doheny, and take it past Sunset Boulevard into the hills, turning right onto tiny Cordell Drive to:

4. **9166 Cordell Drive.** This was the domicile of George Cukor, director of such classics as *The Philadelphia Story, Adam's Rib, Gaslight,* and *My Fair Lady.* The long privacy wall accented with palm trees once enclosed a compound of four houses, including one rented to Spencer Tracy. Katharine Hepburn continued living there for 10 years following Tracy's death—in her arms in the kitchen—in 1967. This cozy enclave was beloved by Cukor; he entertained often by the pool. After his death in 1982, the new owners swore they felt his presence haunting the halls he adored.

Take Doheny Drive back downhill, turning right on Cory Drive, and right again on Sunset Boulevard. As Sunset begins to veer left at the light, stay to the right and take Doheny Road to Schuyler Road. Make a right on Schuyler and follow it up the hill to Readcrest, turning left to:

5. **9377 Readcrest Drive,** former home of actor Fernando Lamas and his wife, swimmer-actress—swimsuit designer Esther Williams.

Turn right when Readcrest meets Lindacrest, then right again onto Beverlycrest. You'll soon see:

6. **9402 Beverlycrest Drive,** the home in which Rock Hudson died of AIDS, a sprawling estate he called "The Castle."

Beverlycrest will return you to Schuyler Road—follow it down the hill to Doheny Road and make a right turn, then curve left onto Foothill and find:

7. **915 Foothill Road,** whose grand gates lead to an estate owned at one time by Mel Brooks, and most recently, by "Ol' Blue Eyes" himself, Frank Sinatra.

On the left side of the street, at the corner of Sunset Boulevard, is:

8. **9521 Sunset Boulevard,** the childhood home of pint-size star Shirley Temple, who had her own miniature playhouse on the grounds.

Turn left onto Sunset, watching between Palm and Hillcrest on the left side of the street for:

9. **9419 Sunset Boulevard.** Imagine MGM "boy wonder" executive Irving Thalberg and his actress wife, Norma Shearer, holding court behind these dense shrubbery walls; this was their estate until Thalberg's untimely death at age 37 in 1936.

Turn right on Hillcrest Road to Santa Monica Boulevard, right to Palm Drive, and right once again. Notice the pleasing symmetry of the landscaping on these streets in the "flats" of Beverly Hills—each north/south drive is planted with a different tree, though clearly not according to name (palm trees line Hillcrest Road, while Palm Drive displays the lavender blooms of jacaranda trees). On Palm you'll find:

10. **508 Palm Drive.** This was home to Marilyn Monroe and Joe DiMaggio during their short marriage in 1954. Two houses up is:

11. **512 Palm Drive,** a modest Mediterranean-style enclave that was blonde bombshell Jean Harlow's last home, where she died in 1937—at the age of 26—of sudden uremic poisoning.

Two blocks further is another former Marilyn Monroe home:

12. **718 Palm Drive.** She briefly shared this ivy-covered house with William Morris agent Johnny Hyde in 1950, the year she began to make a name for herself with small, but pivotal, roles in *The Asphalt Jungle* and *All About Eve.*

Turn back toward Elevado Avenue, turn right to Rexford Avenue, and right again, following Rexford up past Sunset Boulevard to where it intersects Beverly Drive. Make a right turn and look to the left for:

13. **1011 Beverly Drive,** the opulent estate of actress and William Randolph Hearst mistress Marion Davies. Nearly as lavish and excessive as the Santa Monica beach house built for her by Hearst, this mansion is where he died in 1951 (and later she did, in 1961). The driveway is so enormous you might mistake it for a street; stone lions perch atop peach-colored walls guarding the gate, behind which you can see a broad road winding up the hill.

Turn around at Shadow Hill Way and slow down (if traffic allows) on the way back for another look. Turn right at the T-intersection, continuing south on Beverly Drive to Sunset Boulevard, then make a hairpin right turn onto Crescent Drive, where you'll come to:

14. **904 Crescent Drive,** a former home of Gloria Swanson, silent film star and *Sunset Boulevard*'s original Norma Desmond. Across the street are the:

15. **Beverly Hills Hotel and Bungalows,** secluded locale for many legendary trysts, including the rumored Marilyn Monroe/John F. Kennedy affair. Howard Hughes virtually lived here during his Hollywood years, keeping several regular bungalows for his family and staff—including his private food-taster.

Continue to:

16. **1001 Crescent Drive,** an elegant mansion formerly occupied by *Dynasty* star Linda Evans, and owned for many years by Blake Edwards and Julie Andrews.

Follow Crescent as it curves around, taking Oxford Way past Sunset Boulevard onto Rodeo Drive, which is residential here, but becomes Beverly Hills's most extravagant shopping avenue further south. At:

17. **725 Rodeo Drive** was the modest residence of the late, multitalented Gene Kelly.

Turn right on Carmelita, and right onto Bedford, and look for:

18. **620 Bedford Drive,** former residence of Marlene Dietrich. One block farther is:

Hollywood at Home: A Driving Tour

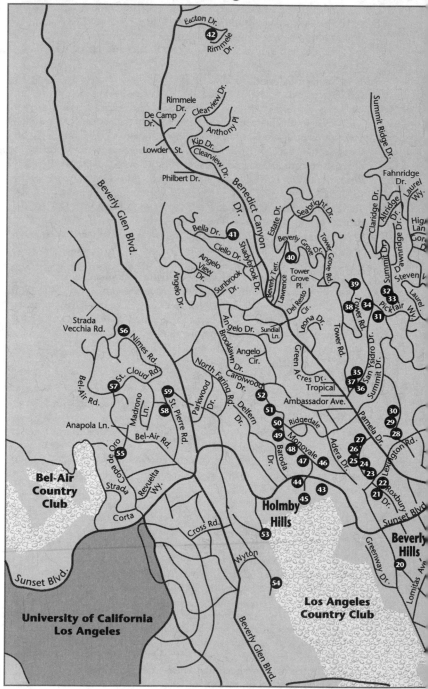

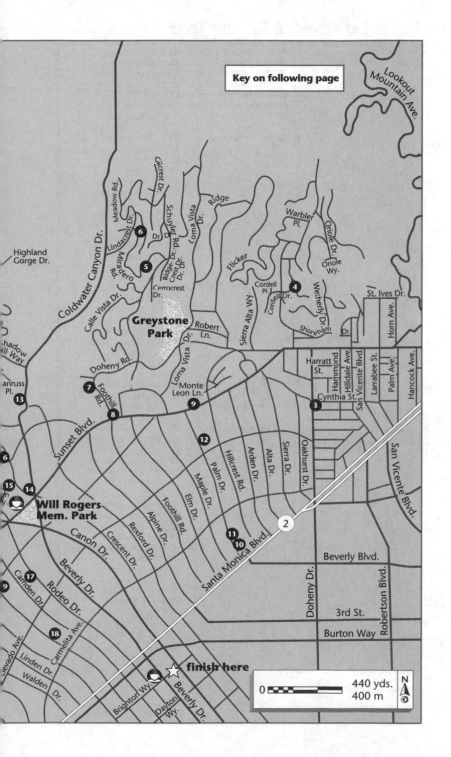

Key on following page

Lookout Mountain Ave.

Gilcrest Dr.
Meadow Rd.
Lindacrest Dr.
Mulhero Rd.
Schuyler Dr.
Warbler Pl.
Oriole Dr.
Ridge
Loma Vista Dr.
Oriole Wy.

Highland Gorge Dr.

⑥
⑤

Calle Vista Dr.

Flicker

Wetherly Dr.

St. Ives Dr.

④

Cordell Pl.
Cordell Dr.

Horn Ave.

Ridge Dr.
Crest Dr.
Crest Dr.
Cerrocrest Dr.

Greystone Park

Robert Ln.

Sierra Alta Wy.

Shoreham Dr.

hadow ill Way

Doheny Rd.

Loma Vista Dr.

Harratt St.
Hammond
Hilldale Ave.
San Vicente Blvd.
Larrabee St.
Palm Ave.
Hancock Ave.

anruss Pl.

⑬

⑦

Foothill Rd.

Monte Leon Ln.

⑨

Cynthia St.

③

⑧

San Vicente Blvd.

Sunset Blvd.

⑫

Hillcrest Rd.
Arden Dr.
Alta Dr.
Sierra Dr.
Oakhurst Dr.

⑥

Palm Dr.

Maple Dr.

⑮ ⑭

Will Rogers Mem. Park

Elm Dr.

Foothill Rd.

②

Alpine Dr.

Canon Dr.

Crescent Dr.

Rexford Dr.

⑪
⑩

Santa Monica Blvd.

Beverly Blvd.

Doheny Dr.

Robertson Blvd.

⑨

⑰

Beverly Dr.

Rodeo Dr.

Camden Dr.

3rd St.

evado Ave.

⑱

Carmelita Ave.

Burton Way

Linden Dr.

Walden Dr.

Brighton Wy.

finish here

Dayton Wy.

Beverly Dr.

0 ▮▮▮▮▮▮ 440 yds.
          400 m

N

169

Hollywood at Home: A Driving Tour

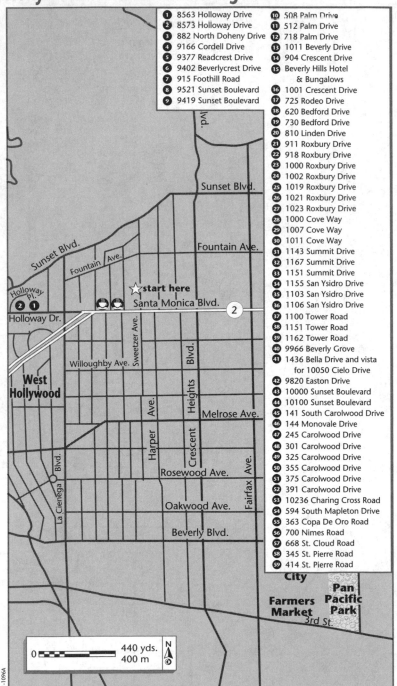

❶	8563 Holloway Drive
❷	8573 Holloway Drive
❸	882 North Doheny Drive
❹	9166 Cordell Drive
❺	9377 Readcrest Drive
❻	9402 Beverlycrest Drive
❼	915 Foothill Road
❽	9521 Sunset Boulevard
❾	9419 Sunset Boulevard
❿	508 Palm Drive
⓫	512 Palm Drive
⓬	718 Palm Drive
⓭	1011 Beverly Drive
⓮	904 Crescent Drive
⓯	Beverly Hills Hotel & Bungalows
⓰	1001 Crescent Drive
⓱	725 Rodeo Drive
⓲	620 Bedford Drive
⓳	730 Bedford Drive
⓴	810 Linden Drive
㉑	911 Roxbury Drive
㉒	918 Roxbury Drive
㉓	1000 Roxbury Drive
㉔	1002 Roxbury Drive
㉕	1019 Roxbury Drive
㉖	1021 Roxbury Drive
㉗	1023 Roxbury Drive
㉘	1000 Cove Way
㉙	1007 Cove Way
㉚	1011 Cove Way
㉛	1143 Summit Drive
㉜	1167 Summit Drive
㉝	1151 Summit Drive
㉞	1155 San Ysidro Drive
㉟	1103 San Ysidro Drive
㊱	1106 San Ysidro Drive
㊲	1100 Tower Road
㊳	1151 Tower Road
㊴	1162 Tower Road
㊵	9966 Beverly Grove
㊶	1436 Bella Drive and vista for 10050 Cielo Drive
㊷	9820 Easton Drive
㊸	10000 Sunset Boulevard
㊹	10100 Sunset Boulevard
㊺	141 South Carolwood Drive
㊻	144 Monovale Drive
㊼	245 Carolwood Drive
㊽	301 Carolwood Drive
㊾	325 Carolwood Drive
㊿	355 Carolwood Drive
51	375 Carolwood Drive
52	391 Carolwood Drive
53	10236 Charing Cross Road
54	594 South Mapleton Drive
55	363 Copa De Oro Road
56	700 Nimes Road
57	668 St. Cloud Road
58	345 St. Pierre Road
59	414 St. Pierre Road

1-1096A

19. **730 Bedford Drive,** where, in 1958, Lana Turner's teenage daughter Cheryl Crane stabbed to death her mother's abusive boyfriend, gangster Johnny Stompanato.

Turn left onto Lomitas Avenue to Linden Drive, turn right, and proceed to:

20. **810 Linden Drive,** which looks exactly as it did the night in 1947 when hoodlum Benjamin "Bugsy" Siegel was gunned down through the living room window. A notorious gangster best remembered for creating Las Vegas from a patch of desert scruff, Siegel had been relaxing in the home of his girlfriend, small-time actress Virginia Hill.

Linden will merge into Whittier Drive; make a right turn onto Sunset Boulevard and take the next left, onto Roxbury Drive, where you'll find:

21. **911 Roxbury Drive,** *Bewitched* star Elizabeth Montgomery's home until her tragic death in 1995, and:

22. **918 Roxbury Drive,** occupied by the actor James Stewart for decades. Stewart turned the adjoining corner lot into a walled garden to indulge his favorite hobby—gardening. Down the street is:

23. **1000 Roxbury Drive,** which was Lucille Ball's simple white home. Disturbed once too often by huge busloads of tourists pouring onto her front lawn, Lucy forced the city of Beverly Hills to create stringent guidelines for tour operators. Her neighbor for many years at:

24. **1002 Roxbury Drive** was another great comedian, Jack Benny. A few houses down and across the street is:

25. **1019 Roxbury Drive,** home of Rosemary Clooney (George's aunt, for all you *ER* fans). Next door is:

26. **1021 Roxbury Drive,** which was the modest home of composer Ira Gershwin, and:

27. **1023 Roxbury Drive,** a newer house built on the site where Spencer Tracy, and later Agnes Moorehead, once resided.

Stay on Roxbury, cross over Benedict Canyon Drive, and make the second left onto Cove Way, in front of:

28. **1000 Cove Way.** This stylish and traditional home was formerly the property of both movie villian Jack Palance and funny man W.C. Fields. Across the street is:

29. **1007 Cove Way,** home to Sidney Poitier, and:

30. **1011 Cove Way,** whose rough-hewn stone exterior suited the moniker of its previous owner, Rock Hudson.

Make a right turn on Summit Drive and follow it up the hill to:

31. **1143 Summit Drive,** former site of a Beverly Hills legend. When Douglas Fairbanks, Sr., and Mary Pickford—Hollywood's favorite couple in the 1920s—moved here, they lived in the only structure in sight, a small hunting lodge. They enlarged the dwelling, adding the first residential swimming pool in Beverly Hills; the gracious hilltop manor became known to the world as "Pickfair." Pickford continued to live here until her death in 1979. In 1990 singer Pia Zadora leveled the 42-room landmark to make way for the larger—and decidedly tackier—mansion you see today. About the only remnants of the glorious original are the stone cherubs adorning the front gate, a gift to the Fairbankses from Charlie Chaplin.

Veer to the right past 1143 and proceed up the street to:

32. **1167 Summit Drive,** home of actress and Elvis widow, Priscilla Presley.

Turn around safely where you can; descending, you'll get a fine view of:

33. **1151 Summit Drive,** home of Sammy Davis, Jr., at the time of his death. Sadly, his family was forced to sell the home and auction off its contents to settle the debts he left behind.

Turn right on Pickfair Way (behind Pia Zadora's house). As Pickfair Way dips to meet San Ysidro Drive, glance straight ahead; atop the hill is.

34. **1155 San Ysidro Drive,** the former Fred Astaire estate. Make a left at the corner, and you'll see his winding driveway on the right. Further down the street is:

35. **1103 San Ysidro Drive,** the last home of Danny Kaye, of which only the impressive gateway is visible, and:

36. **1106 San Ysidro Drive,** the heavily remodeled former home of Rex Harrison. Across the street is:

37. **1100 Tower Road.** The overly theatrical romanesque columns, gargoyles, and garden statuary must have suited Laurence Olivier and Vivien Leigh, who were living here when Leigh won her Best Actress Oscar for *Gone With the Wind*. Make a right turn around the house and continue up Tower to:

38. **1151 Tower Road.** Jay Leno lives here, and it's a sure bet the house has an extensive garage, for Jay lovingly maintains a spectacular collection of vintage automobiles; you might see him motoring about town in one.

Farther up the hill, you'll see the short brick wall defines:

39. **1162 Tower Road,** the estate of the late Michael Landon. A devoted family man, the *Bonanza, Little House on the Prairie,* and *Highway to Heaven* star erected a full-size playground here for his many children and grandchildren; it's easy to see the swings, seesaws, and jungle gyms from the street.

You can turn around in the cul-de-sac at the end of Tower Road and gaze out at the extraordinary city view from what once was John Barrymore's vast estate on this hilltop, appropriately named "Bella Vista" (beautiful view). Backtrack down to where Tower Grove Drive heads up the hill to the right, and follow it up to Beverly Grove Drive; turn left. Just as you emerge at the next minicanyon, look on the left for:

40. **9966 Beverly Grove,** Cary Grant's last home. Slow down, if you can, to look back through the gates to catch a glimpse of the gracious home (entirely remodeled by Grant in 1982), as well as his spectacular view of L.A. and the ocean.

Follow Beverly Grove down the hill to the T-shaped intersection with Beverly Estate Drive, taking it down to Beverly Glen Boulevard. Turn right on Beverly Glen, then left on Cielo Drive, following the road to where it widens slightly for the intersection with a tiny, overgrown spur called Bella Drive. Although technically a public road—and therefore fair game to the curious—there's only one home at the top of this nearly private driveway. But it's worth disturbing the wild rabbits to get to:

41. **1436 Bella Drive.** It has scarcely changed since 1925, when screen heartthrob Rudolph Valentino bought this white-walled estate and named it "Falcon Lair." Valentino's steel pennant emblazoned with the letter "V" still flies atop the house's red-tiled roof; it was last owned by heiress Doris Duke.

Looking down into the canyon from the summit, you can see the site of 10050 Cielo Drive, infamous address of the August 1969 Manson family murder of pregnant actress Sharon Tate and four others. The house itself was torn down in 1994, just after Nine Inch Nails recorded their multiplatinum—and appropriately angst-ridden—album *The Downward Spiral* in it.

One unfortunate houseguest was jet-setting hairstylist Jay Sebring, visiting from further up the canyon, where he lived in a secluded house supposedly haunted by the ghost of movie studio head Paul Bern, who was newly married to starlet Jean Harlow at the time of his death. His death here in 1932 was officially called a suicide, but many speculated about a scandalous murder and cover-up. You can reach the Bern/Sebring house if you're willing to ascend Easton Drive, a narrow and roughly paved alley. Return via Cielo Drive to Benedict Canyon, turn left, and proceed to Easton. Turn right to:

42. **9820 Easton Drive.** The address isn't really visible from the street, but if you go to the end and turn around, you can easily see the two-story Bavarian-style house on your left, set back and above the others.

Return via Benedict Canyon to Sunset Boulevard and make a right turn to:

43. **10000 Sunset Boulevard.** Both Howard Hughes and Vincente Minelli and Judy Garland owned this home, but today it gets the most attention for the whimsical statues adorning the front lawn. The sightseeing couple were the first installed, and tricked many passersby into thinking there was really someone looking over the wall!

Turn left at Carolwood, marked by the bubblegum-pink Spanish-style:

44. **10100 Sunset Boulevard.** It has been owned by singer Rudy Vallee and later by Englebert Humperdinck, but its personality was indelibly stamped in the 1960s by Jayne Mansfield, who chose the color scheme and built a heart-shaped pool in the backyard.

The street dead-ends at:

45. **141 South Carolwood Drive,** an English-style estate named "Owlwood" and owned at various times by Sonny and Cher, Tony Curtis, and movie mogul Joseph Schenck, at whose invitiation Curtis's future *Some Like It Hot* costar Marilyn Monroe occupied a guest house during 1949.

Return to Sunset Boulevard and make a right, then a left onto Ladera Drive, and left on Monovale. You'll come to:

46. **144 Monovale Drive,** the L.A. home of Elvis and Priscilla Presley, who purchased the white cottage in 1972 for a mere $335,000.

Follow Monovale as it merges with Carolwood, and proceed to:

47. **245 Carolwood Drive.** This was the L.A. home of Burt Reynolds and Loni Anderson during their marriage; it once belonged to Beatle George Harrison. Down the street is:

48. **301 Carolwood Drive,** the heavily guarded home of the very private Barbra Streisand, and:

49. **325 Carolwood Drive.** Up the ivy garland–adorned driveway is Clark Gable's former abode. You can't miss:

50. **355 Carolwood Drive,** Walt Disney's home, with its wrought-iron mouse-ear motif on the gate. His widow, Lillian, still lives here. Next you'll see:

51. **375 Carolwood Drive,** home to distinguished actor Gregory Peck, who was probably less than thrilled by the loud partying at:

52. **391 Carolwood Drive** when it was owned by rocker Rod Stewart and his model wife, Rachel Hunter.

Return via Carolwood to Sunset Boulevard and turn right, then turn left onto Charing Cross. Slow down and smile for the sophisticated surveillance system (including cameras, microphones, and guards) at:

53. **10236 Charing Cross Road,** an ostentatious stone manor known since 1971 as the "Playboy Mansion," now reincarnated as the family homestead of Mr. and Mrs. Hugh Hefner and their two small children.

Follow Charing Cross to Mapleton Drive, turn left, and proceed to:

54. **594 South Mapleton Drive.** The community of Holmby Hills was outraged when Aaron Spelling, producer of such successful TV shows as *Charlie's Angels, The Love Boat, Beverly Hills, 90210, Savannah,* and *Melrose Place*—and Tori's dad—razed an estate overlooking the prestigious Los Angeles Country Club and erected this oversized, ostentatious monstrosity.

Past the Spelling residence, turn right on Club View Drive, and right again on Beverly Glen Boulevard. Take Beverly Glen past Sunset Boulevard, straight through the stately entrance to Bel-Air. Turn left at Bellagio Road, then right at Copa de Oro ("cup of gold"). Straight ahead is:

55. 363 Copa De Oro Road, the ornate red-brick mansion of heartthrob Tom Jones, at one time occupied by fellow Las Vegas headliner, the late Dean Martin.

Veer right past the house to the intersection with Bel Air Road, turn right, and then left on St. Cloud Road to Nimes Road. As you approach:

56. 700 Nimes Road, the exotic flowers in varying shades of purple and lavender provide the only clues to the glamorous owner who dwells behind this imposing gate . . . Elizabeth Taylor.

Follow Nimes around and back down to St. Cloud Road, turning left. On the left-hand side is:

57. 668 St. Cloud Road, home to Mr. and Mrs. Ronald Reagan since his departure from the White House. Nancy had the original house number, 666, changed to a less demonic address. If the former president is in residence, the gatehouse will be staffed with armed Secret Service officers.

Continue past Nimes and turn left on St. Pierre. On the right-hand side is:

58. 345 St. Pierre Road, a peach-colored house with green-patina iron fencework. Errol Flynn's alleged statutory rape—the scandal out of which the expression "in like Flynn" was born—took place here. Across the street, diagonally to the left is:

59. 414 St. Pierre Road, which sits abandoned, its carved stone entryway and Mediterranean-tiled patio visible through the overgrowth. As the street curves around the corner, peek into the neglected backyard at the spectacular swimming pool built for original owner Johnny Weissmuller. The athletic swimmer and on-screen Tarzan created a junglelike setting for his daily laps when he and this house were in their prime.

Continuing to the end of the block, you'll find yourself back at Beverly Glen Boulevard. A right turn will lead you to Sunset Boulevard.

WINDING DOWN If all this sightseeing has left your stomach grumbling, stay in the neighborhood and visit one of these local watering holes:

Recently reopened after an extensive restoration, the **Beverly Hills Hotel** has been the unofficial "clubhouse" of the swank Hollywood crowd since it opened in 1912. Katharine Hepburn played tennis here daily, Marlene Dietrich shocked the staid Polo Lounge by strolling in wearing trousers, and Marilyn Monroe and Yves Montand emerged from their 1959 tryst in one of the secluded bungalows to smooch over a milkshake in the **Fountain Coffee Shop** (☎ **310/276-2251**). Stopping in yourself for a sandwich and fountain treat at the shop's counter provides a perfect excuse to stroll these legendary grounds.

Or, try **Nate 'n Al's** delicatessen, at 414 North Beverly Dr. (☎ **310/274-0101**), a regular Beverly Hills fixture for ages. Despite its location among the boutiques of the "Golden Triangle," Nate 'n Al's remains comfortably homey and unchanged, from the sweet condescension of the motherly waitresses to the best pastrami, pickles, and chopped liver in town. And you won't believe the famous faces lining the brown Naugahyde booths—many have had house accounts for decades!

2 Sunset Boulevard!

by Mary Susan Herczog

It's been called the most famous street in America. It inspired a TV show, and a movie, which in turn spawned a Broadway musical hit.

"Sunset BOOO-LA-VAHD!" bellows whoever is playing the musical Norma Desmond these days. It may be kitsch, it may be hokey, it may more often than not be seedy, but for better or worse, Sunset Boulevard is the lifeline of Los Angeles. It's not the fastest way to get around, but if you've got only a few hours in which to try to get a sense of this sprawling, schizophrenic town, the legendary Sunset Boulevard is the way to do it.

Think about it: Sunset begins at Olvera Street, the oldest street in L.A., dating back to when the city was *La Pueblo de la Señora, La Reigna de Los Angeles* ("City of Our Lady, Queen of the Angels"). From there, it winds its way through a fabulous cross-section of everything Los Angeles has to offer, from the good to the bad to the ugly to the glamorous, until it ends, smack at the Pacific Ocean. Movie stars and moguls; immigrants, nouveau riche, and old money; sushi bars and strip joints; punks, parks, and prostitutes—Sunset Boulevard has it all. And then some.

Driving Sunset, you'll get a taste of every flavor of L.A., from conventional tourist sights and a bit of the history of the city to the sordid and sensational. You'll see beautiful old buildings, garish homes, decrepit structures. You can gawk at the spots where John Belushi and River Phoenix shuffled off their mortal coils. You can wave to O.J. You'll get a spectacular view of the Hollywood sign and a glimpse of the stars on the sidewalks (they aren't confined to Hollywood Boulevard). And a few blocks north or south will lead you to a variety of historical or scandalous hot spots.

Naturally, the optimum mode of travel is a convertible, preferably a '62 T Bird. But your style-free rental car gets the job done, as long as it's got a stereo (soundtrack suggestions provided).

Ready? Let's cruise . . .

Start/Finish: This tour is designed to be driven from east to west, beginning downtown at Olvera Street and ending at the Pacific, but you can do it backward if you're more of a deconstructionist than a dreamer. Just reverse the directions where appropriate (west becomes east, right becomes left, and so forth).

Directional Note: You won't be proceeding in a true westerly direction at all times (Sunset Boulevard sometimes heads in a north or south, as the compass points); however, for our purposes, we'll always refer to the direction you're heading as west, since Sunset Boulevard always proceeds in a general westerly direction.

Time: Plan on about 3 hours if you stick strictly to Sunset Boulevard (this allows for some photo-op stops), though it can take longer, depending on the traffic or if you take in some of the suggested side trips. A whole day can easily be devoted to this tour, but it's a day well spent.

Best/Worst Times: Of course, this drive is at its best when the weather is clear and sharp (after a big wind or rain); the hills and mountains stand out like they were cut from glass, the ocean is a shimmering blue green. Smog and haze can radically dull, even obscure, the sights; we do that deliberately to keep more people from moving here (that's our story and we're sticking to it).

Further Reading: For more on the sights along this route, and other unusual sights around Hollywood, check out Ken Schessler's *This Is Hollywood.* It's a comprehensive, regularly updated guide to the history of Hollywood.

Begin at:

1. **Olvera Street** (400–500 N. Main Street), downtown. Los Angeles was founded in 1781, and this is traditionally considered the city's oldest street.

☕ **STARTING OUT** If you need to fuel up before the tour, there are plenty of opportunities for Mexican on Olvera Street, as well as for Chinese a few blocks away in Chinatown (bounded by North Broadway, North Hill Street, Bernard Street, and Sunset Boulevard). A good option is **Yang Chow,** 819 N. Broadway (at Alpine St.; ☎ 213/625-0811), a downtown stalwart that's been serving up well-prepared Mandarin and Szechuan specialties for more than three decades.

Sunset Boulevard originally began a block from Olvera Street, at Spring Street; however, in the last couple years, the first few blocks of the boulevard have been renamed Caesar E. Chavez Avenue. Start at the original beginning anyway, for history's sake (Sunset Boulevard now officially begins in the 900 block).

2. **Your First Side Trip:** Three blocks beyond Spring Street is the corner of Sunset Boulevard and Grand Avenue. **The Music Center,** which includes the Dorothy Chandler Pavilion, frequent home to the Academy Awards, is a left turn away, at 135 N. Grand Ave. Olive Street is one block before Grand; at 751 N. Olive is the spot where William Selig opened the **first movie studio** in Hollywood (there is no plaque).

Now return to Sunset, and crank up "Route 66," by Bobby Troup, on your stereo. Yes, this portion of Sunset Boulevard was once part of the late, lamented, much celebrated American Drive.

3. **Side Trip:** Turn left on Marion, right on Edgeware, and then left onto **Carroll Drive.** This long block of perfectly restored, gingerbread-trimmed Victorian homes is all that remains of fashionable 19th-century Los Angeles. They serve as proof that this city once had as much character as San Francisco, thank you very much. (There are more Victorians one block over, on the less impressive Kellam Street.)

Now return to Sunset and put on some mariachi music as you hit the Hispanic part of the boulevard. It's a little run down, with a mix of sagging apartments and some older, funkier architecture, but has a warm community feel. Or you might want to break into "Take Me Out to the Ballgame"—you'll see signs on the right directing you to the pride of the O'Malleys, Dodger Stadium.

At the corner of Glendale and Sunset boulevards (on the left) is:

4. **Angelus Foursquare Temple,** built by evangelist Aimee Semple McPherson, whose ministry and good works were overshadowed by scandal. McPherson was at the height of her fame when she disappeared for a month in 1926. She was presumed drowned until she turned up and insisted that she had been kidnapped. Her fake story quickly fell apart, and the truth came out: She had rendezvoused with her married lover. McPherson's ministry never recovered from the blow the scandal felled, and she eventually committed suicide in 1944.

5. **Side Trip:** Go right on Glendale Boulevard to no. 1712, on the right, where you'll find the former site of **Mack Sennett's Keystone Cops studio,** where Charlie Chaplin, Fatty Arbuckle, and Gloria Swanson got their starts.

Return to Sunset Boulevard. As you cross Coronado Boulevard, you enter Silverlake, a remarkable multicultural neighborhood with an eclectic mix of arty bohemians, homosexuals, young yuppies in love, budding Sammy Glick Hollywood types, immigrants, and older couples who've been residents for decades. You'll notice that the architecture—much left over from the early days of L.A.—begins to improve; you'll start seeing Hollywood bungalows (many built to house silent screen actors) and Spanish haciendas.

6. **Side Trip:** Just past Silverlake Boulevard and Parkman, turn left on Vendome. Down on the right between 923 and 927 Vendome is a **very steep, very long staircase** (when it's overgrown, it can look deceptively short). Imagine carrying a piano up it. Laurel and Hardy did, in their classic short *The Music Box;* and now there's a plaque honoring it.

   Return to Sunset Boulevard. At 3816 Sunset, on the left, is:

7. **You've Got Bad Taste,** a store owned by Exene Cervenka (former lead singer for seminal Los Angeles punk band, X), featuring strange kitsch items from the last few decades and other twisted finds. On weekends, the store often hosts live shows.

   As you keep driving, if the weather gods are kind, you should get a great view of the Hollywood hills straight ahead. As you cross the little bridge past the corner of Myra and Sunset Boulevard, you can see the hills of Silverlake on your right.

8. **Side Trip:** Make a right at Fountain Avenue. A few yards down, on the right, is a white triangle-shaped building, built in 1916 as a **studio for silent film comedienne Mabel Normand.** Normand, a gifted comic and film pioneer, was best known as Fatty Arbuckle's sidekick and was probably the first female star to direct her own movies. The portrait of her in the movie *Chaplin* does no justice to either her enchanting personality or her career, now largely lost thanks to the disintegration of nitrate films, on which all pre-WWII movies were shot.

   Follow Fountain Avenue east as it curves to the left and becomes Hyperion Avenue. Go left on Griffith Park Boulevard. At the corner is the **Mayfair Market,** which used to be Walt Disney's first official studio, where he made the first Mickey Mouse cartoon, *Steamboat Willie,* and *Snow White and the Seven Dwarfs.* A half-block up on the right are a set of **bungalows** that local legend swears were built by Disney. They certainly look like cottages for Sneezy, Dopey, Doc, et al.

   Keep going to St. George; turn right and take it past the stop sign at Rowena Avenue. St. George dead ends at Waverly Drive; turn left. On the right is **3311 Waverly Drive,** the former home of Manson victims Leo and Rosemary LaBianca.

   Turn around and go back the way you came, admiring the view of Silverlake on your left as you head back on Hyperion/Fountain Avenue.

   Return to Sunset Boulevard. Just past Fountain Avenue on the right is:

9. **KCET,** the Los Angeles PBS affiliate. This lot was built as a movie studio in 1912, and has been in continuous use ever since, changing hands several times (the "East Side Kids/Bowery Boys" made their movies here). Next door to KCET is the **Tiki Ti Room** (☎ 213/669-9381), a bar shack that says it invented the tropical drink. Judge for yourself if you can—the owner keeps his own hours.

   On the northeast corner of the three-way junction of Hillhurst Avenue (as it crosses Sunset going south, it changes names to Virgil Avenue) and Sunset and Hollywood boulevards is the:

10. **Vista Theater,** built in the early '20s and now boasting an interior face-lift that shows off its deco/Egyptian roots. A prime, though smallish, example of early movie palace.

    Diagonally across from the Vista to the left is a:

11. **Vons Supermarket.** Big deal. But wait: In 1916, D.W. Griffith filmed his classic epic *Intolerance* at his studio, which occupied the block on Virgil Avenue between Fountain and Sunset. He built the largest outdoor set ever for the "Babylon" segment of the movie. Afterward, the opulent set just sat there, decaying, towering in the background over the quickly growing skyline of Los Angeles. It was this sight that inspired Kenneth Anger's now-iconic phrase "Hollywood Babylon." So go stand in the parking lot; you're actually smack-dab in the middle of a metaphor for an era.

12. Side Trip: Go right on Hillhurst Avenue for three blocks and turn left on Kingswell. On the left, at **4406 Kingswell,** in his uncle's garage, is where Walt Disney made his first cartoon. Two blocks west on Kingswell, at **no. 4649** (on the right) is the spot where Disney had his first studio, in 1925—this is where the character that became Mickey Mouse was born. (Another building now stands on the spot.)

Continue north on Hillhurst Avenue to Melbourne Avenue, and turn right. At the end of the block is **KABC,** the Los Angeles ABC affiliate, which occupies the site of the former Vitagraph Studios, built in 1917. (As you may have guessed by now, this whole area was the center of the early days of Hollywood, and the silent film era.)

Go north on Hillhurst Avenue for one block; at the southeast corner of Russell is the charming **brown wood Craftsman bungalow** office of Heidi Fleiss's pediatrician father. He's been a neighborhood fixture for decades.

Return to Sunset Boulevard, which veers to the left at the three-way junction (if you continue straight, you end up on Hollywood Boulevard).

13. Side Trip: If you turn right on Vermont Avenue, the next light, and then left at the light on Hollywood Boulevard, on your left is **Barnsdall Park,** which includes the famous Frank Lloyd Wright–designed **Hollyhock House.** It's an idyllic sanctuary, though presently somewhat cluttered up and obscured by subway construction. (If you'd like to visit, see "More City Sights & Attractions" in chapter 7 for details.)

Continue north on Vermont Avenue; on the right, you'll pass Mike D. of the Beastie Boys' shop **X Large,** next to Kim Gordon's (of Sonic Youth) **X Girl** (1766 N. Vermont Ave.; ☎ 213/666-3483 for both stores). Both are hip clothing stores.

Keep going up Vermont Avenue through the gorgeous neighborhood of Los Feliz—when Hollywood was silent, this was the Bel Air and Beverly Hills of the time—and enter **Griffith Park.** The gift of wealthy Colonel Griffith J. Griffith (no, really), an alcoholic seeking to clean up his image after he was imprisoned for shooting his wife in the eye (she lived), it's the largest municipal park in the country.

Keep going on this street as it curves past the **Greek Theater** (another Col. Griffith endowment); eventually you'll hit the **Griffith Observatory.** If it's a clear day, you really can see forever. Admire the **bust of James Dean**—you may recognize the observatory from key moments in *Rebel Without a Cause.*

Return to Sunset Boulevard. If you don't have time for the above detour, just turn your head to the right as you go through the next few lights, and look up at the hill. Isn't the observatory pretty?

The next light is Berendo and Sunset; on the left is the massive, blue . . .

14. Scientology Center, domain of Dianetics guru L. Ron Hubbard, which actually takes up the whole block in all directions. The cult—oops, religion—owns most of the property around here. Scientology is increasing its Hollywood profile; it counts the likes of John Travolta and Tom Cruise among its members. Right next door is a branch of the **Self Realization Fellowship Shrine** (you'll see the bigger version in Pacific Palisades).

You're now entering Hollywood proper, and it ain't pretty. A little dingy, it hardly seems the glamorous place of lore. But then, it never was. X's "Los Angeles" is the soundtrack for this stretch.

At Western Avenue is the site of:

15. William Fox's studio. He eventually merged and the studio became known as Twentieth Century Fox. The original studio took up both sides of the south corner. Not only did Tom Mix shoot bad guys here, but this is where John Wayne got his start.

16. **Side Trip:** One block later, turn right at St. Andrew's Place; go one block, and then left on Harold Way, where you'll find **5620 Harold Way** on the left. This is where Bela Lugosi died.

   Now pop some Glen Miller or Artie Shaw in the tape deck for that nostalgic feel, and return to Sunset Boulevard. On the left, at no. 5858, is:

17. Local station **KTLA,** Channel 5, owned by Gene Autry. This was the original Warner Brothers studios; it was here that Al Jolson helped sink many of his silent film colleagues' careers by making the first talking movie *The Jazz Singer.*

18. **Side Trip:** Turn right on Bronson Avenue, and go north two lights to Franklin Avenue; turn left. The large building on the left is considered the most beautiful in Hollywood. Either a gift from William Randolph Hearst to movie director Thomas Ince's widow to make up for Hearst shooting her husband accidently (official cause of death was stomach ailment), or actually the result of the widow's savvy business dealings—depending on who you believe—its reputation is now permanently tarnished thanks to its present incarnation as the **Scientology Celebrity Center.** Lisa Marie Presley often seeks refuge from her altogether-too-interesting life here.

   Return to Sunset Boulevard. At the southeast corner of Gower Street is:

19. The original home of **Columbia Studios** (founded 1921). Now mostly TV shows are filmed there. Across the street is:

20. **"Gower Gulch,"** where day western players would wait, hoping for a shot in a cowboy picture. It was also the site of the movie studio where bit player Virginia Rappe was working when she achieved her own level of fame by dying—because Fatty Arbuckle, then the most famous actor in Hollywood, was accused (and eventually acquitted) of her "murder."

   Turn your head to the right at the Gower stoplight (and the next couple thereafter). Look up at the hills. There's the:

21. **Hollywood sign.** Built in 1923, and refurbished in the '80s, it used to read Hollywoodland, the name of the development below. In 1932, bit player Peg Entwistle, despondent over her lack of Hollywood success, ensured her immortality by jumping off the letter H. Despite this picturesque method of taking one's own life, she's the only such suicide recorded.

   At the next signal is Vine Street. Look to the right on Vine, at the sidewalk, and you'll see stars—it's part of the famous **Walk of Fame.**

22. **Side Trip:** Turn right at Vine Street and proceed to the **corner of Hollywood and Vine.** It's one of the most famous intersections in the world. It's said that if you stand here long enough, you'll see everyone pass by. (You might have to wait longer these days.) The Brown Derby, the legendary hat-shaped restaurant where all the stars dined—and where Gable proposed to Lombard—was on the northwest corner. (It's now a pawn shop.) Farther north on Vine, on the right, is the round **Capitol Records** building; squint and it looks like a stack of records with a spindle on top.

   Return to Sunset. One block west, on the right, is the:

23. **Hollywood Palladium.** It was the site of the studio that made the first feature length movie (Cecil B. DeMille's *The Squaw Man*), and the spot where Valentino made most of his movies. Once the place to hear the big bands (Lawrence Welk played there for years), now it hosts regular concerts.

   Across the street is the site of the:

24. **Earl Carroll Theater,** where the "most beautiful girls in the world" appeared.

(A "gateway to Hollywood" at the corner of Hollywood Boulevard and LaBrea Avenue pays stylistic tribute to Carroll's girls.) It went through several incarnations after Carroll's plane-crash death in 1948, including a recent mortifying stint as the Chevy Chase Theater, tarted up for Chase's short-lived talk show.

Go 1¹/₂ blocks to the corner of Ivar and Sunset; on the left is the:

25. **Cinerama Dome Theater,** the largest regular (not IMAX) movie screen in the nation. (Try to see a movie here. It's quite an experience.)

The northeast corner of Hudson and Sunset is the:

26. **Hollywood Athletic Club,** recently nicely refurbished; this was the place where Johns Wayne and Barrymore would drink, Valentino would hide from angry wives, and Roman Navarro would tryst. Tyrone Power, Sr., died here in the arms of Tyrone, Jr.

At 6671 Sunset Boulevard, on the right, is the:

27. **Crossroads of the World,** the world's first planned outdoor shopping mall. Yes, it looks like a ship. Across the street, in a strip mall (not nearly as nice or as odd looking), is a great place to:

TAKE A BREAK   Designer Donuts (☎ 213/463-7079), co-owned by Steven Spielberg (the owner is presently suing his illustrious partner). The "fancies" here feed many a TV show star filming down the street. The *Cheers* cast, in particular, loved them.

On the northwest corner of Highland Avenue and Sunset Boulevard is:

28. **Hollywood High,** where both David and Ricky Nelson went to school, as did Lana Turner, Carol Burnett, and Michael Jackson's second wife, Debbie Rowe. Elvis Costello recorded a famous concert here in 1979. Across the street on Highland stood the ice cream shop where someone once asked then-teenaged Turner if she wanted to be in movies; she said she had to ask her mother.

Turn right at Highland if you want to take a **side trip** to:

29. **Hollywood Boulevard.** Note the former **Max Factor building** on the right before the corner of Hollywood Boulevard. Turn left on the boulevard; on the right is **Mann's Chinese Theatre** (formerly Grauman's) and the famous footprints. Notice how tiny the silent actresses' feet were; Mary Pickford was less than five feet tall.

The **Walk of Fame** was started at the corner of Hollywood Boulevard and Highland Avenue in 1960. Now, stars pay for the privilege of seeing their name in sparkly cement.

Continue north on Highland Avenue to Yucca; take a right. At 6735, on the left, stood the **Villa Capri** restaurant (now Luther Vandross Studios), where James Dean had dinner the night before he headed down the highway and never came back.

Continue east on Yucca, turn right on Las Palmas, left on Hollywood Boulevard, and then left on Cherokee, where you'll find **1749 Cherokee Avenue,** on the left, now a vacant lot. L. Frank Baum used his earnings from his beloved *Wizard of Oz* books to build "Ozcot," his dream house, here in 1909. It was here he "crossed the shifting sands" in 1919.

Elizabeth Short lived at **1842 Cherokee Avenue** (on the right) 4 months before she achieved fame in 1946 as the Black Dahlia—of course, she had to be murdered and dismembered to do so.

Return to Sunset Boulevard; LaBrea Avenue is the next light. Just south of Sunset Boulevard, on the left at 1418, is:

30. A series of Tudor-style buildings that now houses **A&M Records.** Built in 1918, it was originally Charlie Chaplin's studio.

31. Side Trip: Go right on LaBrea Avenue to Franklin Avenue; turn right and look for the **Highland Gardens Hotel** (formerly the Landmark), at 7047 on the left. This is where Janis Joplin died.

Head back to Sunset Boulevard. At this point, Sunset becomes Guitar Alley—note all the music stores (including **Guitar Central** and their "Rock Walk" of musicians' handprints). Crank up Guns N' Roses "Welcome to the Jungle"—or if you're feeling more like a goofball, some Van Halen.

On the right, at the corner of Poinsettia, is:

32. Ralph's, the place to see rock stars and wannabes buying red meat, sugar, and alcohol at 3am.

At 7561 Sunset Boulevard was:

33. The early '70s home of now local DJ and ancient scenster Rodney Bingenhiemer's **English Disco,** where sex and drugs and rock 'n' roll was a lifestyle. From here, go to the **corner of Sunset and Courtney:** If you were Hugh Grant, this would be a good place (or perhaps not so good) to pick up a prostitute.

Next, head to the corner of Crescent Heights and Sunset boulevards. At the southeast corner is the:

34. Virgin Megastore. You'll now have to resort to being discovered here, as the the famous Schwab's Drugstore is no more. No one really got discovered there, but Harold Arlen stopped in to write down a melody that struck him while driving—and "Somewhere Over the Rainbow" was born.

Across the street, on the southwest corner, was the site of:

35. Silent star Alla Nazimova's fabulous **Garden of Allah Apartments.** Home to dozens of celebrities and such New York City artistic refugees as Dorothy Parker, Robert Benchley, Harpo Marx, and a struggling-to-stay-sober F. Scott Fitzgerald, it was a wild and yet arty place, immortalized in songs from Don Henley to L.A's own Ringling Sisters.

Right in the middle of Crescent Heights Boulevard (on the triangular cement patch) is the former site of:

36. Pandora's Box. In the '60s, when the club was closed to make this part of Sunset Boulevard wider, a hippie protest against the action turned into a riot. If you can, pop in a cassette or CD of Buffalo Springfield's "For What It's Worth"—the verse beginning "What a field day for the heat" is about this event.

37. Side Trip: At this point, if you're interested, go north on Crescent Heights Boulevard and into **Laurel Canyon** for a glimpse at the golden landscape that was home and nirvana to so many rock musicians and hippies of the late '60s/early '70s.

Back on Sunset Boulevard, about a half-block down at no. 8221, looming over the Strip, is the:

38. Chateau Marmont. A magnificent, stately old hotel, favored by celebrities (from Garbo to Keanu) for decades, it's now most famous for being the spot where John Belushi had one speedball too many. The grounds are striking, and the rooms straight out of *Barton Fink* (Belushi died in Bungalow no. 2). (For a room of your own, see chapter 5, "Accommodations.") Next door is new Hollywood hangout, **Bar Marmont.**

Across Sunset Boulevard is the:

39. Dudley Doo Right Emporium, where Jay Ward's widow still sells Bullwinkle and Nastasha tchotchkes. (A Bullwinkle statue is a little farther west, in front of a psychic's shop.)

Put on the Doors's "L.A. Woman" now; this is the beginning of the Sunset Strip, and it fits. (*An extra trivia tidbit:* The first advertising billboard on the Strip for an album was for the first Doors record.) L.A.'s industry is entertainment, and every part of its cultural development has been reflected along these next couple miles. Once it was lined with glamorous nightclubs; in the '60s and '70s, the sidewalks teemed with teenagers in bellbottoms and spandex, respectively. Now it's upscale rock 'n' roll—and pulsing with considerably less life.

At the corner of Sweetzer Avenue and Sunset Boulevard, on the right, is:

40. **The Source** restaurant, where Woody Allen and Diane Keaton had their last meal in *Annie Hall.*

The corner of King's Road brings you to the:

41. **Hyatt on Sunset**—also known as the "Riot House" thanks to the many rock bands who've turned hotel-staying into performance art here (the TV-tossing capers of such guests as Led Zeppelin are rock 'n' roll legend). Here are also modern day theme restaurants **Thunder Roadhouse** (owned in part by Dwight Yoakam and Peter Fonda) and the **House of Blues** (the corrugated tin on the outside came from a building that stood at the famous Crossroads where bluesman Robert Johnson made his mythical pact with the devil).

42. **Side Trip:** Turn left down La Cienega Boulevard; at the corner of Holloway, on the right, is the **Alta Cienega Motel,** second home to Jim Morrison of the Doors (the Doors', office and studio, where they recorded "L.A. Woman," is across the street and a little to the west, on the south side of Santa Monica Boulevard; it's now an Italian restaurant). Turn right on Holloway; Sal Mineo, one of the stars of *Rebel Without a Cause,* was knifed to death in his garage at 8563 Holloway, on the right. Marilyn Monroe and Shelly Winters shared an apartment at no. 8573, next door.

Back on Sunset, just past La Cienega Boulevard on the right, is the site of:

43. **Ben Frank's 24-hour coffee shop.** In the '60s, it was the hip place to nosh; Arthur Lee and Bryan MacLean conceived of *Love* there, and when auditions were held to cast "The Monkees," the notices asked for "Ben Frank's types." It remained a good place for gawking until 1996, when it sadly closed down for good.

On the other side of Sunset Boulevard is the:

44. **Tiffany Theater,** now surrounded by a mall. To its left was the site of **Dino's,** Dean Martin's nightclub, used as the stand-in for *77 Sunset Strip.* To the right stood the **Trocadero** and the **Mocambo,** fabulous night clubs of the Hollywood glamor years.

During this stretch, as you approach **Tower Records** on the right, look to your right and up past the buildings on Sunset Boulevard. The big cream-colored, awkward-looking apartment building with the jutting balconies at **8787 Shoreham Drive** is where, in 1969, Art Linkletter's daughter Diane, under the influence of LSD, jumped from the sixth floor.

At the corner of Holloway, on the left, is a restaurant (it keeps changing hands) once called:

45. **The Early World.** It's where Diner's Club founder and Reagan kitchen cabinet member Alfred Bloomingdale met Vicki Morgan, starting a bizarre adulterous relationship that ended in palimony, allegations of S&M sex with powerful men, and murder.

Across Sunset Boulevard is the parking lot for:

46. **Spago,** still the restaurant for the beautiful people. (Such as they are. You can dine there, too; see chapter 6.)

Now that you know your way around, let's move on to something simple.

1 8 0 0
C A L L
A T T®

For card and collect calls.

The next light is Larabee. On the left hand corner is the:

47. Viper Room. The small room has gone through many incarnations as a rock club (the London Fog, Filthy McNasty's, the Central), but it's as Johnny Depp's prize that the site became notorious. River Phoenix tossed away a beautiful life and career on the sidewalk outside the Sunset exit.

The next light is Clark, and on the right is:

48. The Whiskey, home to many a famous rock band, like the Doors.

At the corner of Hammond, on the right, is:

49. The Roxy, another landmark rock club.

Next door is the:

50. Rainbow Bar & Grill. Under another name, this is where Vincente Minelli proposed to Judy Garland, and where Marilyn Monroe met Joe DiMaggio on a blind date. As the Rainbow, bands like Led Zeppelin made it their favorite place for debauched behavior. Big-haired rock dudes of varying degrees of fame still hang there.

Two blocks down, also on the right, is the former Gazarri's (now **Billboard Live;** see chapter 10), where such heavy metal bands as Van Halen and Guns 'n' Roses got their start. It's been a club since the '30s.

At the corner of Doheny Drive is where Beverly Hills begins. Suddenly, the landscape becomes considerably more upscale (indeed, from here on out no house you see will sell for much less than a million dollars). The transition is so abrupt that it almost causes a mental car crash. Beverly Hills is green and manicured to within an inch of its life. And everything is big. Really big.

51. A Sordid Side Trip: At Foothill Road, hang a U-turn and go back east on Sunset Boulevard to the next block, Elm. Turn right. At **722 Elm Drive,** on the left, is the former home of Jose and Kitty Menendez, whose sons, Lyle and Erik, were finally convicted of their murder, many years after confessing to it.

Take Elm back to Sunset and turn right. Go one block; on the right is:

52. A huge vacant lot, once the gorgeous mansion of Sheik Al-Fassi. The Sheik bought it in 1978, and horrified his neighbors by painting the statues with anatomical correctness, and adding other tacky elements. (For glimpses of the Sheik's interior decorating skills, rent Steve Martin's *The Jerk.* The mansion scenes later in the movie were shot at the Sheik's home, untouched by set decorator hands.) It burned down in 1980 and was leveled a few years later. The lot is for sale, in case you have some loose change sitting around.

Two more blocks to the west, on the right, is the landmark:

53. Beverly Hills Hotel. It just got a face-lift, turning its famous Pepto-Bismol pink into more of a peach tone. Play the Eagles's "Hotel California" while admiring its inspiration; the top of the three towers is the shot on the cover of the album.

You may want to make an extended trip into this neighborhood if you're interested in seeing the homes of the stars who live in this area; for details, see "Hollywood at Home: A Driving Tour," earlier in this chapter.

Next, check out:

54. 10000 Sunset Boulevard, on the left. Nope, that's not a crowd of people milling about on a stranger's lawn—they're statues. The almost-certainly eccentric folks who live there have been adding figures to their lawn for some years.

Sunset now takes a long hard curve (one of two referred to as the famous "Deadman's Curve"; put on the Jan and Dean song and try not to cut your trip short by wiping out); on the left, at the corner of Carolwood, is:

55. A very large, very pink house, the former home of Marilyn wannabe Jayne Mansfield—pink was her favorite color. Englebert Humperdinck now owns it.

Soon you'll reach Bel Air, which feels somewhat older and warmer than Beverly Hills. Notice how the trees stand taller and wilder. Everything is considerably less landscaped and ostentatious—the difference between old money and nouveau riche, I guess. Notice the:

56. Gates to Bel Air at Beverly Glen Boulevard (and at later intersections) on the right. They have been closed only once, during the 1962 Bel Air fire (though closure was threatened again during the 1992 riots).

At Hilgard Avenue begins the:

57. University of California, Los Angeles (UCLA), on the left. Everything on the left-hand side continues to be UCLA until Veteran Avenue; Westwood Village is south of there.

The next big curve you encounter is the other so called "Deadman's Curve." The freeway you cross is the legendary San Diego Freeway (I-405), bane of all L.A. drivers. This is also the beginning of Brentwood; despite its *Peyton Place*-style reputation of the last couple years, it used to be a low-profile, family-oriented wealthy community.

58. Another Sordid Side Trip: Turn left at Kenter Canyon Avenue. It merges into Bundy Drive, which then dog-legs first to the left across San Vicente Boulevard (admire the famous coral trees down the center), and then to the right. On the right, at the corner of Bundy Drive and Dorothy, is **Nicole Brown Simpson's condo.** Sneer at the lookie-loos taking pictures, and then snap a few yourself. What the heck. You're on vacation.

Return to Sunset.

59. Side Trip: Turn left on Carmelita, the second street after Kenter Canyon (there's no light and it's a small street, so watch for it). The side streets on the left are all called Helena, starting with 18th Helena. Count down to 5th Helena, and turn left to **12305 5th Helena.** This is the house where Marilyn Monroe died.

Return to Sunset again.

60. Your Final Side Trip: Go to Cliffwood, the seventh street after Kenter, and turn right. Turn left on Highwood (the next street), and follow it until it ends at Rockingham Drive. Turn right; two blocks up, on the corner at Ashford, is **O.J. Simpson's house.** (For extra fun, time how long it takes you to drive from Nicole's to O.J.'s. Here's a hint: not very.)

Keep going on Rockingham until it veers to the right and meets Bristol, on the right. At **426 N. Bristol** is the house where Joan Crawford became Mommy Dearest.

Return to Sunset Boulevard once again. At Mandeville Canyon, you'll enter Pacific Palisades. (Notice how the temperature has dropped as much as 20° since Olvera Street, and thank the ocean breeze.) Put on a little Beach Boys— "California Girls" is a good choice—and admire how open, sunny and, well, California-y it all gets.

On the right, about 1.2 miles from Mandeville Canyon, is:

61. Will Rogers State Historic Park, built around the humorist's home. It's a fine place for a picnic, and polo matches are frequently held in the field (for more on the park, see chapter 7).

In another mile, you'll reach the business center of the Palisades. About another 1½ miles after that, you should have your first ocean sighting. Put on Randy

Newman's "I Love L.A." (yes, it's more than a little sarcastic and ironic, but, somehow, it's also just right) as you round the home stretch. (Of course, you've now gone from the East Side to the West Side, while the song sings vice versa, so don't get confused.)

About 2¹/₂ miles from downtown Pacific Palisades—nearly 24 miles from Olvera Street, where you started out—is the final, and perhaps most unexpected, stop on the Sunset tour. On the left is the:

62. Self Realization Fellowship Shrine (watch carefully or you could miss the entrance), founded by guru Paramhansa Yogananda (this is the bigger sibling of the one in Hollywood). The impossibly calm and lovely parklike shrine, complete with lake, is dedicated to meditation and harmony among all religions; it's a surprising find along busy Sunset and well worth taking a walk through. But best of all: Contained in a marble sarcophagus here are the only entombed ashes of Ghandi. The rest were scattered in India; but a portion were sent here as a gift—a most unlikely addition to Los Angeles.

And now, just keep driving. See the water? That's the Pacific Ocean. Don't forget to hit the brakes.

Fittingly, this is the literal end of Western Civilization—and don't think we don't know it and aren't proud. From here on out, it's the mysteries of the Far East.

9 Shopping

Whether you're looking for souvenirs with traditional Southern California images (someone will love that "U.C.L.A. on a clear day" T-shirt), fine goods available only here, cutting-edge Melrose Avenue fashions, Hollywood memorabilia, books on topics of local interest, or some quirky thing that will always remind you of your trip to L.A., I guarantee you'll enjoy the diversity of the city's shopping scene as much as the residents do.

A note on hours: Street shops are generally open Monday through Saturday from 10 or 11am to 5 or 6pm. Many are open Sunday, particularly those near the beaches, movie theaters, or clusters of other stores. In addition, quite a few choose one night a week, often Wednesday or Thursday, to offer extended evening hours. Mall shops take their cue from the anchor department stores; as a rule, they open around 10am and do business till 8 or 9pm. Sundays shave an hour or two off each side, while holiday periods increase mall hours substantially.

Sales tax in Los Angeles is 8.25%; experienced shoppers know to have larger items shipped directly home to save the tax.

1 L.A.'s Top Shopping Streets & Neighborhoods

Here's a rundown of L.A.'s most interesting shopping areas—from the fine and chic to the funky and cheap—along with some highlights of each neighborhood, to give you an idea of what you'll find there. For more details on the shops in these areas and in other parts of town, see "Shopping A to Z," below.

SANTA MONICA & THE BEACHES

Third Street Promenade. 3rd St. from Broadway to Wilshire Blvd., Santa Monica.

Packed with chain stores and boutiques as well as a dozen restaurants and a movie multiplex, Santa Monica's pedestrian-only section of Third Street is one of the most popular shopping areas in the city. It offers the variety and "park-once" convenience of a mall, with the added pleasures of fresh ocean air and a festival atmosphere. The street bustles on into the evening with a seemingly endless assortment of street performers, and an endless parade of souls. Stores stay open late (often till 1 or 2am on the weekends) for the movie-going crowds. Because the Promenade is popular among Santa Monica's younger hipsters, you'll find good CD and music memorabilia stores like **Hear Music, Pyramid Music,** and **Mayhem,** plus avant-garde clothing boutiques like **NaNa.** Browsers of all sorts will appreciate the variety of bookstores along the street, including the truly unique **Hennessey & Ingalls,** a large bookstore devoted to art and architecture. There's plenty of metered parking in structures on the adjacent streets—bring lots of quarters.

Main Street. Between Pacific St. and Rose Ave., Santa Monica and Venice.

The primary strip connecting Santa Monica and Venice, Main Street has a relaxed, beach-community vibe that sets it apart from similar streets; the stores along it straddle the fashion fence between upscale trendy and beach-bum edgy. This stretch south of Pico Boulevard is ideal for strolling, and boasts a healthy combination of mall standards like **Z Gallerie** home furnishings and upscale, left-of-center individual boutiques. Our favorites are **Just In Case,** selling "cruelty-free" handbags and luggage, and **The Bey's Garden** for scented candles, incense, and terrific gift ideas. If you're one of the increasing number of cigar aficionados, the **Royal Cigar Society** sells a variety of stogies and has a smoking lounge inside the shop. You'll also find plenty of casually hip cafés and restaurants, as well as an espresso shop on every block.

Montana Avenue. Between 17th and 7th sts., Santa Monica.

This northern Santa Monica avenue invites window shopping at boutique after boutique, or just people-watching over a cappuccino at an outdoor café. The shopping isn't much more sophisticated than that along Main Street, but the area and crowd make it seem so. This is probably what Beverly Hills was like before it went over the top. There are lots of upscale take-out cafés catering to the many busy yuppies (and on-the-rise celebrities) who make their homes in this part of town.

Santa Monica Place. Colorado Ave. (at 2nd St.), Santa Monica. ☎ **310/394-5451.**

About 140 shops occupy three bright stories anchored by **Robinson's/May** and **Macy's** department stores. The usual mall shops are augmented by more unusual finds like a branch of **Frederick's of Hollywood** and KCET Public Television's **Store of Knowledge,** which has among its wares some thought-provoking and fun stuff for kids. The mall's food pavilion sells an array of fast foods, and includes several health-oriented eateries.

Fisherman's Village. 13763 Fiji Way, Marina del Rey. ☎ **310/823-5411.**

Marina del Rey's waterfront village is touristy, yes—but it's a pleasant waterfront stroll nonetheless. International imports (an umbrella phrase that covers everything from rare $800 Hawaiian Niihau-shell necklaces to $2 plastic coin purses from Hong Kong) are available in shops lining the cobblestoned walks of this Old English whaling village–style shopping center. The stores and restaurants surround an authentic 60-foot-tall lighthouse.

L.A.'S WESTSIDE & BEVERLY HILLS

West Third Street. Between Fairfax and Robertson blvds.

You can shop 'til you drop on this newly trendy strip, which is anchored on the east end by **Farmer's Market.** Many of Melrose Avenue's shops have relocated here, alongside some terrific up-and-comers, several cafés, and the much-lauded restaurant **Locanda Veneta** (see chapter 6, "Dining"). "Fun" is more the catchword here than "funky"; the shops, including the vintage clothing stores, tend a bit more to the refined than they do along Melrose. Two bookstores, **The Traveler's Bookcase** and **The Cook's Library,** make it worth the trip; there's also **Who Makes Sense,** for aromatic oils, candles, and gifts; and **Chado Tea Room,** a genteel Frommer's favorite.

The Beverly Center. 8500 Beverly Blvd. (at La Cienega Blvd.). ☎ **310/854-0070.**

When the Beverly Center opened on L.A.'s Westside, there was more than a bit of concern about the impending "mallification" of Los Angeles. Loved for its convenience and disdained for its penitentiary-style architecture (and the "no validations" parking fee), Beverly Center contains about 170 standard mall shops (leaning a bit toward the high end) anchored on each side by **Macy's** and **Blooomingdales** department stores. You can see it blocks away, looking like a gigantic angular boulder punctuated with the **Hard Rock Cafe's** roof-mounted Cadillac on one corner.

The Sunset Strip. Between La Cienega Blvd. and Doheny Dr., West Hollywood.

The monster-size billboards advertising the latest rock god make it clear that this is rock 'n' roll territory. **Tower Records** and the **Virgin Megastore** dominate a strip lined with trendy restaurants, industry-oriented hotels, and dozens of shops offering outrageous fashions and chunky stage accessories. One anomaly is **Sunset Plaza,** an upscale cluster of Georgian-style shops resembling Beverly Hills at its snootiest. Although the Strip isn't a great place for walking more than a block or two, you might cruise along and stop if something catches your eye.

La Brea Avenue. North of Wilshire Blvd.

This is L.A.'s artiest shopping strip. The stores here are less concentrated; luckily, street parking (at meters—bring a pocketful of quarters) is pretty easy to find, except after 4pm, when the curb lane is put into rush-hour-traffic use. Anchored by the giant **American Rag,** Cie. alterna-complex, La Brea is home to lots of great urban antique stores (dealing in deco, arts and crafts, 1950s Modern, and the like; there's also **Liz's Antique Hardware**), vintage clothiers like hip **Yellowstone Clothing Co.,** and furniture stores like **Mortise & Tenon,** whose simple wood pieces hint at Craftsman and Mission style; one secret pleasure is tiny **Drea Kadilak** millinery. You'll find some of the city's hippest restaurants, such as **Campanile, Citrus,** and many more, on or near this stretch of La Brea Avenue.

Pacific Design Center. 8687 Melrose Ave., West Hollywood, CA 90069. ☎ **310/657-0800.**

Something of an architectural and cultural landmark, the Pacific Design Center is the West Coast's largest facility for interior design goods and fine furnishings. It houses 200 showrooms filled with furniture, fabrics, flooring, wallcovering, kitchen and bath fixtures, lighting, art, and accessories. Locals refer to the PDC as the "Blue Whale" in reference to its exterior, composed entirely of brilliant blue glass. Although businesses here sell to the trade only, the public is welcome to browse. There's also an eclectic Euro-Asian restaurant, **Fusion** (☎ **310/659-6012**). The menu, which offers everything from borscht to pappardelle in rabbit sauce, is the creation of Bruce Marder, of Rebecca's and West Beach Cafe fame.

Rodeo Drive and Beverly Hills's Golden Triangle. Between Santa Monica Blvd., Wilshire Blvd., and Crescent Dr., Beverly Hills.

Sometimes it's fun to see how the other half lives. Everyone knows about Rodeo Drive, Beverly Hills's most famous shopping street; this is where you'll find the couture shops from high fashion's Old Guard—names like **Cartier, Hermés, Louis Vuitton, Tiffany & Co.,** and **Gucci** need no introduction. But believe it or not, the several blocks surrounding Rodeo (known as the "Golden Triangle") also have plenty for you and me, like the nicest **Gap** you're likely to ever see, and comfy-Naugahyde **Nate & Al's** delicatessen (see chapter 6, "Dining"). Check out two examples of the Beverly Hills version of minimalls, each a tiny, tony diorama: the **Rodeo Collection,** 421 N. Rodeo Dr.; and **Two Rodeo,** at Wilshire Boulevard.

Century City Marketplace. 10250 Santa Monica Blvd., Century City. ☎ **310/277-3898.**

This open-air mall, anchored by **Macy's** and **Bloomingdales,** is located on what was once a Twentieth-Century Fox back lot just west of Beverly Hills. Most of the dozens of smaller shops here are upscale chain-store fare: among the offerings are the **Pottery Barn, Ann Taylor, Joan & David,** and **Brentanos,** as well as a giant **Crate & Barrel** and a multiplex with about a hundred (well, not quite) movie screens. If you have to "mall it," this is the most pleasant one in the L.A. area.

HOLLYWOOD

Melrose Avenue. Between Fairfax and La Brea aves.

It's showing some wear—some stretches have become downright ugly—but this is still one of the most exciting shopping streets in the country for cutting-edge fashions and eye-popping people-watching. There are scores of shops selling the latest in clothes, gifts, jewelry, and accessories. Melrose is a playful stroll, dotted with plenty of hip restaurants and funky shops that are sure to shock. Where else could you find green patent-leather cowboy boots, a working 19th-century pocket watch, and an inflatable girlfriend in the same shopping spree?

Hollywood Boulevard. Between Gower St. and La Brea Ave.

One of Los Angeles's most famous streets is, for the most part, a sleazy strip. But along the Walk of Fame, between the T-shirt shops and greasy pizza parlors, you'll find some excellent poster shops, souvenir stores, and Hollywood memorabilia dealers. It's a silly, tourist-oriented strip that's worth getting out of your car for, especially if there's a chance of getting your hands on that long-sought-after Ethel Merman autograph or *200 Motels* poster. Flashy **Frederick's of Hollywood** is celebrating 50 years in Hollywood, and **Musso & Frank Grill,** the Boulevard's touch of class, is nearly 80 years young and still serving steak and martinis to the weary.

DOWNTOWN

Since the late, lamented department store grande dame Bullock's closed in 1993 (her deco masterpiece salons rescued to house Southwestern Law School's library), downtown has become even less of a shopping destination than ever. But savvy Angelenos still go for bargains in the garment and fabric districts, florists and bargain-hunters arrive at the vast **Flower Mart** before dawn for the city's best selection of fresh blooms, and families of all ethnicities and budgets stroll the **Grand Central Market.** Many of the once-splendid streets are lined with cut-rate luggage and cheap electronics storefronts. All in all, shopping downtown can be a gritty but rewarding experience for the adventuresome.

ARCO Plaza, at 505 S. Flower St. (☎ **213/486-3511**), is an underground labyrinth of chain stores and boutiques used primarily by lawyers and other workers from the downtown high-rises. If you're based dowtown, this is a good place to go if you're looking for the basics.

THE SAN FERNANDO VALLEY

Studio City. Ventura Blvd. between Laurel Canyon Blvd. and Fulton Ave.

Long beloved by Valley residents, Studio City is conveniently located, freeway- and canyon-close to Hollywood and the Westside. Ventura Boulevard has a distinct personality in each of several Valley communities it passes through, but Studio City is where you'll find small boutiques and antique stores, quirky little businesses (many dating from the '40s and '50s), and less congested branches of popular chains like **The Gap, Pier 1 Imports,** and **Blockbuster.** Parking is a cinch on the street except during holiday season, when many stores team up to gaily decorate these friendly blocks, often agreeing to mutually observe extended evening hours. The four blocks between Laurel Canyon Boulevard and Whitsett Avenue are the most concentrated, and easily walkable in an afternoon. Start with the city's best pancakes at **Du-par's Coffee Shop** (see chapter 6) and have fun!

Universal CityWalk. Universal Center Dr., Universal City. ☎ **818/622-4455.**

Technically an outdoor mall rather than a shopping area, Universal CityWalk gets mention here because it's so utterly unique. A pedestrian promenade next door to Universal Studios, CityWalk is dominated by brightly colored, outrageously surreal oversize storefronts. The heavily touristed faux street is home to an inordinate number of restaurants, including **B.B. King's Blues Club,** the newest **Hard Rock Cafe,** and a branch of the **Hollywood Athletic Club** featuring a restaurant and pool hall. This is consumer culture gone haywire, an egotistical eyesore that, in terms of shopping, is not worth a special visit; but kids will love the noisy carnival atmosphere and the **Warner Brothers** store.

2 Shopping A to Z
ANTIQUES
L.A.'s Westside & Beverly Hills
Also see **Liz's Antique Hardware** under "Housewares & Interior Design," and **Second Time Around Watch Co.** under "Timepieces," below; for antique globes, see **The Yellow Room,** under "Gifts & Novelties," below.

The Antique Guild. 8800 Venice Blvd., near Culver City. ☎ **310/838-3131.**

Billing itself as "the world's largest antique outlet," the Guild is a veritable warehouse of history, with more than 2 acres of antiques displayed in the former Helms Bakery headquarters. Its buyers regularly purchase entire contents of European castles, beer halls, estates, and mansions. Look for everything from old armoires to chandeliers to stained glass, crystal, china, clocks, washstands, tables, mirrors, and much more.

Memory Lane. 8387 Third St. (At Orlando), Los Angeles. ☎ **213/655-4571.**

This narrow trove of '40s, '50s, and '60s collectibles features such treasures as Formica dinette sets, bakelite radios, cocktail shakers and sets, unusual lamps, and a few well-chosen coats, dresses, and accessories.

Hollywood
Off The Wall. 7325 Melrose Ave., Los Angeles. ☎ **213/930-1185.**

This collection of oversized antiques includes kitschy statues, deco furnishings, carved wall reliefs, Wurlitzer jukeboxes, giant restaurant and gas station signs, pinball machines, and lots and lots of neon.

The San Fernando Valley
For antique jewelry, see **King's Cross** under "Jewelry," below.

Arte de Mexico. 5356 Riverton Ave., North Hollywood. ☎ **818/769-5090.**

Seven warehouses full of carved furniture and wrought iron once sold only to moviemakers and restaurants are now available to the public. One of the most fascinating places in North Hollywood.

The Cranberry House (Studio City Antique Mall). 12318 Ventura Blvd. (2 blocks east of Whitsett), Studio City. ☎ **818/506-8945.**

Under a berry-colored awning, several storefront windows hint at the treasures within this antiques and collectibles store featuring over 100 different sellers. Be sure to haggle . . . even front desk staff are often authorized by the individual dealers to strike a bargain.

✪ Piccolo Pete's Art Deco. 13814 Ventura Blvd. (west of Woodman Ave.), Sherman Oaks. ☎ **818/907-9060.**

A lovely shop selling art nouveau, deco, and Moderne furnishings and art, including clocks, lighting fixtures, pottery, and dinnerware. A recent museum exhibition on art deco wasn't as nice as the perfect specimens in Piccolo Pete's—but expect their prices to reflect that perfection.

ART

Santa Monica & the Beaches

Bergamot Station. 2525 Michigan Ave. (east of Cloverfield Blvd.), Santa Monica. ☎ **310/ 829-5854.**

Once a station for the Red Car trolley line, Bergamot Station's industrial space is now home to about two dozen art galleries, a cafe, a bookstore, and offices. The train yard is located at the terminus of Michigan Avenue east of Cloverfield Boulevard; most of the galleries are closed Mondays. Exhibits change often and vary widely, ranging from a Julius Shulman black-and-white photo retrospective of L.A.'s Case Study Houses to a provocative exhibit of Vietnam War propaganda posters from the U.S. and Vietnam, to whimsical furniture constructed entirely of corrugated cardboard. Here's just a sampling of offerings:

Tables, chairs, beds, sofas, lighting, screens, dressers, and bathroom fixtures are some of the functional art pieces for sale at the **Gallery of Functional Art** (☎ **310/ 829-6990**). Smaller items such as jewelry, watches, flatware, candlesticks, ceramics, and glass are also shown. All work is one of a kind or limited edition.

The **Rosamund Felson Gallery** (☎ **310/828-8488**) is well known for show-casing L.A.–based contemporary artists. This is a good place to get a taste of current trends.

Track 16 Gallery (☎ **310/264-4678**) mounts exhibitions that range from pop art to avant-garde inventiveness. It's always worth seeing what's going on here.

L.A.'s Westside & Beverly Hills

Every Picture Tells A Story. 7525 Beverly Blvd. (between Fairfax and La Brea aves.), Los Angeles. ☎ **213/932-6070.**

This gallery, devoted to the art of children's literature, is frequented by young-at-heart art aficionados as well as parents introducing their kids to the concept of an art gallery. Works by Maurice Sendak (*Where the Wild Things Are*), Tim Burton (*The Nightmare Before Christmas*), and original lithos of *Curious George* and *Charlotte's Web* are featured. Call to see what's going on; they usually combine exhibitions of illustrators with story readings and interactive workshops.

Murray Feldman Gallery. On the plaza at the Pacific Design Center, 8687 Melrose Ave., West Hollywood. ☎ **310/657-0800,** ext. 264.

This is one of the few L.A. galleries dedicated to the decorative arts and architectural design. It's a great excuse to visit the vast Pacific Design Center.

Name That Toon. 8483 Melrose Ave., Los Angeles. ☎ **213/653-5633.**

Several L.A. galleries sell clay, computer, and cel animation art, but none has a better selection than this well-stocked shop, which specializes in original production cels from Disney, Warner Brothers, Hanna-Barbera, Dr. Seuss, and Walter Lantz. Original *Ren & Stimpy* and *Simpsons* art is also available. Phone for information on artists' receptions, lecturers, and other special events.

PaceWildenstein. 9540 Wilshire Blvd., Beverly Hills. ☎ **310/205-5522.**

A stark, modern space ideal for showcasing the oversize contemporary pieces that draw art-minded members of L.A.'s entertainment elite, such as Steve Martin and David Geffen.

BOOKS

Santa Monica & the Beaches

Hennessey & Ingalls. 1254 Third St. Promenade, Santa Monica. ☎ **310/458-9074.**

A bookstore devoted to art and architecture, from magnificent coffee-table photography books to graphic arts titles and obscure biographies of artists and art movements.

L.A. (The Bookstore). 208 Pier Ave. ($\frac{1}{2}$ block east of Main St.), Santa Monica. ☎ **310/ 4-LA-BOOK.**

Fiction or nonfiction, pulp or classic—if it's about the Southland, written by a native author, or has anything to do with L.A., this is the place to find it. Tucked away next to the Novel Cafe, this specialty shop also maintains a Web site for catalog information and other tidbits at **http://www.labooks.com.**

Midnight Special Bookstore. 1318 Third St. Promenade, Santa Monica. ☎ **310/ 393-2923.**

This medium-size general bookshop, located on the Third Street Promenade, is known for its good small-press selection and regular poetry readings.

L.A.'s Westside & Beverly Hills

✪ **Book Soup.** 8800 Sunset Blvd., West Hollywood. ☎ **310/657-1072.**

This has long been one of L.A.'s most celebrated bookshops, selling both mainstream and small-press books and hosting regular book signings and author nights. Book Soup is a great browsing shop; it has a large selection of show-biz books and an extensive outdoor news and magazine stand on one side. The owners recently annexed an adjacent café space so they can better cater to hungry intellectuals. The **Book Soup Bistro** has an appealing bar, a charming outdoor patio, and an extensive menu that includes alphabet soup.

C.G. Jung Bookstore & Library. 10349 W. Pico Blvd. (east of Beverly Glen Blvd.), Los Angeles. ☎ **310/556-1196.**

This bookshop specializes in analytical psychology, folklore, fairy tales, alchemy, dream studies, myths, symbolism, and other related topics. Tapes and videocassettes are also sold.

The Cook's Library. 8373 W. Third St. ☎ **213/655-3141.**

There's a specialty bookshop for everyone in L.A.; this is where the city's top chefs find both classic and deliciously offbeat cookbooks and other food-oriented tomes. Browsing is welcomed, even encouraged, with tea, tasty treats, and rocking chairs.

Dutton's Brentwood Books. 11975 San Vicente Blvd. (west of Montana Ave.), Los Angeles. ☎ **310/476-6263.**

This huge bookshop is well known not only for an extensive selection of new books, but for its good children's section and an eclectic collection of used and rare books. There are over 120,000 in-stock titles at any one time. They host regular author readings and signings, and sell cards, stationery, prints, CDs, and selected software.

Los Angeles Audubon Society Bookstore. 7377 Santa Monica Blvd., West Hollywood. ☎ **213/876-0202.**

A terrific selection of books on nature, adventure travel, and ecology is augmented by bird-watching equipment and accessories. Phone for information on L.A. nature walks. Closed Monday.

Mysterious Bookshop. 8763 Beverly Blvd. (between Robertson and San Vicente blvds.), West Hollywood. ☎ **310/659-2959.**

Over 20,000 used, rare, and out-of-print titles make this the area's best mystery, es-pionage, detective, and thriller bookshop. Author appearances and other special events are regularly hosted.

Traveler's Bookcase. 8375 W. Third St. ☎ **213/655-0575.**

This store, one of the best travel bookshops in the West, stocks a huge selection of guidebooks and travel literature, as well as maps and travel accessories. A quar-terly newsletter chronicles the travel adventures of the genial owners, who know first-hand the most helpful items to carry. Look for regular readings by well-known travel writers.

Hollywood

Samuel French Book Store. 7623 Sunset Blvd. (between Fairfax and La Brea aves.), Holly-wood. ☎ **213/876-0570.**

This is L.A.'s biggest theater and movie bookstore. Plays, screenplays, and film books are all sold here, as well as scripts for Broadway and Hollywood blockbusters. Also in Studio City at 11963 Ventura Blvd. (☎ 818/762-0535).

CAMERA EQUIPMENT

San Fernando Valley

Studio City Camera Exchange. 12174 Ventura Blvd. (1 block west of Laurel Canyon Blvd.), Studio City. ☎ **818/762-4749.**

There's comfort in the '40s architecture of this corner photography store—like an old friend, Studio City Camera is there if you need supplies: film, developing, batteries, frames or albums, and used cameras (some quite collectible). You're also welcome to stop just to talk shop with fellow shutterbugs behind the counter.

CANDLES & OILS

Santa Monica & the Beaches

The Bey's Garden. 2919 Main St. (between Ashland & Pier sts.), Santa Monica. ☎ **310/399-5420.**

This fragrant, esoteric shop specializes in aromatic oils, candles, herbal body treat-ments, and exotic soaps. Check out their porous clay "diffuser" pots: When filled with the essential oil of your choice, they slowly diffuse scent into the room.

L.A.'s Westside & Beverly Hills

Who Makes Sense. 8363 W. Third St., Los Angeles. ☎ **213/651-0311.**

The staff can be a little snooty about their fine line of essential oils, scented lotions, bath crystals, and other gifts, but Who Makes Sense carries just the right thing to pamper yourself or a dear friend. Delicate jewelry and a line of men's products round out the selection, which also includes mirrors, picture frames, and tabletop cherub statues.

CHINA, SILVER & GLASS

L.A.'s Westside & Beverly Hills

Ⓢ **Dishes à la Carte.** 5650 W. Third St. (at La Brea Ave.), Los Angeles. ☎ **213/938-6223.**

Modeled after New York's *Fish's Eddie,* this little ceramics shop carries factory seconds and obsolete patterns of well- and little-known brands alike. You'll find Fiestaware next to locally hand-painted pieces and durable restaurant dishes.

Tiffany & Co. 210 N. Rodeo Dr., Beverly Hills. ☎ **310/273-8880.**

Amid the pieces of crystal and china, shoppers will find an exquisite collection of fine jewelry known the world over for classic styles. Top designers include Elsa Peretti and Paloma Picasso.

CIGARS

Santa Monica & the Beaches

Royal Cigar Society. 2814 Main St., Santa Monica. ☎ **310/581-8555.**

Newly opened in 1996, at the height of the cigar-fancy craze that's sweeping Los Angeles, this store sells a variety of smokes. Patrons are invited to enjoy their purchases in nooks replete with comfortable armchairs and Mission-style furniture. A rear salon is reserved for members.

Downtown

Ⓢ La Plata Cigars. 1026 S. Grand Ave. (between 11th St. and Olympic Blvd.). ☎ **213/747-8561.**

Los Angeles's only cigar factory, family-run La Plata has been hand rolling them since 1947. The public is welcome to visit their compact downtown factory and watch how Cuban artisans create these premium prizes; afterward, enter the shop's humidor to choose from thousands of fresh cigars in all sizes—for about half of what the fancy places charge. Open Monday to Friday 7am to 4:30pm.

DEPARTMENT STORES

L.A.'s Westside & Beverly Hills

Barneys New York. 9570 Wilshire Blvd., Beverly Hills. ☎ **310/276-4400.**

The celebrated New York clothier opened this Beverly Hills satellite shop in 1994, and L.A. is already looking better. Saxophonist and former *Tonight Show* bandleader Branford Marsalis gets his Gaultiers here. **Barney Greengrass,** New York's "sturgeon king," has opened a restaurant on the top floor (see chapter 6, for review).

Neiman Marcus. 9700 Wilshire Blvd., Beverly Hills. ☎ **310/550-5900.**

Distinctive men's and women's fashions, world-famous furs, precious jewels, unique gifts, and legendary personal service have made this one of the area's most successful department stores (despite the "Needless Mark-up").

Nordstrom. In the Westside Pavilion, 10830 W. Pico Blvd., West Los Angeles. ☎ **310/470-6155.** Also in Glendale and Woodland Hills.

Emphasis on customer service has won this Seattle-based chain a loyal following. Equally devoted to women's and men's fashions, the store has one of the best shoe selections in the city, and there are thousands of suits in stock.

Saks Fifth Avenue. 9600 Wilshire Blvd., Beverly Hills. ☎ **310/275-4211.**

Los Angeles's oldest branch of this famous New York–based shop is as opulent as any. Saks sells fashions and gifts for men, women, and children, and has a well-respected restaurant on the top floor.

EDIBLES
BAGELS

Noah's Bagels. 16 Southern California locations, including Santa Monica's Main St. (☎ **310/ 396-4339**), West Hollywood (☎ 310/289-1795), Beverly Hills (☎ 310/550-7392), and Studio City (☎ 818/760-1446).

Stop into Noah's "A Taste of Old New York" for a bagel and a shmear—and a Yiddish refresher course. Large and chewy in the style of New York's legendary H&H bagel bakery, Noah's come in 14 varieties, with your choice of 10 cream cheese "shmears"; since this Bay Area chain set up shop in the Southland, they've quickly established themselves as the best bagel around.

BAKERIES
L.A.'s Westside & Beverly Hills

Mani's Bakery. 8801 Santa Monica Blvd. (at Palm, east of San Vicente Blvd.), West Hollywood. ☎ **310/659-5955.**

If I didn't call it the "sugar-free" bakery, you'd never be able to tell—Mani's recipe wizards are that talented. Cakes, muffins, cookies, and pastries are all sweetened with fruit juice and other alternatives; many are even approved for hard-core diabetics. But all this health-consciousness hasn't kept Mani's from the enormous popularity it enjoys throughout L.A. as both a bakery and hip coffee joint. Best bet: the carrot-pineapple muffin.

Also at 519 S. Fairfax Blvd. (between Third St. and Wilshire Blvd.) in Los Angeles (☎ **213/938-8800**); and in Studio City at 3960 Laurel Canyon Blvd. (south of Ventura Blvd.; ☎ **818/762-7200**).

Downtown

Ⓢ **Phoenix Bakery.** 969 N. Broadway (Chinatown), downtown. ☎ **213/628-4642.**

The freshest, flakiest, sweetest almond cookies are baked right here in the heart of Chinatown; they come in three sizes and cost only pennies each. The bakery is also remarkable for its endless selection of special-occasion cake decorations: whatever theme you desire, from *Pocahontas* to *Sesame Street* to *Star Trek,* they have the plastic figures and accessories to make it memorable.

MARKETS
L.A.'s Westside & Beverly Hills

Farmer's Market. 6333 W. Third St. (at Fairfax Ave.), Los Angeles. ☎ **213/933-9211.**

The city's most famous food carnival is also one of Hollywood's top attractions. Started during the Depression, the outdoor plaza has grown to include spice and candle shops, a friendly outdoor diner, and dozens of stands selling fresh and prepared foods for consumption on or off the premises. Closed evenings.

Downtown

Ⓢ **Grand Central Market.** 317 S. Broadway (between 3rd and 4th sts.), downtown. ☎ **213/624-2378.**

This bustling market, opened in 1917, has watched the face of downtown L.A. change, but has changed little itself. Today it serves Latino families, enterprising restaurateurs, and home cooks in search of unusual ingredients and bargain fruits and vegetables. On weekends you'll be greeted by a lively mariachi band at the Hill Street entrance, near my favorite Market feature: the fruit juice counter, which dispenses

Dressing the Part: Where to Find Hollywood's Hand-Me-Downs

Admit it: You've dreamed of being a glamorous movie or TV star—everyone has. Well, you shouldn't expect to be "discovered" during your L.A. vacation, but you can live out your fantasy by dressing the part. Costumes from famous movies, TV show wardrobes, castoffs from celebrity closets—they're easier to find (and more affordable to own) than you might think.

A good place to start is **Star Wares,** 2817 Main St., Santa Monica (☎ 310/ 399-0224; open daily noon–6pm). This deceptively small shop regularly has leftovers from Cher's closet, as well as celebrity-worn apparel from the likes of Joan Rivers, Tim Curry, and Kathleen Turner. They also stock movie production wardrobes and genuine collector's items. If the $5,000 *Star Trek: The Next Generation* uniform or *Planet Of the Apes* military regalia you covet is out of your price range, don't worry: You can still pick up one of Johnny Depp's *Benny and Joon* outfits, dresses from the closets of Lucille Ball and Greer Garson, or ET's bathrobe, all of which are surprisingly affordable. Many pieces have accompanying photos or movie stills, so you'll know exactly who donned your piece before you.

That isn't the case, however, at **The Place & Co.,** 8820 S. Sepulveda Blvd., Westchester (☎ 310/645-1539; open Mon–Sat 10am–6pm), where the anonymity of their well-heeled clientele (sellers and buyers) is strictly honored. Here you'll find men's and women's haute couture—always the latest fashions, gently worn—at a fraction of the Rodeo Drive prices. All the designers are here—Ungaro, Bill Blass, Krizia, Donna Karan. You may have even seen that Armani suit or Sonia Rykiel gown you find in the racks on an Academy Awards attendee last year!

For sheer volume, you can't beat **It's A Wrap,** 3315 W. Magnolia Blvd., Burbank (☎ 818/567-7366; open Mon–Sat 11am–6pm, Sun 11am–4pm). Every item here is marked with its place of origin, and the list is staggering: *Beverly Hills, 90210; Melrose Place; Seinfeld; Baywatch; All My Children; Forrest Gump; The Brady Bunch Movie;* and so on. Many of these wardrobes (which include shoes and accessories)

---

20 fresh varieties from wall spigots and blends up the tastiest, healthiest shakes in town. Further into the market you'll find produce sellers and prepared food counters, plus spice vendors straight out of a Turkish alley and a grain and bean seller who'll scoop out dozens of exotic rices and dried legumes.

EYEWARE

Santa Monica & the Beaches

Pepper's Eyeware. 2904 Main St. (between Ashland & Pier Sts.), Santa Monica. ☎ 310/ 392-0633.

Lenscrafters they're not, but if you're looking for some truly sophisticated, finely crafted eyeware, this friendly shop is for you. Ask for frames by cutting-edge L.A. designers Bada and Koh Sakai. If you're lucky enough to have perfect vision, consider some stylish shades.

Hollywood

L.A. Eyeworks. 7407 Melrose Ave., Los Angeles. ☎ 213/653-8255. Other locations throughout the L.A. metropolitan area.

This hometown designer has become world famous for its innovative styles and celebrity ad campaign. The shop on Melrose is the original storefront location.

aren't outstanding but for their Hollywood origins: Jerry Seinfeld's trademark polo shirts, for instance, are standard mall-issue. Some collectible pieces, like Sylvester Stallone's *Rocky* stars-and-stripes boxers, are framed and on display.

When you're done at It's A Wrap, stop in across the street at **Junk For Joy,** 3314 W. Magnolia Blvd., Burbank (☎ 818/569-4903; open Tues–Fri 10am– 6pm, Saturday 11am–6pm). A Hollywood wardrobe coordinator or two will probably be hunting through this wacky little store right beside you. The emphasis here is on funky items more suitable as costumes than everyday wear (the store is mobbed each year around Halloween). At press time, they were loaded with '70s polyester shirts and tacky slacks, but you never know what you'll find when you get there.

The grand dame of all wardrobe and costume outlets is **Western Costume,** 11041 Vanowen St., North Hollywood (☎ 818/760-0900; open for rentals Mon– Fri 8am–5:30 pm, for sales Tues–Fri 10am–5pm). In business since 1912, Western Costume still designs and executes entire wardrobes for major motion pictures; when filming is finished, the garments are added to their stagering rental inventory. This place is perhaps best known for outfitting Vivien Leigh in *Gone With the Wind.* Several of Scarlett O'Hara's memorable gowns were even available for rent until they were recently auctioned off at a charity event. Western maintains an outlet store on the premises, where damaged garments are sold at rock-bottom (nothing over $15) prices. If you're willing to do some rescue work, there are definitely some hidden treasures here.

Finally, don't miss **Golyester,** 136 S. La Brea Ave. (☎ 213/931-1339; open Mon–Sat 11am–6pm). This shop is almost a museum of finely preserved (but reasonably priced) vintage clothing and fabrics. The staff will gladly flip through stacks of Vogue magazines from the '30s, '40s, and '50s with you, pointing out the lavish, star-studded original advertisements for various outfits in their stock.

FASHIONS
FOR MEN & WOMEN
Santa Monica & the Beaches
Na Na. 1228 Third St. Promenade, Santa Monica. ☎ 310/394-9690.

This is what punk looks like in the '90s: clunky shoes, knit hats, narrow-striped shirts, and baggy streetwear.

L.A.'s Westside & Beverly Hills
American Rag, Cie. 150 S. La Brea Ave., Los Angeles. ☎ 213/935-3154.

First to draw shoppers back to industrial La Brea back in the early '80s, American Rag has grown from a small vintage clothing store to include trendy new fashions on their own label, as well as adjacent boutiques selling shoes and children's clothes; there's even a kitchen- and housewares shop with a small café in back. Once a best-kept secret of hip teenagers, the American Rag dynasty today draws more tourists than trendsetters.

Gucci. 347 N. Rodeo Dr., Beverly Hills. ☎ 310/278-3451.

An elegant selection of apparel for men and women by one of the best-known and most prestigious names in international fashion is showcased here. In addition to shoes, leather goods, and scarves beautiful enough for framing, the shop offers pricey accessories, like a $7,000 handmade crocodile bag.

Maxfield. 8825 Melrose Ave., West Hollywood. ☎ 310/274-8800.

Some of L.A.'s best-quality avant-garde designs include men's and women's fashions by Yamamoto, Comme des Garçons, Dolce Gabbana, Jil Sander, and the like. Furniture and home accessories are also sold, and the store's provocative window display ranges from sharp political statements to a Jerry Garcia tribute.

North Beach Leather. 8500 Sunset Blvd., West Hollywood. ☎ 310/652-3224.

This San Francisco–based shop has up-to-the-minute fashions from casual to elegant—particularly leather and suede jackets and dresses—at high Sunset Strip prices.

Polo/Ralph Lauren. 444 N. Rodeo Dr., Beverly Hills. ☎ 310/281-7200.

This Beverly Hills shop is the exclusive Los Angeles outlet for Ralph Lauren's Polo collections for men, women, and children. Select home furnishings are also sold.

Hollywood
Boy London. 7519 Melrose Ave., Los Angeles. ☎ 213/655-0302.

Once on the cutting edge of London's King's Road, Boy has toned down a bit, now selling shirts and other clothes emblazoned with its own logo. It's still cool, though.

Retail Slut. 7308 Melrose Ave., Los Angeles. ☎ 213/934-1339.

You'll find new clothing and accessories for men and women at this famous rock 'n' roll shop. The unique designs are for a select crowd (the name says it all); don't expect to find anything for your next PTA meeting here.

FOR MEN
Santa Monica & the Beaches
Mark Michaels. 4672 Admiralty Way, Marina del Rey. ☎ 310/822-1707.

It's not easy to find designer duds when you're 7'3"; Kareem Abdul-Jabbar and other tall guys find theirs at Mark Michaels, a specialty shop that tailor-makes suits, shirts, and slacks.

L.A.'s Westside & Beverly Hills
Billy Martin's. 8605 Sunset Blvd., West Hollywood. ☎ 310/289-5000.

Founded by the legendary Yankee manager in 1978, this chic men's western shop—complete with fireplace and leather sofa—stocks hand-forged silver and gold belt buckles, Lucchese and Liberty boots, and stable staples like flannel shirts.

Downtown
Brooks Brothers. 604 S. Figueroa St., downtown. ☎ 213/629-4200.

Brooks Brothers introduced the button-down collar and single-handedly changed the standard of the well-dressed businessman. This multilevel shop also sells traditional casual wear, including sportswear, sweaters, and shirts. You'll find nothing cutting edge here; this is the quintessential conservative menswear store.

FOR WOMEN
Santa Monica & the Beaches
CP Shades. 2925 Main St., Santa Monica. ☎ 310/392-0949. There's also a boutique in Old Pasadena (see chapter 11).

C.P. Shades is a San Francisco ladies' clothier whose line is carried by many department stores and boutiques; fans will love this store, devoted solely to their loose, casual cotton and linen separates. Their trademark monochromatic neutrals are meticulously arranged within an airy, well-lit store.

L.A.'s Westside & Beverly Hills

Polkadots & Moonbeams. 8367 and 8381 W. Third St. ☎ **213/651-1746.**

This is actually two stores several doors apart, one carrying (slightly overpriced) hip young fashions for women, the other a vintage store with clothing, accessories, and fabrics from the '20s to the '60s, all in remarkable condition.

Hollywood

Betsey Johnson Boutique. 7311 Melrose Ave., Los Angeles. ☎ **213/931-4490.**

The New York–based designer has brought her brand of fashion—trendy, cutesy, body-conscious womenswear in colorful prints and faddish fabrics—to L.A. Also in Santa Monica at 2929 Main St. (☎ 310/452-7911).

The San Fernando Valley

Studio Wardrobe/Reel Clothes. 12132 Ventura Blvd., Studio City. ☎ **818/508-7762.**

You may recognize some of the clothes here from movies and TV shows you've seen; most were worn by stars or extras before being turned over for public sale. Prices range from $10 to $1,000; new shipments arrive every few days.

DISCOUNT

Downtown

Cooper Building. 860 S. Los Angeles St., downtown. ☎ **213/622-1139.**

The centerpiece of downtown's Garment District, the Cooper Building and surrounding blocks are full of shops selling name-brand clothes for men, women, and children at significantly discounted prices.

VINTAGE

Santa Monica & the Beaches

☉ Aardvark's Odd Ark. 58 Market St. (corner of Pacific Ave.), Venice. ☎ **310/392-2996.**

This large storefront near the Venice Beach Walk is crammed with racks of antique and used clothes from the '60s, '70s, and '80s. They stock vintage everything, from suits and dresses to neckties, hats, handbags, and jewelry—and they manage to anticipate some of the hottest new street fashions. There's another Aardvark's at 7579 Melrose Ave.,(☎ **213/655-6769**).

L.A.'s Westside & Beverly Hills

Golyester. 136 S. La Brea Ave., Los Angeles. ☎ **213/931-1339.**

Before opening this ladies' boutique, the owner's friends would take one look at her collection of vintage fabrics and clothes and gasp "Golly, Esther!"—hence the whimsical name. You pay a little extra for the pristine condition of hard-to-find garments like unusual embroidered sweaters from the '40s and '50s, Joan Crawford–style suits from the '40s, and vintage lingerie.

Yellowstone Clothing Co. 712 N. La Brea Ave. (at Melrose Ave.), Los Angeles. ☎ **213/931-6616.**

While they provide plaid Pendleton shirts and flowered '50s sundresses to the followers of grunge style, the best stuff at this Santa Barbara–based vintage clothing shop isn't for sale. The owner's collections of aloha shirts, novelty neckties, and other memorabilia are proudly displayed in cases and on walls; they're the real reason I shop there.

Hollywood
Wasteland. 7428 Melrose Ave., Los Angeles. ☎ **213/653-3028.**

An enormous steel-sculpted facade fronts this L.A. branch of the Berkeley/Haight-Ashbury hipster hangout, which sells vintage and contemporary clothes for men and women. There's lots of leathers and denim as well as some classic vintage, but mostly funky '70s garb. This ultratrendy store is packed with the flamboyantly colorful polyester halters and bell-bottoms from the decade we'd rather forget.

The San Fernando Valley
Playclothes. 13045 Ventura Blvd. (1 block west of Coldwater Canyon Ave.), Studio City. ☎ **818/789-9942.**

Men and women alike will thrill at the pristine selection of vintage clothes housed in this boutique, tucked into a burgeoning antiques row west of Coldwater Canyon Avenue. Playclothes approches its stock with a sense of humor, knowing exactly how each item was worn and accessorized in its heyday.

GIFTS & NOVELTIES
L.A.'s Westside & Beverly Hills
Beverly Hills Baseball Card Shop. 1137 S. Robertson Blvd., Beverly Hills. ☎ **310/278-4263.**

This warehouse of baseball history is home to literally millions of cards, from Ty Cobbs to Lou Gehrigs to Tom Seavers and Mookie Wilsons, plus rare rookie editions and other hard-to-find baseball collectibles. Closed Monday.

GOAT Cadeaux. 306 S. Edinburgh (east of Crescent Heights Blvd. at Third St.). ☎ **213/651-3133.**

Cadeaux means "gifts" in French; this is the kind of shop where you can always find just the right last-minute present. From unusual candles to antique bookends to carved wooden boxes to art deco picture frames, GOAT carries quite a variety—all of it intriguing.

Giorgio Beverly Hills. 327 N. Rodeo Dr., Beverly Hills. ☎ **800/GIORGIO** or 310/274-0200.

Giorgio's signature yellow-and-white-striped awnings mark the home of his apparel, gift, and fragrance collections. Pricey and oh-so-Beverly-Hills, Giorgio logo items are perennially popular L.A. souvenirs.

The Yellow Room. 511 N. Robertson Blvd. (south of Melrose Ave.), Los Angeles. ☎ **310/274-3190.**

Map and globe aficionados shouldn't miss this small antiques store devoted to world globes, maps, and celestial instruments. Prices range from $160 to $8,000 and beyond, so consider a visit just to gaze at ultra-rare collapsing linen globes from England, European wooden globes as ornate as an illuminated manuscript, and a display of unusual telluriums, multigeared contraptions showing the earth and planets in revolution around the sun (represented by a shimmering orb or lit candle).

Hollywood
Condomania. 7306 Melrose Ave., Los Angeles. ☎ **213/933-7865.**

A vast selection of condoms, lubricants, and kits creatively encourage safe sex. Glow-in-the-dark condoms, anyone?

HATS
L.A.'s Westside & Beverly Hills
Drea Kadilak. 463 S. La Brea Ave. (at 6th St.), Los Angeles. ☎ **213/931-2051.**

The art of millinery often seems to have gone the way of white afternoon gloves for ladies; but inventive Drea Kadilak will charm you with her tiny hat shop. Designing in straw, cotton duck, wool felt, and a number of more unusual fabrics, she does her own blocking, will cheerfully take measurements for custom ladies' headware, is reasonably priced, and gives away signature hatboxes for every purchase.

HOUSEWARES & INTERIOR DESIGN
Santa Monica & the Beaches
Z Gallerie. 2728 Main St. (near Hill St.), Santa Monica. ☎ **310/392-5879.**

This California-based chain offers a good selection of framed and unframed poster art, Crate and Barrel–style furnishings, stylish kitchenware, and unusual gift items.

L.A.'s Westside & Beverly Hills
Liz's Antique Hardware. 453 S. La Brea Ave., Los Angeles. ☎ **213/939-4403.**

Stuffed to the rafters with hardware and fixtures from the last 100 years, Liz's thoughtfully keeps a cannister of wet-wipes at the register—believe me, you'll need one after sifting through bags and crates of doorknobs, latches, finials, and any other home hardware you can imagine needing. Perfect sets of Bakelite drawer pulls and antique ceramic bathroom fixtures are some of the more intriguing items. Be prepared to browse for hours, whether you're redecorating or not!

Mortise & Tenon. 444 S. La Brea Ave., Los Angeles. ☎ **213/937-7654.**

For affordable wood furniture with timeless appeal, Angelenos have been flocking to Mortise & Tenon's large, fun showroom. Farm-style tables, vaguely gothic armoires, and faux-Craftsman chairs are complemented by simply styled and affordable accessories, including some refreshingly original CD-storage cabinets.

Hollywood
Brian Jeffrey's Design Greenhouse. 7556 Melrose Ave., Los Angeles. ☎ **213/651-2539.**

This is one of the most beautiful stores on Melrose. Brian Jeffrey's is a professional decorator's dream store for interior plants, baskets and containers, candleholders, and wind chimes. They have floating lotus flowers, pressed eucalyptus, and candles galore. A festival for the senses, the shop is cluttered with terrific visuals, sweet smells, and the sounds of music.

JEWELRY
L.A.'s Westside & Beverly Hills
Cartier. 370 N. Rodeo Dr., Beverly Hills. ☎ **310/275-4272.**

Cartier, one of the most respected names in jewelry and luxury goods, has its Los Angeles outpost near Brighton Way. The boutique's setting is as elegant as the beautifully designed jewelry, watches, crystal, and accessories on display.

Hollywood
Maya. 7452 Melrose Ave., Los Angeles. ☎ **213/655-2708.**

This rather plain-looking store houses a huge—and fascinating—variety of silver and turquoise rings and earrings from South America, Nepal, Bali, and central Asia. The shop's walls are cluttered with Asian and South American ceremonial and ornamental masks.

The San Fernando Valley
King's Cross. 13059 Ventura Blvd. (1 block west of Coldwater Canyon Ave.), Studio City. ☎ **818/905-3382.**

King's Cross sells antique jewelry and furnishings, specializing in crosses, crucifixes, and rosaries made of gold, ivory, and pearl, with an emphasis on Victoriana. Most are vintage models dating from the 1820s to the 1930s. Prices range from $200 to $2,000.

LASER DISCS

San Fernando Valley

Dave's Video The Laser Place. 12144 Ventura Blvd. ($^1/_2$ block west of Laurel Canyon Blvd.), Studio City. ☎ **818/760-3472.**

I don't own a laser-disc player, but friends who do are constantly bemoaning the lack of good outlets to purchase and rent discs. They've followed Dave religiously as he moves up and down the boulevard, expanding his store and selection each time.

LINGERIE

L.A.'s Westside & Beverly Hills

Trashy Lingerie. 402 N. La Cienega Blvd., Hollywood. ☎ **310/652-4543.**

This shop will tailor-fit their house-designed clothes—everything from patent-leather bondage wear to elegant bridal underthings—for you. There's a $2 "membership" fee to enter the store, but, even for browsers, it's worth it.

Hollywood

Frederick's of Hollywood. 6606 Hollywood Blvd., Hollywood. ☎ **213/466-8506.**

Behind the garish pink-and-purple facade lies one of the most well-known panty shops in the world. Everything from spandex suits to "wonder" bras and sophisticated nighties is here. Even if you're not buying, stop in and pick up one of their famous catalogs.

LUGGAGE

L.A.'s Westside & Beverly Hills

Hermés. 343 N. Rodeo Dr., Beverly Hills. ☎ **310/278-6440.**

This Beverly Hills branch of Paris's 160-year-old House of Hermés is known for its superlative handmade leather goods, hand-screened silk ties and scarves, perfumes, and other gift items.

Louis Vuitton. 307 N. Rodeo Dr., Beverly Hills. ☎ **310/859-0457.**

Carrying the largest selection of Vuitton items in the United States, this tony shop stocks luggage, handbags, wallets, and a seemingly endless variety of accessories.

A GREEN ALTERNATIVE

Santa Monica & the Beaches

Just In Case. 2718 Main St., Santa Monica. ☎ **310/399-3096.**

Featuring "cruelty-free" handbags, backpacks, luggage, agendas, wallets, and other items made from fabric and innovative materials like recycled rubber instead of animal skins.

MEMORABILIA

Santa Monica & the Beaches

Mayhem. 1411 Third St. Promenade, Santa Monica. ☎ **310/451-7600.**

This shop sells autographed guitars and other music memorabilia from U2, Nirvana, Springsteen, Bon Jovi, Pearl Jam, and other rockers to collectors, including the owners of the Hard Rock Cafes.

Hollywood

Book City Collectibles. 6631 Hollywood Blvd., Hollywood. ☎ **213/466-0120.**

More than 70,000 color prints of past and present stars are available, along with a good selection of autographs from the likes of Lucille Ball ($175), Anthony Hopkins ($35), and Grace Kelly ($750).

Hollywood Book and Poster Company. 6349 Hollywood Blvd., Hollywood. ☎ **213/465-8764.**

Owner Eric Caidin's excellent collection of movie posters (from about $15 each) is particularly strong in horror and exploitation flicks. Photocopies of about 5,000 movie and television scripts are also sold for $10 to $15 each; the store also carries music posters and photos.

The Last Moving Picture Show. 6307 Hollywood Blvd. (near Vine), Hollywood. ☎ **213/467-0838.**

Movie-related merchandise of all kinds is sold here, including stills from '50s movies and authentic production notes from a variety of films.

MUSIC

Santa Monica & the Beaches

Hear Music. 1429 Third St. Promenade, Santa Monica. ☎ **310/319-9527.**

At the first L.A. branch of Boston's Hear Music chain, albums are grouped by genre, theme, and mood. Headphones are everywhere, so you can test a brand-new disc before you buy.

Pyramid Music. 1340 Third Street Promenade, Santa Monica. ☎ **310/393-5877.**

Seemingly endless bins of used compact discs and cassette tapes line the walls of this long, narrow shop on the Promenade. LPs, posters, cards, buttons, and accessories are also available.

L.A.'s Westside & Beverly Hills

✪ **Rhino Records.** 1720 Westwood Blvd., Westwood. ☎ **310/474-3786.**

This is L.A.'s premier alternative shop, specializing in new artists and independent-label releases. In addition to new releases, there's a terrific used selection; music industry types come here to trade in the records they don't want for the records they do, so you'll be able to find never-played promotional copies of brand-new releases at half the retail price. You'll also find the definitive collection of records on the Rhino label.

Tower Records. 8811 W. Sunset Blvd., Hollywood. ☎ **310/657-7300.**

Tower insists that it has L.A.'s largest selection of compact discs—over 125,000 titles—despite the Virgin Megastore's contrary claim. Even if Virgin has more, Tower's collection tends to be more interesting and browser friendly. And the enormous shop's blues, jazz, and classical selections are definitely greater than the competition's. Open 365 days a year.

Virgin Megastore. 8000 Sunset Blvd., Hollywood. ☎ **213/650-8666.**

Some 100 CD "listening posts" and an in-store "radio station" make this megastore a music lover's paradise. Virgin claims to stock 150,000 titles, including an extensive collection of hard-to-find artists.

The San Fernando Valley
Music & Memories. 5057 Lankershim Blvd., North Hollywood. ☎ **818/761-9827.**

If you're looking for a copy of that Desi Arnaz mambo that you can't get out of your head, or an out-of-print Frank Sinatra record you've been scouring garage sales for, look no further; leave the modern world behind and head to this dusty but friendly mom-and-pop shop.

SHOES
L.A.'s Westside & Beverly Hills
Re-Mix. 7605¹/₂ Beverly Blvd. (between Fairfax and La Brea aves.), Los Angeles. ☎ **213/ 936-6210.**

If you complain that they just don't make 'em like they used to . . . well, they do at Re-Mix. Selling only brand-new (unworn) vintage (1940s–70s) shoes for men and women, Re-Mix is more like a shoe store museum, featuring wingtips, Hush Puppies (the originals), Joan Crawford pumps, and '70s platforms. A rackful of unworn vintage socks all display their original tags and stickers, and the prices are downright reasonable. Celebrity hipsters and hep cats from Madonna to Roseanne are often spotted here.

SPORTS EQUIPMENT
Santa Monica & the Beaches
Horizons West. 2011 Main St. (south of Pico Blvd.), Santa Monica. ☎ **310/392-1122.**

Brand-name surfboards, wet suits, leashes, magazines, waxes, lotions, and everything else you need to catch the perfect wave are found here. Stop in and say hi to Randy, and pick up a free tide table.

Rip City Sports. 2709 Santa Monica Blvd., Santa Monica. ☎ **310/828-0388.**

Jim McDowell's top-rated pro skateboards are some of the world's most coveted. Many are handcrafted with the highest-quality wheels and bearings. Also selling rollerblades, snowboards, and apparel by Stussy and the like.

Downtown
Golf Exchange. 830 S. Olive St. (between 8th and 9th sts.), downtown. ☎ **213/622-0403.**

L.A.'s golf megastore fills 10 rooms with clubs and accessories: An entire room is devoted to golf shoes, another to bags, another to used clubs, and so on. There's also an indoor driving range so you can try before you buy.

TATTOOS
L.A.'s Westside & Beverly Hills
Sunset Strip Tattoo. 8418 W. Sunset Blvd., West Hollywood. ☎ **213/650-6530.**

Cher, Charlie Sheen, Lenny Kravitz, and members of the rock band Guns 'n Roses all got inked at this celeb-magnet parlor, which has been a Sunset Strip fixture for 30 years.

TEA
L.A.'s Westside & Beverly Hills
✪ **Chado Tea Room.** 8422 W. Third St. ☎ **213/655-4681.**

A temple for tea lovers, Chado is designed with a nod to Paris's renowned Mariage Frères tea purveyor. One wall is lined with nooks whose recognizable brown tins are filled with over 250 different varieties of tea from around the world.

Among the choices are 15 kinds of Darjeeling, Indian teas blended with rose petals, and ceremonial Chinese and Japanese blends. They also serve tea meals here, featuring delightful sandwiches and individual pots brewed from any loose tea in the store.

TIMEPIECES

L.A.'s Westside & Beverly Hills

Second Time Around Watch Co. 8840 Beverly Blvd. (west of Robertson Blvd.), Los Angeles. ☎ **310/271-6615.**

The city's best selection of pre-1960s collectible timepieces includes dozens of classic Tiffanys, Cartiers, Piagets, and Rolexes. You might even find an 1850s Patek Philippe pocket watch.

TOYS

Santa Monica & the Beaches

Puzzle Zoo. 1413 Third St. Promenade, Santa Monica. ☎ **310/393-9201.**

Puzzles have proved so popular that the Zoo recently expanded to better accommodate a selection chosen "Best in L.A." by *Los Angeles Magazine*. You'll find the double-sided World's Most Difficult Puzzle, the Puzzle in a Bottle, and collector's serial-numbered Ravensburger series, among others.

L.A.'s Westside & Beverly Hills

F.A.O. Schwarz. In the Beverly Center, 8500 Beverly Blvd., Los Angeles. ☎ **310/659-4547.**

One of the world's greatest toy stores for both children and adults is filled with every imaginable plaything, from hand-carved, custom-painted carousel rocking horses, dolls, and stuffed animals to gas-powered cars, train sets, and hobby supplies. The Barbie collection includes hundreds of models, from a 3-foot-tall, fiber-optically lighted Barbie to a $200 doll dressed by designer Bob Mackie. The standard muscle-bound morphing toys and talking turtles are also available.

Sadie. 167 S. Crescent Heights Blvd., Los Angeles. ☎ **213/655-0689.**

A truly unique toy store for kids and adults, Sadie sells hard-to-find collectible reproductions of classic metal, windup, mechanical, and fashion toys from all over the world. Many are one of a kind.

TRAVEL GOODS

Also see Traveler's Bookcase under "Books," above.

Santa Monica & the Beaches

California Map and Travel Center. 3211 Pico Blvd., Santa Monica. ☎ **310/829-6277.**

Like the name says, this store carries a good selection of domestic and international maps and travel accessories, including guides for hiking, biking, and touring. Globes and atlases are also sold. Visit their Web site at **http://www.mapper.com.**

WINE

Santa Monica & the Beaches

L.A. Wine Co. 4935 McConnell Ave., no. 8, Los Angeles. ☎ **310/306-9463.**

Known for low mark-ups on recent releases, this supplier near Marina Del Rey is one of the best places to buy young wines by the bottle or case with an eye on aging them in your own cellar; they'll ship anywhere in the U.S.

L.A.'s Westside & Beverly Hills

Bel-Air Wine Merchant. 10421 Santa Monica Blvd., West Los Angeles. ☎ **310/474-9518.**

This is an exceedingly knowledgeable yet unpretentious shop with a nationwide clientele. They specialize in old and rare wines, at fair prices.

The Wine Merchant. 9701 Santa Monica Blvd. (at Roxbury Dr.), Beverly Hills. ☎ **310/278-7322.**

"The Wine Merchant to the Stars" is more like it. Linger while looking for the right bottle and you may run into a famous local.

The *L.A. Weekly,* a free weekly paper available at sidewalk stands, shops, and restaurants, is the best place to find out what's going on about town, especially for club happenings. The "Calendar" section of the *Los Angeles Times* is also a good place to find out what's going on after dark.

For weekly updates on music, art, dance, theater, special events, and festivals, call the **Cultural Affairs Hotline** (☎ 213/688-ARTS), a 24-hour directory listing a wide variety of events, most of which are free.

Ticketmaster (☎ 213/480-3232) and **Telecharge** (☎ 800/447-7400) are the major charge-by-phone ticket agencies in the city, selling tickets to concerts, sporting events, plays, and special events.

1 The Performing Arts

CLASSICAL MUSIC & OPERA

Beyond the pop realms (see below), music in Los Angeles generally falls short of that found in other cities. For the most part, Angelenos rely on visiting orchestras and companies to fulfill their classical music appetites; scan the papers to find out who's playing and dancing while you're in the city.

The **Los Angeles Philharmonic** (☎ 213/850-2000) isn't just the city's top symphony; it's the only major classical music company in Los Angeles. Finnish-born music director Esa-Pekka Salonen concentrates on contemporary compositions; despite complaints from traditionalists, he does an excellent job attracting younger audiences. Tickets can be hard to come by when celebrity players like Itzak Perlman, Isaac Stern, Emanuel Ax, and Yo-Yo Ma are in town. In addition to regular performances at the Music Center's **Dorothy Chandler Pavilion,** 135 N. Grand Ave., downtown, the Philharmonic also plays a popular summer season at the **Hollywood Bowl** (see "Concerts Under the Stars," below).

Slowly but surely, the **L.A. Opera** (☎ 213/972-8001) is gaining both respect and popularity with inventive stagings of classic operas, usually with guest divas. The Opera also calls the Music Center home.

The 120-voice **Los Angeles Master Chorale** (☎ 213/626-0624) sings a varied repertoire that includes classical and pop compositions. Concerts are usually held at the Music Center from October to June.

CONCERTS UNDER THE STARS

Also see "The Live Music Scene," below.

✪ **Hollywood Bowl.** 2301 N. Highland Ave. (at Odin St.), Hollywood. ☎ **213/850-2000.**

Built in the early 1920s, the Hollywood Bowl is an elegant Greek-style natural outdoor amphitheater cradled in a small mountain canyon. This is the summer home of the Los Angeles Philharmonic Orchestra; internationally known conductors and soloists often sit in on Tuesday and Thursday nights. Friday and Saturday concerts often feature orchestral swing or pops concerts. The summer season also includes a jazz series; past performers have included Natalie Cole, Mel Torme, Dionne Warwick, and Chick Corea. Other events, from Tom Petty concerts to an annual Mariachi Festival, are often on the season's schedule.

For many concertgoers, a visit to the Bowl is an excuse for an accompanied picnic under the stars; gourmet picnics at the Bowl—complete with a bottle of wine or two—are one of L.A.'s grandest traditions. You can prepare your own, or order a picnic basket with a choice of hot and cold dishes and a selection of wines and desserts from the theater's catering department. À la carte baskets run from $16.95 to $25.95 per person; appetizers and drinks are extra. Call 213/851-3588 the day before you go.

THEATER
MAJOR THEATERS & COMPANIES

The Ahmanson Theater and Mark Taper Forum, the city's top two playhouses, are both part of the all-purpose **Music Center,** 135 N. Grand Ave., downtown. The **Ahmanson** (☎ 213/972-7401) reopened in 1995, after a $71 million renovation that improved acoustics and seating. This theater is active year-round, either with shows produced by the in-house Center Theater Group or with traveling Broadway productions. In-house shows are usually revivals of major Broadway plays, starring famous film and TV actors; I saw *Dangerous Liaisons* with Lynn Redgrave and Frank Langella, and *The Little Shop Around the Corner* with Pam Dawber and Christopher Reeve a few years ago. Traveling shows are usually West Coast premieres of plays such as Neil Simon's *Broadway Bound* or Andrew Lloyd Webber's *Phantom of the Opera;* the renovated theater debuted with *Miss Saigon.* The Ahmanson is so huge that you'll want seats in the front third or half of the theater.

The **Mark Taper Forum** (☎ 213/972-0700) is a more intimate, circular theater staging contemporary works by international and local playwrights. Kenneth Branagh's Renaissance Theatre Company staged their only American productions of *King Lear* and *A Midsummer Night's Dream* at the Mark Taper, to give you an idea of the quality of the shows here. Productions are usually excellent, run with plenty of spirit and no shortage of controversy.

Ticket prices vary depending on the performance. Discounted tickets are usually available on the day of performance for students and seniors.

Big-time traveling troupes and Broadway-bound musicals that don't go to the Ahmanson head instead for the **Shubert Theater** (in the ABC Entertainment Center, 2020 Ave. of the Stars, Century City; ☎ 800/233-3123). This plush playhouse presents major musicals on the scale of *Cats, Sunset Boulevard,* and *Les Misérables.*

Top-quality Broadway-caliber productions are also staged at the **UCLA James A. Doolittle Theater** (1615 N. Vine St., Hollywood; ☎ **213/462-6666** or 213/972-0700).

For a current schedule at any of the above theaters, check the listings in *Los Angeles Magazine* or the "Calendar" section of the Sunday *Los Angeles Times,* or call the box offices directly at the numbers listed above.

SMALLER PLAYHOUSES

Like New York's Off-Broadway or London's fringe, Los Angeles's small-scale theaters often outdo the slick, high-budget shows. Because this is Tinseltown, movie and TV stars sometimes headline, but more often than not, the talent is up and coming. Who knows—the unknown on stage today might be the next David Schwimmer tomorrow.

The **Colony Studio Theater** (1944 Riverside Dr., Silverlake; ☎ 213/665-3011) has an excellent resident company that has played in this air-conditioned, 99-seat, converted silent-movie house for over 20 years. Recent productions include the musical *Candide* and the classic American comedy *The Front Page.*

Actors Circle Theater (7313 Santa Monica Blvd., West Hollywood; ☎ 213/882-8043) is a 47-seater that is as acclaimed as it's tiny. Look for original contemporary works throughout the year.

The **Los Angeles Theater** (615 S. Broadway; ☎ 213/629-2939) is worth a trip no matter what's on. Built in 1931 by cinema architect S. Charles Lee, this grand movie palace was designed in the ornate baroque style of 18th-century France. Live theater began to be staged here in 1995.

In addition to those listed above, there are about 100 other stages of varying quality throughout the city. Tickets for most plays usually cost from $10 to $30. Check newspaper listings for current offerings.

2 The Live Music Scene

by Steve Hochman

Steve Hochman has spent way too many nights in dingy, stiflingly smoky clubs with earplugs stuffed in to deaden the thudding beats and cloying caterwauling emanating from the stage. The sick thing is that often he really enjoys it—though it doesn't hurt that much of the time he gets paid by the *Los Angeles Times* to write about the experience. For more than a decade he has also covered the pop music scene for publications such as *Rolling Stone, Spin, Melody Maker,* and the on-line *HotWired* outlet to the adventure travel magazine *Escape.*

If wearing a T-shirt with a picture of Jake and Elwood Blues on it is your idea of proving to the folks back home that you rock, dude, then you've got it made in L.A. Just stop by the House of Blues on the Sunset Strip—you can squeeze it in between your trips to the Hard Rock Cafe and Planet Hollywood.

That's the mallification of culture for you: rock 'n' roll as a commodity, nicely packaged and marketed like a Big Mac. Soon every city will have one . . . more than 27 billion served. Sure, the House of Blues hosts top-notch acts from around the globe. Some big names of pop, rock, hip-hop, country, and, on occasion, even blues play there. But it's artificial culture, a manufactured scene, and a growing one, with the brand-new Billboard Live club right up on Sunset Strip where Gazzarri's used to be. Tourists flock to this stuff.

And that's fine—if you want to be a tourist. But if you want to experience the real L.A., musically speaking, you're gonna have to dig and scurry. It used to be simple. In the '60s, for example, you might've seen the Byrds at Ciro's, the Doors at the Whisky, or been part of the mob on Sunset after the cops shut down Pandora's Box (the incident that inspired Buffalo Springfield's "For What It's Worth"). If you were there, you witnessed history in the making.

L.A. rock of the '70s also had its essential, defining sights and sounds: You might've witnessed the Eagles learning to fly at the Troubadour or the gatherings of the glitterati—David Bowie and Marc Bolan among them—at Rodney Bingenheimer's English Disco for the first half of the decade, while Van Halen at Gazzarri's (for the rockers) and X or the Germs at the Masque (for the punks) were cornerstones for the second half.

In the early '80s there were the Minutemen, Black Flag, the Dream Syndicate, and the Long Ryders, along with many other post-punks, at Club Lingerie or Raji's; and the hair-band metal of Mötley Crüe and the like dominating club life on the Sunset Strip, with Guns 'n Roses exploding from that scene in the late '80s.

But now? No such luck. If the '60s was the Big Bang, the '90s is all shrapnel: punk-grunge, hip-hop, neo-roots, acid jazz, techno-rave, power pop, folky revivalist, postmetal, performance art, ad nauseum. The idea of having one club, one block, even one region or kind of music that's representative of the community now seems not just anachronistic, but laughable. What's the essence of L.A. in the '90s? The gangsta-rap trinity of Ice Cube, Snoop Doggy Dogg, and Dr. Dre? The South Bay surf-punk of Offspring? The too-eager-to-please coffeehouse singer-songwriters that seem to be on every bus bench? None of the above—not alone, anyway.

And there's certainly no club that is the place to be, nowhere you could simply go hang out with reasonable hopes that something special would transpire. Ciro's is gone. The Masque is a vacant basement. Raji's was torn down after the earthquake. Club Lingerie now houses a Korean disco. The hot club in town is different from night to night—maybe from hour to hour—depending on who's playing at any given time.

That's the bad news. The good news is that L.A., on any given night, offers something for everybody, musically speaking. No matter what your tastes, from major pop stars at the Hollywood Bowl to hot underground faves at Silverlake's Spaceland, from slick cabarets at the Cinegrill to down 'n' gritty blues clubs, from star-studded watering holes à la the Roxbury (famed for altercations invovling Shannen Doherty) to ultrahip S&M fetish clubs like Sin-a-Matic, there's something for you . . . if you know where to look.

And there's the rub. The big events are easy to find, but by the time you get to town, odds are all the good tickets will be gone. But there are a few ways you can try to plan ahead: The Internet is a great source of information, with both **Ticketmaster (http://www.ticketmaster.com,** the nation's biggest ticket-selling service and the bane of Pearl Jam's existence) and concert business trade publication **Pollstar (http://www.pollstar.com)** having Web sites that include tour itineraries of acts that are on, or will be going on, the road. If you can, start checking about six weeks to two months before your trip to see if someone you like is coming to L.A.

Then, the trick is to know when tickets go on sale, which may be a little harder to find out. Try calling one of **Ticketmaster's** L.A.–area numbers (☎ 213/480-3232) first and ask them if they know when the show you're interested in will be sold. If not, you might try calling the publicity department of the artist's record company and explain, nicely, that you're a big fan who will be visiting L.A. when so-and-so is playing and when would tickets be available? (Most of the people at these offices are nice and helpful, but, um, just in case, don't tell them we sent you.) Note that with country acts, tickets usually go on sale far in advance, so you might have to start checking as early as three or even four months ahead. Ticketmaster is starting to sell tickets through the Internet, so if you have that capability, you can order seats right from your desktop.

The smaller clubs are often easier to deal with. Most of the time, you just show up and pay, though many of them also sell through Ticketmaster. The problem here is knowing what, where, and when. And that's where the *L.A. Weekly*, a free publication distributed at stores and restaurants throughout the city, is invaluable, with its comprehensive listings; a new issue is out each Thursday. The *Los Angeles Times's* **Sunday "Calendar"** section also has thorough listings of events, though nowhere near as comprehensive as those you'll find in the *Weekly*.

Also, keep an eye out for **free record store appearances.** Some fairly well-known acts give promotional performances at the big Virgin Megastore and Tower Records outlets on the Strip. Rhino Records in Westwood and Aron's and No Life in Hollywood regularly host alternative and roots acts, as do a few other stores around town, notably the wonderfully twisted (and terrifically named) You've Got Bad Taste, a Silverlake store co-owned by X's Exene Cervenkova.

Of course, if you're hip enough to find your way around this maze, you definitely don't want to look like a tourist, so here are a few tips: Whatever you do, don't seem excited or even too interested in the music—that's a dead giveaway that you're not from around these here parts. If you want to look like a regular, maybe even a music industry weasel or a rock critic, just stand toward the back of the club with your arms folded and maybe nod your head in time with the tunes—but don't overdo it. Of course, don't gawk should you see Madonna or Beck or someone hanging out nearby. If you're really daring, chat loudly throughout the performance, yet still manage to applaud enthusiastically at the end of each song as if you had really been listening. Who knows—maybe you might even be able to pass for a record company executive.

For club shows, see "The Club Scene," below.

THE BIG VENUES

STADIUMS Even plotting out nightlife at the biggest, most obvious level has gotten a bit confusing in recent years. It used to be simple—big outdoor stadium shows were held in one of four places: the **Los Angeles Memorial Coliseum, Dodger Stadium,** the **Rose Bowl** in Pasadena, and, in Orange County, **Anaheim Stadium** (see chapter 11). That's still largely true, though stadium shows seem to come sporadically these days, and the Rose Bowl seems to have risen above the others, with the **Coliseum,** 3911 S. Figueroa St., (☎ 213/748-6136), and its inner-city neighborhood having fallen out of favor due to the 1992 riots and—to add injury to insult—suffering structural damage in the 1994 earthquake.

The famed **Rose Bowl,** 1001 Rose Bowl Dr., Pasadena (☎ **818/577-3100**), shunned rock for years due to resistance from residents of its upscale neighborhood, but in the '90s plain old economics won out, and the surrounding hills have shook to the sounds of the Rolling Stones, Pink Floyd, the Cure, and the Eagles. But the lovely setting is difficult to get to, with only two access roads—so get there early, and have a tailgate party before the show.

The Beatles '66, Elton John '78, and Michael Jackson's "Thriller" concerts are the most famous pop concerts to be held at the squeaky clean **Dodger Stadium,** 1000 Elysian Park Ave. (☎ 213/654-4773), but U2, Depeche Mode, the Cure, and even New Kids on the Block (remember them?) have drawn big crowds more recently. Though the V-shaped stands aren't designed to maximize sightlines to a center-field stage, the general comfort level is high, and this is certainly the most facile stadium in the region in terms of access, parking, and other logistics.

ARENAS   Arena-sized venues also used to be very simple, with the **Great Western Forum,** 3900 W. Manchester Blvd. (at Prarie Ave.), Inglewood (☎ 310/419-3182), ranking with New York's Madison Square Garden as the rock 'n' roll status venue. Once you'd played there, you'd made it. Next in line was the slightly smaller **Los Angeles Sports Arena,** 3939 S. Figueroa St., downtown (☎ 213/748-6136), but like it's adjacent big brother, the Coliseum, it has fallen largely out of favor—as has the Forum somewhat, for much the same neighborhood concerns.

The arrival in 1994 of the **Arrowhead Pond** of Anaheim down in Orange County (see chapter 11) changed the mix somewhat. Comfortable and easy, relatively speaking, the new kid in town is grabbing a lot of the big business—Streisand, Rod Stewart, Green Day among them, as well as nearly every major current country figure (though Garth Brooks, in interest of fairness, split his six 1996 area concerts evenly between the Pond and the Forum).

Rock has returned as a regular feature at the outdoor **Hollywood Bowl** (2301 N. Highland Ave.; ☎ 213/850-2000); it's now drawing some of the acts that would've played the Forum in the past (see "Concerts Under the Stars" in "The Perfoming Arts," below). The most famous amphitheaters in the area, probably in the country, from the early '70s to early '90s it was largely verbotten by the Bowl's operators (the L.A. Philharmonic) and neighbors concerned about noise and marauding rock fans. Now, though, it's back, with Sting, Tom Petty, Rod Stewart, Bonnie Raitt, and Elton John among those who've performed here of late.

AMPHITHEATERS, SHEDS & LARGE THEATERS   The one relative constant in L.A. is the so-called sheds—the amphitheaters that are the staple of national rock and pop concert tours. The two main warriors are the outdoor **Greek Theatre,** in Griffith Park, 2700 N. Vermont Ave. (☎ 213/665-1927), and the indoor **Universal Amphitheatre,** Universal City Dr., Universal City (☎ 818/777-3931), each seating about 6,000. Both are among the most accommodating and comfortable facilities for big-name acts. Nearly as beautiful as the Hollywood Bowl, the Greek books a full season of national acts, from Hootie and the Blowfish to doo wop revivals. Parking can be a problem—not so much getting in as getting out, as cars are stacked in packed lots.

The "Uni Amp" has one advantage over the Greek: With a roof, it can book year-round. Otherwise, it's not as aesthetically pleasing, but it's quite comfortable and, with its semicircle arrangement, no seats are too far from the stage. For some events the "Party in the Pit" offers a general admission section right up next to the stage. In addition to pop stars from Tony Bennett to the Butthole Surfers, the Universal has booked such theater events as *The Who's Tommy.*

On the opposite side of the University of Southern California (USC) from the L.A. Coliseum and Sports Arena is the **Shrine Auditorium,** 665 W. Jefferson Blvd., Los Angeles (☎ 213/749-5123). This 6,300-seat former Shriners hall has long been a major concert site, but now only rarely hosts shows (Bruce Springsteen headlined an acoustic benefit here with Bonnie Raitt and Jackson Browne in 1991). The Shrine has been the L.A. home of the Grammy Awards for years, and has also hosted the Oscars and the Emmys.

Orange County's **Irvine Meadows Amphitheatre,** 8800 Irvine Center Dr., Laguna Hills (☎ 714/855-4515), which holds 15,000 (including general admission lawn way in the back), has been the L.A. area site of Lollapalooza '91, '92, '95, and '96; it also hosts radio station KROQ's often spectacular "Weenie Roast" and KIIS's "Summer Jam" each year, as well as a plethora of touring rock acts. If you're going from L.A. on a weekday, get an early start, since Irvine is located just off one of the heaviest traveled freeway junctions in the country.

MID-SIZE CONCERTS

Virtually every week there's at least one concert at the **Wiltern Theatre,** one of L.A.'s must-sees for architecture fans. Other mid-sized facilities (in the 1,000 to 4,000 capacity range) are a bit more sporadic, but it's a good bet that someone of interest of that size will be in town during any one stay. In addition to the facilities listed below, several others have also been in use of late for moderate-sized rock shows, such as the **Hollywood Grand** (formerly the psuedo-swanky Diamond Club), the elegant art deco **El Rey Theatre,** and the **Henry Fonda Theatre** (also used for legitmate theater engagements). The best way to see what's on at any of these venues is by checking the *L.A. Weekly,* available just about everywhere.

B.B. King's Blues Club. CityWalk, Universal City. ☎ **818/622-5464.**

Despite its setting (on Universal City's Toon Town–ish shopping mall/street, CityWalk), B.B. King's is a bit more "real" than the House of Blues (see below). It's three-floor seating area, resembling an old Southern club, is tastefully decorated, the music stays closer to authentic blues, and the ribs are terrific. Also offers a fine, though overpriced, Sunday gospel brunch.

House of Blues. 8430 Sunset Blvd., West Hollywood. ☎ **213/650-0247.**

Depite its Disneyland-ish decor (the exterior corrugated tin came from a building at the famed "Robert Johnson" crossroads in Mississippi, but still looks like a Pirates of the Carribean set), this club—co-owned by some really strange bedfellows, including, Hard Rock–founder Isaac Tigrett, Jim Belushi, Dan Ackroyd, Aerosmith, and Harvard University—does earnestly honor its namesake music with informative displays and a wealth of colorful folk art. (There's also a slightly surreal touch of spiritual imagery, inspired by Tigrett's Indian guru, Si Baba.) Still, it's permeated with Industry types more interested in being seen than seeing and hearing the music (there's even a Foundations Room upstairs, where the hoity toity can avoid the hoi poloi). Even so, there's enough top-notch music here to keep many who routinely bad-mouth the place coming back, and the food in the upstairs restaurant can be superb (reservations are a must). The Sunday gospel brunch, though a bit overpriced, is a rousing diversion.

Hollywood American Legion Hall. 2035 N. Highland Ave., Hollywood. ☎ **213/960-2035.**

Formerly the home of the "interactive" play *Tamara,* this strange, multiroomed villa-style building just south of the Hollywood Bowl has lately hosted some intriguing modern rock acts in its cozy auditorium, including Perry Farrell's Porno for Pyros, the Presidents of the United States of America, and a stream of techno-rave-type acts. It's a fun place to explore, with a deco-lodge bar downstairs conjuring images of 1920s glory.

Hollywood Palladium. 6215 Sunset Blvd., Hollywood. ☎ **213/962-7600.**

The big band leaders who called this home in the '40s might be horrified to see the chandeliers shaken by alternative rock's top names, and the dance floor turned into a swarming mosh pit. But the 3,000- or 4,000-capacity hall has been for the last decade a key venue for rockers on the way to bigger things, with the likes of Hole, Sonic Youth, and the Red Hot Chili Peppers headlining. Some unruly crowds have brought neighborhood concerns, but tight security—and we mean tight, with everything from lipstick to pens to gum being confiscated in thorough entry searches—has kept the hall open.

John Anson Ford Theatre. 2580 Cahuenga Blvd. West, Hollywood. ☎ **213/464-2826.**

Once, during a late '80s Ramones concert at this lovely al fresco facility, the punk sounds carried across U.S. 101 and into the ears of people who were trying to hear the L.A. Symphony play Beethoven at the Hollywood Bowl. They were not amused, and rock was virtually banned from the Ford for some time. But lately it's been back, and a night with a rising star under the stars (Alanis Morissette played here on her way to superstardom) can be wonderful. Parking, though, is nightmarish—prepare for a long walk uphill.

The Mayan Theatre. 1038 S. Hill St., downtown. ☎ **213/746-4287.**

Perhaps the strangest yet coolest concert venue in town, with elaborate decor in the mode of a Mayan temple (or something). Another fine relic of L.A.'s glorious past, it's relatively new as a pop music house, holding about 1,000 for such performers as PJ Harvey, Ani DiFranco, and—before they got mega-huge—Bush. It's in a part of downtown L.A. that most people never usually go, but there's plenty of parking, and the interior makes it seem like another dimension.

The Palace. 1735 N. Vine St., Hollywood. ☎ **213/461-3504.**

A classic vaudeville house, the 1,200-capacity theater, just across Vine from the famed Capitol Records tower, has been the site of numerous significant alternative rock shows in the '90s, including key appearances by Nirvana and Smashing Pumpkins. But its dominance has been challenged of late by several other venues of similar size.

Pantages Theatre. 6233 Hollywood Blvd., Hollywood. ☎ **213/468-1770.**

Almost as stunning as the Wiltern, but only occasionally used for pop concerts. Bob Dylan did a 5-night stand here in 1993, and Guns 'n Roses used it for a warm-up show in 1992.

Veterans' Wadsworth Theatre. Veteran's Administration Grounds, Brentwood. ☎ **213/ 825-2101.**

Operated by UCLA and just across the San Diego Freeway (I-405) from its campus, this 1,400-seat theater often mixes pop, folk, and world music into a schedule of classical, dance, and stage programs.

○ **Wiltern Theatre.** 3790 Wilshire Blvd., Los Angeles. ☎ **213/380-5005.**

Saved from the wrecking ball in the mid-'80s, this WPA-era art deco showcase is perhaps the most beautiful theater in town. You could have an entertaining evening just sitting and staring at the ornate ceiling—but usually you don't have to. Countless national and international acts have played here, from Jerry Garcia to Joan Osborne, with such nonpop music events as Penn & Teller and top ballet troupes complementing the schedule.

3 The Club Scene

by Heidi Siegmund Cuda

Heidi Siegmund Cuda is the nightclub columnist and a feature writer for the *Los Angeles Times,* a contributing writer to *Entertainment Weekly,* and a pop music critic for *Pulse!* magazine. She has also contributed to *Playboy, Rolling Stone, Esquire,* and a wealth of other publications. With Ice-T, she co-authored *The Ice Opinion* (St. Martin's Press), a first-person narrative detailing the rapper's view of America, politics, and urban culture.

The L.A. club scene is truly something-for-everybody territory, from blues fanatics to leather freaks. But be fair warned: You're not in Kansas anymore. Or for that matter, San Francisco. Friendlier cities greet out-of-towners with arms extended and advice at hand. Travel to the City by the Bay, and a waiter might tip you off to the best restaurant or the hottest dance club for that moment in time. Sit in a Los Angeles cafe, however, and be grateful if you're acknowledged. It's nothing personal—it's more a matter of Social Darwinism. This is a town where only the strongest—and the most resourceful—survive, and too many folks are angling to get out of the cattle line, past the velvet rope and into clubland's hot zones.

The competition is compounded by L.A.'s short attention span. What might have been the hip ticket last week could be belly-up by the time you find the door. That said, don't lose all hope. A smart visitor has ammo: This guide, along with a current *L.A. Weekly* (which can be found for free at numerous 'round town outlets on Thursdays), offers a plethora of dance and music club info for the adventurous at heart.

LIVE MUSIC

Al's Bar. 305 S. Hewitt St., downtown. ☎ **213/625-9703.** 21 and over; cover varies.

Al's is the last of a dying breed of downtown hellholes that regularly attracts fun underground music. If you can brave the neighborhood, which is sketchy at best, a good time can almost always be had here.

Alligator Lounge. 3321 Pico Blvd., Santa Monica. ☎ **213/453-8477.**

An unassuming dive with a neighborhood feel, the Alligator has become one of the top sites for emerging roots and alternative music in recent years, as well as weekly New Music Mondays hosted by avant-garde guitarist Nels Cline with challenging music that crosses rock, jazz, and classical forms performed by Cline and his band,as well as guests drawn from the creme of category-busting musicians.

The Ash Grove. 250 Santa Monica Pier, Santa Monica. ☎ **310/656-8500.**

Ed Pearl has resurrected his old club—an essential venue in L.A.'s early '60s folk and blues surge—in new digs on the Santa Monica Pier, right next to the historic carousel. Look for many of the people who, as youngsters, learned their trade at the original Ash Grove, including Ry Cooder, Taj Mahal, David Lindley, and Jackson Browne, to be among the regulars at the new one.

Bar Deluxe. 1710 N. Las Palmas Ave., Hollywood. ☎ **213/469-1991.** 21 and over; generally no cover.

This is the club to go to when you're looking for a hassle-free, no-lines affair. This dimly lit, black and red, voodoo-meets-hoodoo haven specializes in surf, blues, and rockabilly bands and is as comfortable as an old pair of Doc Martens.

Billboard Live. 9039 Sunset Blvd., West Hollywood. ☎ **310/786-1712.** Cover varies.

With a gala opening in August 1996 that closed down the Sunset Strip for the first time in history—so thousands of revelers could help Tony Bennett celebrate the birth of this three-tier, $5¹/₂ million club—this club promises to breathe some life into the legendary Strip. Located on the former site of the seminal rock 'n' roll club Gazzari's, Billboard Live's ambitions loom large. Among its state-of-the-art distinctions: Two gigantic exterior "Jumbotrons," which reveal the on-stage performances to passersby and, during the day, feature continuous music programming; a unique "industrial plush" interior design (think corrugated metal draped in velvet); a "Tequila Library," where card-carrying members can order any tequila concoction under el sol; and numerous monthly performances selected from *Billboard's* "Heatseekers" charts, so you can be the first to see the Next Big Thing. Ultimately, the 400-capacity club, the first of a dozen Billboard Live venues scheduled to be built over the next 4 years, is an excellent live music showcase.

Coconut Teaszer. 8117 Sunset Blvd., West Hollywood. ☎ **213/654-4773.**

In some ways a carryover of the '80s, prealternative rock ethos, with hard-rockin' dudes mostly trying to impress record company talent scouts. A good place for local acts that you've never heard of, and most likely will never hear of again. But who knows—the night you're there may be the night a future superstar is discovered.

Doug Weston's Troubadour. 9081 Santa Monica Blvd., West Hollywood. ☎ **310/276-6168.** All ages; cover varies.

The Troubadour has worked long and hard to shed its creepy '80s spandex-'n'-big-hair image, and it's emerged vibrant and vigorous once again. Turning 40 in 1997, the club counts the Byrds and the Eagles among the bands that virtually formed here, and even in the metal years saw Mötley Crüe and others rise to the big time. Today the Troub can be counted on for excellent sound, and a wide array of up-and-coming break-out bands and already made-its. A fine, fine venue.

Dragonfly. 6510 Santa Monica Blvd., Hollywood. ☎ **213/466-6111.** 21 and over; cover varies.

Not one to miss a trend, Dragonfly went from being a dance club scene that offered live music to becoming a live music scene that offers dancing. Currently, the hip venue in the heart of Hollywood is attacking its band bookings with a vengeance. From "surprise" shows by top-notch local acts such as Rage Against the Machine and Porno for Pyros to surprising national acts—Run-D.M.C. at an alternative music club!—Dragonfly is soaring. Guests should also enjoy its cool outdoor patio and pillow room.

FM Station Live. 11700 Victory Blvd., North Hollywood. ☎ **818/769-2220.** 21 and over; cover varies.

This is Hessian heaven, NoHo style. The last of the headbanger havens, FM Station keeps metal alive by booking tribute bands nearly 5 nights a week. Acts to look for are the Atomic Punks (a Van Halen cover band) and Sticky Fingers (you guessed it, a Rolling Stones tribute act). But no matter who's on stage at FM Station, it's always good time rock 'n' roll.

The Foothill Club. 1922 Cherry Ave., Signal Hill (near Long Beach). ☎ **310/494-5196.** 21 and over; cover varies.

Although it's off the beaten path, this club, in a community adjacent to Long Beach, is a special venue that deserves a special mention. It's been around since the beginning of time—country time, that is (Merle Haggard, Hank Williams, Sr., and Johnny

Cash played here in their prime)—and still retains a bit of cowpoke flavor on Fridays and Saturdays. The ultimate show at this revamped punk and rockabilly venue is the Supersuckers and Reverend Horton Heat, who play here fairly regularly.

Hell's Gate. 6423 Yucca St., Hollywood. ☎ **213/463-9661.** 21 and over; cover varies.

With rumors of its imminent demise constant, this divey dive in the heart of Hollywood's crack district might not exist one day—and it'll be a sad passing. Although there's nothing stellar about Hell's Gate (the decor is postapocalyptic *Mad Max*-esque), it's got a lot of heart, and books lots of bands before anyone else gets hip to 'em.

Hollywood Moguls. 1650 N. Schrader Blvd., Hollywood. ☎ **213/465-7449.** 18 and over; cover varies.

Visualize a warehouse-size venue with weird art, a center stage, theater screenings, and lots of live music, and you've got Moguls. From announced performances by the Red Hot Chili Peppers to scheduled dates by such touring acts as the Flaming Lips, this eclectic night spot keeps getting more interesting as time goes by. Live and digital music booked nightly, as well as comedy and movie screenings.

Jabberjaw. 3711 W. Pico Blvd., Los Angeles. ☎ **213/732-3463.** All ages; cover varies.

This sweaty, arty coffeehouse is only fun if you like the national indie rock scene and a lot of java (no alcohol is served). When temperatures begin to soar, so does the discomfort factor, but guests are granted a reprieve on the club's outdoor patio. Nevertheless, this club is so tied in to the indie scene, a regular can cancel his subscription to *Flipside*.

Jack's Sugar Shack. 1707 Vine St., Hollywood. ☎ **213/466-7005**.

Jack doesn't mess around. The *Gilligan's Island* meets *Love Boat* decor combined with a select booking policy makes this nightclub a tasty treat. Less interested in trends than in quality music, Jack's books national and local blues, country and western, and alternative music and is the current host to Ronnie Mack's Barndance, an always free Tuesday-night affair of alternative country music.

Lava Lounge. 1533 La Brea Ave., Hollywood. ☎ **213/876-6612.** 21 and over; cover varies.

Described by its lovely owner, a former set decorator, as a "Vegas in hell" motif, the interior of this small bar and performance space located in a très-ugly strip mall is very inventive. Think tiki-tacky coupled with big city chic. Live music includes jazz and surfabilly, and live regulars include Quentin Tarantino.

LunaPark. 665 N. Robertson Blvd., West Hollywood. ☎ **310/652-0611.** Cover varies, none–$10.

Proprietor Jean-Pierre Boccarra has turned this bilevel retaurant/performance space into one of the most unpredictable yet reliable venues in the area—not just for music, which ranges from up-and-coming sensations (Ani DiFranco played her first L.A. show here) to global music stars (Cape Verde's "barefoot diva" Cesaria Evora), but for performance art, cabaret, and comedy, too.

McCabe's. 3101 Pico Blvd., Santa Monica. ☎ **213/828-4497.** All ages; ticket prices vary.

Since the early '70s, the back room of this earthy guitar shop has been the leading folk club in L.A., and possibly west of the Mississippi. Bonnie Raitt, Jackson Browne, and Linda Ronstadt are among those who played here early in their careers, and top-flight folk, country and even rock musicians still return regularly to perform in an unbeatable, low-key, almost living room–esque setting.

The Opium Den. 1605 Ivar St., Hollywood. ☎ **213/466-7800.** 21 and over; cover varies.

Brent Bolthouse, an über-promoter on the Hollywood night life circuit, opened his first club on the site of the old Gaslight so his friends would have a comfortable, quality venue to perform in. With pals who appear in nearly every issue of *People*, this works in everyone's favor. Live alternative music is scheduled seven nights a week, with late-night dance parties occurring on Thursday, Friday, and Saturday. Standout performances include the Geraldine Fibbers, Rickie Lee Jones, Spain, and X.

Pan at the Faultline. 4216 Melrose Ave., Silverlake. ☎ **213/662-LOVE** or 213/660-0889. 21 and over; cover varies.

The precursor to Spaceland, Pan moved over to its current location, a gay leather bar, and voila—a star was born. Combining the fetish underground with local and national underground bands makes for interesting bedfellows. Add a decent sound system and a dash of style—this is not only one good-looking leather venue but interested parties can purchase all the fetish accoutrements on Visa and Amex at the club boutique—and you've got one of the coolest underground scenes in L.A. Pan held bimonthly—usually the second and fourth Thursday—plus all day on some Saturdays. Call for info.

Roxy. 9009 Sunset Blvd. ☎ **213/276-2222.**

Veteran record producer/executive Lou Adler opened this Sunset Strip club in the mid '70s with concerts by Neil Young and a lengthy run of the premovie *Rocky Horror Picture Show*. Since, it has remained among the top showcase venues in Hollywood—though it's lost its unchallenged preeminence among cozy clubs to increased competition from the revitalized Troubadour and such new entries as the House of Blues.

Spaceland at Dreams. 1717 Silverlake Blvd., Silverlake. ☎ **213/413-4442.** 21 and over; cover varies.

In less than a year, promoter Mitchell Frank took over a spacious, dowdy bar on the eastern edge of Hollywood and turned it into one of the most happening night spots in Los Angeles. With his eclectic booking (everyone from the Foo Fighters and the Beasties to hometown faves Extra Fancy), Frank built a scene from scratch; Spaceland now rivals such Hollywood fixtures as the Whisky and Roxy as a place to see and be seen.

Union. 8210 Sunset Blvd., West Hollywood. ☎ **213/654-1001.** 21 and over; Thurs–Tues no cover, Wed $5 cover.

Otherwise known as the club that books avant garde acid jazz artiste Toledo every Monday night, the Union is a comfortable bilevel venue with an outdoor patio and a piano bar. Averaging 5 nights of live music weekly, guests will hear acid jazz, straight jazz, and blues. On Wednesdays, promoter Brent Bolthouse takes over with "Soap," an inspired cocktail lounge atmosphere. But if you want something to remember L.A. by, see Toledo on Mondays. A true original.

✪ Viper Room. 8852 Sunset Blvd., West Hollywood. ☎ **310/358-1880.** 21 and over; cover varies.

This place is so delightfully hot you might get singed on the way out. Definitely a club to witness firsthand before exiting town—despite what you might have heard: Yes, Johnny Depp owns it (with partner Sal Jenco) and yes, River Phoenix overdosed here, and the combo either attracts or repulses clubgoers. But hands down, the Viper Room has the most varied and exciting live music bookings in town. From Johnny Cash to Iggy Pop, the small, bilevel venue doesn't disappoint. The expensive sound system is a delight to true music fans, and there's enough stars on hand nightly to keep gazers excited.

The Whisky. 8901 Sunset Blvd., West Hollywood. ☎ **310/535-0579.** All ages; cover varies.

If you don't go to any other club in L.A., you must a go-go to The Whisky. The bilevel venue personifies L.A. rock 'n' roll, from Jim Morrison to X to Guns 'n Roses. Every trend has passed through this club, and it continues to be the most vital venue of its kind. Recently, an in-house booker was hired to bring more local music to the club, which already offers one of the best local showcases in town: Bianca's Hole on Monday nights, an always-free night of mostly L.A. bands.

DANCE CLUBS & BARS

To give outsiders an idea of the lightning speed with which dance clubs come and go in this town, the Roxbury doesn't even register on the map this year. It's still there, but folks aren't lining up like they used to, so we can't recommend it this time out. But no worries: There's plenty of sonic offerings to take its place, but best to move quickly and precisely. Take great pains to follow the recommended nights closely— you'll be glad you did.

In addition to what's listed below, the brand-new behemoth known as **Billboard Live,** 9039 Sunset Blvd., West Hollywood (☎ **310/786-1712**), offers late-night dancing Wednesday to Sunday nights after 11pm. You must be 21 or over; cover varies. For details, see "Live Music," above.

Bossa Nova. Thursdays at the Pink, 2810 Main St., Santa Monica. ☎ **310/392-1077.** 21 and over; $10 cover.

DJs and label execs Jason Bentley and Bruno Guez bring their eclectic music tastes to this happening nightclub each week and guest DJs (including Tricky) round out the mood, which includes electronic, acid jazz, and more interesting musical treats than you can shake a stick at. An aural pleasure for all music fans.

Cherry. Fridays at the Love Lounge, 657 N. Robertson Blvd., West Hollywood. ☎ **310/659-0472.** 21 and over; $10 cover.

DJ Mike Messex's Friday night gig finds him digging deep into the '80s for loads of glam rock, New Wave, and disco, keeping the dance floor packed all evening. Promoter Bryan Rabin knows how to keep the energy level high, with selective live performances—often with a homoerotic edge—as well as theme nights. A celebration of *Showgirls* was a must-see.

The Derby. 4500 Los Feliz Blvd., Los Feliz. ☎ **213/663-8979.** 21 and over; $5 cover.

This east Hollywood swing club is one class-A joint. The luscious club, located at a former Brown Derby site, was restored to its original luster and detailed with a heavy '40s edge. This would explain the inordinate number of guests who come decked out in garb from that era to swing the night away to such musical acts as Big Bad Voodoo Daddy and the Royal Crown Revue (whose popularity soared after weekly bookings at the club).

Dragstrip 66. The second Saturday of each month at Rudolpho's, 2500 Riverside Dr., Silverlake. ☎ **213/969-2596.** 21 and over; $10–$20 cover.

Note the cover disparity: If you ain't in drag, prepare to pay for it (and wait in line a wee bit longer than the more fashionably hip). This all-time great drag club, located in a Mexican restaurant, switches themes each month ("Chicks with Dicks" was a standout), and offers up every type of music—except disco and Liza. That's entertainment.

Caffeine Nation: L.A's Other Bar Scene

What cocaine was to disco, coffee is to grunge—not just the drug of choice, but the fuel of the culture. Actually, it's just the latest application of the sacred bean to boho lifestyle (imagine Maynard G. Krebs without access to a coffeehouse). Today, though, coffee has gone beyond cliche and into ubiquitousness, with funky little coffeehouses practically on every corner—in addition, of course, to the Starbucks that are overrunning the city.

L.A.'s romance with '90s coffee culture is hardly unique; every major urban city in America is similarly enthralled. But a few of L.A.'s coffeehouses are distinctly Angeleno in their funky characters, which basically range from seedy funky to arty funky. They're definitely worth checking out if you're craving a half-caf cap nonfat with a twist—and maybe some music or poetry to go with it.

The Abbey, 692 N. Robertson Blvd. (☎ 310/289-8410), in the heart of West Hollywood, is really a cafe, offering full meals. But it's also perhaps the best casual hangout in this heavily gay neighborhood, with desserts galore. Lingering over an iced mocha on the patio with a few friends makes for a perfect evening time-waster.

With a bit more of a bar atmosphere than the usual coffeehouse, scene veteran **Bourgeois Pig,** 5931 Franklin Ave. (☎ 213/962-6366), on a hot business strip at the Hollywood/Los Feliz border, is a youth and show-biz drone favorite. An added draw is the terrific newsstand next door.

Predating the coffeehouse explosion, the comfortable, relatively unpretentious **Highland Grounds,** 742 N. Highland Ave., Hollywood (☎ 213/466-1507), set

El Floridita. 1253 N. Vine St., Hollywood. ☎ **213/871-8612.** 21 and over; cover varies.

This Cuban restaurant-cum-salsa joint is hot, hot, hot. Despite its modest strip lot locale, the tiny club attracts the likes of Jennifer Lopez, Sandra Bullock, Jimmy Smits, and Jack Nicholson, and the hippest nights continue to be Monday and Thursday, when Johnny Polanco and his swinging N.Y.-flavored salsa band get the dance floor jumpin'.

The Garage. 4519 Santa Monica Blvd., Silverlake. ☎ **213/683-3447.** 21 and over; cover varies.

Another key Silverlake club, this one sprung up from the underground and remains firmly planted therein. With a wide variety of weekly dance club promotions, this sparkling erstwhile garage attracts a comfortable gay/straight clientele with such events as Sucker, a Sunday beer bust hosted by drag diva Miss Vaginal Creme Davis; Hai Karate, a dazzling Friday night funky fest; and Ultra Saturdays, with hot Hollywood DJ Victor Rodriguez spinning deep house and soul.

The Gate. 643 N. La Cienega Blvd., West Hollywood. ☎ **310/289-8808.** 21 and over; cover varies.

This is one despicable club, but folks seem to migrate here anyway. Perhaps the demise of Beverly Hills's Tatou encouraged the migration. Most famous for its repeated mentions in Faye Resnick's ode to Nicole Brown Simpson, the Gate attracts the chemically altered, surgically enhanced Eurotrash bimbos and himbos, who enjoy its elaborate decor and gargoyles a-plenty. Dancing is scheduled Wednesday through Saturday—and don't wear shorts if you want to get in.

the L.A. standard with a vast assortment of food and drink—not just coffee—and often first-rate live music, ranging from nationally known locals, such as Victoria Williams, to open-mike Wednesdays for all-comers. The ample patio is often used for readings and record release parties.

The two cozy, adjacent rooms known as **Onyx/Sequel,** 1804 N., (Vermont Ave.; no phone), in the Los Feliz district, offer generally friendly service, as well as a decent line-up of soup, sandwiches, and desserts to go with the beverages. Owner John has long supported local performers and visual artists, giving a home to spoken word and music nights that have drawn such luminaries as Ann Magnuson and Beck. But if you're looking for something fancy, go elsewhere. *Caveat:* The art on the walls generally tends toward the scary tortured-soul variety, which doesn't always sit well after a double espresso.

Airy and comfy, **Equator,** 22 Mills Place (☎ 818/564-8656), a brick room on a busy alleyway in the heart of resurgent Old Town Pasadena, has withstood the challenge of a Starbucks that moved in a block away. The menu—with smoothies, soup, and desserts in addition to a wide variety of coffee drinks—and the friendly service keep people coming back. The post-Haring art on the walls contributes to the distinctive character of the place, which has been used for scenes in such films and TV shows as *Beverly Hills, 90210* and *A Very Brady Sequel.* (For complete coverage of Pasadena, see chapter 11, "Side Trips from Los Angeles.")

—Steve Hochman

The Gem. 7302 Melrose Ave., Hollywood. ☎ **213/932-8344.** 21 and over; no cover.

This is a good example of a club that requires some resourcefulness—i.e., get there early, and expect to wait outside until the doorman deems you worthy. By virtue of its intimate size, the Gem is primarily a private club. This doesn't stop hoards of public citizens from lining up outside, on the off chance that they might get in to experience some disco, soul, hip-hop, and trip-hop on the Gem's tiny raised dance floor. Truly a diamond in the rough, the lovely, detailed Gem gives Melrose's trendy shopping district its first decent nightclub. Relatively speaking, it's worth the wait.

Kontrol Faktory. Mondays at the Probe, 836 N. Highland Ave., Hollywood. ☎ **818/303-4634.** 18 and over; $3–$5 cover.

This popular industrial music club is the best in its genre. Kontrol Faktory features hours of music by such artists as KMFDM, Skinny Puppy. and Nine Inch Nails, and its self-scarring audience is as interesting to watch as a Fellini film. Wait, no: They're more interesting, because they're real people. Located in the gloomy, cavernous, multileveled Probe—also the home of the Wednesday night gothic scene **Helter Skelter** and Friday's **Stigmata,** an alternative techno scene—Kontrol Faktory is appropriately located and perfectly not well.

Saturday Night Fever. Saturdays at the Diamond Club, 7070 Hollywood Blvd., Hollywood. ☎ **213/848-9300** for location. 21 and over; $10 cover.

For nearly 5 years now, this weekly disco party continues to be the biggest Saturday night dance bash in Hollywood. Although it's moved numerous times since its inception, it continues to outgrow each venue, and the last consistent spot was at the Roxbury. Fever's currently going off at the Diamond Club, but owner Brent Bolthouse indicated at press time he plans to move it yet again. Wherever it lands, it's sure to be the bomb: With popular L.A. DJ Mike Messex behind the main console, the temperature's always sizzling.

Soul Mama. Fridays at Checca, 7323 Santa Monica Blvd., Hollywood. ☎ **213/850-7471.** 21 and over; $15 cover.

L.A. used to be chock full of decent hip-hop clubs, but in the past few years, they've dropped like flies. Until things straighten up, Soul Mama—with its ample supply of hip-hop, funk, and old school soul—will have to suffice.

7969. 7969 Santa Monica Blvd., West Hollywood. ☎ **213/654-0280.** 21 and over; cover varies.

Here's a fetish club that can't miss: Saturdays feature Sin-A-Matic, L.A.'s long-running, popular S&M industrial dance club, complete with whipping room. Mondays and Fridays offer a drag party. 7969's most popular night to date is Thursdays Grand Ville, a sexy dance club with a midnight striptease—emphasis on "tease." Also quite popular, among the ladies, that is, is Michelle's XXX Revue, a Tuesday night lesbian hangout with an enormous number of topless women.

4 Cocktail Bars

Four Seasons Hotel Los Angeles. 300 S. Doheny Dr. (at Burton Way), Los Angeles. ☎ **310/273-2222.** No cover.

The sprawling lobby bar of this slightly pretentious but always eventful hotel serves as both celebrity magnet and unofficial parlor for monied regulars who virtually live in the high-rise. Decorated in the same comfortable but unremarkable neutral tones as the rest of the hotel, the bar is actually comprised of several sitting rooms and an outdoor patio, through which waft the sounds of the house pianist tinkling the ivories. The bartenders here have seen it all—no request is too outrageous, from a platter of oysters courtesy of the hotel's restaurant to a bowl of water for a canine companion (dogs served on patio only). The current cigar trend has found a home here: You may select from the bar's expansive humidor, but stay away if the smoke will offend you (or your dry cleaner).

Good Luck Bar. 1514 Hillhurst Ave. (between Hollywood and Sunset blvds.), Los Angeles. ☎ **213/666-3524.** No cover.

Until they installed a flashing sign—which simply reads "LUCK"—only locals and hipsters knew about this Kung Fu–themed room in the Los Feliz/Silverlake area. The dark red windowless interior boasts Oriental ceiling tiles, fringed Chinese paper lanterns, sweet-but-deadly drinks like the "Yee Mee Loo" (translated as "blue drink"), and a jukebox with selections from Thelonius Monk to Cher's "Half Breed." The spacious sitting room, furnished with mismatched sofas, armchairs, and banquettes, provide a great atmosphere for conversation or romance. Arrive early to avoid the throngs of L.A. scenesters.

Lounge 217. 217 Broadway (between Second and Third sts.), Santa Monica. ☎ **310/281-6692.** Cover varies.

A lounge in the true sense of the word, these plush Art Deco surroundings just scream "martini"—and the bartenders stand ready to shake or stir up your favorite. Comfortable seating lends itself well to intimate socializing, or enjoying Monday's classical guitarist; Thursday night brings a torch singer and cigar bar. Come early on the weekends, when Lounge 217 hosts a more raucous late-night crowd.

Windows On Hollywood. In the Holiday Inn, 1755 No. Highland Ave., Hollywood. ☎ 213/462-7181. No cover.

There's nothing like a revolving bar/restaurant to enjoy a panoramic view of the city; this one is 23 floors above the heart of Hollywood. While it scores low on the hipness scale, we're glad trendy bar-hoppers have taken their scene elsewhere, freeing up the prime window tables for you and me. The slowly revolving outer circle will show you downtown's skyline, the lights of Hollywood, and the hills to the north; the noncirculating center offers entertainment and dancing. If you're lucky, there'll be some young Sinatra wannabe providing a schmaltzy soundtrack for your cocktail hour.

5 Comedy & Cabaret

Except for the Cinegrill, which is in its own league, each of the following venues claims—and justly so—to have launched the careers of the comics that are now household names. The funniest up-and-comers are playing all the clubs (except for the Groundlings, which is an improvisation group), so you're probably best off choosing a club for its location. In addition to the clubs below, check out **Hollywood Moguls,** 1650 N. Schrader Blvd., Hollywood (☎ 213/465-7449), a live music club that also books comedy acts (see "The Live Music Scene," above).

The Cinegrill. 7000 Hollywood Blvd., in the Hollywood Roosevelt Hotel, Hollywood. ☎ 213/466-7000.

There's something going on every night of the week here, at one of L.A.'s most historic hotels. Some of the country's best cabaret singers pop up here regularly. The Cinegrill draws locals with a zany cabaret show and guest chateuses from Eartha Kitt to Cybill Shepherd.

Comedy Store. 8433 Sunset Blvd., West Hollywood. ☎ 213/656-6225.

You can't go wrong here: New comics develop their material, and established ones work out the kinks from theirs, at owner Mitzi Shore's (Pauly's mom) landmark venue.

The Best of the Comedy Store Room, which seats 400, features professional stand-ups continuously on Friday and Saturday nights. Several comedians are always featured, each doing about a 15-minute stint. The talent here is always first rate, and includes comics who regularly appear on the *Tonight Show* and other shows.

The Original Room features a dozen or so comedians back-to-back nightly. Sunday night is amateur night: Anyone with enough guts can take the stage for 3 minutes, so who knows what you'll get?

The Belly Room alternates between comedy stage and piano bar, with Wednesday nights reserved for the "Gay and Lesbian Comedy Show."

Groundling Theater. 7307 Melrose Ave. Los Angeles. ☎ 213/934-9700.

L.A.'s answer to Chicago's Second City has been around for over 20 years, yet remains the most innovative and funny group in town. Their collection of skits changes every year or so, but they take new improvisational twists every night, and the satire is often savage. In the current production, O.J. meets the Menendez brothers, and Universal CityWalk takes a hilarious beating. The Groundlings were the springboard to fame for Pee-Wee Herman, Elvira, and former *Saturday Night Live* stars Jon Lovitz, Phil Hartman, and Julia "It's Pat" Sweeney. Trust me—you haven't laughed this hard in ages. Phone for show times and reservations.

Igby's Comedy Cabaret. 11637 W. Pico Blvd., West Los Angeles. ☎ **310/477-3553.**

Igby's is the best spot for comedy on the Westside. There's not a bad seat in the place. The comics are well "stacked," so the night usually becomes racier the later it gets. You can order from a full dinner menu during the show, as long as you don't mind eating right under the comedian's nose.

The Improvisation. 8162 Melrose Ave., West Hollywood. ☎ **213/651-2583.**

A showcase for top stand-ups since 1975, the Improv offers something different each night. The club's own television show, *A&E's Evening at the Improv,* is now filmed at the Santa Monica location. Although there used to be a fairly active music schedule, the Improv is now mostly doing what it does best—showcasing comedy. Owner Bud Freedman's buddies—like Jay Leno, Billy Crystal, and Robin Williams—hone their skills here more often than you would expect. But even if the comedians on the bill the night you go are all unknowns, they won't be for long. Shows are at 8pm Sunday and Thursday, at 8:30 and 10:30pm Friday and Saturday.

6 Late-Night Bites

L.A. is no 24-hour town. Surprisingly, the city has only about a dozen bonafide restaurants that are open after hours; even fewer serve all night. If you want a serious meal after 2am, head for one of the following places, all of which are open 24 hours: **Pacific Dining Car,** 1310 W. 6th St. (at Witmer St.), downtown (☎ 213/483-6000) is the place for a well-marbled, patiently aged New York steak any time of day or night; for westsiders, there's a Santa Monica location at 2700 Wilshire Blvd. (one block east of 26th St.; ☎ 310/453-4000). The **Original Pantry Cafe,** 877 S. Figueroa St. (at 9th St.; ☎213/972-9279) has been serving huge portions of comfort food around the clock for more than 60 years; in fact, they don't even have a key to the front door. **Jerry's Famous Deli,** 12655 Ventura Blvd. (at Coldwater Canyon Blvd.), Studio City (☎ 818/980-4245), is where Valley hipsters go to relieve their late-night munchies.

Kate Mantilini, 9101 Wilshire Blvd. (at Doheny Dr.), Beverly Hills (☎ 310/278-3699), serves up stylish fare until 1am most weeknights, and to 3am on weekends. The trendy-comfy **Swingers,** attached to the Beverly Laurel Motor Hotel at 8020 Beverly Laurel Motor Hotel at 8020 Beverly Blvd. (west of Fairfax Ave.; ☎ 213/653-5858), keeps L.A. hipsters happy with its retro comfort food 'til 2am on weeknights, and 4am Friday and Saturday nights.

If you're looking for an after-hours hangout during the week, **Du-par's Coffee Shop,** 12036 Ventura Blvd. (1 block east of Laurel Canyon), Studio City (☎ 818/766-4437), probably isn't the place to go; they're only serving blue-plate specials 'til 1am. However, come the weekend, they're slingin' hash until 4am.

In addition to the restaurants mentioned above (see chapter 6, "Dining," for details on each), another late-night option is **Canter's Fairfax Restaurant, Delicatessen & Bakery,** 419 N. Fairfax Ave. (☎ 213/651-2030), a Jewish deli that's been a hit with late-nighters since it opened more than 65 years ago. If you show up after the clubs close, you're sure to spot a bleary-eyed celebrity or two alongside the rest of the after-hours crowd, chowing down on a giant pastrami sandwich, matzoh-ball soup, potato pancakes, or another deli favorite. Try a potato knish with a side of brown gravy—trust me, you'll love it.

Side Trips from Los Angeles

The area within a 100-mile radius of Los Angeles is one of the most diverse regions in the world: There are arid deserts, rugged mountains, industrial cities, historic towns, alpine lakes, rolling hillsides, and sophisticated seaside resorts. You'll also find an offshore island that's been transformed into the ultimate city-dweller's hideaway, not to mention the Happiest Place on Earth.

1 Pasadena & Environs

11 miles NE of Los Angeles

Pasadena is part of the greater Los Angeles area, but this community is so far removed from the rest of the city, both physically and in spirit, that we think of it as a side trip.

Founded by Midwesterners fleeing the cold winter of 1873, by the turn of the 20th century Pasadena had grown into a warm resort destination nestled among the orange groves. The tear-down epidemic which swept Los Angeles mercifully passed over Pasadena, allowing the city a refreshing old-time feel. Historic homes along tree-lined streets coexist with a revitalized downtown respectful of its old brick and stone commercial buildings.

Angelenos flock here to shop and dine, enjoying the opportunity to stroll a compact, manageable downtown area. Best known to the world as the site of the Tournament of Roses Parade each New Year's Day, Pasadena is also home to the California Institute of Technology. Caltech's scientists are the first to report earthquake activity worldwide. In addition, the school boasts 22 Nobel Prize winners among its alumni, and the Caltech-operated Jet Propulsion Laboratory is the birthplace of America's space program. Pasadena offers a richly diverse arts and entertainment scene, and is a favorite location for feature films and TV.

ESSENTIALS

GETTING THERE If you are flying to L.A., and are planning to make Pasadena or another San Fernando or San Gabriel Valley town your base, see if you can land at the quiet, convenient **Burbank–Glendale–Pasadena Airport**, 2627 N. Hollywood Way, Burbank (☎ 818/840-8840). See chapter 2 for more airport and airline information.

California's first freeway, the 6-mile Arroyo Seco Parkway, opened in 1940, linking downtown Los Angeles and Pasadena. It later

---

Area Code Change Notice

Please note that, effective June 14, 1997, the area code for Pasadena and the San Gabriel Valley is scheduled to change to **626.** You will be able to dial 818 until January 17, 1998, after which you will have to use 626.

---

connected to greater L.A.'s planned 1,500-mile freeway system as the **Pasadena Freeway (Calif. 110).** Narrower and curvier than modern freeways, the Pasadena Freeway, with its lush, overgrown landscaping, now seems like a quaint relic of an earlier era. Though bumper-to-bumper during rush hours, it's refreshingly traffic-free in the late morning, and a lot of fun to drive. If you approach Pasadena from the San Fernando Valley, take the Calif. 134 Freeway east and exit directly onto Colorado Blvd.

VISITOR INFORMATION   For a free destination guide and information, contact the **Pasadena Convention and Visitors Bureau,** 171 S. Los Robles Ave., Pasadena, CA 91101 (☎ 818/795-9311; fax 818/795-9656). They are open Monday to Friday from 8am to 5pm and Saturday from 10am to 4pm. There's also a city-run Web site (**http://www.ci.pasadena.ca.us**) which offers tourist information as well as business and government listings.

SPECIAL EVENTS   In addition to the attractions listed below, there are many seasonal events in Pasadena. If you can't visit on January 1 for the **Tournament of Roses Parade,** floats are parked on public display in nearby **Victory Park** (along Altadena Drive one block north of Orange Grove Boulevard) on January 1st or 2nd. Once you take an up-close look you'll finally understand why the commentators gush each year about all those carefully placed chrysanthemums and mustard seeds.

If you can't make the Tournament of Roses Parade at all, the **Doo-Dah Parade** on the Sunday following Thanksgiving began in 1977 as its irreverant counterpart.

The annual **Pasadena Showcase House of Design** from mid-April to mid-May (☎ 818/792-4661) is extremely popular; each year one of Pasadena's splendid historic mansions is given the fancy designer treatment, rooms turn out hilarious as often as sublime. The tour admission fee benefits the Pasadena Junior Philharmonic.

GETTING AROUND   Street parking can be scarce around the few blocks at the core of Old Town, but there are abundant public garages with friendly rates (often less than the change you'd feed your meter anyway). Look for the Old Pasadena Parking signs.

An alternative is to take advantage of the free Arts Buses which run along Colorado Boulevard and Green Street through Old Town and the Lake Avenue shopping district. Shuttles come every 20 minutes (12 minutes during lunchtime) between 11am and 8pm Monday to Saturday.

EXPLORING THE AREA

Various tours spotlighting architecture or neighborhoods are lots of fun, given this area's history of wealthy estates and ardent preservation. Call **Pasadena Heritage** (☎ 818/793-0617) for a schedule of guided tours, or pick up "Ten Tours of Pasadena," self-guided walking or driving maps available at the Visitor's Bureau (see "Essentials," above). For a quick but profound architectural fix, stroll past Pasadena's grandiose and baroque **City Hall,** 100 N. Garfield Ave., 2 blocks north of Colorado Boulevard; closer inspection will reveal its classical colonnaded courtyard, formal gardens, and spectacular tiled dome.

Pasadena

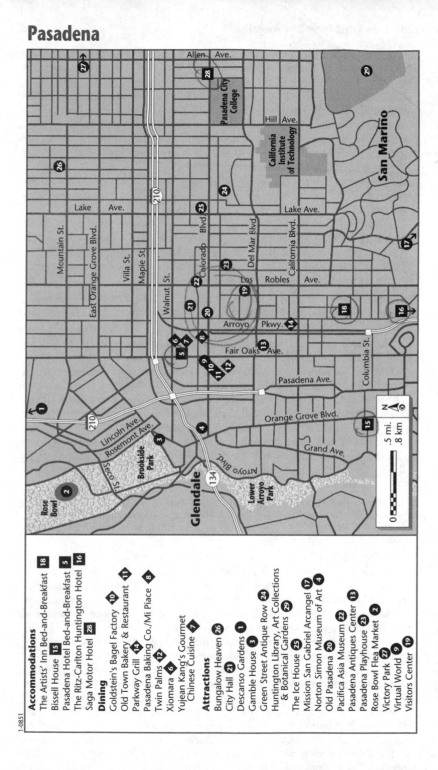

Accommodations
The Artists' Inn Bed-and-Breakfast 18
Bissell House 15
Pasadena Hotel Bed-and-Breakfast 5
The Ritz-Carlton Huntington Hotel 16
Saga Motor Hotel 28

Dining
Goldstein's Bagel Factory 10
Old Town Bakery & Restaurant 11
Parkway Grill 14
Pasadena Baking Co./Mi Piace 8
Twin Palms 12
Xiomara 6
Yujean Kang's Gourmet
Chinese Cuisine 7

Attractions
Bungalow Heaven 26
City Hall 21
Descanso Gardens 1
Gamble House 3
Green Street Antique Row 24
Huntington Library, Art Collections
& Botanical Gardens 29
The Ice House 25
Mission San Gabriel Arcangel 17
Norton Simon Museum of Art 4
Old Pasadena 20
Pacifica Asia Museum 22
Pasadena Antiques Center 13
Pasadena Playhouse 23
Rose Bowl Flea Market 2
Victory Park 27
Virtual World 9
Visitors Center 19

227

1-0851

Descanso Gardens. 1418 Descanso Dr., La Cañada. ☎ **818/952-4402** or 818/952-4401. Admission $5 adults, $3 students and seniors (over 62), $1 children 5–12, children under 5 free. Daily 9am–4:30pm.

Camellias—evergreen flowering shrubs from China and Japan—were the passion of amateur gardener E. Manchester Boddy, who began planting them here in 1941. Today, his Descanso Gardens contain more than 100,000 camellias in over 600 varieties, blooming under a 30-acre canopy of California oak trees. The shrubs now share the limelight with a 5-acre Rose Garden, home to hundreds of varieties.

This is really a magical place, with paths and streams that wind through the towering forest, bordering a lake and bird sanctuary. Each season features different plants: daffodils, azaleas, tulips, and lilacs in the spring; chrysanthemums in the fall; and so on. Monthly art exhibits are held in the garden's hospitality house.

There's also a beautifully landscaped Japanese-style teahouse which serves tea and cookies on Saturday and Sunday from 11am to 4pm. Free docent-guided walking tours are offered every Sunday at 1pm; guided tram tours, which cost $1.50, run Tuesday through Friday at 1, 2, and 3pm, and on Saturday and Sunday at 11am and 1, 2, and 3pm. Picnicking is allowed in specified areas.

✪ **Gamble House.** 4 Westmoreland Place, Pasadena. ☎ **818/793-3334.** Admission $5 adults, $4 seniors, $3 students, children under 12 free. Thurs–Sun noon–3pm. Closed holidays.

The huge two-story Gamble House, built in 1908 as a California vacation home for the wealthy family of Procter and Gamble fame, is a sublime example of Arts-and-Crafts architecture. Designed by the famous Pasadena-based Greene and Greene architectural team, the interior abounds with handcraftsmanship, including intricately carved teak cornices, custom-designed furnishings, elaborate carpets, and a fantastic Tiffany glass door. No detail was overlooked. Every oak wedge, downspout, air vent, and switchplate contributes to the unified design. Admission is by 1-hour guided tour only, which departs every 15 minutes. No reservations are necessary.

If you can't fit the tour into your schedule, but have a love of Craftsman design, visit the well-stocked bookstore and gift shop located in the former garage (you can also see the exterior and grounds of the house this way). They are open Tuesday through Saturday 10am to 4:30pm and Sunday 11:30am to 4:30pm.

✪ **The Huntington Library, Art Collections and Botanical Gardens.** 1151 Oxford Rd., San Marino. ☎ **818/405-2141.** Admission $7.50 adults, $6 seniors ages 65 and above, $4 students and children under 12, free for children under 12. Tues–Fri noon–4:30pm, Sat–Sun 10:30am–4:30pm. Closed major holidays.

The Huntington Library is the jewel in Pasadena's crown. The 207-acre hilltop estate was once home to industralist and railroad magnate Henry E. Huntington (1850–1927), who bought books on the same massive scale that he acquired businesses. The continually expanding collection includes dozens of Shakespeare's original works; Benjamin Franklin's handwritten autobiography; a Gutenberg Bible from the 1450s; and the earliest known manuscript of Chaucer's *Canterbury Tales.* Although these rarer works are only available to visiting scholars, the library has a regularly changing (and always excellent) exhibit showcasing different items in the collection.

If you prefer canvas to parchment, Huntington also put together a terrific 18th-century British and French art collection. His most celebrated paintings are Gainsborough's *The Blue Boy* and *Pinkie,* a companion piece by Sir Thomas Lawrence depicting the youthful aunt of Elizabeth Barrett Browning. These and other works are displayed in the stately Italianate mansion on the crest of this hillside estate, so you can also get a glimpse of its splendid furnishings.

But it's the botanical gardens which draw most locals to the Huntington. The Japanese Garden is complete with traditional open-air Japanese house, koi-filled stream, and serene Zen garden; the cactus garden is exotic, the jungle garden intriguing, the lily ponds soothing—and plentiful benches scattered about encourage you to sit and enjoy.

Because the Huntington surprises many with its size and the wealth of activities to choose from, first-timers might want to start by attending one of the regularly scheduled 12-minute introductory slide shows; or take the more in-depth 1-hour garden tour, given each day at 1:00pm.

I also recommend you tailor your visit to include the popular English high tea served Tuesday to Sunday from 1:30 to 3:30pm. The charming tearoom overlooks the Rose Garden (home to 1,000 varieties displayed in chronological order of their breeding), and since the finger sandwiches and desserts are served buffet-style, it's a genteel bargain (even for hearty appetites) at $11 per person. Phone 818/683-8131 for reservations.

Mission San Gabriel Arcangel. 537 W. Mission Dr., San Gabriel. ☎ **818/457-3035.** Admission $3 adults, $1 children 6–12 years, children under 6 free. Daily 9am–4:30pm (Oct–May); 10am–5:30pm (June–Sept). Closed holidays.

Founded in 1771, Mission San Gabriel Arcangel still retains its original facade, notable for its high oblong windows and large capped buttresses that are said to have been influenced by the cathedral in Cordova, Spain. The mission's self-contained compound encompasses an aqueduct, a cemetery, a tannery, and a working winery. Within the church stands a copper font with the dubious distinction of being the first one used to baptize a Native Californian. The most notable contents of the mission's museum are Native American paintings depicting the Stations of the Cross, painted on sailcloth, with colors made from crushed desert flower petals. The mission is about 15 minutes south of Pasadena.

Norton Simon Museum of Art. 411 Colorado Blvd., Pasadena. ☎ **818/449-6840.** Admission $4 adults, $2 students and seniors, children under 12 free. Thurs–Sun noon–6pm; bookshop, Thurs–Sun noon–5:30pm.

Named for a food-packing king and financier who reorganized the failing Pasadena Museum of Modern Art, the Norton Simon Museum has become one of California's most important museums. Comprehensive collections of masterpieces by Degas, Picasso, Rembrandt, and Goya are augmented by sculptures by Henry Moore and Auguste Rodin, including *Burghers of Calais,* which greets you at the gates. The "Blue Four" collection of works by Kandinsky, Jawlensky, Klee, and Feininger is particularly impressive, as is a superb collection of Southeast Asian sculpture. *Still Life with Lemons, Oranges, and a Rose* (1633), an oil by Francisco de Zurbarán, is one of the museum's most important holdings. One of the most popular pieces is Mexican artist Diego Rivera's *The Flower Vendor/Girl with Lilies.*

Pacific Asia Museum. 46 N. Los Robles Ave., Pasadena. ☎ **818/449-2742.** Admission $3 adults, children under 12 free. Free for everyone on the third Saturday of each month. Wed–Sun 10am–5pm.

The most striking aspect of this museum is the building itself. Designed in the 1920s in Chinese Imperial Palace style, it's rivaled in flamboyance only by Mann's Chinese Theatre in Hollywood (see chapter 7). Rotating exhibits of Asian art span the centuries, from 100 B.C. to the current day. This manageably sized museum is usually worth a peek.

Virtual World. In the One Colorado Mall, 35 Hugus Alley (Colorado & Fair Oaks blvds.), Pasadena. ☎ **818/577-9896.** Admission $7 Mon–Fri before 5pm, $8 after 5pm; $9 Sat–Sun. Mon–Fri 10am–9pm, Sat–Sun 10am–8pm.

This is the ultimate "easy side trip" from Los Angeles. Several different adventures are offered at the world's first virtual reality play center, including a run through the

Yesteryear Revisited, Arts & Crafts Style: Bungalow Heaven

Long adored by "bungalowners" and nostalgic architecture buffs, Pasadena's Bungalow Heaven is now a formally preserved slice of Southern California history. This charming neighborhood's nickname became its official designation in 1989, when determined homeowners and preservationists succeeded in having a Landmark District created to encompass the approximately 900 pre-Depression-era bungalows here.

Ironically, the bungalow, inexpensive to construct and often sold in kits, was never intended to be a lasting part of the landscape. Easterners had been drawn to the unspoiled beauty, abundant fruits, and hospitable climate of Pasadena (a Chippewa word meaning "crown of the valley") since Victorian times. In the first few decades of the 20th century, Midwesterners, looking for a warm, economically friendly place to settle down, work, and raise families, came in droves—hence the prevalence of street names like Michigan, Madison, Peoria, and Wabash. Their desire for affordable housing, coupled with the growing Arts and Crafts movement in design, proved fertile ground for the growth of bungalow neighborhoods.

Around the turn of the century, many artists, designers, and architects were beginning to reject the stifling ornateness of Victorian style and to stress simplicity, organic motifs, and natural materials in their work. The philosophy of this new Arts and Crafts movement grew to emphasize lifestyle, inspiring a greater appreciation of and interaction with nature. The distinctive elements of the bungalow illustrate this trend: Abundant windows, expansive porches, and limited indoor space all extend the living area to include the outdoors. The widespread use of raw natural materials, such as exposed beams, rough-hewn boulders, and simple clay tiles, reflects a respect for nature shaped by Southern California's Spanish, Mexican, and Japanese heritage. And bungalow design spoke directly to the climate: There were overhanging eaves for daylight shading and lots of windows for cross-ventilation—summertime necessities prior to air-conditioning. The interiors were outfitted along the same lines; the furniture style was often called "mission" because it resembled the stark simplicity of the nearby Spanish missions.

North Mentor Avenue defines the western border of Bungalow Heaven and boasts the oldest home in the neighborhood, number 714. Built in 1883, this eerie ramshackle Victorian still awaits the attention of a restorer. At 775 North Mentor, don't miss a striking 1913 example of an "airplane bungalow," whose wide lower gables resemble the spreading wings of a plane, topped with the second-story "cockpit." Over on North Michigan Avenue, notice the unusual entrance to number 875, a Craftsman bungalow from 1909, whose front door passes right through the wide, lopsided brick chimney. Stroll these blocks and choose your own favorites.

Bungalow Heaven, easily reached from the Calif. 134 and I-210 freeways, is centered around McDonald Park, between Lake and Hill avenues north of Orange Grove Boulevard. The **Bungalow Heaven Neighborhood Association** conducts a house tour each April, with detailed histories of each of the homes open to visitors during the tour. But feel free to check out the neighborhood whenever you're in Pasadena—without bothering the residents, of course. For more information, call the BHNA at **818/585-2172.**

mining tunnels of Mars in the year 2053 and a jousting tournament on the fictitious desert planet Solaris VII. Many of the virtual worlds are set up like intergalactic war games, where you don heavy helmets and try to "neutralize" your friends. After the VR adventure, you can review your game from various angles on videotape.

SHOPPING

Pretty, compact Pasadena lends itself perfectly to many travelers' number 1 pastime: shopping. The city's recent renovation efforts have focused unabashedly on creating an alternative to L.A.'s behemoth shopping malls, so Pasadena's streets are a true pleasure to stroll. As a general rule, stores are open 7 days a week from about 10am, and, while some close at the standard 5 or 6 o'clock, many stay open till 8 or 9pm to accommodate the pre- and post-dinner/movie crowd.

OLD PASADENA   The focus of consumerism is along Colorado Boulevard between Pasadena Avenue and Arroyo Parkway, where you'll see the ongoing regentrification of a once-dingy downtown. It's known as **Old Pasadena,** and some old-time residents hate it as much as the scores of visitors love it. In our opinion it's one of the best parts about the L.A. area, but we hope they retain more of the "mom-and-pop" businesses currently being pushed out by the likes of Banana Republic, Urban Outfitters, Crate & Barrel, J. Crew, Victoria's Secret, Barnes & Noble, and Armani Exchange. As you move eastward, however, the mix does begin to include more eclectic shops and galleries comingling with dusty, preyuppie relics.

  Penny Lane, 12 W. Colorado Blvd. (☎ 818/564-0161), a new and used CD store, also has a great selection of music magazines and kitschy postcards. The selection is less picked-over here than at many record stores in Hollywood. Around the corner at **Rebecca's Dream,** 16 S. Fair Oaks Ave. (☎ 818/796-1200), men and women can both find vintage clothing treasures in this small and meticulously organized (by color scheme) store. Be sure to look up; vintage hats adorn the walls. Around the corner is the **Del Mano** gallery of contemporary crafts, 33 E. Colorado Blvd. (☎ 818/793-6648), and it's a whole lot of fun to see the creations—some whimsical, some exquisite—of American artists working with glass, wood, ceramics, or jewelry.

  On the corner of Colorado and Raymond, even if you don't stop in, have a look at **Crown City Loan & Jewelry,** a pawn shop which survived regentrification as musty as ever! Their haphazard window display (wooden elephant carvings, assorted wristwatches, an old accordion) thumbs its nose at the order all around. Further down is **Tournament Souvenirs,** 88 E. Colorado Blvd. (☎ 808/395-7066), which is exactly as it sounds: Rose Parade and Rose Bowl clothing, hats, pennants, glassware, and sports sippers for anyone visiting during the 51 other weeks of the year. Around the corner is a duo of related stores, **Distant Lands Bookstore and Outfitters,** 54 and 62 S. Raymond Ave. (☎ 818/449-3220). The bookstore has a terrific selection of maps, guides, and travel-related literature, while the recently opened outfitters two doors away offers everything from luggage and pith helmets to space-saving and convenient travel accessories.

  TAKING A BREAK   Serious shopping requires occasional periods of rest and refreshment, and there's no place better than one of Pasadena's many, many coffee cafés. In addition to the ubiquitous **Starbucks,** 117 W. Colorado Blvd. (☎ 818/577-4622), there's sleek, spacious **Espresso Cabaret,** 17 E. Colorado Blvd. (☎ 818/584-6505), and the outdoor patio at **Micah's,** 88 N. Fair Oaks at Holly (☎ 818/795-9733). But our favorite is **Chatz of Pasadena,** 53 E. Union St. (☎ 818/584-9110), tucked away one block north of busy Colorado Boulevard. It's cozy and friendly, the kind of place which runs out of the best muffins early but never takes down old flyers from the cluttered bulletin board on the wall by the door.

OTHER SHOPPING VENUES   In addition to Old Town Pasadena, there are numerous good hunting grounds in the surrounding area. For example, antique hounds might want to head to the **Green Street Antique Row,** 985 to 1005 E. Green St., east of Lake Avenue, or **Pasadena Antique Center,** South Fair Oaks Boulevard south of Del Mar. Each has a rich concentration of collectibles dealers, and can captivate browsers for hours.

You never know what you'll find at the **Rose Bowl Flea Market,** at the Rose Bowl, 991 Rosemont Ave., Pasadena (☎ 818/577-3100). Built in 1922, the horseshoe-shaped Rose Bowl is one of the world's most famous stadiums, home to UCLA's football Bruins, the annual Rose Bowl Game, and an occasional Super Bowl. California's largest monthly swap meet, on the second Sunday of every month from 9am to 3pm, is a favorite of Los Angeles antique hounds (who know to arrive as early as 6:30am for the best finds). Antique furnishings, clothing, jewelry, and other collectibles are assembled in the parking area to the left of the entrance, while the rest of the flea market surrounds the exterior of the Bowl. Here, look for everything from used surfboards and car stereos to one-of-a-kind lawn statuary and bargain athletic shoes. Admission is $5.

Book lovers will want to prowl through the rare and out-of-print treasures at **The Browser's Bookshop,** 659 E. Colorado Blvd. at El Molino (☎ 818/585-8308), or its dusty neighbor **House of Fiction,** 663 East Colorado Blvd. (☎ 818/449-9861). For a world-class selection of big band, swing, pop vocalist, soundtracks and other non–rock 'n' roll CD's, don't miss **Canterbury Records,** 805 E. Colorado, corner of Hudson (☎ 818/792-7184).

Anglophiles will delight in **Rose Tree Cottage,** 824 E. California Blvd., just west of Lake Avenue (☎ 818/793-3337), and their charming array of all things British. This cluster of historic Tudor cottages surrounded by traditional English gardens holds three gift shops and a tearoom, where a superb $19.50 high tea is served thrice daily amongst the knick-knacks (and supervised by the resident cat, Miss Moffett). In addition to imported teas, linens, and silver trinkets, Rose Tree Cottage sells homemade English delicacies like steak and kidney pies, hot cross buns, and shortbread. They are also the local representative of the British Tourist Authority and offer a comprehensive array of travel publications.

WHERE TO STAY

In the following listings, parking is free unless otherwise noted.

EXPENSIVE

✪ **The Ritz-Carlton Huntington Hotel.** 1401 S. Oak Knoll Ave. (west of Elliott), Pasadena, CA 91109. ☎ **800/241-3333** or 818/568-3900. Fax 818/568-3700. 355 rms, 22 suites, 6 cottages. A/C MINIBAR TV TEL. $145–$240 double; suites from $350. AE, DC, MC, V. Parking $12.

Built in 1906 and still one of America's grandest hotels, the Spanish-Mediterranean Huntington gained popularity early on among celebrated writers, entertainers, political and business leaders, even royalty. Set on 23 meticulously landscaped acres, it seems a world apart from downtown Los Angeles, though it's only about 20 minutes away. Closed for 6 years after a particularly destructive earthquake, the hotel reopened in 1991 as a full replica of itself under the Ritz-Carlton banner. Each oversized guest room is dressed in conservatively elegant Ritz-Carlton style, with marble baths, thick carpets, terry robes, and the like. Behind the hotel is a bucolic Japanese garden that's great for strolling.

Dining/Entertainment: Locals of senior-citizen status love to celebrate in the Georgian Room, where continental meals are prepared by a classically trained French chef. The less formal Grill serves traditional fare in a comfortable clublike setting. The Cafe serves all day, either indoors or out; it's best on Sundays, for champagne brunch. High tea is served daily in the Lobby Lounge.

Services: Concierge, 24-hour room service, nightly turndown, baby-sitting.

Facilities: Olympic-size outdoor heated pool, small exercise room, outdoor Jacuzzi, sundeck, three lighted tennis courts, car-rental desk, mountain bike rental, pro shop, full service spa/salon, shopping promenade.

MODERATE

The Artists' Inn Bed-and-Breakfast. 1038 Magnolia St., South Pasadena, CA 91030. ☎ and fax **818/799-5668.** 5 rms. A/C. $100–$120 double, additional person $20. Rates include full breakfast. AE, MC, V.

This Victorian-style inn, an unpretentious yellow-shingled home pleasantly furnished with wicker throughout, was built in 1895 as a farmhouse. Each of the five rooms is thematically decorated to reflect the style of a particular artist or period, including Impressionist, Fauve, and Van Gogh. The English Room, fitted with good quality antique furnishings and cheerful rose-patterned wallpaper, is the best room in the house; it's also the only one with a king-size bed. The Italian Suite has a queen bed and adjoining sun room with twin beds, a perfect choice for families. The Inn is on a quiet residential streeet 5 minutes from the heart of downtown.

Bissell House. 201 Orange Grove Ave. (corner of Columbia St.), South Pasadena, CA 91030. ☎ **818/441-3535.** 4 rooms. AC. $100–$150 double. Rates include full breakfast on weekends, expanded continental breakfast weekdays, plus afternoon snack and all-day beverages. AE, MC, V.

Hidden behind tall hedges which carefully isolate it from busy Orange Grove Avenue, this 1887 gingerbread Victorian is furnished with antiques and offers a delightful taste of life on what was once Pasadena's "Millionaire's Row." All rooms have private bath with both shower and tub (one an antique claw-foot, one a private whirlpool). There's a swimming pool and Jacuzzi on the beautifully landscaped grounds, and a downstairs library offers telephone and fax machine for guests' use.

INEXPENSIVE

Pasadena Hotel Bed & Breakfast. 76 N. Fair Oaks Ave. (between Union & Holly sts.), Pasadena, CA 91103. ☎ **800/653-8886** or 818/568-8172. Fax 818/793-6409. 10 rms., 1 with half-bath. AC, TV, TEL. $65–$165 double. Rates include continental breakfast. AE, MC, V. Parking $5.

This old-style hostelry is definitely not for everyone. In true turn-of-the-century rooming house style, the guest rooms have washbasins; all but one must share hallway bathrooms (three full, two half). Part of the attraction here is to the well-restored, National Historic Register building, and part to the hotel's flawless location: It's the only accommodation literally in the heart of Old Pasadena. Guest quarters are small but comfortable, and all are second-story exterior rooms. The central sitting room/lounge is elegant and welcoming, and there is a lively coffeehouse in the courtyard behind the hotel where you can enjoy your breakfast and complimentary afternoon teas. Shuttle buses to the Rose Bowl depart one block away during major events.

Saga Motor Hotel. 1633 E. Colorado Blvd. (between Allen and Sierra Bonita aves.), Pasadena, CA 91106. ☎ **818/795-0431.** 69 rms, 1 suite. A/C TV TEL. $62–$69 double; $75 suite. Rates include continental breakfast. AE, CB, DC, MC, V.

This motel is a 1950s relic of old Route 66, a little bland by modern standards but with far more character than most others in its price range. The rooms are small, clean, and simply furnished with just the basics. The best rooms are in the front building surrounding the gated swimming pool, which is shielded from the street and inviting in warm weather. The grounds are attractive and surprisingly well kept, if you don't count the astro-turf "lawn" around the pool. The motel is about a mile from the Huntington Library and within 10 minutes of both the Rose Bowl and Old Pasadena.

WHERE TO DINE

During the past decade or so, Pasadena has grown into one of the premier dining destinations for Angelenos "in the know." Superstar chefs have fled the super competitive Westside restaurant scene to shine in this friendly suburb. As a result, there are many excellent and affordable eateries, plus a profusion of coffeehouses and casual bakery/cafes. Remember, this isn't really out-of-town, and no one thinks twice about hopping on the freeway for dinner and a movie.

EXPENSIVE

Parkway Grill. 510 S. Arroyo Parkway (at California Blvd.), Pasadena. ☎ **818/795-1001.** Reservations recommended. Main courses $8–$23. AE, CB, DC, MC, V. Mon–Fri 11:30am–2:30pm, Mon–Thurs 5:30–11pm, Fri–Sat 5pm–midnight, Sun 10am–2pm and 5–11pm. CALIFORNIA ECLECTIC.

This quintessentially Southern California restaurant has been one of the LA area's top-rated spots since it opened in 1985, quickly gaining a reputation for avant-garde flavor combinations and gourmet pizzas to rival Spago's. Although some critics find many of chef Hugo Molina's dishes too fussy, others thrill to appetizer innovations like lobster-stuffed cocoa crepes or Dungeness crab cakes with ginger cream and two salsas. The star entrees are meat and game from the iron mesquite grill, followed by richly sweet (and substantial) desserts. The interior is vibrantly colored and architecturally, well, eclectic; for the building once knew life as a transmission shop! Located where the old Arroyo Seco Parkway glides into an ordinary city street, the Parkway Grill is within a couple minutes' drive from Old Pasadena and thoughfully offers free valet parking.

✪ **Xiomara.** 69 N. Raymond Ave. (1 block north of Colorado Blvd.), Pasadena. ☎ **818/796-2520.** Reservations recommended. Main courses $18–$23; fixed-price menu $25. AE, MC, V. Mon–Fri 11:30am–2:30pm; Mon–Sat 5:30–10:30pm, Sun 5–10:30pm. COUNTRY FRENCH.

By any other name, Xiomara (SEE-o-ma-ra) would still be one of the top restaurants in Los Angeles, despite the fact that it has never made Zagat's "top rated" list. Chef Patrick Healy's best dishes are rustic country concoctions like sausage-laden cassoulet, and veal shanks braised so long the meat practically falls off the bone. Chicken is simmered for an eternity in a sealed cast-iron pot with artichokes and carrots. The nightly fixed-price meal, a three-course menu determined by the chef's mood and the fresh ingredients at hand, is a remarkably good value. A long list of obscure country wines complements the menu. The dining room, a sleek black bistro setting, is as pleasing as the food, fitted with comfortable armchairs, and presided over by the enthusiastic Xiomara herself. An oyster and clam bar features oyster shooters, ceviche, and a large selection of raw oysters and clams on the half shell.

MODERATE

✪ **Twin Palms.** 101 W. Green St. (at Delacey Ave.), Pasadena. ☎ **818/577-2567.** Reservations recommended on weekends. Main courses $9–$17. AE, CB, DC, MC, V. Mon–Thurs 11:30am–midnight, Fri–Sat 11:30–1:30am, Sun 10:30am–midnight. MEDITERRANEAN/FRENCH.

Twin Palms is able to seat nearly 400 at spacious tables (no postage-stamp two-seaters here!) shaded by the fronds of 100-year-old palm trees. It's also busy, having become a hit with recession-weary Angelenos who come here for some of the best-value meals in the entire L.A. area. The quasi-outdoor and tented space creates a festival atmosphere augmented by two lively bars, and a bandstand with entertainment every night except Monday. Or come Sundays until 1:30pm for the "Gospel Brunch," during which Twin Palms also offers alternative entertainment for children. Co-owner/chef Michael Roberts is as well known for his celebrity backers (including Kevin Costner) as he is for the French "comfort food" he created as a backlash against pricey haute cuisine. Everyone talks about the salt cod mashed potato brandade, a delicious appetizer that's big enough to serve four—for only $5. The best main courses come off the crackling rotisserie and outdoor grill; they include juicy, roasted sage-infused pork and honey-glazed coriander-scented duck. Sautéed dishes and salads are not as successful. A number of exciting wines are priced well, under $20.

Yujean Kang's Gourmet Chinese Cuisine. 67 N. Raymond Ave. (between Walnut St. and Colorado Blvd.), Pasadena. ☎ 818/585-0855. Reservations recommended. Main courses $14–$21. AE, MC, V. Daily 11:30am–2:30pm, and 5–10pm. CHINESE CONTEMPORARY.

Many Chinese restaurants put the word "gourmet" in their name, but few really mean—or deserve—it. Not so at Yujean Kang, where Chinese cuisine is taken to an entirely new level. A master of "fusion" cuisine, the eponymous chef/owner snatches bits of techniques and flavors from both China and the West, comingling them in an entirely fresh way. Can you resist such provocative dishes as "Ants on Tree" (beef sautéed with glass noodles in chili and black sesame seeds), or lobster with caviar and fava beans, or Chilean sea bass in passion-fruit sauce? Kang is a wine aficionado and has assembled a magnificent cellar of California, French, and particularly German wines. Try pairing a German Spatlese with tea-smoked duck salad. The red-wrapped dining room is less subtle, but just as elegant as the food.

INEXPENSIVE

Goldstein's Bagel Bakery. 86 W. Colorado Blvd. (corner of Delacey Ave.), Old Pasadena. ☎ 818/79-BAGEL. Most items under $3. AE, MC, V. Mon–Thurs and Sun 6am–9pm, Fri–Sat 6am–10:30pm. BAKERY/DELI.

Join the locals who storm Goldstein's each morning for freshly baked (in the authentic New York style, they'll assure you) bagels; reliable Plain and Onion are as good as exotic Honey Oat Raisin or Banana Nut. In addition to six flavored cream cheeses, you can choose a bagel sandwich prepared with your choice of every deli ingredient under the sun. Centrally located in the heart of Old Pasadena, this is a good choice for snacks and light meals without interrupting the rhythm of your day.

Old Town Bakery & Restaurant. 166 W. Colorado Blvd. (at Pasadena Ave.), Pasadena. ☎ 818/792-7943. Main courses $5–$11. DISC, MC, V. Sun–Thurs 7:30am–10pm, Fri–Sat 7:30am–midnight. CONTINENTAL.

Set back from the street in a quaint fountain courtyard, this cheery bakery is an especially popular place to read the morning paper over one of their tasty breakfasts like pumpkin pancakes or zesty omeletes. The display counters are packed with cakes, muffins, scones, and other confections, all baked expressly for this shop. The rest of the menu is a mish-mosh of pastas, salads, and the like, borrowing heavily from Latin and Mediterranean cuisines. Old Town Bakery is a great place to spy on local Pasadenans in their natural habitat.

Pasadena Baking Company/Mi Piace. 25-29 E. Colorado Blvd. (east of Fair Oaks Ave.), Old Pasadena. ☎ 818/796-9966 or 818/795-3131. Bakery items under $3, main courses $6–$15.

AE, MC, V. Mon–Thurs 7am–11pm, Fri 7am–midnight, Sat 8am–midnight, Sun 8am–11pm. BAKERY/ITALIAN CAFE.

This little café holds just a handful of small tables, which spill out onto the sidewalk during nice weather (which is to say 90% of the time). Their particularly large—and sweet-smelling—selection of fresh pastries, tarts, truffles, cakes, and candies are all proudly displayed. There's also an assortment of fresh breads and a fresh fruit stand to accompany their breakfast and lunch menu.

Mi Piace is the adjoining casual trattoria, offering the usual pastas and Northern Italian dishes done unusually well. The Baking Company commandeers their sidewalk tables during breakfast, but starting around 11:30am it's not unusual to see Pasadena locals enjoying an espresso with their dogs tethered to a table leg!

PASADENA AFTER DARK

Espresso Bar. 1039 E. Green St. (near Catalina). ☎ **818/577-9113.** Coffee drinks and baked goodies $1–$4. No credit cards.

This simply named coffeehouse has been around so long that it almost seems as though Pasadena grew up around it. Formerly hidden down a hard-to-find alleyway, their new location is on Green Street's Antique Row—outside of Old Town but close to Pasadena City College. Open mike nights are popular with beat poets and singers, and bands play Friday and Saturday nights to an eclectic crowd lounging on the hodge-podge of dingy furniture typical of Espresso Bar's Greenwich Village ambiance. There's a spacious upstairs loft, and a beverage menu with some exotic entries like steamed milk with molasses.

Gordon Biersch Brewery & Restaurant. 41 Hugus Alley (in One Colorado). ☎ **818/449-0052** or 818/449-0067.

The Pasadena branch of the Northern California chain is one of the most successful brewpubs in Southern California. The wood-and-brick interior is large and noisy, and the food woefully uneven, but their house Pilsner and dark Bavarian-style brews are great and the atmosphere upbeat. Go for drinks and an appetizer, then head to a real restaurant for dinner.

The Ice House. 24 N. Mentor Ave. ☎ **818/577-1894;** Annex 818/577-9133.

Pasadena's best-known comedy and music club since 1960 claims to have launched the careers of Robin Williams, Steve Martin, David Letterman, and Lily Tomlin, among others. There are usually three acts nightly, with two shows on Friday and three shows on Saturday. The Ice House Annex presents blues, improvisational theater, and intimate performance art shows. Phone for the latest.

The Muse. 54 E. Colorado Blvd. (near Fair Oaks), Pasadena. ☎ **818/588-1030.**

This nightclub in the core of Old Town will draw you in with it's wild, Gaudi-esque bar furniture and decor. Kind of like Toontown for the 21-and-over crowd (but generally not too much over!). In back are some pool tables, and there's dancing until 2am Friday and Saturday.

Pasadena Playhouse. 35 S. El Molino Ave. (near Colorado Blvd.). ☎ **818/356-7529.**

One of the most highly acclaimed professional theaters in L.A., Pasadena Playhouse was founded in 1917, is a registered historic landmark, and has served as the training ground for many theatrical, film, and television stars, including William Holden and Gene Hackman. Productions are staged both on the main theater's elaborate Spanish Colonial Revival stage and in a smaller theater on the second floor. Call to find out what's on.

2 Long Beach & the *Queen Mary*

21 Miles S of Downtown L.A.

The fifth-largest incorporated city in California, Long Beach consists mostly of business and industrial areas interspersed with unremarkable neighborhoods. The city is best known as the permanent home of the former cruise liner *Queen Mary* (see "What to See and Do" and "Where to Stay," below) and for the annual Long Beach Grand Prix in mid-April, whose star-studded warm-up race sends the likes of young hipster Jason Priestly (*Beverly Hills, 90210*) and perennial racer Paul Newman burning rubber through the streets of the city. Although Long Beach is too far away to be considered part of Los Angeles as a tourist destination, and it's not as attractive as most of the smaller coastal communities to either the north or south, the *Queen Mary* makes a trip here worthwhile.

ESSENTIALS

GETTING THERE   See chapter 2 for airport and airline information. When driving from Los Angeles on either I-5 or I-405, take I-710 south; it follows the Los Angeles River on its path to the ocean and leads directly to both downtown Long Beach and the Queen Mary Seaport.

ORIENTATION   Most of seaside Long Beach is in vast San Pedro Harbor, L.A.'s busy industrial port. Terminal Island sits right in the middle. To the west across pretty Vincent Thomas bridge is the city of San Pedro, home to the nautical and touristy **Ports O' Call Village.** The *Queen Mary* is docked near the eastern end of Long Beach, looking out over the actual "long beach" extending along peaceful, affluent Belmont Shore to tiny Long Beach Marina, home to charming Naples Island (see Gondola Getaway below).

VISITOR INFORMATION   Contact the **Long Beach Area Convention & Visitors Bureau,** One World Trade Center, #300 (☎ 800/4LB-STAY or 310/436-3645). There's a city-run Web site at **http://www.ci.long-beach.ca.us,** which offers, in addition to business and government information, a section with tourism listings. For further information on the **Long Beach Grand Prix,** call 310/981-2600 or visit their Web site at **http://www.longbeachgp.com.**

THE *QUEEN MARY* & OTHER PORT ATTRACTIONS

The *Queen Mary.* Pier J (at the end of I-710), Long Beach. ☎ **562/435-3511.** Admission $10 adults, $8 seniors 55 and over and military, $6 children 4–11, under 4 free. Daily 10am–6pm (last entry at 5:30pm). Extended summer hours. Charge for parking.

It's easy to dismiss the *Queen Mary* as a barnacle-laden tourist trap, but it is the only surviving example of this particular kind of 20th-century elegance and excess. From staterooms paneled lavishly in now-extinct tropical hardwoods, to miles of hallway handrails made of once-pedestrian Bakelite and perfectly preserved crew quarters which are an art-deco homage, wonders never cease aboard this luxury liner. Stroll the teakwood decks with just a bit of imagination, and you're back in 1936 on the maiden voyage from Southampton, England. Kiosk displays of photographs and memorabilia are everywhere, and the ship has been virtually unaltered since her heyday. Especially evocative is the first-class observation lounge, a Streamline Moderne masterpiece you might recognize from *Barton Fink, Beverly Hills 90210,* and others. Regular admission includes a self-guided tour. For an additional $6 for adults or $3 for kids, you can take a behind-the-scenes guided tour of the ship, peppered with worthwhile anecdotes and details.

Area Code Change Notice

Please note that, effective January 25, 1997, the area code for Long Beach, previously in the 310 area, has changed to **562**. You will be able to dial 310 until July 26, 1997; after that date, you will have to use 562.

Gondola Getaway. Naples Island, Long Beach. ☎ **562/433-9595.** One-hour cruise $55 for two. Daily 11am–11pm.

Since 1982 these authentic Venetian gondolas have been snaking the human-made canals of Naples Island, under gracefully arched bridges and past the gardens of resort cottages. Feel free to bring your beverage of choice, for they send you out with a nice basket of bread, cheese, and salami plus wine glasses and a full ice bucket. Perhaps your traditionally clad oarsman will sing an Italian aria, or relate the many tales of marriage proposals by romance-minded passengers (some not-so-successful!).

Shoreline Village. 407 Shoreline Dr. (at Pine Ave. across the channel from the *Queen Mary*). ☎ **562/435-2668** or 562/432-3053 for information. Open daily 10am–9pm, or later in summer and holidays.

If you've seen the real thing in New England you won't be overly impressed, but Long Beach likes to promote this cluster of shops, restaurants, and waterside cafés as a replica 19th-century seaport village. But our favorite surprise was an ornate merry-go-round handcarved in 1906 by Charles Looff, master carousel maker who helped build The Pike, an old-fashioned seaside amusement park which stood on this spot in the 1930s. The 62 wooden carousel animals include not only horses but leaping camels, giraffes, and rams, all illuminated by glittering Austrian crystal; rides are $1.

The Tall Ship *Californian*.

Literally the flagship of the Nautical Heritage Society, the *Californian* sails from Long Beach between late August and mid-April (it's based in northern California during summer). At 145 feet long, this two-masted wooden cutter-class vessel offers barefooters the opportunity to help raise and lower eight sails, steer by compass, and generally experience the "romance of the high seas." Landlubbers will want to choose the 4-hour day sail for $75 ($113 for two), including lunch, while old salts can take 2-, 3- or 4-day cruises out to Catalina or the Channel Islands at $140 per person per day. For reservations, call 800/432-2201. Overnight sails should be booked well in advance.

WHERE TO STAY

✪ **Hotel *Queen Mary*.** 1126 Queen's Hwy. (end of I-710), Long Beach, CA 90802-6390. ☎ **800/437-2934**, 562/432-6964, or 562/435-3511. Fax 562/437-4531. 365 rooms, 17 suites. A/C TV TEL. $75–$160 double; suites from $350. AE, DC, EURO, MC, V. Charge for parking.

Although the *Queen Mary* is considered the most luxurious ocean liner ever to sail the Atlantic, with the largest rooms ever built aboard a ship, the quarters aren't exceptional when compared to those on terra firma today, nor are its amenities. The idea is to enjoy the novelty and charm of the original bathtub watercocks ("cold salt," "cold fresh," "hot salt," "hot fresh"). The ship's beautifully carved interior is a festival for the eye and fun to explore, plus the weekday rates are hard to beat. Three on-board restaurants are overpriced but convenient, and the original shopping arcade has a decidedly British feel (one shop sells great *Queen Mary* souvenirs). An elegant Sunday champagne brunch—complete with ice sculpture and harpist—is served in the ship's Grand Salon, and it's always worth having a cocktail in the Art Deco Observation Bar. If you're too young or too poor to have traveled on the old luxury liners, this is the perfect opportunity to experience the romance of an Atlantic crossing—and with no seasickness, cabin fever, or week of formal dinners.

WHERE TO DINE

Belmont Brewing Company. 25 Thirty-Ninth Place (at the Belmont Pier), Long Beach. ☎ **562/433-3891.** Main courses $5–$11. AE, CB, DC, MC, V. Mon–Fri 11:30am–9:30pm, Sat-Sun 10:30am–10pm (bar untill midnight daily). BREWPUB/AMERICAN.

This brewed-on-premises beer restaurant's outdoor patio has a million-dollar harbor view of the *Queen Mary*, fiery sunsets, and the pier's unusual chameleon streetlamps. The five house brews include "Top Sail" (amber) and "Long Beach Crude" (porter). The menu conists of salads, sandwiches, pizzas, pasta, and Happy Hour appetizer favorites, including a deep-fried whole onion "flower" served with sweet-spicy dipping sauce.

Papadakis Taverna. 301 W. Sixth St. (at Centre St.), San Pedro. ☎ **562/548-1186.** Reservations recommended. Main courses $8–$16. CB, DC, MC, V. Sun–Thurs 5–9pm, Fri–Sat 5–10pm. GREEK.

The food here rates higher than the ambiance—even genial host John Papadakis's hand-kissing greeting doesn't soften the blunt lines and bright lights of this banquet room–like space decorated with equal parts Aegean murals and football art (in deference to Papadakis's glory days as a USC football legend). The waiters dance and sing loudly when they're not bringing plates of *spanikopita* (spinach filled filo pastries) or thick, satisfying *tsatziki* (garlic-laced cucumber and yogurt spread) to your table. Servings are very generous, prices reasonable, and the wine list has something for everyone.

Parker's Lighthouse. 435 Shoreline Village Dr., Long Beach. ☎ **562/432-6500.** Reservations recommended on weekends. Lunches $6–$15, dinners $9–$27. AE, DC, DISC, MC, V. Mon–Thurs 11am–10pm, Fri 11am–11pm, Sat 3–11pm, Sun 3:30–9:30pm. SEAFOOD GRILL.

Built to look like a giant Cape Cod lighthouse, Parker's fits right into the Shoreline Village motif. It's actually kind of fun to wind upstairs to one of three dining levels, including the circular bar on the top floor which looks out over the harbor and the behemoth *Queen Mary*. The main dining room specializes in mesquite-fired fresh seafood, but also offers steaks and chicken.

3 Santa Catalina Island

22 miles W of mainland Los Angeles

Santa Catalina—which everyone calls simply Catalina—is a small, cove-fringed island famous for its laid-back inns, largely unspoiled landscape, and crystal-clear waters. Many devotees consider it Southern California's alternative to Capri or Malta. Because of its relative isolation, out-of-state tourists tend to ignore it; but those who do show up have plenty of elbow room to boat, fish, swim, scuba, and snorkel. There are miles of hiking and biking trails, plus golf, tennis, and horseback-riding.

Catalina is so different from the mainland that it almost seems like a different country, remote and unspoiled. In 1915, the island was purchased by William Wrigley, Jr., the chewing gum manufacturer, in order to develop a fashionable pleasure resort. To publicize the new vacation land, Wrigley brought big-name bands to the Avalon Ballroom and moved the Chicago Cubs, which he owned, to the island for spring training. His marketing efforts succeeded, and this charming and tranquil retreat became—and still is—a favorite vacation resort for mainlanders.

Today about 86% of the island remains undeveloped, owned and preserved by the Santa Catalina Island Conservancy. Some of the specacular outlying areas can only be reached by arranged tour (see "Exploring the Island," below).

ESSENTIALS

GETTING THERE   The most common way to get to and from the island is via the *Catalina Express* (☎ 562/519-1212), which operates up to 20 daily departures year-round to Catalina from San Pedro and Long Beach. The trip takes about an hour. One-way fares from San Pedro are $17.75 for adults, $16 for seniors, $13 for children 2 to 11, and $1 for infants. Long Beach fares are about $2 higher for all except infants, who are still charged $1. The trip is an additional $1.80 if you travel to Two Harbors. The Catalina Express departs from the Sea/Air Terminal at Berth 95, port of L.A. in San Pedro; from the Catalina Express port at the Queen Mary in Long Beach; and from the Catalina Express port at 161 N. Harbor Dr. in Redondo Beach. Call for information and reservations.

Catalina Cruises (☎ 800/CATALINA) also ferries passengers from Long Beach to Avalon Harbor—they have the best rates going (about $5 cheaper than above) because they run monstrous 700-passenger boats which take longer to make the crossing (about 1 hour and 50 minutes). But they do offer twice-daily sailings during the high season, plus frequent runs to Twin Harbors. If you want to save money, particularly if you're staying overnight and don't have to maximize your island time, Catalina Cruises is the choice for you.

Note: Luggage on the *Catalina Express* is limited to 50 pounds per person; reservations are necessary for bicycles, surfboards, and dive tanks; and there are restrictions on transporting domestic pets. Call for information.

Island Express Helicopter Service, 900 Queens Way Dr., Long Beach (☎ 562/510-2525; fax 562/510-9671), flies from Long Beach or San Pedro to Catalina in about 15 minutes. They fly on demand between 8am and sunset year-round, charging $66 each way. If you just want an airborne tour of Catalina, they'll spend 10 to 30 minutes showing you island sights. There's a four-passenger minumum and the cost is $50–$90 per person.

ORIENTATION   The picturesque town of Avalon is the island's only city. Named for a passage in Tennyson's Idylls of the King, Avalon is also the port of entry for the island. From the ferry dock you can wander along Crescent Avenue, the main road along the beachfront, and easily explore adjacent side streets.

Visitors are not allowed to drive cars on the island. There are only a limited number of autos permitted; most residents motor around in golf carts (many of the homes only have golf cart-sized driveways). But don't worry—you'll be able to get everywhere you want to go by renting a cart yourself or just hoofing it, which is what most visitors do.

Northwest of Avalon is the village of Two Harbors (see below), accessible only by boat or the most intrepid of hikers. Its twin bays are favored by pleasure yachts from L.A.'s various marinas, so there's more camaraderie and a less touristy ambiance overall.

VISITOR INFORMATION   The **Catalina Island Chamber of Commerce and Visitor's Bureau,** P.O. Box 217, Avalon, CA 90704 (☎ 310/510-1520; fax 310/510-7606), located on the Green Pleasure Pier, distributes brochures and information on island activities, including sightseeing tours, camping, hiking, fishing, and boating. It also offers information on hotels and boat and helicopter transport. Call for a free 100-page visitor's guide.

The Santa Catalina Island Company-run **Visitor's Information Center,** which is just across from the Chamber of Commerce, on Crescent Avenue (☎ 310/510-2000), handles hotel reservations, sightseeing tours, and other island activities.

There's also a colorful Internet site at **http://www.catalina.com** which offers current news from the *Catalina Islander* newspaper in addition to updated activities, events, and general information.

GETTING AROUND If you want to explore the area around Avalon beyond where your feet can comfortably carry you, try renting a mountain bike or tandem from **Brown's Bikes,** 107 Pebbly Beach Rd., Avalon (☎ 310/510-0986), or even a gas-powered golf cart from **Cartopia,** 615 Crescent Avenue, Avalon (☎ 310/510-2493), where rates are $30 per hour.

EXPLORING THE ISLAND

ORGANIZED TOURS The Santa Catalina Island Company's **Discovery Tours,** Avalon Harbor Pier (☎ 800/626-7489 or 310/510-TOUR), operates several motorcoach excursions that depart from the tour plaza in the center of town on Sumner Avenue.

The Skyline Drive tour basically follows the perimeter of the island and takes about 1³/₄ hours. Trips leave several times a day from 11am to 3pm and cost $18 for adults, $16 for seniors, and $10 for children 3 to 11.

The Inland Motor Tour is more comprehensive; it includes some of the 66 square miles of preserve owned by the Santa Catalina Island Conservancy. You'll see El Rancho Escondido, and probably have a chance to view buffalo, deer, goats, and boars. Tours, which take about 3³/₄ hours, leave at 9am; from June to October, they leave at other times too. Tours are $29 for adults, $26 for seniors, and $16 for children 3 to 11; free for children under 3.

Other excursions offered by the company include the 40-minute Casino Tour, which explores Catalina's most famous landmark; the 50-minute Avalon Scenic Tour, a 9-mile introductory tour of the town; and the 1-hour Flying Fish Boat Trip, during which an occasional flying fish lands right on the boat.

Check with the Catalina Island Company for other tour offerings, as well as for information on multiple excursion packages.

VISITING TWO HARBORS If you want to get a better look at the rugged natural beauty of Catalina and escape the throngs of beachgoers, head over to Two Harbors, the ¹/₄-mile "neck" at the island's northwest end which gets its name from the "twin harbors" on each side, known as the Isthmus and "Cat" Harbor. An excellent starting point for campers and hikers, Two Harbors offers just enough civilization for the less intrepid traveler.

The Banning House Lodge (☎ 310/510-7265) is an 11-room bed-and-breakfast overlooking the Isthmus. The clapboard house was built in 1910 for Catalina's pre-Wrigley owners, and has seen duty as girls' camp, army barracks, and on-location lodging for moviestars like Errol Flynn and Dorothy Lamour. The innkeepers are gracious, the atmosphere peaceful and isolated. Call from the pier and they'll even drive you up to the lodge.

Everyone eats at **Doug's Harbor Reef** (☎ 310/510-7265) down on the beach. This nautical/South Seas–themed saloon/restaurant serves breakfast, lunch, and dinner, the latter being hearty steaks, ribs, swordfish, chicken teriyaki, and buffalo burgers in the summer. The house drink is sweet "buffalo milk," a potent concoction of vodka, creme de cacao, banana liqueur, milk, and whipped cream.

Avalon Casino and Catalina Island Museum. At the end of Crescent Ave. ☎ **310/ 510-2414.** Museum admission $1.50 adults, $1 seniors, 50¢ ages 6–11; children under 5 free. Daily 10:30am–4pm.

The Avalon Casino is the most famous structure on the island, and one of its oldest. Built in 1929 to house a ballroom and theater, its massive circular rotunda topped with a red-tile roof is its most notable feature. The Avalon Casino is widely known for its beautiful art deco ballroom, which once hosted the Tommy Dorsey and Glen Miller orchestras and other top bands. You can see the inside of the building by attending a ballroom event or watching a film (the Casino is Avalon's primary movie theater). Otherwise, admission is by guided tour only, operated daily by the Santa Catalina Island Company (see "Organized Tours," above).

The Catalina Island Museum, located on the ground floor of the Casino, features exhibits on island history, archaeology, and natural history—they also have a contour relief map of the island which can be helpful to anyone planning to venture into the interior.

SNORKELING, DIVING & KAYAKING

Snorkeling, scuba-diving, and sea kayaking are among the main reasons mainlanders head to Catalina. Purists will prefer the less-spoiled waters of Two Harbors, but Avalon's many coves have plenty to offer as well. **Banana Boat Riders,** 107 Pebbly Beach Rd., Avalon (☎ 800/708-2262 or 310/510-1774), offers snorkel gear and sea kayak rentals, as well as half- and full-day excursions to Two Harbors and other island coves. **Catalina Divers Supply** (☎310/510-0330 or 800/353-0330) offers guided snorkel and scuba tours with certified instructors, in addition to gear rental at three Avalon locations. **Descanso Beach Ocean Sports** (☎ 310/510-1226) offers sea-kayak and snorkel rentals with instruction, plus specialty expeditions and kids' programs.

At Two Harbors, sit-on-top beginner kayaks as well as advanced touring types can be rented at **Two Harbors Kayak Center** (☎ 310/510-7265). They offer instruction and guided tours of the secluded coves on the northern end of the island.

WHERE TO STAY

Catalina's accommodations range from old-salt motels to yachting-set luxury. If you plan to stay overnight, be sure to reserve a room in advance, since most places fill up pretty quickly during the summer and holiday seasons. **Catalina Island Accommodations** (☎ 310/510-3000) might be able to help you out in a pinch; they're a reservations service with updated info on the whole island. Here are three of the most noteworthy places to stay.

Catalina Island Inn. 125 Metropole, north of Crescent Ave. (P.O. Box 467), Avalon, CA 90704. ☎ **800/246-8134** or 310/510-1623. Fax 310/510-7218. 35 rms, 1 minisuite. TV TEL. May–Sept, holidays, and weekends, $89–$179 double; $189 minisuite. Oct–Apr except holidays and weekends, $45–$99 double; $155 minisuite. All rates include continental breakfast. AE, DISC, MC, V.

Innkeepers Martin and Bernadine Curtin provide clean, comfortable rooms simply furnished with a vaguely tropical motif. Many rooms have balconies with views of the harbor, and you can't beat the location right in the center of bustling Avalon.

✪ **The Inn on Mt. Ada.** 398 Wrigley Rd. (P.O. Box 2560), Avalon, CA 90704. ☎ **310/ 510-2030.** 6 rms, 2 suites. June–Oct and weekends, $320–$490 double; $490–$590 suite. Mon–Thurs and Nov–May, $230–$370 double; $370–$470 suite. Rates include 3 meals. MC, V.

When William Wrigley, Jr., purchased Catalina Island in 1921, he built this remarkably ornate Georgian Colonial mansion as his summer vacation home. In 1985, several local residents signed a 30-year lease for the estate and lovingly transformed it into one of the finest small hotels in California. The opulent inn has several ground-floor salons, a fireplaced club room, a deep-seated formal library, and a wickered sunroom where tea, cookies, and fruit are always available. Once the master bedroom, the best guest room is the Grand Suite fitted with a fireplace and a large private patio. Room 2 has a queen-size four-poster bed, a fireplace, and a sitting lounge with wingback chairs. Amenities include bathrobes. TVs are available on request, but there are no telephones in the rooms. A hearty full breakfast, a light deli-style lunch, and a beautiful multicourse dinner complemented by a limited wine selection are included in the tariff.

Zane Grey Pueblo Hotel. Off Chimes Tower Rd., north of Hill St. (P.O. Box 216), Avalon, CA 90704. ☎ **800/378-3256** or 310/510-0966. 17 rms. April–Oct, $75–$125 double; Nov–Mar, $59 double. Rates include continental breakfast. AE, MC, V.

You'll have the most superb views on the island from this Shangri-la mountain retreat, the former home of novelist Zane Grey, who spent his last 20 years in Avalon. He wrote many books here, including *Tales of Swordfish and Tuna,* which tells of his fishing adventures off Catalina Island.

The hotel has teak beams that the novelist brought from Tahiti on one of his fishing trips. Most of the rooms also have large windows and ocean or mountain views. They have all been renovated with new furniture, carpeting, and ceiling fans. An outdoor patio has an excellent view. The original living room has a grand piano, a fireplace, and a TV. The hotel also has a pool and sundeck, with chairs overlooking Avalon and the ocean. Coffee is served all day, and there's a courtesy bus to town.

WHERE TO DINE

The Busy Bee. 306 Crescent Ave. (north of Pleasure Pier). ☎ **310/510-1983.** Reservations not accepted. Main courses $7–$15. AE, CB, DC, DISC, MC, V. Summer, daily 8am–10pm. Winter, daily 8am–8pm. AMERICAN.

The Busy Bee, an Avalon institution since 1923, is located right on the beach. The fare is light deli style. The extensive menu offers breakfast, lunch, and dinner at all times. The restaurant grinds its own beef, cuts its own potatoes for french fries, and makes its own salad dressings. Even if you're not hungry, come here for a drink; it's Avalon's only waterfront bar.

El Galleon. 411 Crescent Ave. ☎ **310/510-1188.** Reservations recommended on weekends. Main courses $11–$37 at dinner. AE, DISC, MC, V. Daily 11am–2:30pm and 5–10pm. Bar daily 10am–1:30am. AMERICAN.

El Galleon is large, warm, and woody, complete with portholes, rigging, anchors, wrought-iron chandeliers, oversize leather booths, and tables with red-leather captain's chairs. There's additional balcony seating, plus outdoor café tables overlooking the ocean harbor. Lunch and dinner feature seafood. Favorite dinner dishes include fresh swordfish steak and broiled Catalina lobster tails in drawn butter. "Turf" main dishes range from country-fried chicken to broiled rack of lamb with mint jelly.

Sand Trap. Avalon Canyon Rd. (north of Tremont St.). ☎ **310/510-1349.** Reservations not accepted. Main courses $4–$12. No credit cards. Daily 7:30am–3:30pm. CALIFORNIA-MEXICAN.

This local favorite is a great place to escape from the bayfront crowds. Enjoy breakfast, lunch, or snacks while overlooking the golf course. Specialties of the house include delectable omelets served until noon and soft tacos served all day. Either can be made with any number of fillings. Burgers, sandwiches, salads, and chili are also served. Beer and wine are available.

4 Disneyland & Other Anaheim Area Attractions

27 miles SE of downtown Los Angeles

The sleepy Orange County town of Anaheim grew up around Disneyland, the West's most famous theme park. Now, even beyond this Happiest Place on Earth, the city and its neighboring communities are kid central. Otherwise unspectacular, sprawling suburbs have become a playground of family-oriented hotels, restaurants, and unabashedly tourist-oriented attractions. Among the nearby draws are Knott's Berry Farm, another family-oriented theme park, in nearby Buena Park. At the other end of the scale is the Richard Nixon Library and Birthplace, a surprisingly compelling presidential library and museum, just 7 miles northeast of Disneyland in Yorba Linda.

ESSENTIALS

GETTING THERE   Los Angeles International Airport (LAX) is located about 30 minutes from Anaheim via I-5 south (see chapter 2). If you're heading directly to Anaheim and want to avoid Los Angeles altogether, try to land at **John Wayne International Airport** (☎ 714/252-5200) in Irvine, Orange County's largest airport. It's about 15 miles from Disneyland. The airport is served by Alaska, American, Continental, Delta, Northwest, TWA, and United Airlines. Check to see if your hotel has a free shuttle to and from either airport, or call one of the following commercial shuttle services (fares are generally $10 one way from John Wayne or $12 from LAX): **L.A. Xpress** (☎ 800/I-ARRIVE); **Prime Time** (☎ 800/262-7433); **SuperShuttle** (☎ 714/517-6600). Rental cars located at John Wayne Airport include **Budget** (☎ 800/221-1203) and **Hertz** (☎ 800/654-3131).

VISITOR INFORMATION   The **Anaheim/Orange County Visitor and Convention Bureau,** at 800 W. Katella Ave. (P.O. Box 4270), Anaheim, CA 92803 (☎ 714/999-8999), can fill you in on area activities and shopping shuttles. They are located just inside the Convention Center (across the street from Disneyland), next to the dramatic cantilevered arena, and welcome visitors Monday to Friday from 8:30am to 5:30pm. **The Buena Park Convention and Visitors Office,** 6280 Manchester Blvd., Suite 103 (☎ 800/541-3953 or 714/562-3560), will provide specialized information on their area, including Knott's Berry Farm.

DISNEYLAND

Disney was the originator of the mega–theme park. Opened in 1955, Disneyland remains unsurpassed. Despite constant threats from pretenders to the crown, Disneyland and its sister park, Walt Disney World in Orlando, Florida, remain the kings of the theme parks. At no other park is fantasy elevated to an art form. Nowhere else is as fresh and fantastic every time you walk through the gates, whether you're 6 or 60—and no matter how many times you've done it before. There's nothing like Disney Magic.

The park stays on the cutting edge by continually updating and expanding, while still maintaining the hallmarks that make it the world's top amusement park (a term coined by Walt Disney himself). Look for the most recent Disney additions during your visit—*Toontown,* an interactive cartoon area added in 1993, and 1995's *Indiana Jones Adventure,* a high-tech thrill that's not to be missed—no matter how long you have to wait in line. Also look for live-action musical extravaganzas based on Disney's most recent animated features, *The Lion King, Pocahontas,* and *The Hunchback of Notre Dame.* It was "lights out" in 1996 for the Main Street Electrical Parade's 20-year run, but at press time plans were already in the works for a completely new nighttime spectacular.

GETTING THERE   Disneyland is located at 1313 Harbor Blvd. in Anaheim. It's about an hour's drive from downtown Los Angeles. Take I-5 south to the well-marked Harbor Boulevard exit.

ADMISSION, HOURS & INFORMATION   Admission to the park, including unlimited rides and all festivities and entertainment, is $34 for adults and children over 12, $26 for children 3 to 11, and $30 for seniors 60 or better; children under 3 are free. Parking is $6. Two- and three-day passes are also available; in addition, many area accommodations offer lodging packages which include one or more day's park admission.

Disneyland is open every day of the year, but operating hours vary, so we recommend you call for information which applies to the specific day(s) of your visit. Generally speaking, the park is open from 9 or 10am to 6 or 7pm on weekdays, fall through spring; and from 8 or 9am to midnight or 1am on weekends, holidays, and during winter, spring, or summer vacation periods.

For information, call 714/781-4565 or 213/626-8605, ext. 4565. If you've never been to Disneyland before and would like to get a copy of their *Souvenir Guide* to orient yourself to the park before you go, write to **Disneyland Guest Relations,** P.O. Box 3232, Anaheim, CA 92803. Or, pick up a copy of *The Unofficial Guide to Disneyland* (Macmillan Travel) at your local bookstore.

DISNEY TIPS   Disneyland is busiest from mid-June to mid-September, and on weekends and holidays year-round. Peak hours are from noon to 5pm; visit the most popular rides before and after these hours and you'll cut your waiting times substantially. If you plan on arriving during a busy time, purchase your tickets in advance and get a jump on the crowds at the ticket counters.

Disneyland's attendance falls dramatically during the wintertime, so the park offers discounted (about 25% off) admission to Southern California residents who may purchase up to six tickets per zip code verification. If you will be visiting the park with someone who lives here, be sure to take advantage of this money-saving opportunity.

Many visitors tackle Disneyland systematically, beginning at the entrance and working their way clockwise around the park. But a better plan of attack is to arrive early and run to the most popular rides first—the Indiana Jones Adventure, Star Tours, Space Mountain, Big Thunder Mountain Railroad, Splash Mountain, the Haunted Mansion, and Pirates of the Caribbean. Lines for these rides can last an hour or more in the middle of the day.

TOURING THE PARK

The Disneyland complex is divided into several themed "lands," each of which has a number of rides and attractions that are, more or less, related to that land's theme.

Main Street U.S.A., at park's entrance, is a cinematic version of turn-of-the-century small-town America. This whitewashed Rockwellian fantasy is lined with gift shops, candy stores, a soda fountain, and a silent theater that continuously runs early Mickey Mouse films. You'll find the practical things you might need here, too, such as stroller rentals and storage lockers. Because there are no rides here, it's best to tour Main Street during the middle of the afternoon, when lines for rides are longest, and in the evening, when you can rest your feet in the theater that features "Great

Disneyland

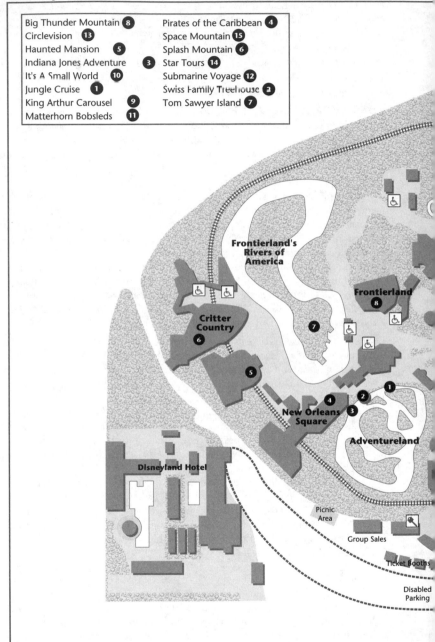

Big Thunder Mountain **8**
Circlevision **13**
Haunted Mansion **5**
Indiana Jones Adventure **3**
It's A Small World **10**
Jungle Cruise **1**
King Arthur Carousel **9**
Matterhorn Bobsleds **11**

Pirates of the Caribbean **4**
Space Mountain **15**
Splash Mountain **6**
Star Tours **14**
Submarine Voyage **12**
Swiss Family Treehouse **2**
Tom Sawyer Island **7**

Frontierland's
Rivers of
America

Frontierland
8

Critter
Country
6

7

5

4 **2** **1**

New Orleans
Square
3

Adventureland

Disneyland Hotel

Picnic
Area

Group Sales

Ticket Booths

Disabled
Parking

1-0853

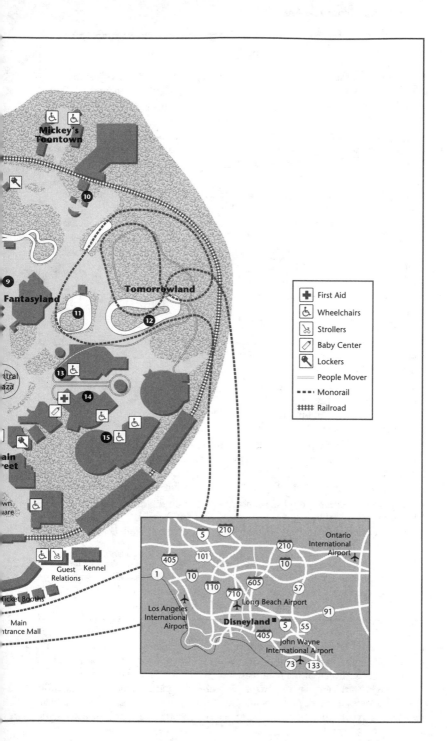

Mickey's
Toontown

10

Fantasyland

9

Tomorrowland

11

12

Central
Plaza

13

14

15

Main
Street

Town
Square

Guest
Relations

Kennel

Ticket Booths

Main
Entrance Mall

First Aid
Wheelchairs
Strollers
Baby Center
Lockers
People Mover
Monorail
Railroad

5   210

210

Ontario
International
Airport

405   101

10

1

10

110   605   57

Los Angeles
International
Airport

710   Long Beach Airport

91

Disneyland   5   55

405

John Wayne
International
Airport

73   133

247

Disney Dossier

Believe it or not, the Happiest Place on Earth keeps more than a few skeletons—as well as some just plain interesting facts—in its closet. Did you know that:

- Disneyland was carved out of orange groves; original plans called for carefully chosen individual trees to be left standing and included in the park's landscaping. On groundbreaking day, July 21, 1954, each tree in the orchard was marked with a ribbon—red to be cut and green to be spared. But the bulldozer operator went through and mowed down every tree indiscriminately . . . no one had foreseen his color blindness.

- Disneyland designers utilized forced perspective in the construction of many of the park's structures to give the illusion of height and dramatic proportions while keeping the park a manageable size. The buildings on **Main Street U.S.A.,** for example, are actually 90% scale on the first floor, 80% on the second, and so forth. The stones on **Sleeping Beauty Castle** are carved in diminishing scale from the bottom to the top, giving it the illusion of towering height.

- The faces of the **Pirates of the Caribbean** were modeled after some of the early staff of Walt Disney Imagineering, who also lent their names to the second-floor "businesses" along **Main Street U.S.A.**

- Walt Disney maintained two apartments inside Disneyland. His private apartment above the **Town Square Fire Station** has been kept just as it was when he lived there.

- The elaborately carved horses on Fantasyland's **King Arthur Carousel** are between 100 and 120 years old; Walt Disney found them lying neglected in storage at Coney Island in New York, and brought them home to be carefully cleaned and restored.

- **It's A Small World** was touted at its opening as "mingling the waters of the oceans and seas around the world with Small World's Seven Seaways." This was more than a publicity hoax—records from that time show such charges as $21.86 for a shipment of sea water from the Caribbean.

- The peaceful demeanor of Disneyland was broken during the summer of 1970 by a group of radical Vietnam protesters who invaded the park. They seized **Tom Sawyer Island** and raised the Vietcong flag over the fort before being expelled by riot specialists.

- **Indiana Jones: Temple of the Forbidden Eye,** Disneyland's newest attraction, won't be experienced the same way by any two groups of riders. Like a sophisticated computer game, the course is programmed with so many variables in the action that there are 160,000 possible combinations of events.

Moments with Mr. Lincoln," a patriotic (and animatronic) look at America's 16th president. There's always something happening on Main Street; stop in at the information booth to the left of the main entrance for a schedule of the day's events.

You might start your day by circumnavigating the park by train. An authentic 19th-century steam engine pulls open-air cars around the park's perimeter. Board at the Main Street Depot and take a complete turn around the park, or disembark at any one of the lands.

Adventureland is inspired by the most exotic regions of Asia, Africa, India, and the South Pacific. There are several popular rides here. This is where you'll find the Swiss Family Treehouse. On the Jungle Cruise, passengers board a large authentic-looking Mississippi River paddleboat and float along an Amazon-like river. En route, the boat is threatened by "animatronic" wild animals and hostile natives, while a tour guide entertains with a running patter. A spear's throw away is The Enchanted Tiki Room, one of the most sedate attractions in Adventureland. Inside, you can sit down and watch a 20-minute musical comedy featuring electronically animated tropical birds, flowers, and "tiki gods."

The Indiana Jones Adventure is Adventureland's newest ride. Based on the Steven Spielberg series of films, this ride takes adventurers into the Temple of the Forbidden Eye, in joltingly realistic all-terrain vehicles. Riders follow Indy and experience the perils of bubbling lava pits, whizzing arrows, fire-breathing serpents, collapsing bridges, and the familiar cinematic tumbling boulder (this effect is very realistic in the front seats!). Disney "imagineers" reached new heights with the design of this ride's line which, take my word for it, has so much detail throughout its twisting path that 30 minutes or more simply flies by.

New Orleans Square, a large, grassy, gas lamp—dotted green—is home to the Haunted Mansion, the most high-tech ghost house I've ever seen. The spookiness has been toned down so kids won't get nightmares anymore, so the events inside are as funny as they are scary. Even more fanciful is Pirates of the Caribbean, one of Disneyland's most popular rides. Here, visitors float on boats through mock underground caves, entering an enchanting world of swashbuckling, rum-running, and buried treasure. Even in the middle of the afternoon you can dine by the cool moonlight and to the sound of crickets in the Blue Bayou Restaurant, the best eatery in the land.

Critter Country is supposed to be an ode to the backwoods—a sort of Frontierland without those pesky settlers. Little kids like to sing along with the animatronic critters in the musical Country Bear Jamboree show. Older kids and grown-ups head straight for Splash Mountain, one of the largest water flume rides in the world. Loosely based on the Disney movie *Song of the South,* the ride is lined with about 100 characters who won't stop singing "Zip-A-Dee-Doo-Dah." Be prepared to get wet, especially if someone sizable is in the front seat of your log-shaped boat.

Frontierland gets its inspiration from 19th-century America. It's full of dense "forests" and broad "rivers" inhabited by hearty looking (but, luckily, not smelling) "pioneers." You can take a raft to Tom Sawyer's Island, a do-it-yourself play island with balancing rocks, caves, and a rope bridge, and board the Big Thunder Mountain Railroad, a runaway roller coaster that races through a deserted 1870s gold mine. You'll also find a petting zoo and an Abe Lincoln–style log cabin here; both are great for exploring with the little ones.

On Saturdays, Sundays, holidays, and vacation periods, head to Frontierland's Rivers of America after dark to see the FANTASMIC! show—a mix of magic, music, live performers, and sensational special effects. Just as he did in *Sorcerer's Apprentice,* Mickey Mouse appears and uses his magical powers to create giant water fountains, enormous flowers, and fantasy creatures. There's plenty of pyrotechnics, lasers, and fog, as well as a 45-foot-tall dragon that breathes fire and sets the water of the Rivers of America aflame. Cool.

Mickey's Toontown, opened in 1993, is a colorful, wacky, whimsical world inspired by the Roger Rabbit films. This is a gag-filled land populated by toons. There are several rides here, including Roger Rabbit's CarToonSpin, but these take a backseat to Toontown itself—a trippy smile-inducing world without a straight line or right angle in sight. This is a great place to talk with Mickey, Minnie, Goofy, Roger Rabbit, and the rest of your favorite toons. You can even visit their "houses" here. Mickey's red-shingled house and movie barn is filled with props from some of his greatest cartoons.

Fantasyland has a storybook theme and is the catchall "land" for all the stuff that doesn't quite seem to fit anywhere else. Most of the rides here are geared to the under 6 set, including the King Arthur Carousel, Dumbo the Flying Elephant ride, and the Casey Jr. Circus Train, but some, like Mr. Toad's Wild Ride and Peter Pan's Flight, grown-ups have an irrational attachment to as well. You'll also find Alice in Wonderland, Snow White's Scary Adventures, Pinocchio's Daring Journey, and more in Fantasyland. The most lauded attraction is It's a Small World, a slow-moving indoor river ride through a saccharine nightmare of all the world's children singing the song everybody loves to hate. For a different kind of thrill, try the Matterhorn Bobsleds, a zippy roller coaster through chilled caverns and drifting fog banks. It's one of the park's most popular rides.

Tomorrowland may now seem a bit dated, but it still offers some of the park's best attractions. Space Mountain, a pitch-black indoor roller coaster, is one of Disneyland's best rides. Star Tours, the original Disney/George Lucas joint venture, is a 40-passenger StarSpeeder that encounters a spaceload of misadventures on the way to the Moon of Endor, achieved with wired seats and video effects (not for the queasy); the line can last an hour or more, but it's worth the wait. In addition to all this, you can take a dive in a submarine and soar in a rocket jet in Tomorrowland; there's also a huge video arcade.

The "lands" themselves are only half the adventure. Other joys include roaming Disney characters, penny arcades, restaurants and snack bars galore, summer fireworks, mariachi and ragtime bands, parades, shops, marching bands, and much more. Oh yeah—there's also the storybook Sleeping Beauty Castle . . . can you spot the evil witch peering from one of the top windows?

KNOTT'S BERRY FARM

Cynics say that Knott's Berry Farm is for people who aren't smart enough to find Disneyland. Well, there's no doubt that visitors should tour Disney first, but it's worth staying in a hotel nearby so you can play at Knott's during your stay.

Like Disneyland, Knott's Berry Farm is not without its historical merit. Rudolph Boysen crossed a loganberry with a raspberry, calling the resulting hybrid the "boysenberry." In 1933, Buena Park farmer Walter Knott planted the boysenberry, thus launching Knott's Berry Farm on 10 acres of leased land. When things got tough during the Great Depression, Mrs. Knott set up a roadside stand, selling pies, preserves, and home-cooked chicken dinners. Within a year, she was selling 90 meals a day. Lines became so long that Walter decided to create an Old West Ghost Town as a diversion for waiting customers.

The Knott family now owns the farm that surrounds the world-famous Chicken Dinner Restaurant, an eatery serving over a million fried meals a year. And Knott's Berry Farm is the nation's third-most-attended family entertainment complex (after the two Disney parks, of course).

During the last half of October, locals flock to Knott's Berry Farm. Why? Because the entire park is revamped as "Knott's *Scary* Farm"—the ordinary attractions are made spooky and haunted, every grassy area is transformed into a graveyard or gallows, and even the already scary rides get special surprise extras, like co: ghouls who grab your arm in the middle of a roller-coaster ride!

GETTING THERE   Knott's Berry Farm is located at 8039 Beach Blvd. in Buen, Park. It's about an hour's drive from downtown Los Angeles, and about a 5-minute ride north on I-5 from Disneyland. From I-5 or Calif. 91, exit south onto Beach Boulevard. The park is located about half a mile south of Calif. 91.

ADMISSION, HOURS & INFORMATION   Admission to the park, including unlimited access to all rides, shows, and attractions, is $29 for adults and children over 12, $19 for seniors over 60 and children ages 3 to 11, free for children under 3. Admission is $14 for everyone after 4pm. Like Disneyland, Knott's offers discounted admission during off-peak seasons for Southern California residents, so if you're bringing local friends or family members along, be sure to take advantage of the bargain. Also like Disneyland, Knott's Berry Farm's hours vary from week to week, so you should call about the day you plan to visit. Generally speaking, the park is open during the summer every day from 9am to midnight. The rest of the year, they open at 10am and close at 6 or 8pm, except Saturdays when they stay open until 10pm. Knott's is closed Christmas Day. Special hours and prices are in effect during Knott's Scary Farm in late October. For recorded information, call **714/ 220-5200.**

TOURING THE PARK

Knott's Berry Farm still maintains its original Old West motif. It's divided into five "Old Time Adventures" areas.

Old West Ghost Town, the original attraction, is a collection of refurbished 19th-century buildings that have been relocated from actual deserted Old West towns. Here, you can pan for gold, ride aboard an authentic stagecoach, ride rickety train cars through the Calico Mine, get held up aboard the Denver and Rio Grande Calico Railroad, and hiss at the villain during a melodrama in the Birdcage Theater.

Fiesta Village has a south-of-the-border theme that means festive markets, strolling mariachis, and wild rides like Montezooma's Revenge and Jaguar!, a huge new roller coaster that includes two heart-in-the-mouth drops and a loop that turns you upside down.

The Roaring '20s Amusement Area contains Sky Tower, a parachute jump drop with a 20-story free-fall. Other white-knuckle rides include XK-1, an excellent flight simulator "piloted" by the riders; and Boomerang, a state-of-the-art roller coaster that turns riders upside down six times in less than a minute. Kingdom of the Dinosaurs features extremely realistic Jurassic Park–like creatures. It's quite a thrill, but it may scare the little kids.

Wild Water Wilderness is a $10-million, $3^1/2$-acre attraction styled like a turn-of-the-century California wilderness park. The top ride here is a white-water adventure called Bigfoot Rapids, featuring a long stretch of artificial rapids; it's the longest ride of its kind in the world.

Camp Snoopy will probably be the youngsters' favorite area. It's meant to re-create a wilderness camp in the picturesque High Sierra. Its six rustic acres are the playgrounds of Charles Schulz's beloved beagle and his pals, Charlie Brown and Lucy, who greet guests and pose for pictures. The rides here, including Beary Tales Playhouse, are tailor made for the 6-and-under set.

Thunder Falls, Knott's newest area, contains Mystery Lodge, a truly amazing high-tech, trick-of-the-eye attraction based on the legends of local Native Americans. Don't miss this wonderful theater piece.

ıd special activities are scheduled throughout the day. Pick up a
·ket booth.

BEYOND THE THEME PARKS

 .-cate these attractions, see map on p. 261 of this chapter.

Crystal Cathedral. 12141 Lewis St., Garden Grove. ☎ **714/971-4000.**

This angular, mirror-sheathed church (think movie *Superman's* Fortress of Solitude),
otherwise known as the Garden Grove Community Church, is a shocking architectural oddity, with nine-story-high doors and a vast, open interior that's shaped like
a four-pointed star. Opened in 1980, it's the pulpit for televangelist Robert Schuller,
who broadcasts sermons and hymns of praise on radio and television to an international audience of millions. Each Sunday, an overflow crowd listens to the service
blaring from loudspeakers into the parking lot. Annual Christmas and Easter pageants
feature live animals, floating "angels," and other theatrics. A $5 million stainless steel
carillon, which began ringing in 1991, has prompted some of the cathedral's neighbors to complain that they want less joyful noise and more peace on earth.

Medieval Times Dinner & Tournament. 7662 Beach Blvd., Buena Park. ☎ **800/899-6600**
or 714/521-4740. Admission $33–$36 adults, $23–$26 children 12 and under. Shows Mon–
Thurs at 7pm; Fri at 6:30 and 8:45pm; Sat at 6 and 8:15pm, Sun at 5 and 7:15pm. Call for
reservations (be sure to inquire about auto club discounts).

Guests crowd around long wooden tables and enjoy a four-course banquet of roast
chicken, ribs, herbed potatoes, and pastries—all eaten with your hands in medieval
fashion, of course. More than 1,100 people can fit into the castle, where sword fights,
jousting tournaments, and various feats of skill are performed by colorfully costumed
actors, including fake knights on real horseback. It's kind of ridiculous, but kids of
all ages love it. A word of warning . . . the horses (and horseplay) kick up lots of dirt,
so if you have any allergies to dust or animal dander, keep an eye on the nearest exit.

Movieland Wax Museum. 7711 Beach Blvd. (Calif. 39), Buena Park. ☎ **714/522-1155.**
Admission $12.95 adults, $10.55 seniors, $6.95 children 4–11, free for children under 4. Daily
9am–7pm. Discount combination admission includes Ripley's Believe It Or Not (across the
street).

At this goofy museum, located one block north of Knott's Berry Farm in Buena Park,
you can see wax-molded figures of all your favorite film stars, from Bela Lugosi as
Dracula and Marilyn Monroe in *Gentlemen Prefer Blondes,* to Leslie Nielsen in the
Naked Gun movies. "America's Sweetheart," Mary Pickford, dedicated the museum
on May 4, 1962; it has risen steadily in popularity ever since, with new stars added
yearly, taking their place next to the time-tested favorites. The museum was created
by film addict Allen Parkinson, who saw to it that some of the most memorable
scenes in motion pictures were re-created in exacting detail in wax. In the seemingly
unrelated Chamber of Horrors, you almost expect the torture victims to scream "tourist trap!" Discount combination admission tickets include the new **Ripley's Believe
It Or Not Museum** across the street—grown-ups yawn but young kids marvel at the
"astounding" facts presented in a sensational manner.

Richard Nixon Library and Birthplace. 18001 Yorba Linda Blvd., Yorba Linda. ☎ **714/
993-5075.** Fax 714/528-0544. Admission $5.95 adults, $3.95 seniors, $2 children 8–11; chil-
dren under 8 free. Mon–Sat 10am–5pm, Sun 11am–5pm.

Although he was the most vilified U.S. president in modern history, there's always
been a warm place in the hearts of Orange County locals for Richard Nixon. This
presidential library, located in Nixon's boyhood town, celebrates the roots, life, and

legacy of America's 37th president. The 9-acre site contains the modest farmhouse where Nixon was born, manicured flower gardens, a modern museum containing presidential archives, and the final resting place of both Nixon and his wife, Pat.

Displays include videos of the famous Nixon-Kennedy TV debates, an impressive life-size statuary summit of world leaders, gifts of state (including a gun from Elvis Presley), and exhibits on China and Russia. There's also an exhibit of the late Pat Nixon's sparkling First Lady gowns. There's a 12-foot-high graffiti-covered chunk of the Berlin Wall, symbolizing the defeat of Communism, but hardly a mention of Nixon's leading role in the anti-Communist "witch hunts" of the 1950s. There are exhibits on Vietnam, yet no mention of Nixon's illegal expansion of that war into neighboring Cambodia. Only the Watergate Gallery is relatively forthright, where visitors can listen to actual White House tapes and view a montage of the president's last day in the White House.

WHERE TO STAY
VERY EXPENSIVE

✪ **Disneyland Hotel.** 1150 W. Cerritos Ave. (west of the Disneyland parking lot), Anaheim, CA 92802. ☎ **714/778-6600.** Fax 714/965-6597. 1,136 rms, 62 suites. A/C MINIBAR TV TEL. Rooms $155–$250; suites from $425. AE, MC, V. Parking $10.

The "Official Hotel of the Magic Kingdom," attached to Disneyland via a monorail system that runs right to the hotel, is the perfect place to stay if you're doing the park. You'll be able to return to your room anytime you need to during the day, whether it's to take a much-needed nap or to change your soaked shorts after your Splash Mountain Adventure. Best of all, hotel guests get to enter the park early almost every day and enjoy the major rides before the lines form. The amount of time varies from day to day, but usually you can enter 1 1/2 hours early. Call ahead to check the schedule for your specific day.

The theme hotel is a wild attraction unto itself. The rooms aren't fancy, but they're comfortably and attractively furnished like a good-quality business hotel. Many rooms feature framed reproductions of rare Disney conceptual art, and The Disney Channel is free on TV, naturally. The beautifully landscaped hotel is an all-inclusive resort, offering six restaurants, five cocktail lounges, every kind of service desk imaginable, a "wharfside" bazaar, a walk-under waterfall, and even an artificial white sand beach. Disneyland has also just taken over the adjoining Pacific Hotel, whose Asian tranquility (including a fine and pricey Japanese restaurant) brings a slightly higher tariff.

When you're planning your trip, inquire with the hotel about multiday packages that allow you to take on the park at your own pace.

Dining/Entertainment: The best restaurant is Stromboli's, an Italian/American eatery that serves all the pasta staples. Kids love Goofy's Kitchen, where the family can enjoy breakfast and dinner with the Disney characters.

Services: Concierge, room service, shoeshine, laundry, nightly turndown, babysitting, express checkout.

Facilities: Three large outdoor heated pools, complete health club, putting green, shuffleboard and croquet courts, sundeck, special children's programs, beauty salon, and 20 shops and boutiques.

Sheraton Anaheim Hotel. 1015 W. Ball Rd. (at I-5), Anaheim, CA 92802. ☎ **800/ 325-3535** or 714/778-1700. Fax 714/535-3889. 500 rooms, 26 suites. A/C MINIBAR TV TEL. $90–$190 double; $220–$280 suite. AE, CB, DC, MC, V. Free parking, shuttle to Disneyland.

This hotel rises to the festive theme-park occasion with its fanciful English Tudor architecture, a castle which lures business conventions, Disney-bound families, and area high-school proms equally successfully. Public areas are quiet and elegant—intimate gardens with fountains and koi ponds, plush lobby and lounges—which can be a pleasing touch after a frantic day at the amusement park. Rooms are modern and unusually spacious, but otherwise not distinctive; a large swimming pool is located in the center of the complex, surrounded by attractive landscaping.

Dining/Entertainment: The Garden Court Bistro offers indoor and outdoor ambiance, while the California Deli is open from 6am to midnight and serves standard delicatessan fare. There's also a wood & tapestry cocktail lounge.

Services: Concierge, room service, overnight shoe shine, laundry services, nightly turndown.

Facilities: Outdoor heated pool, sundeck, gift shop.

MODERATE

Anaheim Plaza Hotel. 1700 S. Harbor Blvd., Anaheim, CA 92802. ☎ **800/228-1357** or 714/772-5900. Fax 714/772-8386. 300 rms. & suites. A/C TV TEL. $79–$119 double; suites from $175. AE, DISC, DC, MC, V. Free parking, shuttle to Disneyland.

You can easily cross the street to Disneyland's main gate, or you can take advantage of the Anaheim Plaza's free shuttle to the Park. Once you return, however, you'll appreciate the way this 30-year-old hotel's clever design shuts out the noisy world. In fact, the seven two-story garden buildings remind me of 1960s Waikiki more than busy Anaheim. The olympic-size heated outdoor pool and whirlpool are unfortunately surrounded by astro-turf, but new management was doing a total room renovation in 1996, so there's always hope. They won't change a thing about the light-filled modern lobby, or the friendly rates. The hotel will still offer room service from the casual The Cafe in the lobby, plus laundry valet and coin-operated laundry.

Buena Park Hotel. 7675 Crescent Ave. (at Grand), Buena Park, CA 90620. ☎ **800/422-4444** or 714/995-1111. Fax 714/828-8590. 350 rooms and suites. AC TV TEL. $89–$99 double; $175–$250 suite. AE, DC, DISC, MC, V. Free parking, shuttle to Disneyland.

Within easy walking distance of Knott's Berry Farm, the Buena Park Hotel also offers a free shuttle to Disneyland just 7 miles away. The pristine lobby has the look of a business-oriented hotel, and that it is. But vacationers can also benefit from the elevated level of service designed for the business traveler. Be sure to inquire about Executive Club rates as well as Knott's or Disneyland package deals. Rooms in the 9-story tower are tastefully decorated, and facilities and services include room service, charming heated outdoor pool and spa, two restaurants and a 50s-60s dance club, and car-rental desk.

Candy Cane Inn. 1747 S. Harbor Blvd., Anaheim, CA 92802. ☎ **800/345-7057** or 714/774-5284. Fax 714/772-5462. 173 rooms. A/C TV TEL. $70–$84 double. Rates include breakfast. AE, DC, DISC, MC, V. Free parking, shuttle to Disneyland.

Take your standard U-shaped motel court with outdoor corridors, spruce it up with cobblestone drive- and walkways, old-time streetlamps, flowering vines engulfing the balconies of attractively painted rooms, and you have the Candy Cane. The face-lift worked, making this motel near Disneyland's main gate a real treat for the stylish bargain-hunter. Guest rooms are decorated in bright floral motifs with comfortable furnishings, including queen-size beds and a separate dressing and vanity area. Complimentary breakfast is served in the courtyard, where you can also splash around in a heated pool, spa, or kids' wading pool.

Howard Johnson Hotel. 1380 S. Harbor Blvd., Anaheim, CA 92802. ☎ **800/422-4228** or 714/776-6120. Fax 714/533-3578. 320 rms. A/C TV TEL. $64–$94 double. AE, CB, DC, DISC, MC, V. Free parking.

The hotel occupies an enviable location, directly opposite Disneyland, and a cute San Francisco trolley car runs to and from the park every 30 minutes. Rooms are divided among several low-profile buildings, all with balconies opening onto a central garden with two heated pools for adults and one for children. Garden paths lead under eucalyptus and olive trees to a splashing circular fountain. During the summer, you can see the nightly fireworks display at Disneyland from the upper balconies of parkside rooms. Try to avoid rooms in the back buildings, for they get some freeway noise. Services and facilities include in-room movies and cable, room service from the attached Coco's Restaurant, gift shop, game room, laundry service plus coin laundry room, airport shuttle, and family lodging/Disney admission packages . . . we think it's pretty classy for a HoJo's.

Inn at the Park. 1855 S. Harbor Blvd. (south of Katella), Anaheim, CA 92802. ☎ **800/ 421-6662** or 714/750-1811. Fax 714/971-3626. 500 rooms. AC TV TEL. $120–$145 double. AE, DC, DISC, MC, V. Free parking, shuttle to Disneyland.

Although the Inn is on the Anaheim Convention Center Complex (across the street from Disneyland) and draws primarily a business crowd, there is much to appeal to the leisure traveler. Contemporary and comfortable rooms in the 12-story tower all have balconies overlooking either Disneyland or the hotel's luxurious pool area, which includes a large heated pool, deluxe spa, attractive sundeck, and snack/cocktail bar gazebo. The hotel offers guest laundry and valet, activities desk, room service and gift shop, plus the Old West frontier-themed Overland Stage Restaurant, serving up steak and seafood, plus a few colorful game selections.

The Jolly Roger Hotel. 640 W. Katella Ave. (west of Harbor Blvd.), Anaheim, CA 92802. ☎ **800/446-1555** or 714/772-7621. Fax 714/772-2308. 225 rooms, 11 suites. AC TV TEL. $65–$118 double; $78–$185 suite. AE, DC, DISC, MC, V. Free parking, shuttles to Disneyland.

The only thing still sporting a buccaneer theme here is the adjoining Jolly Roger Restaurant, and that's just fine. The comfortable but blandly furnished rooms are in either an older, two-story L-shaped motel or two newer five-story annexes. We prefer the older units for their quiet and also for the palm-shaded heated pool in the center of it all. Across the driveway is the swashbuckling restaurant where dinner will set you back a few doubloons. The all-day coffee shop is more reasonable, and there's nightly entertainment and dancing in the lounge. Conveniently located across the street from Disneyland, the Jolly Roger also has meeting and banquet rooms, plus a second pool, spa, beauty salon, and gift shop.

INEXPENSIVE

Best Western Anaheim Stardust. 1057 W. Ball Rd., Anaheim, CA 92802. ☎ **800/ 222-3639** or 714/774-7600. Fax 714/535-6953. 103 rooms, 18 suites. A/C TV TEL. $58–$70 double; $95 suite. Rates include full breakfast. AE, DC, DISC, MC, V. Free parking.

Located on the back side of Disneyland, this modest hotel will appeal to the budget-conscious traveler who isn't willing to sacrifice absolutely everything. All rooms have refrigerator and microwave, breakfast is served in a refurbished train dining car, and you can relax by the large outdoor heated pool and spa while doing wash in the laundry room. Large family suites will accommodate virtually any brood, and shuttles run regularly to the park.

Colony Inn. 7800 Crescent Ave. (west of Beach Blvd.), Buena Park, CA 90620. ☎ **800/ 98-COLONY** or 714/527-2201. Fax 714/826-3826. 130 rooms (sleep up to 4) and suites (sleep up to 8). A/C TV TEL. $49–$98 double/suite. AE, MC, V. Free parking.

Although it's composed of two modest U-shaped motels, the recently refurbished Colony Inn has a lot to offer. It's the closest lodging to Knott's Berry Farm's south entrance and is just 10 minutes away from Disneyland. They cheerfully offer discount coupons for Knott's and other nearby attractions, as well as complimentary coffee and donuts to jump-start your morning. Rooms are spacious and comfortably outfitted with conservatively styled furnishings. There are two pools, two wading pools for kids, two saunas, and a coin-operated laundry on the premises.

WHERE TO DINE

Inland Orange County isn't known for its restaurants, most of which are branches of reliable California or national chains you'll easily recognize. We've listed a few intriguing options, but if you're visiting the area just for the day, you'll probably eat inside the theme parks; there are plenty of restaurants to choose from at both Disneyland and Knott's Berry Farm. At Disneyland, in the Creole-themed **Blue Bayou,** you can sit under the stars inside the Pirates of the Caribbean ride—no matter what time of day it is. At Knott's, try the fried chicken dinners and boysenberry pies at Mrs. Knott's historic **Chicken Dinner Restaurant.** For the most unusual dinner you've ever had with the kids, see **Medieval Times** (see "Attractions Beyond the Theme Parks," above).

EXPENSIVE

Chanteclair. 18912 MacArthur Blvd. (opposite John Wayne Airport), Irvine. ☎ 714/752-8001. Reservations required. Main courses $15–$24. AE, CB, DC, MC, V. Mon–Fri 11am–3pm; Mon–Sat 6–11pm. CONTINENTAL/FRENCH.

Chanteclair is expensive and a little difficult to reach, but it's worth seeking out. Designed in the style of a provincial French inn, the rambling stucco structure is built around a central garden court and houses several dining and drinking areas, each with its own unique ambiance. The antique-furnished restaurant has five fireplaces. At lunch, you might order grilled lamb chops with herb-and-garlic sauce, chicken-and-mushroom crêpes, or Cajun charred ahi. Dinner is a worthwhile splurge that might begin with a lobster bisque with brandy or Beluga caviar with blinis. For a main dish, I recommend the rack of lamb with thyme sauce and roasted garlic.

Mr. Stox. 1105 E. Katella Ave. (east of Harbor Blvd.), Anaheim. ☎ 714/634-2994. Reservations recommended on weekends. Main courses $12–$23. AE, DC, MC, V. Mon–Fri 11am–2:30pm; Mon–Sat 5:30–10pm, Sun 5–9pm. AMERICAN.

Hearty steaks and fresh seafood are served in an early California manor-house setting here at Mr. Stox. Specialties include roast prime rib and mesquite-broiled fish, veal, and lamb. Chef Scott Raczek particularly excels at reduction sauces and innovative herbal preparations. Sandwiches and salads are also available. Homemade breads and desserts, such as chocolate-mousse cake, are unexpectedly good. Mr. Stox has an enormous and renowned wine cellar, and there's live entertainment every night.

MODERATE

Felix Continental Cafe. 36 Plaza Square (intersection of Chapman and Glassell), Orange. ☎ 714/633-5842. Reservations recommended for dinner. Main courses $6–$14. AE, DC, MC, V. Mon–Thurs 7am–9pm, Fri 7am–10pm; Sat 8am–10pm; Sun 8am–9pm. CUBAN/SPANISH.

If you like the re-created Main Street in the Magic Kingdom, then you'll love the historic 1886 town square in the city of Orange, on view from the cozy sidewalk tables outside Felix Continental Cafe. Dining on traditional Cuban specialties and watching traffic spin around the magnificent fountain and rosebushes of the plaza evokes old Havana or Madrid rather than the cookie-cutter Orange County communities just blocks away. The food receives glowing praise from restaurant reviewers and loyal locals alike.

Peppers Restaurant and Nightclub. 12361 Chapman Ave. (west of Harbor Blvd.), Garden Grove. ☎ **714/740-1333.** Reservations recommended on weekends. Main courses $9–$14. AE, CB, DC, DISC, MC, V. Mon–Thurs 11am–10pm; Fri–Sat 11am–11pm; Sun 10am–10pm. CALIFORNIA-MEXICAN.

This colorful Californian/Mexican–themed restaurant just south of Disneyland looks like a partying kind of place, and it doesn't disappoint. The varied menu features mesquite-broiled dishes and fresh seafood daily. Mexican specialties include lots of variations of tacos and burritos, but the grilled meats and fish are best, especially Pepper's signature King Fajitas with crab legs or lobster tails. Dancing is available nightly to Top 40 hits starting at 9pm, and Monday nights a Mexican group plays live music. There's a free shuttle to and from six area hotels between 6pm and the nightclub closing time of 2am.

Renata's Caffe Italiano. 227 E. Chapman Ave. (corner of Grand), Orange. ☎ **714/771-4740.** Reservations recommended for dinner. Main courses $8–$15. AE, MC, V. Mon–Thurs 11am–9pm, Fri 11am–10pm; Sat–Sun 4–10pm. Closed Sunday in summer. ITALIAN.

Near Felix Cafe in the historic plaza district, owner Renata Cerchiari draws a steady stream of regulars with good if not great contemporary Italian specialties. We found the charming patio dining in this small town atmosphere a welcome change from Orange County's frantic pace (particularly if you're staying by the amusement parks), and the wide selection of appetizers and pasta dishes more authentic and reasonably priced than anywhere else, although the creamy Caesar salad wins higher marks than the disappointing cannoli.

INEXPENSIVE

Belisle's Restaurant. 12001 Harbor Blvd. (at Chapman), Garden Grove. ☎ **714/750-6560.** Main courses $3–$23. MC, V. Sun–Thurs 7am–midnight, Fri–Sat 7am–2am.

Harvey Belisle's modest pink cottage has been doling out "Texas-size" portions of diner-style food since before Disneyland opened in 1955. This is the place to bring a ravenous football team, or just your hollow-legged teenage boys. Portions are enormous—we can't say that enough; from the four-egg omeletes accompanied by mountains of hash browns to the 12-oz. chicken fried steak to a chocolate eclair the size of a log, we think Paul Bunyan would feel right at home. Just say "fill 'er up"!

5 The Orange Coast

Whatever you do, don't say "Orange County." The mere name evokes images of smoggy industrial parks, cookie-cutter housing developments, and the staunch Republicanism that prevail behind the so-called orange curtain.

We're talking instead about the Orange Coast, one of Southern California's best-kept secrets, a string of seaside jewels which have been compared with the French Riviera or the Costa del Sol. Forty-two miles of beaches offer pristine stretches of sand, tide pools teeming with marine life, ecological preserves, charming secluded coves, quaint pleasure-boat harbors, and legendary surfers atop breaking waves. Whether your bare feet want to stroll a funky wooden boardwalk or your gold card gravitates toward a yachtclub, you've come to the right place.

ESSENTIALS

GETTING THERE   See chapter 2 for airport and airline information. By car from Los Angeles, take I-5 or I-495 south. The scenic, shore-hugging Pacific Coast Highway (Calif. 1, or just P.C.H. to the locals) links the Orange Coast communities from Seal Beach in the north to Capistrano Beach just south of Dana Point, where it merges with I-5. To reach the beach communities directly, take the following freeway exits: **Seal Beach:** Seal Beach Blvd. from I-405. **Huntington Beach:** Beach Blvd./Calif. 39 from either I-405 or I-5. **Newport Beach:** Calif. 55 from either I-405 or I-5. **Laguna Beach:** Calif. 133 from I-5. **San Juan Capistrano:** Ortega Hwy./Calif. 74 from I-5. **Dana Point:** Pacific Coast Hwy./Calif. 1 from I-5.

VISITOR INFORMATION   The **Seal Beach Chamber of Commerce,** 201 8th St., corner of Central (☎ 310/799-0179), is open Monday to Friday from 10am to 2pm.

The **Huntington Beach Conference & Visitors Bureau,** 101 Main St., Suite A2 (☎ 800/SAY-OCEAN or 714/969-3492; fax 714/969-5592) makes up for being really hard to find by genially offering tons of information, enthusiasm, and personal anecdotes. They're at the corner of PCH and Main Street—from the rear parking lot take the elevator to the second floor. Open Monday to Friday from 8:30am to noon and 1:30to 5pm. Their Internet Web site is at **http://www.imark.com/hbcvb**.

The **Newport Beach Conference & Visitors Bureau,** 3300 W. Coast Hwy. (☎ 800/94-COAST or 714/722-1611; fax 714/722-1612), distributes brochures, sample menus, a calendar of events, and their free and very helpful Visitor's Guide. Call or stop in Monday through Friday 8am to 5pm. Internet Web site is at **http://www.newport.lib.ca.us/default.htm**.

The **Laguna Beach Visitors Bureau,** 252 Broadway (☎ 800/877-1115 or 714/497-9229), is in the heart of town and distributes lodging, dining, and art gallery guides. They're open Monday through Friday 9am to 5pm and Saturday 10am to 4pm. Their Internet Web site is at **http://www.orangecounty.com/lagunabeach**.

The **San Juan Capistrano Chamber of Commerce,** 31931 Camino Capistrano, Suite D (☎ 714/493-4700), is located in El Adobe Plaza at the corner of Camino Capistrano and Del Abispo, conveniently within walking distance of the Mission. They're open Monday to Friday from 8:30am to 4pm, and print a sepia-tone *Walking Tour Guide* to historic sites. Their Internet Web site with lots of helpful links is at **http://www.sanjuancapistrano.com**.

The **Dana Point Chamber of Commerce,** 24681 La Plaza, #120 (☎ 800/290-DANA or 714/496-1555), is open Monday to Friday 9am to 4:30pm and carries some restaurant and lodging info as well as a comprehensive *Recreation Brochure.*

DRIVING THE ORANGE COAST

You'll most likely be exploring the coast by car, so we cover the beach communities in order, from north to south. Keep in mind, however, that if you're traveling the interstates between Los Angeles and San Diego, the Pacific Coast Highway (Calif. 1) is a splendidly scenic detour which adds less than an hour to the commute. So pick out a couple of destinations, and go for it.

Seal Beach, on the border between Los Angeles and Orange Counties and neighbor to Long Beach's Naples harbor, is geographically isolated both by the adjacent U.S. Naval Weapons Station and the self-contained Leisure World retirement community. As a result, the charming beach town appears untouched by modern development—Orange County's answer to small-town America. Taking a stroll down Main Street is a walk back in time which culminates in the Seal Beach Pier. Although there are no longer clusters of the sunbathing, squalking seals which gave the town its name, old-timers fish hopefully, lovers stroll swooningly, and families cavort by the seaside, perhaps capping off the afternoon with an old-fashioned double dip from **Main Street Ice Cream & Yogurt** at the corner of Main Street and Ocean Avenue, where the walls are decorated with sepia-toned photographs of Seal Beach's yesteryear.

Huntington Beach is probably the largest Orange Coast city; it stretches quite a ways inland and has seen the most urbanization. To some extent, this has changed the old boardwalk and pier to a modern outdoor mall where cliques of gang kids coexist with families and the surfers who continue to flock here, for Huntington is legendary in surf lore. Hawaiian surfer Duke Kahanamoka brought the sport here in the 1920s, and some say the breaks around the pier and Bolsa Chica are the best in California. The world's top wave-riders flock to Huntington each August for the rowdy but professional **U.S. Open of Surfing** (call 310/286-3700 for information). If you'll be around during Christmastime, try to see the gaily decorated marina homes and boats in Huntington Harbour by taking the **Cruise of Lights,** a 45-minute narrated sail through and around the harbor islands. The festivities generally last from mid-December until Christmas; call 714/840-7542 for schedules and ticket information.

The name **Newport Beach** conjures comparisons with Rhode Island's Newport, where the well-to-do enjoy seaside living with all the creature comforts. That's the way it is here too, on a less grandiose scale. From the million-dollar Cape Cod–style cottages on sunny Balboa Island in the bay, to elegant shopping complexes like Fashion Island (surrounded by ultramanicured country club lawns) and South Coast Plaza (an *über*-mall with valet parking, car detailing, limo service, and concierge), this is where fashionable socialites, right-wing celebrities, and business mavens can all be found. Alternately, you could explore Balboa peninsula's historic Pavilion and old-fashioned pier; or board a passenger ferry to Catalina Island.

Laguna Beach, whose breathtaking geography is marked by bold elevated headlands, coastal bluffs, and pocket coves, is known as an artist enclave, but the truth is Laguna has became so in (read: expensive) that it drove most of the true Bohemians out. Their legacy remains with the annual **Festival of the Arts and Pageant of the Masters** (see "A Special Arts Festival," below), as well as a proliferation of art galleries intermingling with high-priced boutiques along the town's cozy streets. In warm weather Laguna Beach has an overwhelming Mediterranean-island ambiance which makes everyone feel beautifully, idly rich.

San Juan Capistrano, nestled in the verdant headlands just inland of Dana Point, is defined by Spanish missions and its loyal flock of swallows. The "mission" architecture is authentic, and history abounds here. Consider San Juan Capistrano a compact, life-size diorama illustrating the evolution of a western small town from Spanish mission era to secular rancho period, into statehood and the 20th century. Ironically, Mission San Juan Capistrano (see "Seeing the Sights," below) is once again the center of the community, just as the founding friars intended 200 years ago.

Dana Point, the last town south, has been called a "marina development in search of a soul." Overlooking the harbor stands a monument to 19th-century author Richard Henry Dana, who gave his name to the area and described it in *Two Years Before the Mast.* Activities generally center around yachting and Dana Point's jewel of a harbor. Nautical themes are everywhere; particularly charming are the series of streets named for old-fashioned shipboard lights, a rainbow which includes "Street of the Amber Lantern," the "Violet Lantern," the "Golden Lantern," and so on. Bordering the harbor is Doheny State Beach (see "Beaches and Nature Preserves," below), which wrote the book on seaside park and camping facilities.

BEACHES AND NATURE PRESERVES

Bolsa Chica Ecological Reserve (☎ 714/897-7003), in Huntington Beach, is a 300-acre restored urban salt marsh that's haven to more than 200 bird species, as well as a wide variety of protected plants and animals. Naturalists come to spot herons and egrets as well as California horn snails, jackknife clams, sea sponges, common jellyfish, and shore crabs. An easy 1^1/$_2$-mile loop trail begins from a parking lot on Pacific Coast Highway (Calif. 1) 1 mile south of Warner Boulevard; docents lead a narrated walk every first Saturday. The trail heads inland, over Inner Bolsa Bay and up Bolsa Chica bluffs. It then loops back toward the ocean over a dike that separates the Inner and Outer Bolsa Bays and traverses a coastal sand dune system. This beautiful hike is a terrific afternoon adventure. The Bolsa Chica Conservancy has been working since 1978 on reclaiming the wetlands from oil companies who began drilling here 70 years ago. It is an ongoing process, and you can still see those "seesaw" drills dotting the outer areas of the reserve. Although Bolsa Chica State Beach across the road has superb facilities, fantastic surfing, and well-equipped campsites, you might find that the hulking offshore oil rigs spoil the view.

Huntington City Beach, adjacent to Huntington Pier, is a haven for volleyball players and surfers; dense crowds abound, but at least so do amenities like outdoor showers, beach rentals, and restrooms. Just south of the city beach is 3-mile-long **Huntington State Beach.** Both popular beaches have lifeguards and concession stands seasonally. The state beach also has restrooms, showers, barbecue pits, and a waterfront bike path. Main entrance is at Beach Boulevard, plus access points all along Pacific Coast Highway (Calif. 1).

Newport Beach runs for about 5 miles and includes both Newport and Balboa piers. There are outdoor showers, restrooms, volleyball nets, and a vintage boardwalk that just may make you feel like you've stepped 50 years back in time. **Balboa Bike and Beach Stuff** (☎ 714/723-1516), at the corner of Balboa and Palm near the pier, can rent you a variety of items, from pier fishing poles to bikes, beach umbrellas, and bodyboards. **Southwind Kayak Center,** 2801 W. Pacific Coast Hwy. (☎ 800/768-8494 or 714/261-0200), rents sea kayaks for use in the bay or open ocean at rates of $8 to $10 per hour; instructional classes are available on weekends only. They also conduct bird-watching kayak expeditions into Upper Newport Bay Ecological Reserve at rates of $40 to $65.

Crystal Cove State Park, which covers 3 miles of coastline between Corona Del Mar and Laguna Beach plus extends up into the hills around El Moro Canyon, is a good alternative to the more popular beaches for you seekers of solitude. There are, however, lifeguards and restrooms. The beach is a winding sandy strip, backed with grassy terraces; high tide sometimes sections it into coves. The entire area offshore is an underwater nature preserve. There are four entrances including Pelican Point and El Moro Canyon. For more information, call 714/494-3539 or 714/848-1566.

Salt Creek Beach Park lies below the palatial Ritz-Carlton Laguna Niguel; guests who tire of the pristine swimming pool venture down the staircase on Ritz Carlton Drive to wiggle their toes in the sand. The setting is marvelous, wide white sand beaches looking out toward Catalina Island (why do you think Ritz-Carlton built here?). There are lifeguards, restrooms, a snack bar, and convenient parking near the hotel.

Doheny State Beach in Dana Point has long been known as a premiere surfing spot and camping site. Just south of lovely Dana Point Marina (enter off Del Abispo Street), Doheny has the friendly vibe of beach parties in days gone by: Tree-shaded lawns give way to wide beaches, and picnicking and beach camping are encouraged. There are 121 sites for both tents and RVs, and a state-run Visitor's Center featuring several small aquariums of sea and tidepool life. For more information and camping availability, call 714/492-0802.

Anaheim Area Attractions & the Orange Coast

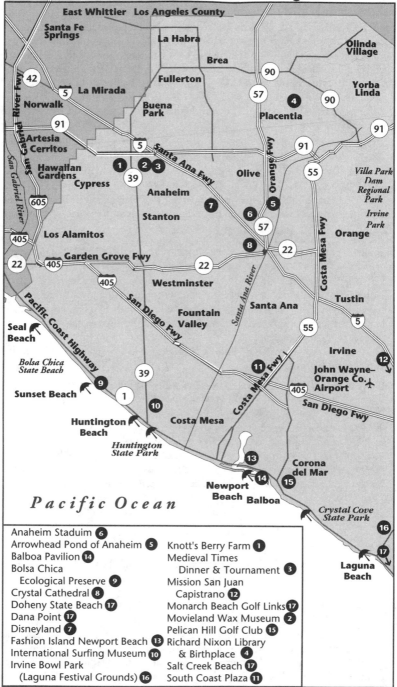

Anaheim Stadium **6**
Arrowhead Pond of Anaheim **5**
Balboa Pavilion **14**
Bolsa Chica
   Ecological Preserve **9**
Crystal Cathedral **8**
Doheny State Beach **17**
Dana Point **17**
Disneyland **7**
Fashion Island Newport Beach **13**
International Surfing Museum **10**
Irvine Bowl Park
   (Laguna Festival Grounds) **16**

Knott's Berry Farm **1**
Medieval Times
   Dinner & Tournament **3**
Mission San Juan
   Capistrano **12**
Monarch Beach Golf Links **17**
Movieland Wax Museum **2**
Pelican Hill Golf Club **15**
Richard Nixon Library
   & Birthplace **4**
Salt Creek Beach **17**
South Coast Plaza **11**

1-0854

BIKING & GOLFING

BICYCLE RENTALS   Bicycling is the most popular beach activity up and down the coast. A slower-paced alternative to driving, it allows you to enjoy the clean fresh air and notice smaller details of these laid-back beach towns and harbors. Bikes and safety equipment are available for rent at **Zack's Too,** Pacific Coast Highway at Beach Boulevard, **Huntington Beach** (☎ 714/536-2696); **Balboa Bike & Beach Stuff,** 601 Balboa Blvd., Newport Beach (☎ 714/723-1516); **Laguna Beach Cyclery,** 240 Thalia St. (☎ 714/494-1522); and **Dana Point Bicycle,** 34155 Pacific Coast Hwy. (☎ 714/661-8356).

GOLF   Many golf course architects use the geography of the Orange Coast to its full advantage, molding challenging and scenic courses from the rolling bluffs. Two beautiful courses open to the public are **Monarch Beach Golf Links,** 23841 Stonehill Dr., Dana Point (☎ 714/240-8247), and **Pelican Hill Golf Club,** 22651 Pelican Hill Rd. South, Newport Beach (☎ 714/760-0707). Both offer holes with breathtaking views of the ocean (remember, the break is always toward the water!).

SEEING THE SIGHTS

International Surfing Museum. 411 Olive Ave., Huntington Beach. ☎ **714/960-3483.** Admission $2 adults, $1 students, children under 6 free. Mid-June to late Sept, daily noon–5pm; rest of year, Wed–Sun noon–5pm.

Nostalgic Gidgets and Moondoggies shouldn't miss this monument to the laid-back sport which has become synonymous with California beaches. There are gargantuan longboards from the sport's early days, memorabilia of Duke Kahanamoka and the other surfing greats represented on the "Walk of Fame" near Huntington Pier, and a gift shop where a copy of the "Surfin'ary" can help you bone up on your surfer slang even if you can't hang ten.

Balboa Pavilion. 400 Main St., Balboa, Newport Beach. ☎ **714/673-5245.** From Calif. 1, turn south onto Newport Blvd. (which becomes Balboa Blvd. on the peninsula); turn left at Main St.

This historic cupola-topped structure, a California Historical Landmark, was built in 1905 as a bathhouse for swimmers in ankle-length bathing costumes. Later during the Big Band era, dancers rocked the Pavilion doing the "Balboa Hop." Now it serves as the terminal for Catalina Island passenger service, harbor and whale-watching cruises, and fishing charters. The surrounding boardwalk is the Balboa Fun Zone, a collection of carnival rides, game arcade, and vendors of hot dogs and cotton candy. For Newport Harbor or Catalina cruise information, call 714/673-5245; for sportfishing and whalewatching information, call 714/673-1434.

Balboa Island.

The charm of this pretty little neighborhood isn't diminished by knowing that the island was manmade—and it certainly hasn't affected the price of real estate. Tiny clapboard cottages in the island's center and modern houses with two-story windows and private docks along the perimeter make a colorful and romantic picture. You can drive onto the island on Jamboree Road to the north, or take the three-car ferry from Balboa Peninsula (about $1 per vehicle). It's generally more fun to park and take the ferry as a pedestrian, since the tiny alleys they call streets are more suitable for strolling, there usually are crowds, and parking spaces are scarce. Marine Avenue, the main commercial street, is lined with small shops and cafés which evoke a New England fishing village. Refreshing shaved ices sold by sidewalk vendors will relieve the heat of summer.

Mission San Juan Capistrano. Ortega Hwy. (Calif. 74), San Juan Capistrano. ☎ **714/ 248-2049.** Admission $4 adults, $3 children and seniors. Daily 8:30am–5pm. Closed Thanksgiving, Christmas, and Good Friday.

The 7th of the 21 California coastal missions, Mission San Juan Capistrano is continually being restored, a mix of old ruins and working buildings that are home to small museum collections and various adobe rooms that are as quaint as they are interesting. The intimate mission chapel with its ornate baroque altar is still regularly used for religious services, and the mission complex is the center of the community, hosting performing arts, children's programs, and other cultural events year-round.

This mission is best known for its swallows, who are said to return to nest each year at their favorite sanctuary. According to legend, the birds wing their way back to the mission annually on March 19, St. Joseph's Day, arriving here at dawn; they are said to take flight again on October 23, after bidding the mission farewell. In reality, however, you can probably see the well-fed birds here any day of the week, winter or summer.

A SPECIAL ARTS FESTIVAL

A 60-year tradition in arts-friendly Laguna, the **Festival of Arts and Pageant of the Masters** is held each summer throughout July and August. It's pretty large now, including the formerly "alternative" Sawdust Festival across the street and the unique Pageant of the Masters. Amidst the artists exhibiting (and selling) original works in every medium, local volunteers perform a series of tableaux vivants, re-creating well-known paintings by posing perfectly still in accurate costumes and elaborate makeup against carefully re-created backdrops. The pageant is one-of-a-kind, creating an extraordinary sense of two-dimentionality. Musical entertainment ranging from jazz ensembles to ethnic groups perform throughout the day, and there are workshops for adults and children, plus demonstrations of printmaking, raku (japanese pottery), and other arts. The festival grounds are at 650 Laguna Canyon Rd., Laguna Beach (☎ **800/487-3378** or 714/494-1145 for advance tickets). Grounds admission is $3 adults, $2 seniors and students. Pageant tickets cost $15 to $40, depending on performance night and seat location. Check it out on the Web at **http://www.coolsville.com/festival**.

SHOPPING

Just as the communities along the coast range from casually barefoot summer playgrounds to meticulously groomed yacht-clubby enclaves, so does the shopping scene stretch to both ends of the spectrum.

Seal Beach, indifferent to tourists, has charming low-tech shops designed to service the year-round residents, while Huntington Beach offers a plethora of surf and water-sport shops, reflecting its sporty nature. Both Huntington and Balboa have more than their share of T-shirt and souvenir stands, while tony Newport Beach has been called "Beverly Hills south" because of the many European designer boutiques and high-priced shops there. Corona Del Mar, immediately south of Newport Beach on Calif. 1, is more like "Pasadena south," with branches of stylish but affordable L.A. boutiques sharing several fun blocks with local boutiques and services. Laguna Beach is art gallery intensive; there are too many to list, but most are along Pacific Coast Highway or Ocean, Forest, and Park Avenues. Reflecting a wide range of artistic media, their wares can also come from all over the country—try to purchase the work of local artists unavailable elsewhere. There's little shopping in Dana Point and mostly Mission-themed souvenirs in San Juan Capistrano. Shoppers from all over the Southland flock to the two excellent malls listed below. If that isn't to your taste, a drive along Pacific Coast Highway will yield many other opportunities for browsing and souvenir purchases.

Fashion Island Newport Beach. 401 Newport Center Dr., Newport Beach. ☎ **714/ 721-2000.** Mon–Fri 10am–9pm, Sat 10am–7pm, Sun 11am–6pm.

Not an island at all, this shopping center is located next to the harbor and designed to resemble an open-air Mediterranean village. A pretty upscale village, that is, with tiled streets and plazas dotted with strolling pull-cart vendors and lined with upscale stores and boutiques, including Neiman-Marcus and Macy's department stores as well as Baywatch (they sell timepieces) and other specialty shops.

South Coast Plaza. 3333 Bristol St. (at I-405), Costa Mesa. ☎ **800/782-8888** or 714/ 435-2000. Mon–Fri 10am–9pm, Sat 10am–7pm, Sun 11am–6:30pm.

South Coast Plaza is one of the most upscale shopping complexes in the world, and it's so big that it's a day's adventure unto itself. This beautifully designed center is home to some of fashion's most prominent boutiques, including Emporio Armani, Chanel, Alfred Dunhill, and Coach, beautiful branches of the nation's top department stores such as Saks Fifth Avenue and Nordstrom, and outposts of the best high-end specialty shops like Williams Sonoma, L.A. Eyeworks, and Rizzoli Booksellers.

The mall is home to many impressive works of art, including a 1.6-acre environmental sculpture by Isamu Noguchi. In between shoe-store browsing or sale-rack pillaging, you can stroll along the sculpture garden path, climb its hill, listen to its rushing water, cross its bubbling stream, and wonder at the sculpture's striking geometric forms from the garden benches. Not the usual rest in the food court, is it?

Speaking of food, here you won't find Hot-Dog-On-A-Stick among the forty or so restaurants scattered throughout. Wolfgang Puck Cafe, Morton's of Chicago, Ghiradelli Soda Fountain, Planet Hollywood, and Scott's Seafood Grill lure the hungry away from Del Taco and McDonald's.

WHERE TO STAY
VERY EXPENSIVE

Four Seasons Hotel Newport Beach. 690 Newport Center Dr., Newport Beach, CA 92660. ☎ **800/332-3442** or 714/759-0808. Fax 714/760-8073. 221 rms, 64 suites. A/C MINIBAR TV TEL. $260–$300 double; suites from $350. AE, DC, MC, V. Valet parking $13.50.

This polished and professional member of the world-class Four Seasons group gets the highest marks for its comprehensive facilities and impeccable service. Rooms, conservatively designed in inoffensive beiges, have lovely touches like terry robes, oversize closets, and marble baths. Most have small balconies, even though the Newport skyline is nothing special to look at. Butlers are on call around the clock. Because of their larger size, rooms with two double beds are the hotel's best value. Guests are encouraged to bring their pets; doggie biscuits and food are always available.

Dining/Entertainment: The Pavilion Restaurant, serving California-French cuisine, is popular with locals at lunch. The poolside Cabana Cafe enjoys a nice garden setting. Afternoon tea and evening cocktails are served in the Gardens Cafe and Lounge.

Services: Concierge, 24-hour room service, overnight laundry and shoeshine, nightly turndown, complimentary transportation to and from John Wayne Airport.

Facilities: Large outdoor heated pool, small fitness club, Jacuzzi, sundeck, two outdoor lighted tennis courts, business center, gift shop.

☉ **The Ritz-Carlton Laguna Niguel.** 1 Ritz-Carlton Dr., Dana Point, CA 92629. ☎ **800/ 241-3333** or 714/240-2000. Fax 714/240-1061. 393 rms and suites. A/C MINIBAR TV TEL. $215–$485 double; $500–$1,100 suites. Children under 18 stay free. Weekday and special packages available. AE, DC, DISC, MC, V. Parking $15.

Old World meets Pacific Rim at this glorious hotel, majestically set among gardens, terraces, and fountained gardens on a 150-foot-high bluff above a 2-mile-long beach. There's a beautiful limestone fireplace in the elegant, silk-lined lobby, and lush foliage abounds throughout the interior. A ravishingly arched lounge is perfect for watching the sun set over the Pacific. The service, in Ritz-Carlton style, is unassuming and impeccable. Some guests, however, might find the hotel's palatial airs out of keeping with the beachy location.

The spacious rooms are outfitted with sumptuous furnishings and fabrics; despite their generous size, however, some are overfurnished to the point of being cramped. All rooms come with a terrace, and some even have fireplaces. The most expensive rooms overlook the blue Pacific below. All come with three phones (with voice mail), a refrigerator, a shoe polisher, and a safe. The Italian marble bathrooms are equipped with double vanities, hair dryers, and bathrobes.

Dining/Entertainment: The Dining Room is the most elegant of the hotel's four restaurants, offering Continental/French cuisine served by a knowledgeable staff. The gracious setting features subdued lighting, European chandeliers, and original paintings. Dine by the numbers, choosing from two- to seven-course prix-fixe dinners with matching wines from their formidable cellar. There's also a clubby lounge for nightcaps and five bars (two with nightly entertainment).

Services: Twice-daily maid service (they'll even stick a bookmark in the appropriate page of your *TV Guide*), car-rental desk, masseur, baby-sitting, children's programs, regular shuttle to and from the beach and the golf course, and room service (on Rosenthal china, no less); the two staffers for every room are generally alert in responding to requests.

Facilities: Beach with lifeguard, game room, lawn games, sauna, steam room, whirlpool, beauty salon, day-care center, 24-hour business center; first-rate sports facilities include a smart fitness center with unisex steam rooms and a public golf course designed by Robert Trent Jones II.

EXPENSIVE

Surf & Sand Hotel. 1555 S. Coast Hwy. (south of Laguna Canyon Rd.), Laguna Beach, CA 92651. ☎ **800/524-8621** or 714/497-4477. 155 rms, 2 penthouses. MINIBAR TV TEL. Apr–Oct, $200–$275 double; from $475 penthouse. Nov–Mar, $190–$240 double; from $375 penthouse. AE, CB, DC, DISC, MC.

The fanciest hotel in Laguna Beach has come a long way since it started life in 1937 as a modest little hostelry with just 13 units. Still occupying the same fantastic oceanside location, it now features dozens of top-of-the-line luxurious rooms that, despite their standard size, feel enormously decadent. Done entirely in white—from walls to linens to furnishings—they're very bright and beachy, and every one has a private balcony with an ocean view, a marble bath, and plush robes; some have whirlpool tubs. Try to get a deluxe corner room.

Dining/Entertainment: Splashes Restaurant (see "Where to Dine," below) serves three meals daily in a beautiful oceanfront setting. Towers offers contemporary northern Italian cuisine for dinner. Because the windows don't open, a sound system was installed to pipe in the sounds of the surf below.

Services: Concierge, room service, dry cleaning, overnight laundry, complimentary morning newspaper, nightly turndown.

Facilities: Outdoor heated pool, gift shop, salon, boutique.

MODERATE

Blue Lantern Inn. 34343 Street of the Blue Lantern, Dana Point, CA 92629. ☎ **800/ 950-1236** or 714/661-1304. Fax 714/496-1483. 29 rooms. AC, TV, TEL. $125–$275 double. Rates include full breakfast. AE, MC, V.

A newly constructed three-story New England–style gray clapboard inn, the Blue Lantern is a pleasant cross between romantic B&B and sophisticated small hotel. Almost all of the rooms, which are decorated with reproduction traditional furniture and plush bedding, have a balcony or deck overlooking the harbor. All have a fireplace and Jacuzzi tub. Have your breakfast here in private (clad perhaps in the fluffy robe provided), or choose to go downstairs to the sunny dining room which also serves complimentary afternoon tea. There's an exercise room, and cozy lounge with menus for many area restaurants. The friendly staff welcomes you with homebaked cookies at the front desk.

Doryman's Inn Bed & Breakfast. 2102 W. Ocean Front, Newport Beach, CA 92663. ☎ **800/634-3303** or 714/675-7300. 8 rms, 2 suites. A/C TV TEL. $135–$230 double; from $185 suite. Rates include breakfast. AE, MC, V.

Doryman's rooms are both luxurious and romantic, making this one of the nicest B&Bs to be found anywhere. Rooms are outfitted with French and American antiques, floral textiles, beveled mirrors, and cozy furnishings. Every room has a working fireplace and a sunken marble tub (some have Jacuzzi jets). King- or queen-size beds, lots of plants, and good ocean views round out the decor. Doryman's location, directly on the Newport Beach Pier Promenade, is also enviable, though some may find it a bit too close to the action. Breakfast includes fresh pastries and fruit, brown eggs, yogurt, cheeses, and international coffees and teas.

Vacation Village. 647 S. Coast Hwy., Laguna Beach, CA 92651. ☎ **800/843-6895** or 714/ 494-8566. Fax 714/494-1386. 100 rms, 38 suites. TV. $80–$155 double; from $175 suite. AE, CB, DC, DISC, MC, V.

Vacation Village has something for everyone. This cluster of seven oceanfront and near-the-ocean motels offers rooms, studios, suites, and apartments. Most of the accommodations are standard motel fare: bed, TV, table, basic bath. The best rooms are oceanfront in a four-story structure overlooking the Village's private beach. Umbrellas and backrests for beachgoers are available in summer. There's a restaurant on the premises, and facilities include a private beach, two pools, and a whirlpool.

WHERE TO DINE
EXPENSIVE

Splashes Restaurant and Bar. In the Surf and Sand Hotel, 1555 S. Coast Hwy., Laguna Beach. ☎ **714/497-4477.** Reservations recommended. Main courses $16–$22. DC, DISC, MC, V. Daily 7am–10pm. MEDITERRANEAN.

Splashes is truly stunning. Almost directly on the surf, this light and bright restaurant basks in sunlight and the calming crash of the waves. At dinner, a basket of fresh-baked crusty bread prefaces a long list of appetizers that might include wild-mushroom ravioli with lobster sauce, or sautéed Louisiana shrimp with red chiles and lemon. Gourmet pizzas also make great starters; they come topped with interesting combinations like grilled lamb, roasted fennel, artichokes, mushrooms, and feta cheese. Main courses change daily and might offer baked striped bass and braised duck in a Cabernet.

MODERATE

Five Feet. 328 Glenneyre, Laguna Beach. ☎ **714/497-4955.** Reservations recommended on weekends. Main courses $14–$24. AE, MC, V. Fri 11:30am–2:30pm; Sun–Thurs 5–10pm, Fri–Sat 5–11pm. CALIFORNIA/ASIAN.

Chef/proprietor Michael Kang has created one of the area's most innovative and interesting restaurants, combining the best in Californian cuisine with Asian technique and ingredients. If the atmosphere were as good as the food, Five Feet would be one of the best restaurants in California. Main courses run the gamut from tea-smoked filet mignon topped with Roquefort cheese and candied walnuts to a hot Thai-style mixed grill of veal, beef, lamb, and chicken stir-fried with sweet peppers, onions, and mushrooms in curry-mint sauce. Unfortunately, the dining room's gray-concrete walls are not much to look at, and the exposed vents on an airplane hangar-scale wooden ceiling just look unfinished, not trendy industrial. Fourtunately this unspectacular decor is brightened by an exceedingly friendly staff and unparalleled food.

Harbor Grille. 34499 Street of the Golden Lantern, Dana Point. ☎ **714/240-1416.** Reservations suggested on weekends. Main courses $8–$18. AE, DC, MC, V. Mon–Sat 11:30am–10pm, Sun 9am–10pm. SEAFOOD.

In a business/commercial mall right in the center of pretty Dana Point Marina, Harbor Grille is enthusiastically recomended by local inns for mesquite-broiled, ocean-fresh seafood. Hawaiian mahi-mahi with a mango chutney baste is on the menu, along with Pacific swordfish, grilled shark steaks, and teriyaki chicken.

Las Brisas. 361 Cliff Dr. (off P.C.H. north of Laguna Canyon), Laguna Beach. ☎ **714/ 497-5434.** Reservations recommended. Main courses $8–$17. AE, MC, V. Mon–Sat 8am–10:30pm, Sun 9am–10:30pm. MEXICAN.

Boasting a breathtaking view of the Pacific, Las Brisas is popular for sunset drinks and alfresco appetizers—so much so that it can get pretty crowded during the summer months. Affordable during lunch but pricey at dinner, the menu consists mostly of seafood recipes from the Mexican Riviera. Even the standard enchiladas and tacos get a zesty update with crab or lobster meat and fresh herbs. Calamari steak is sautéed with bell peppers, capers, and herbs in a garlic butter sauce, and king salmon is mesquite broiled and served with a creamy lime sauce. Although a bit on the touristy side, Las Brisas can be a fun part of the Laguna Beach experience.

Twin Palms. 630 Newport Center Dr., Newport Beach. ☎ **714/721-8288.** Reservations suggested. Main courses $9–$17. AE, CB, DC, MC, V. Sun–Wed 11:30am–10pm, Thurs–Sat 11:30am–1am. MEDITERRANEAN/FRENCH.

Opened in late 1995, this sister restaurant to one of Pasadena's most popular eateries seems to be leading the Newport Beach pack as well. From the famous original started by, among others, movie star Kevin Costner, comes the high-tented, palm-accented, huge circuslike space which is Twin Palms' trademark. Amidst this festival atmosphere you can enjoy the French "comfort food" original chef Michael Roberts created as a backlash against pricey haute cuisine. Favorites include juicy, roasted sage-infused pork and honey-glazed coriander-scented duck from the rotisserie grill, as well as the popular salt cod mashed potato brandade appetizer. Sautéed dishes and salads are not as successful, but Twin Palms has brought its traditional Sunday "Gospel Brunch" to the new location.

INEXPENSIVE

El Adobe de Capistrano. 31891 Camino Capistrano (near the Mission), San Juan Capistrano. ☎ **714/493-1163** or 714/830-8620. Dinners $8–$15; lunch $5–$10. AE, DISC, MC, V. Mon–Thurs 11:30am–10pm, Fri–Sat 11:30am–11pm, Sun 10:30am–2:30pm and 4–10pm. CLASSIC MEXICAN.

This restaurant is housed in a historic landmark 1778 Spanish adobe near San Juan Capistrano's main attraction, the Mission. Understandably touristy, there's some interesting history inside, like the enclosed lobby which was originally a dirt pathway between two buildings. A former dungeon jail cell makes a fine wine cellar, and El Adobe proudly offers a menu combination named "the President's Choice" after Richard Nixon, who visited often from his summer White House at the shore nearby. Hot plates overflow with cheesy combinations featuring chile relleños, tamales, and enchiladas topped with rich, red sauce. Dinner selections also include steak and seafood.

Ruby's, 1 Balboa Pier, Balboa. ☎ **714/675-7829.** Most items under $5. AE, MC, V. Sun–Thurs 7am–10pm, Fri–Sat 7am–11pm. AMERICAN DINER.

With their trademark red and white hamburger stand decor sprouting up all over the Southland, Ruby's is fast becoming a local institution. Housed in a former baithouse, the Balboa Pier Ruby's is the original, and several others can be found on or near the end of Orange Coast piers, including Seal Beach, Huntington, and Laguna. Ruby's sells nostalgia and food in equal measure. Their hamburgers, fries, milkshakes, and flavored sodas are reasonably priced, and the fun, kid-friendly atmosphere really suits the surroundings.

6 Santa Barbara

by Erika Lenkert

A native San Franciscan, Erika Lenkert worked for HarperCollins before becoming a freelance writer. She co-authors *Frommer's San Francisco* and *Frommer's California* and has contributed to dozens of other travel guides. Erika is currently seeking her fortune in both San Francisco and Hollywood; her Siamese cats are along for the ride.

Between the Santa Ynez Mountains and the Pacific, charming, spoiled Santa Barbara is coddled by wooded mountains, caressed by baby breakers, and sheltered from tempestuous seas by rocky offshore islands. And it's just far enough from Los Angeles to make the big city seem at once remote and accessible. There are few employment opportunities, and real estate is expensive here, so demographics have favored college students and rich retirees, thought of by the locals as the "almost wed and almost dead."

Downtown Santa Barbara is distinctive for its Spanish-Mediterranean architecture; all the structures sport matching red-tile roofs. But it wasn't always this way. Santa Barbara had a thriving Native American Chumash population for hundreds, if not thousands, of years. The European era began in the late 18th century, around a Presidio (fort) that's been reconstructed in its original spot. The earliest architectural hodgepodge was destroyed in 1925 by a powerful earthquake that leveled the business district. Out of the rubble rose the Spanish-Mediterranean town of today, a stylish planned community that continues to rigidly enforce its strict building codes.

ESSENTIALS

GETTING THERE By car, U.S. 101 runs right through Santa Barbara; it's the fastest and most direct route from north or south (2 hours from Los Angeles, 6 hours from San Francisco).

By train, **Amtrak** (☎ 800/USA-RAIL) offers daily service to Santa Barbara. Trains arrive and depart from the **Santa Barbara Rail Station,** 209 State St. (☎ 805/963-1015). Fares can be as low as $20 from Los Angeles.

ORIENTATION State Street, the city's primary commercial thoroughfare, is the geographic center of town. It ends at Stearns Wharf and Cabrillo Street; the latter runs along the ocean and separates the city's beaches from touristy hotels and restaurants.

VISITOR INFORMATION The **Santa Barbara Visitor Information Center,** 1 Santa Barbara St., Santa Barbara, CA 93101 (☎ 805/965-3021 to order a free destination guide), is on the ocean, at the corner of Cabrillo Street. They distribute maps, literature, an events calendar, and excellent advice. Be sure to ask for their handy guide to places of interest and public parking. The office is open Monday to Saturday from 9am to 4pm and Sunday from 10am to 4pm; it closes one hour earlier in winter and one hour later in July and August.

Also make sure you pick up a copy of *The Independent,* an excellent free weekly paper with a comprehensive listing of events. It's available in shops and from sidewalk racks around town.

SEEING THE SIGHTS

County Courthouse. 1100 Anacapa St. ☎ **805/962-6464.** Free admission. Mon–Fri 8am–5pm, Sat, Sun, and holidays 10am–5pm.

Even murderers are afforded exquisite surroundings in stunning Santa Barbara, for the courthouse is the most flamboyant example of Spanish-Mediterranean architecture in the entire city. Built in 1929 to mimic a much older style, the ornate building is Santa Barbara's literal and figurative centerpiece. There are great views of the ocean, mountains, and the city's terra-cotta tile roofs from the observation deck atop the clock tower. A free guided tour is offered on Wednesday and Friday at 10:30am and Monday to Saturday at 2pm.

Moreton Bay Fig Tree. Chapala and Montecito sts.

Santa Barbara's best-known tree has a branch spread that would cover half a football field, and its roots run under more than an acre of ground. It is, hands down, the largest of its kind in the world. It's so broad, in fact, that an estimated 10,000 people could stand in its shade. Planted in 1877, it's a native of Moreton Bay in eastern Australia. The tree is related to both the fig and rubber tree, but produces neither figs nor rubber. Once in danger of being leveled for a proposed gas station and later threatened by excavation for nearby U.S. 101, the revered tree now shelters Santa Barbara's homeless community.

Santa Barbara Botanic Garden. 1212 Mission Canyon Rd. ☎ **805/682-4726.** Admission $3 adults, $2 children 13–19 and seniors (over 64), $1 children 5–12, children under 5 free. Mon–Fri 9am–5pm, Sat–Sun 9am–6pm.

The gardens, about 1¹/₂ miles north of the mission, encompass 65 acres of native trees, shrubs, cacti, and wildflowers, and more than 5 miles of trails. They're at their aromatic peak just after spring showers. Docent tours are offered daily at 2pm, with additional tours on Thursday, Saturday, and Sunday at 10:30am.

Santa Barbara Mission. Laguna and Los Olivos sts. ☎ **805/682-4713** or 805/682-4151. Admission $3 adults, free for children under 16. Daily 9am–5pm.

Established in 1786 by Father Junípero Serra and built by the Chumash Indians, this is a very rare example in physical form of the blending of Indian and Hispanic spirituality. Called the "Queen of the Missions" for its twin bell towers and graceful beauty, this hilltop mission overlooks the town and the Channel Islands beyond. Brochures are available in six languages, and docent-guided tours can be arranged in advance ($1 extra per person).

Santa Barbara Museum of Art. 1130 State St. ☎ **805/963-4364.** Admission $4 adults, $3 seniors (over 65), $1.50 children 6–16, children under 6 free. Free for everyone Thurs and the first Sun of each month. Tues–Sat 11am–5pm, Thurs 11am–9pm, Sun noon–5pm.

A trip here feels like an exclusive visit to the private galleries of a wealthy art collector. Works by Monet and other mid-quality oils by Dalí, Picasso, Matisse, Chagall, and Rousseau are displayed on a rotating basis in rooms that, for the most part, are ample, airy, and well lit. Quantitatively, the museum's strengths lie in early 20th-century western American paintings and 19th- and 20th-century Asian art. Qualitatively, the best are the antiquities and Chinese ceramics collections. Many pieces are often on loan to other museums, but good temporary exhibits show a high degree of reciprocity. Some awkward arrangements don't always make sense, and lighting could be improved on the placards. For the most part, though, SBMA is a jewel of a museum. Free docent-led tours are given Tuesday to Sunday at 1pm. Focus tours are held on Wednesday and Saturday at noon. A new wing to be completed in 1997 is slated to include more galleries, a larger gift shop, and a café.

Santa Barbara Museum of Natural History. 2559 Puesta del Sol Rd. (2 blocks uphill from the mission). ☎ **805/682-4711.** Admission $5 adults, $4 seniors and teens, $3 children. Mon–Sat 9am–5pm, Sun and holidays 10am–5pm.

This museum focuses on the study and interpretation of Pacific Coast natural history, which includes mammals, birds, marine life, plants, insects, and displays ranging from fossil ferns to the complete skeleton of a blue whale. Native American history is emphasized in exhibits including basketry, textiles, and a full-size replica of a Chumash canoe. An adjacent planetarium projects sky shows every Saturday and Sunday.

Santa Barbara Zoological Gardens. 500 Ninos Dr. ☎ **805/962-5339,** or 805/962-6310 for a recording. Admission $5 adults, $3 seniors and children 2–12, children under 2 free. Daily 10am–5pm; last admission is 1 hour prior to closing. Closed Thanksgiving, Christmas.

When you're driving around the bend on Cabrillo Beach Boulevard, look up—you might spot the head of a giraffe poking up through the palms. This is a thoroughly charming, pint-sized place, where all 700 animals can be seen in about 30 minutes. Most of the animals live in natural, open settings. The zoo has a children's Discovery Area, a miniature train ride, and a small carousel. The picnic areas (complete with barbecue pits) are underutilized and especially recommendable.

Stearns Wharf. At the end of State St.

In addition to a small collection of second-rate shops, attractions, and restaurants, the city's 1872-vintage pier offers terrific inland views and good drop-line fishing. The Dolphin Fountain at the foot of the wharf was created by local artist Bud Bottoms for the city's 1982 bicentennial.

BEACHES

Santa Barbara has an array of beaches perfect for stretching out on a towel, playing volleyball (a very popular sport around here), or frolicking seaside. **Hendry's Beach,** at the end of Cliff Drive, is popular with families, boogie-boarders who come to ride the excellent beach breaks, and sunset strollers. **Cabrillo Beach** is a wide swath of clean white sand that hosts beach umbrellas, sand-castle builders, and spirited volleyball games. A grassy, parklike median keeps the noise of busy Cabrillo Boulevard away. On Sundays, local artists set up shop beneath the palms.

Note: A tragic oil spill off the coast of Santa Barbara in 1969 left surfers and sea critters dodging gobs of floating tar for the next 20 years. Although the area has finally cleared up, the staining brown substance still finds its way onto clothes and skin from time to time even if you don't go in the water (that's why the Four Seasons Biltmore hotel includes "Tar Off" in its baskets of toiletry goodies).

Downtown Santa Barbara

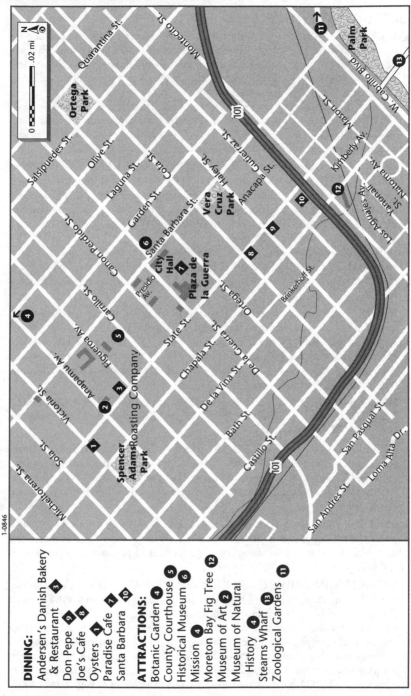

1-0846

DINING:
Andersen's Danish Bakery & Restaurant **3**
Don Pepe **9**
Joe's Cafe **8**
Oysters **1**
Paradise Cafe **7**
Santa Barbara **10**

ATTRACTIONS:
Botanic Garden **4**
County Courthouse **5**
Historical Museum **6**
Mission **4**
Moreton Bay Fig Tree **12**
Museum of Art **2**
Museum of Natural History **4**
Stearns Wharf **13**
Zoological Gardens **11**

OUTDOOR ACTIVITIES

BICYCLING A relatively flat, palm-lined 2-mile coastal pathway runs along the beach and is perfect for biking. More adventurous riders can peddle through town, up to the mission, or to Montecito, the next town over. The best mountain bike trail begins at the end of Tunnel Road, and climbs up along a paved fire road before turning into dirt trail to the mountaintop.

Beach Rentals, 22 State St. (☎ 805/966-6733), rents well-maintained 1-speeds. They also have tandem bikes and surrey cycles that can hold as many as four adults and two children. Rates vary depending on equipment. Bring your driver's license or passport to expedite your rental. They're open daily from 8am to dusk.

GOLF At the **Santa Barbara Golf Club,** 3500 McCaw Ave., at Las Positas Road (☎ 805/687-7087), there's a great 6,009-yard, 18-hole course and driving range. Unlike many municipal courses, the Santa Barbara Golf Course is well maintained and was designed to present a moderate challenge for the average golfer. Greens fees are $24 Monday to Friday and $28 on weekends ($17 for seniors). Optional carts rent for $20 for 18 holes, $10 for nine.

The 18-hole, 7,000-yard course **Sandpiper,** at 7925 Hollister Ave. (☎ 805/968-1541), a scenic oceanside course, has a pro shop and driving range, plus a coffee shop. Greens fees are $60 Monday to Friday and $80 on Saturday and Sunday. Carts cost $24.

HIKING The hills and mountains surrounding Santa Barbara have excellent hiking trails. One of my favorites begins at the end of Tunnel Road. Take Mission Canyon Road past the mission, turn right onto Foothill Road, and take the first left onto Mission Canyon Drive. Bear left onto Tunnel Road and park at the end (where all the other cars are). You can buy a trail map at the Santa Barbara Visitor Information Center (see "Essentials," above).

HORSEBACK RIDING Several area stables rent horses, including **Circle Bar B Ranch,** 1800 Refugio Rd. (☎ 805/968-3901), and **Rancho Oso,** Paradise Road, off Calif. 154 (☎ 805/964-8985).

POWER BOATING & SAILING The **Sailing Center of Santa Barbara,** at the Santa Barbara Breakwater (☎ 800/350-9090 or 805/962-2826), rents sailboats from 13 to 50 feet, as well as power boats and jet-skis. Both crewed and bare-boat charters are available by the day or hour. Sailing instruction for all levels of experience is also available.

SKATING The paved beach path that runs along Santa Barbara's waterfront is perfect for skating. **Beach Rentals,** 22 State St. (☎ 805/966-6733), located nearby, rents both in-line and conventional roller skates. The $5 per hour fee includes wrist and knee pads.

SPORT FISHING, DIVE CRUISES & WHALE WATCHING **Sea Landing,** at the foot of Bath Street and Cabrillo Boulevard (☎ 805/963-3564), makes regular sport fishing runs from specialized boats. They also offer a wide variety of other fishing and diving cruises. Food and drink are served on board, and rental rods and tackle are available. Rates vary according to excursion; call for reservations.

Whale-watching cruises are offered from February through April, when California gray whales make their migratory journey from Baja California, Mexico, to Alaska. Tours are $24 for adults and $14 for children; sightings of large marine mammals are guaranteed.

SHOPPING

State Street from the beach to Victoria Street is the city's main thoroughfare, and has the largest concentration of shops. Many specialize in T-shirts and postcards, but there are a number of boutiques as well. If you get tired of strolling, hop on one of the electric shuttle buses (25¢) that run up and down State Street at regular intervals.

Also check out **Brinkerhoff Avenue** (off Cota Street, between Chapala and De La Vina Streets), Santa Barbara's "antique alley." Most shops here are open Tuesday to Sunday from 11am to 5pm. **El Paseo** (814 State St.) is a picturesque shopping arcade reminiscent of an old Spanish street. Built around an 1827 adobe home, the mall is lined with charming shops and art galleries.

WHERE TO STAY

Before you even begin calling around for reservations, keep in mind that Santa Barbara's accommodations are expensive—especially in summer. Then decide whether you'd like to stay beachside (even more expensive) or downtown. The town is small, but not small enough to happily stroll between the two areas.

Hot Spots Accommodations, 36 State St., Santa Barbara, CA 93101 (☎ 805/564-1637), a one-stop shop for hotel and B&B rooms, keeps an updated list of what's available in all price categories. There's no charge for their services. Significantly discounted rates are often available at the last minute, when hotels need to fill their rooms. Another option is **Accommodations Reservations Service** (☎ 800/292-2222), a company that books rooms along California's coast from Oxnard to Monterey. The service is free and has information on all price ranges.

VERY EXPENSIVE

✪ **Four Seasons Biltmore.** 1260 Channel Dr., (at the end of Olive Mill Rd.), Santa Barbara, CA 93108. ☎ **800/332-3442** or 805/969-2261. Fax 805/969-4682. 234 rms, 24 suites. A/C MINIBAR TV TEL. $199–$475 double; suites from $650. Extra person $30. Special midweek and package rates available. AE, DC, MC, V.

The tattoo-and-lace taste of the now long-divorced couple Heather Locklear (*Melrose Place*) and Tommy Lee (Mötley Crüe) may have raised a few eyebrows in their day, but they regained my faith by getting married at the beach club next door from here (and later indulging in the hotel's infamously decadent Sunday brunch). But they weren't the first to celebrate in the area—other Hollywood highbrows such as Greta Garbo, Errol Flynn, and Bing Crosby also knew that the Biltmore is one of the most beautiful hotels in the country.

Today the hotel still captivates guests with Spanish Revival architecture, hand-painted Mexican tiles, and 19 acres of incredibly landscaped oceanfront gardens, but its aura is much lighter, warmer, and even greener with flora and fauna almost everywhere you look. Frankly, its beauty is beyond description, especially in the common areas such as the Patio restaurant, which has an oceanfront view, indoor and outdoor seating, and a retractable atrium roof. Guest rooms are appropriately less elaborate but come complete with the most comfortable beds, fluffy towels and robes, and the kind of bath soaps you can't help but pack in your luggage when you depart. They also come with striking views of the mountains or the ocean, and some have Spanish balconies and/or fireplaces, or private patios; all come with VCRs. If you've got the bucks, you can't do better than this.

Dining/Entertainment: This is resort dining at its finest. Elegant La Marina offers surprisingly innovative specialties. The Patio is more casual, serving three meals daily and Santa Barbara's best Sunday brunch. La Sala is a comfortable lounge serving afternoon tea and evening cocktails; there's live jazz on Wednesday and Friday nights.

Services: Concierge, 24-hour room service, overnight shoe shine, laundry services, twice-daily maid service including nightly turndown, in-room movies.

Facilities: Two outdoor heated pools, three lighted tennis courts, two health clubs, putting green, shuffleboard and croquet courts, beachfront cabanas, sundeck, complimentary bicycle rental, special children's programs, beauty salon, and gift shop.

☺ San Ysidro Ranch. 900 San Ysidro Lane (off U.S. 101), Montecito, CA 93108. ☎ **800/ 368-6788** or 805/969-5046. Fax 805/565-1995. 43 cottages, 15 suites. MINIBAR TV TEL. $240– $475 double; suites from $575. AE, MC, V.

Since 1940, when Vivien Leigh and Laurence Olivier were married here, San Ysidro Ranch has won raves as one of Southern California's most distinguished hotels. Over the years, guests from Groucho Marx to Winston Churchill signed the register at this quiet, beautifully landscaped 540-acre retreat. If the guest list's not impressive enough already, John and Jacqueline Kennedy spent their honeymoon here in 1953.

The 100-year-old hotel comprises about a dozen freestanding cottages nestled near the base of their own private mountain. Many rooms have been recently refurbished, but all maintain their traditional French country style and are decorated with antiques. All have working fireplaces, coffeemakers, computer jacks, and CD players; most have private decks or patios, and some have outdoor hot tubs. Weddings are held most weekends in truly magnificent jasmine- and honeysuckle-edged gardens, which explode year-round with color.

Dining/Entertainment: The Stonehouse is a charming candlelit restaurant, which has stumbled through some recent chef changes but is still one of Santa Barbara's best. The Plow and Angel bar is a good place for drinks; there's live music on weekends.

Services: Concierge, room service, laundry, in-room massage, twice-daily maid service, bike rentals, newspaper delivery,

Facilities: Outdoor heated pool, two tennis courts, badminton, croquet, hiking trails, kids' playground.

EXPENSIVE

Montecito Inn. 1295 Coast Village Rd., Santa Barbara, CA 93108. ☎ **800/843-2017** or 805/ 969-7854. Fax 805/969-0623. 50 rms, 10 suites. $150–$195 double; suite from $205. Rates include continental breakfast. Two-night minimum on weekends. AE, DISC, MC, V. From U.S. 101, take Olive Mill Rd. exit, turn west on Olive Mill Rd. to Coast Village.

This Mediterranean-style inn isn't at 95% capacity year-round just because Charlie Chaplin built it in 1928 to serve as Hollywood elite's romantic retreat. It's in demand because it's professional and charming. Rooms are not as impressive as some of the common areas adorned with Chaplin memorabilia, but are well appointed with French-provincial-style furnishings, floral prints, and hand-painted tiles in the small bathrooms; some have VCRs and refrigerators. New luxury suites are eye-poppingly lavish, with large living and bedrooms and Italian marble bathrooms bigger than many hotel rooms I've seen; Jacuzzi tubs and fireplaces put them over the top. The only drawback is the lack of views. Out back there's a small heated pool, spa, and sauna. Athletic folks will enjoy the free touring bikes and exercise room.

The Upham. 1404 De La Vina St. (at Sola St.), Santa Barbara, CA 93101. ☎ **800/727-0876** or 805/962-0058. Fax 805/963-2825. 50 rms, 4 suites. TV TEL. $125–$190 double; suites from $255. Rates include continental breakfast. AE, CB, DC, DISC, MC, V.

This upscale B&B located right in the heart of town celebrated its 125th anniversary in 1996. What's kept it so popular for so long? It could be the great service—it keeps the business people happy. Or maybe the European atmosphere, which makes the foreigners feel right at home. Or per chance it's the accommodations themselves— they have private entrances and are distinctively outfitted with some truly impressive antiques and brass or four-poster beds; many even have private porches and fireplaces. My only complaint: my room was desperate for a paint job. Combined with the complimentary continental breakfast and evening wine and cheese served in the lobby and garden (with a feisty cat who hangs out at the gazebo), the Upham is a charming alternative to other downtown hotels. Louie's at the Upham, a cozy restaurant, is open for lunch and dinner.

MODERATE

Highly recommendable, moderately priced accommodations are to be had at the **Best Western Encina Lodge and Suites** (☎ 800/526-2282 or 805/682-7277) and **Tropicana Inn and Suites** (☎ 800/468-1988 or 805/966-2219).

✪ Bath Street Inn. 1720 Bath St. (north of Valerio St.), Santa Barbara, CA 93101. ☎ **800/ 341-BATH,** 800/549-BATH in California, or 805/682-9680. 12 rms. TV TEL. $95–$175 double. Up to 25% off midweek. Rates include breakfast. AE, MC, V.

This is one of the cutest, most meticulously cared for B&Bs I've ever seen. The minute I walked in, a gracious innkeeper guided me to the redwood patio for a glimpse of an amazing wisteria canopy in bloom (luckily guests can have breakfast beneath the blooms). I was then treated to fresh-baked cookies, which are served with tea and wine each afternoon. After my snack, I wandered from room to room, astonished by the exquisite details of each nook and cranny throughout the three-story Victorian (two unique features include a semicircular "eyelid" balcony and a hipped roof). Each adorable (and immaculate) room is intimately and individually decorated with antiques, colorful wallpaper, and fresh flowers—and it has a private bath. Some include a Jacuzzi and/or a VCR. Common areas are equally attractive and include a third-floor reading nook with a VCR (there's a video library downstairs). No smoking is allowed in the house.

INEXPENSIVE

All the best buys fill up fast in the summer months, so be sure to reserve your room— even if you're just planning to stay at the nice, reliable **Motel 6** (☎ 800/466-8356 or 805/564-1392) near the beach, or the good-value **Sandpiper Lodge** (☎ 805/ 687-5326) just a little farther away—well in advance.

Casa del Mar. 18 Bath St., Santa Barbara, CA 93101. ☎ **800/433-3097** or 805/963-4418. Fax 805/966-4240. 14 rms, 7 suites. TV TEL. $79–154 double; suite from $114. Extra person $10. Rates include continental breakfast and wine and cheese social. Midweek discounts available. $10 extra per pet. AE, DC, DISC, MC, V. From northbound U.S. 101, exit at Cabrillo, turn left onto Cabrillo and head toward the beach. Bath is second street on right after the wharf. From southbound U.S. 101, take the Castillo exit, turn right on Castillo, left on Cabrillo, turn left at Bath.

Very similar to the Franciscan Inn and just a half block away (even closer to the beach), Casa del Mar is another good-value motel with one- and two-room suites. Decor is old Spanish Mediterranean with a mish-mash of furnishings. Many rooms have kitchenettes, fridges, and stoves. The Jacuzzi here stays open half an hour later than the Francisan's.

⑤ Franciscan Inn. 109 Bath St. (at Mason St.), Santa Barbara, CA 93101. ☎ **805/963-8845.** Fax 805/564-3295. 53 rms, 25 suites. TV TEL. $65–$99 double; suites from $85. Extra person $8. Rates include continental breakfast. AE, CB, DC, MC, V.

One of the best bargains beachside can be found one block from the shore at the Franciscan. The exterior is motel-like. Inside, rooms are a quirky combination of country pine furnishings and floral and plaid prints. In some cases, the decor just doesn't work, but the immaculate recently renovated rooms and the price more than make up for it. Several rooms have fully equipped kitchenettes and/or balconies and most bathrooms come with tub. All have coffeemakers, computer jacks, VCRs (hair dryers are available upon request). Suites come complete with a living room, a separate kitchen, and sleeping quarters for up to four adults, one has a fireplace. Breakfast, afternoon appetizers, and a complimentary newspaper are included in the price, as is the use of the heated outdoor pool, Jacuzzi, and coin-operated laundry. Reservations should be made well in advance, especially for May through September.

Orange Tree Inn. 1920 State St., Santa Barbara, CA 93101. ☎ **800/LEM-ORNG** or 805/569-1521. 44 rms, 2 suites. A/C TV TEL. $65–$150 double; suites from $90. AE, DISC, MC, V.

I'd personally prefer to stay by the beach, but if you want cheap downtown accommodations, you're safe with the Orange Tree. Don't get too excited, though: It is a motel, after all. Still, rooms are newly renovated and have new carpets, bedspreads, and TVs. Most have balcony or patio; some have bathtubs. Guests also get free local calls and use of the pool.

WHERE TO DINE
EXPENSIVE

Oysters. In Victoria Court, 9 W. Victoria St. (at State St.). ☎ **805/962-9888.** Reservations recommended on weekends. Main courses $9–$16. AE, DC, DISC, MC, V. Tues–Sat 11:30am–2:30pm; Tues–Thurs and Sun 5–9pm, Fri–Sat 5–10pm. CALIFORNIAN.

Whether you're in the intimate and formal dining room or basking on the sunny patio, you're sure to enjoy a well-prepared feast here. Most popular are the sautéed oysters with bacon, scallops, spinach, mushrooms, and hollandaise; the fresh fish of the day (a few choices and a selection of preparations); and cappellini with shrimp, artichoke, tomato, sweet peppers, and basil. For dessert, even the richest chocolate mousse cake should be passed up for the restaurant's home-churned ice cream.

✪ **Pan e Vino.** 1482 E. Valley Rd., Montecito. ☎ **805/969-9274.** Reservations required. Pastas $8–$10; meat and fish dishes $11–$18. AE, MC, V. Mon–Sat 11:30am–9:30pm, Sun 5:30–9:30pm. ITALIAN.

The perfect Italian trattoria, Pan e Vino offers food as authentic as you'd find in Rome. The simplest dish, spaghetti topped with basil-tomato sauce, is so delicious it's hard to understand why diners would want to occupy their taste buds with more complicated concoctions. But this kitchen is capable of almost anything. A whole artichoke appetizer, steamed, chilled, and filled with breading and marinated tomatoes, is absolutely fantastic. Pasta puttenesca, with tomatoes, anchovies, black olives, and capers, is always tops. Pan e Vino gets high marks for its terrific food, attentive service, and casual atmosphere. Although many diners prefer to eat outside on the intimate patio, some of the best tables are in the charming, cluttered dining room.

✪ **Wine Cask.** In El Paseo Center, 813 Anacapa. ☎ **805/966-9463.** Reservations recommended. Main courses lunch $8–$12; dinner $17–$23.50. AE, DC, MC, V. Mon–Thurs 10am–9pm, Fri–Sat 10am–10pm, Sun 10am–9pm. ITALIAN.

Take a 15-year-old wine shop, a large dining room with a big stone fireplace, a few large abstract paintings, and hand-stenciled gold-leaf 1920s historic-landmark ceiling, and outstanding Italian fare. Mix them with an attractive staff and clientele, and you've got the Wine Cask—the most popular upscale dining spot in Santa

Barbara. Whether you go for the dining room (request fireside for romance) or patio dining (yes, there are heat lamps), you'll be treated to such heavenly creations as lamb sirloin with twice-baked au gratin potatoes, green beans, baby carrots, port wine, and a roasted garlic demi-glaze. Other options include potato and proscuitto-wrapped local halibut with sautéed spinach and shiitake mushrooms, cioppino sauce, and rouille; or grilled marinated chicken breast in a red-wine reduction with prosciutto, wild mushrooms, fresh rosemary and sage. The wine list reads like a novel, with over 1,000 wines (ranging from $14 to $1,400), and has deservedly received the *Wine Spectator* award for excellence. There's also a happy hour at the beautiful maple bar from 4 to 6pm daily. This place is so in-the-know they sell cigars, too.

MODERATE

Brophy Bros. Clam Bar & Restaurant. Yacht Basin and Marina (at Harbor Way). ☎ **805/966-4418.** Reservations not accepted. Main courses $9–$16. AE, MC, V. Sun–Thurs 11am–10pm, Fri–Sat 11am–11pm. SEAFOOD.

First-class seafood combined with an unbeatable view of the marina makes dining here a favorite for both tourists and locals. Dress is casual, service is excellent, portions are huge, and everything on the menu is good. Favorites include New England clam chowder, cioppino (California fish stew), and any one of an assortment of seafood salads. The scampi is consistently good, as is all the fresh fish. A nice assortment of beers and wines is available. But be forewarned: The wait at this small place can be up to 2 hours on a weekend night.

Joe's Cafe. 536 State St. (at Cota St.). ☎ **805/966-4638.** Reservations recommended. Main courses $9–$17. AE, DISC, MC, V. Mon–Thurs 11am–11:30pm, Fri–Sat 11am–12:30am, Sun noon–9pm. AMERICAN.

Joe's may not be the hottest gourmet eatery in town, but it's been around so long (since 1928), it seems coming here is a generationally passed habit with locals and college students alike. The feel is hunting lodge–cum–picnic and offers fare you'd expect from an old-school establishment: plenty of red meat dishes (five different steak options), Southern-fried chicken, and a shrimp dish and garden burger thrown in for good measure. Meals come with a barrage of side dishes. Weekends, the full bar turns out plenty of strong cocktails and late-night dinners to partying students.

⑤ Montecito Cafe. 1295 Coast Village Rd. (off Olive Mill Rd.). ☎ **805/969-3392.** Reservations recommended. Main courses $7–$13. AE, MC, V. Daily 11:30am–2:30pm and 5:30–10pm. CALIFORNIA NOUVEAU.

Overlooking Montecito's shopping street, the light and airy Montecito Cafe provides diners a high-quality California culinary experience at an affordable price (some say it's the best value in town). Menu items include broiled oysters with lemon cream and goat cheese, a walnut-filled pork chop with lemon herb sauce, and penne pasta with scallops, shrimp, and mussels in a saffron broth. The petit dining room itself is pleasantly simple—well-set tables, a wall of windows, plants, a small fountain, and original art—it's the perfect place to impress a date.

Your Place. 22A N. Milpas St. (at Mason St.). ☎ **805/966-5151.** Reservations recommended. Main courses $7–$13. AE, DC, MC, V. Tues–Thurs and Sun 11am–10pm, Fri–Sat 11am–11pm. THAI.

There are an unusually large number of Thai restaurants in Santa Barbara, but when locals argue about which one is best, Your Place invariably ranks high on the list. Traditional dishes are prepared with the freshest ingredients and represent a wide cross section of Thai cuisine. It's best to begin with tom kah kai, a hot-and-sour chicken soup with coconut milk and mushrooms, ladled out of a hotpot tableside, enough for two or more. Siamese duckling, a top main dish, is prepared with sautéed vegetables, mushrooms, and ginger sauce. Like other dishes, it can be made mild, medium, hot, or very hot.

INEXPENSIVE

Andersen's Danish Bakery and Restaurant. 1106 State St. (near Figueroa St.). ☎ **805/ 962-5085.** Reservations recommended on weekends. Breakfast $4–$8; lunch $5–$8. No credit cards. Wed–Mon 8am–8pm. DANISH.

Remember how ice cream parlors used to look? Well, pink and frilly does not describe this bakery's sweets, but old-style, family-restaurant decor does. Grandma will feel at home here and kids won't have a problem finding something they like on the menu (especially when it comes to dessert). Authentically Danish, Ms. Andersen greets you herself (when she's not baking) and offers substantial (and cheap!) portions of New York Steak, chicken or crab salad, and an array of other edibles (including an honest-to-goodness smörgasbord). Seating provides great State Street people-watching from both in- and outdoor tables.

La Super-Rica Taqueria. 622 N. Milpas St. (between Cota and Ortega Sts.). ☎ **805/ 963-4940.** Reservations not accepted. Main courses $3–$6. No credit cards. Sun–Thurs 11am– 9:30pm, Fri–Sat 11am–10pm. MEXICAN.

Following celebrity chef Julia Child's lead, aficionados have deemed this place the state's best Mexican eatery. Excellent soft tacos are the restaurant's real forte. Unfortunately portions can be quite small—you have to order two or three items in order to satisfy an average hunger. There's nothing grand about La Super-Rica except the food; you might want to get your order to go and take it to the beach.

SANTA BARBARA AFTER DARK

To find out what's going on while you're in town, check the free weekly *The Independent,* or call the following venues direct: the **Center Stage Theater,** upstairs at the Paseo Nuevo Shopping Center, Chapala and De La Guerra Sts. (☎ 805/963-0408); the **Lobero Theater,** 33 E. Canon Perdido St. (☎ 805/963-0761); the **Arlington Theater,** 1317 State St. (☎ 805/963-4408); and the **Earl Warren Showgrounds,** at Las Positas Road. and U.S. 101 (☎ 805/687-0766).

Backstage. 18 E. Ortega. ☎ **805/730-7383.** Cover free–$7.

Santa Barbara's most cutting-edge alternative nightclub enjoys a Los Angeles–style warehouse setting and a mixed gay/straight crowd. Under high ceilings are two bars, a pool table, an indoor fountain, and one of the largest dance floors in town. Regular theme nights are interspersed with occasional live local bands.

Madhouse. 434 State St. ☎ **805/962-5516.** No cover.

Young singles pack into this warehouse-cum-cocktail lounge that's eclectically decorated with Eastern rugs and interesting trinkets hanging overhead. Order a drink from one of the beautiful young bartenders or forge your way to the back room—a heated covered patio that's jazzed up with colorful hanging lamps— where there's another bar and a little extra elbow room.

Mel's. 6 W. De La Guerra St. (in the Paseo Nuevo Mall). ☎ **805/963-2211.** No cover.

The compact bar of this old drinking dive in the heart of downtown attracts a good cross section of regulars.

The Wildcat Lounge. 15 W. Ortega. ☎ **805/962-7970.** No cover.

On a side street off State Street downtown, this small bar with retro funky decor, a CD jukebox, and a pool table keeps young local singles coming back for more.

Appendix

Useful Toll-Free Numbers

AIRLINES

Air Canada
800/776-3000 in the Continental U.S.
800/268-7240 in Canada

Alaska Airlines
800/426-0333

America West Airlines
800/235-9292

American (and American Eagle)
800/433-7300

British Airways
800/247-9297 in the Continental U.S.
0345/222-111 in Britain

Continental Airlines
800/525-0280

Delta Airlines
800/221-1212

Hawaiian Airlines
800/367-5320 from the Continental U.S.
800/838-1555 from Hawaii

Northwest Airlines
800/225-2525

Reno Air
800/736-6247

Skywest Airlines
800/453-9417

Southwest Airlines
800/435-9792

Trans World Airlines (TWA)
800/221-2000

United (and United Express)
800/241-6522

USAir (and USAir Express)
800/428-4322

Virgin Atlantic Airways
800/862-8621 in the Continental U.S.
0293/747-747 in Britain

CAR RENTAL COMPANIES

Alamo Rent A Car
800/327-9633
Avis Rent A Car
800/331-1212
Budget Rent A Car
800/527-0/00
Dollar Rent A Car
800/421-6868
Enterprise Rent-A-Car
800/325-8007
Hertz Rent A Car
800/654-3131
National Car Rental
800/328-4567
Thrifty Car Rental
800/367-2277

MAJOR HOTEL & MOTEL CHAINS

Best Western
800/528-1234
Comfort Inns
800/228-5150
Courtyard by Marriott
800/443-6000
Days Inn
800/DAYS-INN (800/329-7466)
Embassy Suites
800/EMBASSY (800/362-2779)
Hampton Inns
800/HAMPTON (800/426-7866)
Hilton Hotels
800/HILTONS (800/445-8667)
Holiday Inn
800/HOLIDAY (800/465-4329)
ITT Sheraton
800/325-3535
La Quinta Motor Inns
800/531-5900
Marriott Hotels
800/228-9290
Quality Inns
800/228-5151
Radisson Hotels International
800/333-3333
Ramada Inns
800/2-RAMADA (800/272-6232)
Super 8 Motels
800/800-8000
TraveLodge
800/578-7878

GROUND TRANSPORTATION

Amtrak
800/USA-RAIL (800/872-7245)
Automobile Association of America (AAA)
800/336-4357
Greyhound/Trailways
800/231-2222
Prime Time Airport Shuttle
800/262-7433

VISITOR INFORMATION

Beverly Hills Visitors Bureau
800/345-2210
Buena Park Convention & Visitors Bureau
800/541-3953
Dana Point Chamber of Commerce
800/290-3262 (800/290-DANA)
Huntington Beach Conference & Visitors Bureau
800/SAY-OCEAN (800/729-6232)
Laguna Beach Visitors Bureau
800/877-1115
Long Beach Area Convention & Visitors Bureau
800/4-LB-STAY (800/452-7829)
Newport Beach Conference & Visitors Bureau
800/94-COAST (800/942-6278)
West Hollywood Convention & Visitors Bureau
800/368-6020

Index

FROMMER'S COMPLETE TRAVEL GUIDES

(Comprehensive guides to destinations around the world, with selections in all price ranges—from deluxe to budget)

FROMMER'S FRUGAL TRAVELER'S GUIDES

(The grown-up guides to budget travel, offering dream vacations at down-to-earth prices)

Australia from $45 a Day	India from $40 a Day
Berlin from $50 a Day	Ireland from $45 a Day
California from $60 a Day	Italy from $50 a Day
Caribbean from $60 a Day	Israel from $45 a Day
Costa Rica & Belize from $35 a Day	London from $60 a Day
Eastern Europe from $30 a Day	Mexico from $35 a Day
England from $50 a Day	New York from $70 a Day
Europe from $50 a Day	New Zealand from $45 a Day
Florida from $50 a Day	Paris from $65 a Day
Greece from $45 a Day	Washington, D.C. from $50 a Day
Hawaii from $60 a Day	

FROMMER'S PORTABLE GUIDES

(Pocket-size guides for travelers who want everything in a nutshell)

Charleston & Savannah	New Orleans
Las Vegas	San Francisco

FROMMER'S IRREVERENT GUIDES

(Wickedly honest guides for sophisticated travelers)

Amsterdam	Miami	Santa Fe
Chicago	New Orleans	U.S. Virgin Islands
London	Paris	Walt Disney World
Manhattan	San Francisco	Washington, D.C.

FROMMER'S AMERICA ON WHEELS

(Everything you need for a successful road trip, including full-color road maps and ratings for every hotel)

California & Nevada	Northwest & Great Plains
Florida	South Central & Texas
Mid-Atlantic	Southeast
Midwest & the Great Lakes	Southwest
New England & New York	

FROMMER'S BY NIGHT GUIDES

(The series for those who know that life begins after dark)

Amsterdam	Los Angeles	New York
Chicago	Miami	Paris
Las Vegas	New Orleans	San Francisco
London		

WHEREVER YOU TRAVEL, *H*ELP IS NEVER FAR AWAY.

From planning your trip to providing travel assistance along the way, American Express® Travel Service Offices are always there to help.

Los Angeles

American Express Travel Service
327 North Beverly Drive
Beverly Hills
310/274-8277

American Express Travel Service
8493 W. 3rd St. at La Cienega Blvd.
Los Angeles
310/659-1682

American Express Travel Service
301 East Ocean Boulevard
Long Beach
310/432-2029

San Pedro Travel Service, Inc. (R)
243L8 South Western Avenue
San Pedro
310/833-5265

American Express Travel Service
The Hilton Center, 901 West 7th Street
Los Angeles
213/627-4800

American Express Travel Service
1250 4th Street
Santa Monica
310/395-9588

American Express Travel Service
267 Del Amo Fashion Center
Hawthorne Blvd. at Carson St., Torrance
310/542-8631

Travel

http://www.americanexpress.com/travel

**American Express Travel Service Offices
are located throughout California.
For the office nearest you, call 1-800-AXP-3429.**